P9-CKX-656

The Achievement of

WILLIAM FAULKNER

Books by Michael Millgate

WILLIAM FAULKNER
AMERICAN SOCIAL FICTION: JAMES TO COZZENS
THE ACHIEVEMENT OF WILLIAM FAULKNER

The Achievement of
WILLIAM FAULKNER

MICHAEL MILLGATE

Random House   *New York*

Grateful acknowledgment is extended to the Estate of William Faulkner for the use of the copyrighted material from his works. The chapter on *Pylon* was first published in *The Michigan Quarterly Review,* III (1964).

TO JANE

PREFACE

THE principal object of this study has been to offer a critical review of Faulkner's overall achievement, to develop independent analyses of each of his novels and short story volumes, and to view each book in the context of his career as a whole. In order to establish that context as firmly as possible, I have opened with an extended account of those aspects of Faulkner's life which seemed relevant to an understanding of his work, especially as that work changed and developed in the course of time. This account is not offered as a biography, nor even as a biographical sketch; it does not pretend to explore Faulkner's elusive and intensely private personality; its intention is rather to draw together published material, to supplement this with additional information, and thus to provide the present generation of Faulkner students with a straightforward, reasonably comprehensive, and adequately documented narrative of Faulkner's literary career.

In this attempt to chart what Faulkner wrote, when he wrote it, and in what general circumstances, I have been greatly aided by the generosity of Faulkner's daughter and literary executor, Mrs. Jill Faulkner Summers, in allowing me to make substantial quotations from her father's letters and literary manuscripts. My debt to her is a large one, and I am particularly happy to acknowledge it. I take pleasure, too, in thanking Mr. Malcolm Cowley for permission to quote from his own letters to Faulkner at the time of the preparation of *The Portable Faulkner*. I should like at the same time to extend my thanks to those institutions and individuals who gave me access to Faulkner materials in their possession: the William Faulkner Foundation and the Alderman Library of the University of Virginia; Yale University Library; Princeton University Library; the Humanities Research Center of the University of Texas; the University of Mississippi Library; the Arents Collection of the New York Public Library; Mr. Linton Massey; Mr. T. Holtzman; Mr. William B. Wisdom. I am especially grateful for the help and advice of Mr. John Cook Wyllie and Miss Anne Freudenberg at the University of Virginia, Mr. Warren Roberts and Mrs. Ann Bowden at the University of Texas, and Mr. Donald Gallup at Yale. My thanks are also due to the United States Department of State, whose award of a Foreign Specialist grant made possible my research visit to America; to the

School of English of the University of Leeds, which granted me leave of absence during the period of the grant; and to the editors of A Review of English Literature and the Michigan Quarterly Review, for permission to republish material which first appeared in those journals. Mrs. Margaret Woodward did an admirable job of typing the greater part of the book and Miss Audrey Stead, with equal efficiency, helped me out in a moment of crisis.

Professor Robert Bloom gave valuable criticism and encouragement during the preparation of the manuscript; Professor Walter Isle commented on portions of the proofs; Professor James B. Meriwether not only read and criticised the book both in manuscript and in proof but displayed a quite extraordinary generosity in giving me freely of his time, his advice, and his own immense knowledge of Faulkner. Professor Meriwether, Professor Walter B. Rideout, and Mr. Gordon Price-Stephens all magnanimously allowed me to make use of the results of their own research, and my debts to them, to Professor Joseph L. Blotner, to Mr. Robert Coughlan, to Mr. Albert Erskine, and to Mr. Thomas L. McHaney are further acknowledged in the notes. Also mentioned in the notes are many people who helped me in various ways, usually with information about some period of Faulkner's career, and I take this opportunity of expressing my gratitude for their assistance and for their patience. Not mentioned in the notes, but equally to be thanked, are Professor Douglas Grant, Mr. D. W. Jefferson, Professor James W. Silver, Professor Douglas Day, Professor George P. Garrett, and the other colleagues who have contributed to my understanding of Faulkner and his work. Perhaps this is the best place to say how much I have profited from discussing Faulkner with Mr. Malcolm Cowley and with Professor Cleanth Brooks and how much I regret that the latter's William Faulkner: The Yoknapatawpha Country appeared in England too late for me to be able to draw upon its insights and its wisdom. There remains only the pleasant task of acknowledging the discriminating criticism and untiring assistance which I have received from my wife at every stage of the composition of the book, and also the specifically scholarly debt I owe to her own work on Faulkner. If this study should prove to be of value to students of Faulkner, then it is to my wife and to Professor Meriwether that much of the credit will properly belong.

CONTENTS

TEXTUAL NOTE

THE list below, arranged in chronological order, gives the year of
original publication of each of Faulkner's books and the publication
details of the text used in the present study for purposes of quotation
or reference. These texts, in all cases, are either first editions or subsequent impressions, direct or by photo-offset, from the original plates
(see James B. Meriwether, "The text of Faulkner's books: an introduction and some notes," *Modern Fiction Studies*, IX [Summer 1963],
159-170). The sources for quotations from other works of Faulkner's
(stories and articles in periodicals, etc.) are supplied in the notes. For
further bibliographical information readers should consult James B.
Meriwether's *William Faulkner: A Check List* (Princeton, New
Jersey, 1957) and the same author's *The Literary Career of William
Faulkner: A Bibliographical Study* (Princeton, New Jersey, 1961).
For the convenience of English readers, the list below also gives, in
parentheses, the publication details of the first English editions;
asterisks indicate English texts which were reproduced by photo-
offset from the American first edition or issued in sheets from that
edition (see Meriwether, *The Literary Career*, pp. 99-116).

1924. *The Marble Faun.* Boston: The Four Seas Company, 1924.
1926. *Soldiers' Pay.* New York: Liveright Publishing Corporation,
     1951. (London: Chatto and Windus, 1930).
1927. *Mosquitoes.* New York: Boni and Liveright, 1927. (London:
     Chatto and Windus, 1964).
1929. *Sartoris.* New York: Random House, 1962. (London: Chatto
     and Windus, 1932*).
1929. *The Sound and the Fury.* New York: Jonathan Cape and
     Harrison Smith, 1931. (London: Chatto and Windus, 1931).
1930. *As I Lay Dying.* New York: Jonathan Cape and Harrison
     Smith, 1930. (London: Chatto and Windus, 1935).
1931. *Sanctuary.* New York: The Modern Library, 1932. (London:
     Chatto and Windus, 1931).
1931. *These 13.* New York: Jonathan Cape and Harrison Smith,
     1931. ([Entitled *These Thirteen*] London: Chatto and
     Windus, 1933*).
1931. *Idyll in the Desert.* New York: Random House, 1931.
1932. *Miss Zilphia Gant.* [Dallas:] Book Club of Texas, 1932.
1932. *Light in August.* [Norfolk, Conn.:] New Directions, 1947.
     (London: Chatto and Windus, 1933*).

1933. *A Green Bough.* New York: Harrison Smith and Robert Haas, 1933.

1934. *Doctor Martino and Other Stories.* New York: Harrison Smith and Robert Haas, 1934. (London: Chatto and Windus, 1934*).

1935. *Pylon.* New York: Harrison Smith and Robert Haas, 1935. (London: Chatto and Windus, 1935).

1936. *Absalom, Absalom!.* New York: The Modern Library, 1951. (London: Chatto and Windus, 1937*).

1938. *The Unvanquished.* New York: Random House, 1938. (London: Chatto and Windus, 1938).

1939. *The Wild Palms.* New York: Random House, 1939. (London: Chatto and Windus, 1939).

1940. *The Hamlet.* New York: Random House, 1940. (Chatto and Windus, 1940).

1942. *Go Down, Moses [and Other Stories.]* [Last three words of the title deleted in all impressions subsequent to the first.] New York: Random House, 1942. ([Original title retained in all impressions.] London: Chatto and Windus, 1942).

1948. *Intruder in the Dust.* New York: Random House, 1948. (London: Chatto and Windus, 1949*).

1949. *Knight's Gambit.* New York: Random House, 1949. (London: Chatto and Windus, 1951).

1950. *Collected Stories of William Faulkner.* New York: Random House, 1950. (London Chatto and Windus, 1951*).

1951. *Notes on a Horsethief.* Greenville, Mississippi: Levee Press, 1951.

1951. *Requiem for a Nun.* New York: Random House, 1951. (London: Chatto and Windus, 1955).

1954. *A Fable.* New York: Random House, 1954. (London: Chatto and Windus, 1955).

1955. *Big Woods.* New York: Random House, 1955.

1957. *The Town.* New York: Random House, 1957. (London: Chatto and Windus, 1958).

1959. *The Mansion.* New York: Random House, 1959. (London: Chatto and Windus, 1961).

1962. *The Reivers.* New York: Random House, 1962. (London: Chatto and Windus, 1962).

ACKNOWLEDGMENTS

Grateful acknowledgment is made to Faulkner's English publishers, Messrs. Chatto and Windus Ltd., and to the William Faulkner Estate for permission to quote from Faulkner's works; also to the University of North Carolina Press, the Princeton University Press, and the University of Virginia Press for permission to quote substantially from other published sources.

THE CAREER

THE CAREER

WILLIAM CUTHBERT FAULKNER was born at New Albany, Mississippi, on September 25, 1897, eldest of the four sons of Murry C. and Maud Butler Falkner. In view of the many explanations which have been offered for the change in Faulkner's spelling of his name, it is useful to have his own testimony on the subject, contained in a letter which he wrote to Malcolm Cowley in 1945:

> The name is 'Falkner'. My great-grandfather, whose name I bear, was a considerable figure in his time and provincial milieu. He was a prototype of John Sartoris: raised, organized, paid the expenses of and commanded the 2nd Mississippi Infantry, 1861-2, etc. Was a part of Stonewall Jackson's left at 1st Manassas that afternoon; we have a citation in James Longstreet's longhand as his corps commander after 2nd Manassas. He built the first railroad in our county, wrote a few books, made grand European tour of his time, died in a duel and the county raised a marble effigy which still stands in Tippah County. The place of our origin shows on larger maps: a hamlet named Falkner just below the Tennessee line on his railroad.
>
> My first recollection of the name was, no outsider seemed able to pronounce it from reading it, and when he did once pronounce it, he always wrote the 'u' into it. So it seemed to me that the whole outside world was trying to change it, and usually did. Maybe when I began to write, even though I thought then I was writing for fun, I secretly was ambitious and did not want to ride on grandfather's coat-tails, and so accepted the 'u', was glad of such an easy way to strike out for myself. I accept either spelling. In Oxford it usually has no 'u' except on a book. The above was always my mother's and father's version of why I put back into it the 'u' which my greatgrandfather, himself always a little impatient of grammar and spelling both, was said to have removed. I myself really dont know the true reason. It just seemed to me that as soon as I got away from Mississippi, I found the 'u' in the word whether I wished it or not. I still think it is of no importance, and either one suits me.[1]

Faulkner was fully aware of his great-grandfather's literary reputation, although Colonel William Clark Falkner's most successful book, the novel called *The White Rose of Memphis*, seems too pedestrian to have seriously influenced his descendant, who once spoke of it, indeed, as a bad book: his great-grandfather had done a little of everything in his time and it was natural that he should also want to try his hand at writing.[2] Of much greater importance to Faulkner were those qualities in Colonel Falkner and those aspects of his active and often violent life which provided the basis for the figure of Colonel John Sartoris in books like Sartoris and The Unvanquished: Faulkner must have been attracted above all by the Colonel's determination to leave his mark on the world, by his considerable success in doing so, and by the part he played in the Civil War and its aftermath. The building of the railroad, in particular, seized Faulkner's imagination: he referred to it many times in his early fiction and used it as the main axis of his legendary Yoknapatawpha County.

It was in 1871 that Colonel Falkner began construction of a narrow-gauge line between his home town of Ripley in Tippah County, where his monument now stands, and the Tennessee town of Middleton, twenty-five miles to the north; at a later stage the line was extended southwards to New Albany and Pontotoc, Mississippi. Originally called the Ripley Railroad, the name was changed the following year to the Ripley, Ship Island, and Kentucky, and in 1889, only a month before his death at the hands of Richard J. Thurmond, his former partner, Colonel Falkner became president of a new company into which the Ripley, Ship Island, and Kentucky railroad was merged; the Gulf and Chicago railroad, as it was now called, was "in name, the embodiment of his dream to link the Gulf with the Great Lakes."[3] The Gulf and Chicago remained in the possession of the Falkner family until 1902; the line was subsequently changed to standard-gauge, and in 1917, after various changes of ownership, it was eventually brought into the Gulf, Mobile and Northern system. Faulkner's grandfather, "Colonel" John Wesley Thompson Falkner, a man of considerable political influence in northern Mississippi, was president of the railroad until it was sold; he later acted as counsel for it and for the Illinois Central. John Faulkner, the second of the Falkner brothers and himself a novelist, recalled in his memoir, My Brother Bill, that "Grandfather had not wanted the railroad to begin with. He had an extensive criminal practice at the law that left him no spare time to manage anything else, let alone a railroad. Dad was the only one who wanted it and except for a misunderstanding would have bought it when Grandfather sold it in 1902."[4] While the railroad was still in the family, Murry Falkner worked for it in many capacities—as fireman, engineer, conductor, and, at the time when Faulkner was born, as general passenger agent at New Albany. In 1898 he was appointed treasurer and auditor to the company and moved with his wife and baby son to Ripley; four years later, after the railroad had been sold, he moved again, this time to Oxford, Mississippi, his wife's home town and the place where his own father had gone into legal practice when the death of the old Colonel and its aftermath of local dissension and bitterness had made life in Ripley uncomfortable for the Falkners.[5]

In Oxford Murry Falkner first bought a cottonseed-oil mill and an ice plant; later he ran a livery stable for several years, a Standard Oil agency for a much briefer period, and then a hardware business on the Square; after the First World War he became secretary and business manager of the University of Mississippi, which stands on the outskirts of Oxford.[6] John Faulkner's memoir recreates many incidents in the childhood of the Falkner brothers and gives an impression of their background of assured comfort and social position, of their active and often adventurous lives—they were early trained to hunting and the use of guns, and there were always ponies, horses, and other animals about the place—and of the leadership which William, with his superior age and inventiveness, naturally assumed.[7] Faulkner himself told Malcolm Cowley that, as the eldest of four boys, he had found it easy to escape his mother's influence: "I more or less grew up in my father's livery stable ... my father thought it was fine for me to apprentice to the business. I imagine I would have been in the livery stable yet if it hadn't been for [the] motor car." In the same letter, Faulkner told Cowley that he had gone through grammar (i.e. junior) school, but had stayed at high school for only two years and failed to graduate: according to his own testimony he went to school only during the fall term and only in order to play on the football team. Faulkner said that when his family "caught on" to his truancy he was taken into his grandfather's bank—the First National Bank of Oxford, of which "Colonel" J. W. T. Falkner was the first president—as a book-keeper.[8] Phil Stone, writing in the *Oxford Magazine* in 1934, spoke of this episode as a "futile effort to make a banker out of the present William Faulkner. I think the old gentleman had too much sense to expect success in this endeavor except by a miracle but the family couldn't get Bill to do anything else so they thought they would try banking on him and see if it would take."[9] According to John Faulkner, however, the year in the bank was a happy period in William's life, when he seemed contented with the prospect of a settled career and when his relationship with Estelle Oldham, the girl whom he wanted to marry, seemed to be firmly established.[10] Supplying autobiographical information to *Forum* magazine in 1930, Faulkner summarised his life up to this point with humorous inaccuracy: "Born male and single at early age in Mississippi. Quit school after five years in seventh grade. Got job in Grandfather's bank and learned medicinal value of his liquor. Grandfather thought janitor did it. Hard on janitor."[11]

His years since leaving school Faulkner had spent under the energetic—though irregular and entirely unpaid—tuition of Phil Stone, a young Oxford lawyer[12] of literary tastes, who was to exercise an extremely important formative influence on Faulkner's early career. Their two families had long been friendly—Stone speaks of the affection which existed between his own mother and Faulkner's maternal grandmother[13]—and it was about 1914 that Stone, who was the elder by four years, seems first to have realised that Faulkner had literary interests of his own, and, indeed, an unmistakable literary talent: as Stone told Robert Coughlan many years later, "Anybody could have seen that he had a real talent. It was perfectly obvious."[14] Perhaps Stone made his most important contribution to the fostering of this talent by suggesting to Faulkner what he might read and, often, by supplying the books themselves. John Faulkner recalled: "The Stones had a big old Studebaker touring car, a seven-passenger affair. Phil loaded it with books for Bill to read and turned the car over to him. Bill would go out on some country road, a side road where it was quiet, and park the car and spend the day reading."[15] Richard P. Adams, who has accumulated impressive evidence of the range of Faulkner's early reading, speaks of Stone supplying Faulkner especially with French poetry, with modern English poetry, and with copies of such magazines as *Poetry*, *The Dial*, and *The Little Review*.[16] Stone's interests were broader than this, however, and in the early 1920's, when he and Faulkner were still close, Stone was buying a great variety of books from the Brick Row Bookshop, in New Haven. Among those he purchased in 1922, for example, were the three Joseph Hergesheimer novels which Faulkner reviewed for *The Mississippian* in December 1922; *Moby Dick*, which Faulkner certainly knew well; Elie Faure's *History of Art*, which Faulkner mentions in an unpublished work called "Elmer"; as well as *The Education of Henry Adams*, Fitzgerald's *The Beautiful and Damned*, Huxley's *Chrome Yellow* and *Leda*, Lawrence's *Tortoises* and *Aaron's Rod*, Cather's *My Ántonia*, and Percy Lubbock's *The Craft of Fiction*.[17]

The relationship between the voluble Stone and the taciturn Faulkner must have been a curious one in some ways, and the apparent passivity of the younger man, his willingness to accept the position of listener, learner, recipient, and protégé, undoubtedly led Stone to exaggerate in his own mind, and in public and private statements, the real extent of his influence on Faulkner and on Faulkner's work. He seems never to have understood the essential quality of Faulkner's genius and to have been unable, or unwilling, to see that by the early nineteen-thirties he had become a novelist of major stature. In his prefatory remarks to the series of articles on Faulkner which he contributed to the *Oxford Magazine* in 1934 he wrote: "That William Faulkner has talent, talent of a high order, I have no doubt. I am equally sure that as yet he has shown no trace of genius and, I am sorry to say, I have grave doubts that he ever will be a genius. I even have disquieting fears that so far as concerns literary achievement he has gone as far as he will ever go."[18] Inevitably, Faulkner grew beyond

Stone, and it is clear that he had never been as receptive of Stone's literary views and aesthetic theories as Stone himself imagined; at the same time, Stone's friendship, criticism, and encouragement played an extremely important part in getting Faulkner started as a writer, and there is a sense in which Stone could justly claim to have assisted the birth and early growth of Faulkner's career in the dual role of "midwife" and "wet nurse".[19] Stone might with equal justice have claimed the roles of promoter and publicity agent, since for many years he was an outspoken advocate of Faulkner's work and did whatever he could to get it published. Writing in 1942 of local reactions to Faulkner, particularly during the early 1920's, Stone said:

> He had an aristocratic, superior appearance—which most people considered an affectation—and an aloof reserve and an arrogant snappishness when someone tried to get familiar. So he was considered affected, peculiar, a crank, or a harmless ne'er-do-well. And thus he became "Count No Count."
>
> The old families of Oxford tolerated him because, after all, he was a member of the Faulkner family. Also some of them had black sheep in their own families. But they did not invite him to their houses, as a rule, and my frequent statements that he was a writer of ability and would one day be more famous than Stark Young (another native son) and would cause many people to come to Oxford because it was the home of William Faulkner—such statements provoked guffaws from the general public and polite, derisive smiles from the old families.[20]

When in 1931 Louis Cochran, who had known Faulkner at the University of Mississippi in the years immediately following the First World War, sent Stone the draft of an article on Faulkner which he later contributed to the Memphis *Commercial Appeal*, Stone understandably rejected as "bunk" a statement that Faulkner had lacked help and sympathy in his early years as a writer: "I lent him books, read every line he ever wrote, criticised it and revised some of it. This was an almost daily routine of his literary training for years and years. God only knows how many thousands of lines of his verse that I have read and some of it was pretty poor at that." In the same letter Stone remarked: "I doubt if it was his early ambition to be a poet as much as it was my ambition for him to be one," and it is significant that even in December 1931, after the publication of *The Sound and the Fury*, Stone should be telling Cochran to look out for the publication of Faulkner's forthcoming book of verse, *A Green Bough*, as an expression of the qualities in Faulkner's work which Stone most admired.[21]

Whether under Stone's influence or not, Faulkner undoubtedly saw himself at the beginning of his career as primarily a poet, though with potentialities as a graphic artist. So far as is known, his first published work was the drawing of a couple dancing which appeared in the 1916-1917 volume of *Ole Miss*, the University of Mississippi annual. He published two more drawings in *Ole Miss* a year later, and it was not until the following year, on August 6, 1919, that he published his first poem, "L'Apres-Midi d'un Faune", in *The New Republic*. Later that same year the University of Mississippi newspaper, *The Mississippian*, published a slightly different version of "L'Apres-Midi d'un Faune", three more poems, and Faulkner's first published story, "Landing in Luck."[22]

The story is a pleasant and lightly amusing product of Faulkner's own experiences at a Royal Air Force flying training school in Canada, and although the hero, the incompetent flyer who turns a crash into a triumph, is not specifically identified as an American, his nationality is suggested by his manner of speech and by the fact that he privately alludes to his instructor as "Blasted Englishman."[23] In April 1918 Faulkner had gone to New Haven, Connecticut, where he lived with Stone, then about to graduate from Yale Law School, and worked for a short while as a clerk in the factory of the Winchester Arms Company.[24] John Faulkner states that Faulkner's departure from Oxford was prompted by Estelle Oldham's engagement to Cornell Franklin, then concluding his studies at the University of Mississippi, and that in June, while Faulkner was still away, the marriage took place and the couple left for the Philippines, where the Franklins had a family business.[25] It was apparently after the wedding that Faulkner enlisted in the Royal Air Force as a cadet pilot, made a brief visit to Oxford, and left in July to begin training in Canada.[26] If we may judge from comments made much later in life, Faulkner had long wanted to take part in the war: "This was 1915 and '16; [he wrote in 1953] I had seen an aeroplane and my mind was filled with names: Ball, and Immelmann and Boelcke, and Guynemer and Bishop, and I was waiting, biding, until I would be old enough or free enough or anyway could get to France and become glorious and beribboned too."[27] According to some accounts, he had previously tried to join the aviation branch of the United States Signal Corps but been turned down because he had not had two years of college education.[28]

An extant notebook of technical data which Faulkner kept during his flying training bears on its front page the identification:

> 173799 William Faulkner
> Royal Air Force
> Course 42, 4 School of Aeronautics
> University of Toronto
> Canada

The notes themselves are neatly kept, but on two sides of a sheet detached from the notebook are several sketches of girls and of men in uniform, similar in style to those Faulkner was later to contribute to *Ole Miss*.[29] The Armistice came before Faulkner's training had been finally concluded, but it has been suggested that he and the rest of his particular course were allowed to complete their training and qualify for their wings.[30] Faulkner returned to Oxford that December of 1918, but it was not until March 9, 1920, that the *London Gazette* formally announced his appointment as an Honorary 2nd Lieutenant.[31] Faulkner never got to Europe during the war, but he apparently underwent basic training as a pilot and it is just possible that he was injured in a flying accident. Phil Stone told a story of a crash on Armistice Day itself, when Faulkner and another cadet pilot got drunk.[32] John Faulkner spoke of the crash as occurring during a celebration on the day Faulkner's course graduated,[33] while Faulkner himself, in one of his letters to Cowley, hinted that the crash had occurred during an unauthorised flight.[34] Many years before, when Henry Nash Smith tried to draw him on the subject of his flying exploits, Faulkner replied: "I just smashed them up."[35]

In the years following the war Murry Falkner, as an administrative officer of the University of Mississippi, had a house on the campus, and it was natural that Faulkner should play some part in student activities. Indeed, for one brief period—the 1919-1920 academic year and the first two months of the following semester—Faulkner was formally enrolled as a student.[36] He did well in French and fairly well in Spanish but badly in English, possibly because of his dissatisfaction with the way the course was taught: A. Wigfall Green, in an early article on Faulkner, drew attention to the attack in *Mosquitoes* on the stultification of academic teaching of literature.[37] Faulkner told Cowley that he had entered the University at his father's request and against his own inclination, and that since he had not graduated from high school he was able to enroll only "by special dispensation for returned troops." He said that he left the University because he found he liked it no more than he had high school, and added, with a phrase full of significance for his later work: "Rest of education undirected reading."[38] The results of this reading began to appear in the poems he was writing at this period. *The Marble Faun*—which Faulkner dated from the spring and early summer of 1919, but much of which he may have written later[39]—owes a general debt to English pastoral and lyric verse, from Shakespeare to Swinburne, while the poems actually published at this time suggest the influence of Swinburne, of more recent English poets, such as Oscar Wilde, Ernest Dowson, and the early Yeats, and, more especially, of the French symbolists—in February and March 1920, for example, Faulkner published in *The Mississippian* no less than four adaptations of poems by Verlaine.[40]

Carvel Collins's account of this period of Faulkner's career records some of the protests and parodies which these early poems provoked,[41] and it is clear that Faulkner, largely by his own choice, was a controversial figure on the University of Mississippi campus. He had been in the R.A.F., he was a more sophisticated poet than any of his contemporaries, and he was already dedicated to a literary career; he also indulged in a good deal of self-dramatisation, dressing in eccentric fashion and playing, perhaps overplaying, his various roles of ex-pilot, poet and artist. At the same time, he did not cut himself off from campus activities. He was active in the publication of *The Mississippian* and the *Ole Miss* annual, as well as contributing to them a series of poems, articles and drawings, and he took a leading part in the foundation of the Marionettes, the University dramatic society, in September 1920 : in a list of members of the society which appeared in *Ole Miss* for 1920-1921 Ben Wasson, later to become Faulkner's first literary agent, is named as president and William Falkner [sic] as a property man.[42] It was in the same year that Faulkner wrote and "published"—elaborately writing out and illustrating half a dozen copies for his friends—a highly formal play in one act called *Marionettes*.[43] The action, if it can be so called, concerns Pierrot's seduction of Marietta and subsequent abandonment of her, and in the light of Faulkner's later work it is possible to see Marietta as a type of the woman bereft and patiently waiting who recurs in *Idyll in the Desert* and elsewhere; the concluding episodes of the play, narrated by the Spirit of Autumn, include the moment of arrested movement when Pierrot stands poised on a hilltop, looking back at Marietta, holding his fate momentarily in his hands. The chief importance of the play, however, lies in its combination of text with related illustrations and in its overall stylisation of language, action and line. The stage directions, which appear on the second of the two pages reproduced in James B. Meriwether's *The Literary Career of William Faulkner*, give some inkling of the formality of the piece :

> The sky is a thin transparent blue, a very light blue merging into white with stars in regular order, and a full moon. At the back center is a marble colonnade, small in distance, against a regular black band of trees; on either side of it is the slim graceful silhouette of a single poplar tree. Both wings are closed by sections of wall covered with roses, motionless on the left wall is a peacock silhouetted against the moon. . . .[44]

The facing illustration, which partly reflects these directions, is very much in the Beardsley manner, and it seems likely that one source of Faulkner's inspiration, both for the stylisation and vague, *fin de siècle* sensuality of the play itself and for the manner of its "publication," may have been the edition of Wilde's *Salomé*, with illustrations by Beardsley, which was in his library at the time of his death.[45]

Faulkner at this time was living at home and largely dependent on his father for financial support, but he also earned money by doing casual jobs of various kinds. Phil Stone said that Faulkner, "a good carpenter and a good housepainter," could "make almost anything on Earth with his hands,"[46] while Faulkner himself often mentioned housepainting as one of the things he had done to raise money. John Faulkner told a story of Faulkner painting the steeple of the Law School building at the University ("No one else would paint the steeple so Bill did. He tied himself to it with ropes and painted it from top to bottom"),[47] and it is perhaps worth noting that this building, subsequently occupied by the Geology Department, stands near to the campus statue of the Confederate Soldier, and that it was on this statue, rather than on the one in the Square at Oxford, that Faulkner later modelled the statue in his fictional town of Jefferson.[48] Faulkner once told an interviewer that it was because he had earned a hundred dollars from painting during the summer of 1920 that he was able to act on Stark Young's suggestion that he go to New York: "Young said I should go to New York. He said that was the place to be. Well, that was an idea.... So with sixty dollars of my stake spent for railroad fare I went to New York."[49] Years later, Stark Young spoke of finding Faulkner in "rebellious mood" in the summer of 1920,[50] and Faulkner must have seized on the invitation as an available outlet for his restlessness some time following his withdrawal from the University that November. He stayed with Young, who found him a job at Lord & Taylor's store in the Doubleday Bookshop managed by Elizabeth Prall, in whose house they were both living and who married Sherwood Anderson shortly afterwards.[51] Faulkner later said that he "got fired" from the job because he was "a little careless about making change or something"; according to Young, Faulkner simply "drifted back South."[52] Elizabeth Prall Anderson herself, interviewed by Walter B. Rideout in 1959, recalled that Faulkner at that time was very reserved, looking like an Englishman, with his chin tucked down toward his collar. She insisted, however, that he was an excellent book salesman, almost insulting customers who picked up what he considered worthless books, and pressing better books upon them with the words, "Don't read that trash, read this." As a result, people bought whole piles of new books. It was true, she said, that Faulkner didn't keep his accounts straight, but a good accounts secretary did that for him.[53]

In December 1921 Faulkner was in Oxford, where he took up an appointment first as temporary and subsequently as permanent postmaster at the University of Mississippi.[54] Phil Stone wrote to Louis Cochran in 1931 that "Major L. E. Oldham, now his Father-in-law, got him the appointment and I forced Bill to take the job over his own declination and refusal." Stone adds, in words which aptly sum up

all the tales told of Faulkner's shortcomings in his official capacity:
"He made the damndest postmaster the World has ever seen."[55]
Faulkner retained the job until his resignation in the autumn of 1924
—the Certificate of Outgoing Postmaster, signed "W. C. Falkner," is
dated October 31, 1924[56]—after the complaints of dissatisfied customers had finally provoked an official reprimand. In his 1930 letter to
Forum Faulkner gave his version of the affair as follows: "Family
got job: postmaster. Resigned by mutual agreement on part of two
inspectors; accused of throwing all incoming mail into garbage can.
How disposed of outgoing mail never proved. Inspectors foiled."
Faulkner must have been glad to be free of a job he had never enjoyed,
but the shadow of the post office was to pursue him yet a little longer.
Among the Faulkner papers in the Alderman Library is a series of
letters relating to an amount, first given at $21.85, later as $38.25,
which the auditors had noted as outstanding from Faulkner's final
balance sheet as postmaster. Faulkner's father replied to the first letter,
which was dated October 19, 1925, saying that his son was abroad
and that he hoped a settlement could be delayed until his return. The
General Accounting Office wrote back to ask Murry Falkner to see
personally that his son sent the amount due, and on March 3, 1926,
wrote again to Faulkner himself, warning that if the money were not
paid it would be necessary to collect it from his bondsmen. At this
point Phil Stone must have intervened, for there is a letter to Stone
from Congressman B. G. Lowrey stating that he had looked into the
matter, established that the post office authorities were in the right,
and learned from them that they regarded the discrepancy as a simple
mathematical error, in no way unusual or reprehensible. The fact that
printed form letters were used for all the official communications
would seem to support this view, and presumably the matter was
finally settled by the payment of the outstanding amount.

During his term as postmaster, Faulkner was again very much a
part of the campus scene, and student publications of the time contained many allusions to "Count Falkner's" notorious inefficiency and
inactivity.[57] Outside office hours he continued his walks and discussions with Phil Stone, played golf, at which he excelled, and ran
for a time the local Scout troop, until, as he told Cowley, his retire-
ment was requested on "moral" grounds, apparently a humorous
allusion to the objections to his drinking which seem to have been
made.[58] Faulkner seems to have been a success as a scoutmaster, and
his fondness for children and his gift for gaining their friendship
and affection have often been insisted upon. Mrs. Brown, the widow
of Professor Calvin Brown, one of Faulkner's teachers at the University
of Mississippi, told Coughlan: "He was wonderful, too, with children.
He's always liked children and known how to talk with them, tell them
stories, and get along with them; they respond to him. That was an
outstanding characteristic I remember from those times, and the other

was his intellectual groping."[59] To Mrs. Brown's daughter, Margaret, Faulkner presented at about this time, or a little later, the unpublished story, "The Wishing-Tree".[60] The story of what happened to a little girl called Daphne on her birthday, "The Wishing-Tree" is a fantasy of magical happenings and wishes granted, with certain elements somewhat in the manner of *Alice in Wonderland* and others which point to a relationship with another unpublished story, "Mayday": towards the end of "The Wishing-Tree" Daphne and her friends enter "the valley through which, in the old days, young Sir Galwyn of Arthgyl, with the green design called Hunger at his right hand and the red design called Pain at his left hand, had ridden."[61] It is in this valley that they find the Wishing-Tree itself, with the good Saint Francis standing beside it.

A number of other unpublished stories may also date from this period. In 1958, for example, Faulkner said that "Love," "Adolescence," and "Moonlight" had all been written in the early 1920's, though he suggested that the last might have been written as early as 1919.[62] In "Love,"the least distinguished of the three, the story of Beth Gordon's relationship with Bob Jeyfus, an ex-pilot whose claims to have seen war service in France are unjustly doubted, is combined with a highly melodramatic sub-plot involving an irresistibly handsome Major, his wily Oriental servant, and a passionate Italian maid who tries to trick the Major into drinking a love-potion. The opening sentence establishes the manner, and possibly the date, of the piece: "In 1921 Beth came across the flagged terrace, her geranium colored dress taut with fury." "Adolescence" is a slightly sentimentalised treatment of a young girl's conflicts with her stepmother and grandmother, and of her gradual growth out of childhood: a simple, innocent friendship between the girl and a boy of her own age is soured when the grandmother finds the two of them outdoors, sleeping naked together under a blanket. The girl's name, Juliet Bunden, and the fact that her mother, her father's first wife, had been a school-teacher from another part of the country, suggests a remote relationship to one of the central elements of *As I Lay Dying*, while the scene of sleeping outdoors in some ways foreshadows Donald Mahon's youthfull seduction of Emmy in *Soldiers' Pay*. A more immediate and interesting anticipation of *Soldiers' Pay* is provided by "Moonlight," which Faulkner described in 1958 as "about the first short story I ever wrote." The carbon typescript version in the Alderman Library is incomplete, but the story opens in a drug-store in a Southern town: it is Saturday night, the stores are still open, and "the courthouse among its elms and fronted by the marble Confederate soldier, was like a postcard."[65] Two boys, Robert Binford and his friend George, have been talking about girls; they then meet Cecily, who is apparently Robert's sister, and Robert soon departs, leaving George and Cecily together. Tension arises between them over the unspoken suggestion that they should make love, taking advantage of the opportunity offered by an empty house, but it relaxes again when George makes it clear that he will not insist on the love-making.

Faulkner undoubtedly wrote short stories and other prose during the early 1920's: in 1922, for example, he contributed to *The Missis-sippian* a prose sketch called "The Hill," as well as two literary articles and two book reviews.[66] But he still thought of himself primarily as a poet, and several of the poems later included in *A Green Bough* (1933) appear to have been written during the later months of 1924.[67] In June 1922 Faulkner had published one of his poems, "Portrait," in the New Orleans "little magazine," *The Double Dealer*, and he probably knew before the end of 1924 that the magazine had accepted another poem, "Dying Gladiator," and a literary article, "On Criticism," for publication in the issue of January-February 1925.[68] This interest in his work probably encouraged Faulkner to hope for a wider audience than the one that had been available to him in campus periodicals, and in the last months of 1924 he must have looked forward eagerly to the publication of his first book, *The Marble Faun*. The nineteen poems which comprise this pastoral cycle apparently represent a distillation of a much greater quantity of verse in the same mode and the same octosyllabic couplets; the cycle had been extensively revised from time to time, however, and the published version is actually longer than the bound typescript version which Faulkner prepared, apparently in several copies, in the early 1920's.[69]

The publication of *The Marble Faun* seems to have been financed by Phil Stone. In his first letter to the Four Seas Publishing Company of Boston, on May 13, 1924, Stone inquired what financial contribution would be required towards the publication of these poems by "a young man whom I consider to have a great deal of talent."[70] The sum of $400 was asked for, and eventually raised, and Stone then entered into negotiations about the details of publication, acting throughout on behalf of Faulkner himself, whom he had appropriately described as "not so very keen at attending to business." The book was published in mid-December, 1924, and Faulkner left shortly after Christmas for New Orleans, apparently intending to take a ship to Europe. Writing to the Four Seas on November 5, Stone suggested that they buy for $250 cash the publishing rights to the collection of articles which Faulkner planned to write during his forthcoming trip to Europe: "we would not make this proposition if it were not for that fact that Mr. Faulkner is accumulating all the money he can for his stay in Europe, as he expects to be there at least two or three years." In fact, Faulkner delayed his departure for Europe for several months, settling temporarily in New Orleans, where he wrote *Soldiers' Pay*, his first novel.

Some of Faulkner's first contacts in New Orleans were with members of the group of writers and artists who circulated about *The Double*

Dealer, which had already published one of his pieces and was about to publish two more. *The Double Dealer*, edited by Basil Thompson and Julius Weis Friend, had begun publication early in 1921 "with no policy whatever but that of printing the very best material it can procure, regardless of popular appeal, moral or immoral stigmata, conventional or unconventional technique, new theme or old."[71] The magazine lived up to its principles, publishing during its six years of existence work by Ernest Hemingway, Ezra Pound, Sherwood Anderson, Allen Tate, Hart Crane, Malcolm Cowley, and John Crowe Ransom, as well as by Faulkner himself and by several other young writers later to become well known. Understandably, its office on the disused third floor of 204 Baronne Street, just over a block away from Canal Street, the central artery of New Orleans, became one of the centres of the city's literary and artistic life,[72] which enjoyed something of a renaissance during the early 1920's. Among the writers then living in the city were Roark Bradford, author of several novels, including *Ol' Man Adam and his Chillun*, later used by Marc Connelly as the basis of the play *The Green Pastures*; Lyle Saxon, known especially for his writings on New Orleans and Louisiana; Oliver La Farge, novelist,[73] anthropologist and champion of the American Indian; John McClure, poet and journalist, one of the founders of *The Double Dealer*, referred to as "the ballad-maker" in Sherwood Anderson's novel *Dark Laughter*;[74] and, above all, Sherwood Anderson himself, then at the height of his reputation. Anderson spent the early months of 1922 in New Orleans, living at 708 Royal Street in the heart of the French Quarter, which he described to Gertrude Stein as "the most civilized place I've found in America,"[75] and he returned with his new wife, Elizabeth Prall Anderson, in the summer of 1924, taking this time an apartment in the Pontalba Building on the south side of Jackson Square.[76]

According to Hamilton Basso, who was contributing to *The Double Dealer* while still a student at Tulane, Anderson was the "Royal Personage" among "all those who made the French Quarter a sort of Creole version of the Left Bank. We weren't a literary clique, we weren't a movement, and God knows we weren't a school. What held us together was simply mutual friendliness and good will."[77] Other accounts of New Orleans at this time stress the prevailing element of mutual admiration: "We're all internationally famous locally," one of them is said to have remarked in a moment of disenchantment,[78] and James K. Feibleman, probably the youngest among a predominantly young group, recalls in his memoirs:

> The office of *The Double Dealer* was a strange place in those days. Itinerant literary men, restless painters, and all manner of odd fish drifted in and out, submitting manuscripts, borrowing money, and talking interminably about art. Here among second-rate

men the aesthetics of the day was aired a thousand times, revealing itself behind and within the most casual as well as the most profound observations.[79]

These last remarks have considerable significance for Faulkner, since it was presumably in New Orleans that he first became fully aware of some of the most fashionable of contemporary intellectual influences, notably those emanating from Freud, Frazer and Joyce. "Everybody talked about Freud when I lived in New Orleans," said Faulkner in 1956, "but I have never read him."[80] Again, Faulkner may not actually have read Frazer or Joyce at this time, but he certainly heard their names mentioned repeatedly in many discussions in cafés and restaurants, in the apartments of his friends, in the offices of *The Double Dealer* or of the *Times-Picayune* newspaper. Some hint of this appears in his reply to the question about Joyce which Henry Nash Smith asked him in 1932 :

> "You know," he smiled, "sometimes I think there must be a sort of pollen of ideas floating in the air, which fertilizes similarly minds here and there which have not had direct contact. I had heard of Joyce, of course," he went on. "Someone told me about what he was doing, and it is possible that I was influenced by what I heard."[81]

Faulkner told Smith that he still had not read *Ulysses*, although he had a copy of the 1924 printing of the book on his table—perhaps the copy, bearing his autograph, with the date "1924," which he owned at the time of his death.[82] On subsequent occasions he insisted that he had written *The Sound and the Fury* before reading *Ulysses*, but that he had read *Dubliners* and *A Portrait of the Artist* by then and knew about *Ulysses* from excerpts and from what his friends had told him.[83] The mention of excerpts lends support to the suggestion of Richard P. Adams that Faulkner saw the extracts from *Ulysses* which appeared between 1918 and 1920 in *The Little Review*, to which Phil Stone is said to have subscribed,[84] while the friend most likely to have told Faulkner what Joyce was doing was Sherwood Anderson, who met Joyce in 1921, apparently received a copy of *Ulysses* soon after it was published, and later said of his own novel, *Dark Laughter*, finished while Faulkner was in New Orleans, that he had deliberately based its prose rhythms upon those of *Ulysses*.[85] On the other hand, Faulkner's wife, interviewed in 1931, said that her husband had made her read *Ulysses* twice while they were on their honeymoon;[86] since they were married in June 1929, eight or nine months after Faulkner had finished *The Sound and the Fury* but before he had corrected the galley proofs, Mrs. Faulkner's remarks offer strong, though not conclusive, evidence that Faulkner had read *Ulysses* at an earlier date than he himself ever admitted, and that this reading may conceivably have preceded, if not the inception, at least the final completion of *The Sound and the Fury*. Since by September 1925 Anderson was lending *Ulysses* around to his friends, Faulkner may actually have read the book, as well as talked about it, during his New Orleans visit; the date on Faulkner's own copy suggests an even earlier reading, but it is not impossible, in view of Faulkner's habitual casualness about dates, that the "1924" was inscribed at some later period and involved some degree of accidental, or even deliberate, inaccuracy.[87]

During the six months which he spent in New Orleans, Faulkner lived in a ground-floor apartment at 624 Orleans Alley, the pedestrian thoroughfare, now referred to as "Pirate's Alley," which runs from Jackson Square to Royal Street between the Cabildo and St. Louis Cathedral. In the same building his close friend, the artist William Spratling, had an attic apartment which Oliver La Farge once referred to as the "main gathering place" of the writers and artists in the Quarter.[88] Another apartment was occupied by the future Mrs. John McClure, who recalls that Faulkner behaved so quietly and spoke so rarely that she and her friends usually took little notice of him. Much of the time he spent shut up in his room, especially during the period when, as later appeared, he was writing *Soldiers' Pay*.[89] When he was not writing Faulkner was generally to be found walking about the streets and quays of the city or sitting with friends, drinking hard but remaining a listener rather than a participator in most of the conversations. He also found time to do some flying with a "barnstorming" group which visited New Orleans,[90] to spend at least one weekend on "a river boat,"[91] and, conceivably, to collect the bootlegging experiences on which he drew for the story "Once Aboard the Lugger," for a section of the piece on "Mississippi" which he wrote for *Holiday* magazine in 1954, and for reminiscent remarks in numerous interviews given over the years.[92]

Nor was *Soldiers' Pay* itself the only immediate literary product of this period. In the volume entitled *New Orleans Sketches*, Carvel Collins has collected the various stories and prose sketches which Faulkner contributed to *The Double Dealer* and the *Times-Picayune* during 1925, while *The Double Dealer* followed its publication of a poem and article in the issue of January-February 1925 with another poem and a further article in the April issue of the magazine. This latter article, "Verse Old and Nascent: A Pilgrimage," is primarily interesting for its account of the development of Faulkner's tastes in poetry and its indication of the influences which may have operated upon his own work, but it incidentally reveals the considerable extent of Faulkner's acquaintance with contemporary verse; he refers specifically to E. A. Robinson, Robert Frost, Richard Aldington, and Conrad Aiken as poets he has learned to admire, adding, perhaps a little arrogantly: "I no longer try to read the others at all."[93] The stories and sketches, as Collins points out,[94] are particularly of interest for their occasional anticipations of Faulkner's mature work, but they also reveal, as do the poems Faulkner wrote at this period, a young writer diligently seeking his own style and manner, experimenting somewhat self-consciously in a variety of different modes, and trying to find his own voice through a series of temporary apprenticeships. Two important influences at this time would seem to have been Oscar Wilde and George Moore,[95] whose prose dealt in much the same "decadent" and symbolist currency as Faulkner had met with in his reading of modern French verse. But Faulkner was now trying his hand at many different styles, and it may well have been the sheer virtuosity of the eleven brief sketches which appeared in the January-February issue of *The Double Dealer* which provoked Sherwood Anderson into telling Faulkner: "You've got too much talent. You can do it too easy, in too many different ways. If you're not careful, you'll never write anything."[96]

Faulkner's decision to postpone his visit to Europe and spend some time in New Orleans seems to have been a direct consequence of his meeting with Sherwood Anderson, now married to Faulkner's New York benefactress, Elizabeth Prall. The period of intimacy between the two men dates from after Anderson's return to New Orleans, following a lecture tour, on March 3, 1925,[97] but they seem to have met earlier than this. Elizabeth Prall Anderson, interviewed in 1959, was certain that Faulkner and Phil Stone had come to New Orleans to see her, and hence Sherwood Anderson, before Christmas 1924, and that they had all had so much fun for a couple of weeks that Faulkner subsequently returned for a longer visit.[98] There is evidence to substantiate these recollections. Anderson apparently drew upon his first meeting with Faulkner, and upon certain elements of Faulkner's appearance and personality, in his story "A Meeting South," published in *The Dial* for April 1925: it has long been assumed that David, the little, delicately-built Southern poet with the war-wound and the admiration for Shelley was based on Faulkner, and Phil Stone, writing to Four Seas in March 1925, stated categorically that Faulkner was the "original" of the forthcoming story.[99] But Otto K. Liveright. at that time Anderson's New York literary agent, acknowledged receipt of the manuscript of "A Meeting South" in a letter to Anderson dated from New York on November 12, 1924.[100] Since Faulkner was engaged with his post office duties until the end of October, it seems reasonable to infer that Faulkner first met Anderson during a visit made to New Orleans, in company with Phil Stone, at the beginning of November 1924.

Faulkner's longer visit to New Orleans apparently began early in January 1925; Anderson must have left at the very beginning of the year in order to keep the first appointment of his lecture tour at Cleveland, Ohio, on January 4.[101] In late February Faulkner was temporarily back in Oxford, possibly to fulfil his obligations as a member of the staff of *The Scream*, a humour magazine published at the University of Mississippi: *The Scream* published three of Faulkner's drawings in May 1925, and George W. Healy, later editor of the New Orleans *Times-Picayune*, recalled in 1962 that when he was editor of *The Scream* Faulkner approached him with some poems: "Bill also had some cartoons that he had drawn and I liked the cartoons better than the poems."[102] In March 1925 Faulkner and Anderson met again when the latter returned from his lecture tour, and in the following month Phil Stone, writing to Four Seas, reported that Faulkner and Anderson were writing a novel in collaboration.[103] No direct trace of Anderson's influence appears in *Soldiers' Pay*, although the final passage about the Negro church is faintly reminiscent of Anderson's treatment of Negroes in *Dark Laughter*, and Elizabeth Prall Anderson was later to declare: "Nobody could influence Bill Faulkner."[104] There are, it is true, curious similarities between some of the story ideas which Anderson outlined in a letter to Otto Liveright on March 25, 1925, and certain elements in some versions of Faulkner's long, unpublished story, "Elmer",[105] but it seems more likely that Faulkner had told Stone something of the Al Jackson letters which he and Anderson exchanged, probably at about this time, and which he later adapted for incorporation into *Mosquitoes*. From the two Al Jackson letters which have been published— one by Faulkner, the other, apparently a reply, by Anderson—it is clear that they were not items of correspondence but deliberate literary exercises in the tall tale genre.[106] That Faulkner and Anderson may have intended at one time to work them up into a book is suggested by Faulkner's response to a question about the Al Jackson stories during one of the recorded class-sessions at the University of Virginia in 1958:

> They never were printed. We invented those people and it was the sort of thing that you think of and you do so much talking and laughing about it that the desire, the will to put it down has evaporated. We never did get around to putting that down. We'd write letters to one another about it and just swap lies about it face to face, but we never did get things put down on paper.[107]

The friendship between Anderson and Faulkner during the months while they were in New Orleans together was close and affectionate: "He was one man I know that I could have shared a desert island with," Faulkner once said. "We would have got along."[108] Faulkner often told how the example of Anderson's pleasant routine of morning work and subsequent relaxation first attracted him to the idea of becoming a novelist; there was obviously an element of humorous exaggeration in the story—Faulkner had determined to be a writer long before he went to New Orleans—but it is quite possible that his friendship with Anderson helped to turn his attention to novel-length fiction, though perhaps not for the first time.[109] It has usually been assumed that Faulkner was also exaggerating when he spoke of Anderson's recommending *Soldiers' Pay* to his own publisher, Horace Liveright, without having read a word of it; Elizabeth Prall Anderson, however, confirmed Faulkner's story when Rideout questioned her about it in 1959. Faulkner, she said, had hesitated to give her the manuscript of *Soldiers' Pay* for Anderson to read because he thought Anderson was too busy. But she took it to Anderson, who said that he *was* too busy. When she still insisted that he should look at the manuscript, Anderson sent it off to Liveright, recommending it without reading it.[110] There is, at any rate, no doubt that Anderson was largely instrumental in securing publication of *Soldiers' Pay*: "I am glad you are going to publish Faulkner's novel," Anderson wrote to Horace Liveright on August 28, 1925. "I have a hunch this man is a comer. Will tell you a lot about him when I see you in late October or November."[111]

That Faulkner was grateful to Anderson, admired him as a man, and valued his advice, is abundantly clear from the moving article he wrote for the *Atlantic Monthly* in June 1953, but he seems always to have had severe reservations about much of Anderson's work, and he did not hesitate to voice them in the article on Anderson published in the *Dallas Morning News* on April 26, 1925.[112] Faulkner's early realisation that Anderson's way was not to be his way must always have been a source of strain in their relationship, and Faulkner was bound eventually to break out of the role of protégé in which he was cast: in certain ways the relationship was similar to that with Stone, Anderson doing the talking—to "anyone, anywhere," as Faulkner said later[113]—and Faulkner the listening. The break between Anderson and Faulkner has usually been attributed to the publication, late in 1926, of *Sherwood Anderson & Other Famous Creoles: A Gallery of Contemporary New Orleans*. This collection of Spratling's caricatures of Anderson, Lyle Saxon, John McClure, Roark Bradford, and other figures of the New Orleans literary and artistic world, concluded with a drawing of Spratling and Faulkner working at the same table; Faulkner holds a glass in his left hand and has a bottle wedged under his left arm and three jugs of whiskey under his chair.[114] What is supposed to have upset Anderson is the introduction to the volume, written by Faulkner in a parody of what Faulkner himself later called Anderson's "primer-like" style. Speaking also on this latter occasion of Hemingway's parody of Anderson in *The Torrents of Spring*, Faulkner observed: "Neither of us—Hemingway or I—could have touched, ridiculed, his work itself. But we had made his style look ridiculous; and by that time, after *Dark Laughter*, when he had reached the point where he should have stopped writing, he had to defend that style at all costs because he too must

have known by then in his heart that there was nothing else left."[115]
This cannot, however, have been the only or even the most important
source of disagreement between Anderson and Faulkner, since
Sherwood Anderson & Other Famous Creoles was not published until
December 1926, while Anderson's letter to Horace Liveright of April
19, 1926, makes it clear that a definite break between Faulkner and
himself had already taken place and that they were no longer in
correspondence:

> I saw in the *New York Times* a very good review of the Faulkner
> novel. I hope you will have sales enough of this novel to encourage
> both Faulkner and yourself. I do not like the man personally very
> much, but I have a hunch on that he is a man who will write the
> kind of novels that will sell. He is modern enough and not too
> modern; also he is smart. If I were you, I would do what I could
> to encourage him to keep at work. If you want to do so, why don't
> you write him a letter telling him some of the things I have
> said about him, as it may buck him up, particularly if this first
> novel does not have much sale? You see what I mean. He may
> be a little bit like a thoroughbred colt who needs a race or two be-
> fore he can do his best. He was so nasty to me personally that I
> don't want to write him myself, but would be glad if you
> were to do it in this indirect way, as I surely think he is a good pros-
> pect.[116]

It is characteristic of Anderson's honesty that he should be so scrupu-
lous in separating his personal feelings about Faulkner from his
valuation of him as a writer. It is not clear what provoked Anderson's remarks about Faulkner's "nastiness," although it is, of course,
possible that he had seen a draft of the yet unpublished introduction
to Spratling's book, or that he had gained some inkling of Faulkner's
intention to caricature him in *Mosquitoes*, or that Faulkner had made
some other gesture of literary independence. Faulkner's offence may,
on the other hand, have been of a more personal nature, and Elizabeth
Prall Anderson, who said she knew of no reason for a rift between
Faulkner and Anderson, nevertheless spoke of one which sprang up
between Faulkner and herself. When Ferdinand Schevill, a close friend
of Anderson's, came to visit them in New Orleans, Faulkner was in-
vited in to meet him; Mrs. Anderson thought that Faulkner behaved
very rudely towards Schevill, but when she later spoke to him about
the matter Faulkner denied that he had been rude at all.[117] If this
disagreement with Anderson's wife affected Faulkner's relationship
with Anderson himself, then their estrangement may well have begun
even while Faulkner was in New Orleans. Yet no hint of ill-feeling
accompanies the mention of Faulkner's name in Anderson's letter to
Horace Liveright of August 28, 1925, or in his earlier letter to Phil

Stone, of August 17, in which he offered to write a blurb for the dust jacket of *Soldiers' Pay* if Liveright published it, as he had not at that date finally decided to do.[118] Thus there still seem grounds for thinking that Anderson and Faulkner may have parted on reasonably good terms when the latter left for Europe, in company with Spratling, on July 7, 1925, as a passenger aboard the freighter *West Ivis*.[119]

Some echoes from this voyage are perhaps to be detected in various versions of "Elmer," on which Faulkner worked in Paris later that summer.[120] In one typescript version, Elmer, a young man suddenly come into money and determined to be an artist, sails from New Orleans to Italy on a freighter. The books he takes with him are Clive Bell, Elie Faure's *The Outline of Art*, and "six novels in the familiar readable American vein—six sedgments [sic] of sweetness and light like a custard pie in 6 identical slices."[121] Notable among the crew is the Second Officer, who asks Elmer if he has read Kipling and tells him that "in Paris you can see the Louver."[122] As the ship approached land, Elmer "began to feel human again, i.e. to remember that after all he was still heir to the emotions of loneliness and impatience, to what circumstance and his fellow man could do to him." In mid-ocean Elmer had not felt lonely:

> There was really very little time to be lonely at sea. After twenty [sic] days on a freighter pushing one empty horizon before and drawing another one behind, empty too save for a green carpet of wake unrolling across that blue monotone as though before a great cathedral prepared for an elegant wedding in high life, Elmer forgot how to be anything except hungry and sleepy: his one emotional response was that of a fat unenergetic pleasure like that of a bright lazy child, at the sight of a lone busy ship far away or a porpoise or a spouting whale.[123]

During the actual voyage in the *West Ivis* Faulkner seems to have done a good deal of writing: Carvel Collins suggests that the last of the sketches for the *Times-Picayune* may have been written on shipboard, and there exist manuscripts of poems dated at various stages of the voyage.[124]

The *West Ivis* reached Genoa on August 2.[125] After spending some time in northern Italy and passing through Switzerland[126]—Myrtle, one of the characters in "Elmer", finds that living in Switzerland was "like living at a country club where they only had dances once a week"[127]—Faulkner arrived in Paris, where he lived at 26 Rue Servandoni,[128] a street running from St. Sulpice to the Luxembourg Gardens, close to the Rue Guynemer, named after the French air ace of the First World War,[129] and to the Luxembourg Galleries, where, as Richard P. Adams suggests, he may well have seen, and been influenced by, the paintings of Cézanne and other post-impressionists then hanging there.[130] According to William C. Odiorne, the photographer, who knew Faulkner when he was in Paris, Faulkner and Spratling arrived together but Faulkner stayed after Spratling had gone on elsewhere. Odiorne recalls seeing Faulkner from time to time, usually in cafés, but remembers nothing particularly significant about their conversations together, simply that they idled around, as people did in Paris.[131] Odiorne also speaks of Faulkner making a brief trip to England at one stage, and one version of "Elmer" includes some rather improbable scenes, set in England, which might have been prompted by such a visit.[132] In a complete short-story version of the "Elmer" material, "Portrait of Elmer Hodge", now in the Massey Collection at the University of Virginia, Elmer on arriving in Paris is first taken by his Italian guide, Angelo, to an expensive and very gloomy hotel catering especially to rich Americans, but eventually finds himself a place in the Rue Servandoni, where the harried, scolding landlady reminds him of his mother. In another version of the story Paris is evoked as with a painter's eye and there are references to several painters, including Cézanne, Degas, Manet, Matisse and Picasso; Paris is also described as "that homely informal garden where the ghost of George Moore's dead life wanders politely in a pale eroticism."[133]

"Portrait of Elmer Hodge" apparently represents Faulkner's attempt at some later stage to salvage a long story out of what he had originally intended as a novel. At the opening of the story Elmer and Angelo are sitting in a café in Montparnasse, and in a series of flashbacks we learn the story of Elmer's life: his love for his vanished sister Jo ("they had never heard from Jo and ... for all they knew she might be Gloria Swanson or J. P. Morgan's wife");[134] his early wanderings, during the course of which he acquires a bastard son in Houston; his war service, brought to an abrupt end when he fails to throw a grenade far enough in training; his rise to sudden wealth when his father discovers an oil-well in his back yard; his meeting with Myrtle, of whom we are told in another version that she was "like a star, clean and young and unattainable for all of her—Henry James would have called it vulgarity—humanness";[135] his meeting with Angelo, who got him out of jail in Venice; his painting of his first picture, in order that in asking the best master in Paris to accept him as a student he need not go empty-handed. At the beginning of the final section, Elmer suddenly rises from the table at the café and hurries off, with Angelo in pursuit. As they cross the Luxembourg Gardens, it becomes clear that Elmer is making for his lodgings in order to use the lavatory. When he arrives, the landlady tells him that Myrtle and her mother have come; he tells her to ask them to wait and rushes for the lavatory, where he experiences ecstatic relief but finds there is no paper. Sadly, he takes the painting from his pocket, and the story ends with what is apparently an ironic reference to the death of Elmer's ambitions as a painter: "Yet still within the formal twilight of the trees the bugle sounds, measured, arrogant, and sad."[136]

Faulkner told James B. Meriwether in 1958 that he had written "Elmer" in Paris in 1925 but left it unfinished because, although funny, it was "not funny enough."[137] The judgment was surely correct. The various versions of "Elmer" have moments of lively comedy, but for the most part the humour is of that self-conscious, effortful kind which Faulkner was to employ, with only moderate success, in Mosquitoes. Moreover, the material with which he was attempting to work seems to have been too close to him in time, and too nearly autobiographical, as if, balked of his scheme for writing articles about his European trip, he had determined to transpose his experiences and impressions into fictional form. It is not surprising that "Elmer" remained unfinished. It belongs with Mosquitoes as a product of that brief period when Faulkner had found his vocation but not yet his subject, and its interest lies mainly in its autobiographical elements, and in its occasional hints of characters, episodes, and images which appear in more developed form in later works: for instance, a manuscript fragment entitled "Growing Pains" begins, "In Jefferson, Miss., Elmer was in the fourth grade. . . ." An anticipation of the Quentin section of The Sound and the Fury appears in one of the typescript versions, where we learn that Elmer collected cigar stubs as a child and had a passion for other phallic symbols, such as "long tapering whips fixed pliant and slenderly recovering in their sockets on the dashboards of buggies; and he would stand in a dull trance staring at a factory smokestack."[138] Elmer's father is described as "that inverted Io with hookworm and a passionate ambitious wife for gad-fly", while Elmer's sister, called at one point Jo-Addie, seems in "her fierce integral pride" to relate back to the girl in "Adolescence" and forward to Addie Bundren in As I Lay Dying.[139]

Faulkner's failure to proceed very far with his novel of an American in Paris—or, possibly, his sense that this was not the kind of writing which suited his particular gifts—may have had something to do with the early conclusion of the European trip he had once intended to last for two or three years, or even longer. It may simply have been that he was too deeply a Mississippian to take readily to expatriation. He certainly seems to have had few contacts with the various expatriate groups in Paris at that time, and indeed to have known few literary figures of any kind. When asked at the University of Virginia whether he had met Joyce in Paris, Faulkner replied: "I knew Joyce, I knew of Joyce, and I would go to some effort to go to the café that he inhabited to look at him. But that was the only literary man that I remember seeing in Europe in those days."[140] A more immediate factor influencing Faulkner's decision to return home may well have been shortage of money: if there is any foundation for John Faulkner's suggestion that Faulkner worked for a French newspaper while he was in Paris,[141] then one can only surmise that the job was a very temporary one. In November 1925, at all events, Phil Stone was writing to the Four Seas company asking them to pay the money due to the author of *The Marble Faun*: "Mr. Faulkner has been writing me for this money...."[142] Faulkner must have left for home soon after writing to Stone since in December 1925 he arrived back in Oxford—just in time for Christmas with his family,[143] and in good time for the publication, on February 25, 1926, of his first novel, *Soldiers' Pay*.

Soldiers' Pay had a mixed reception: it got some good reviews, but it did not sell well. In the meantime, Faulkner had turned to new projects. It was probably in the early months of 1926 that he began work on a novel, or possibly a story, with the title "The Devil Beats His Wife." He seems not to have got very far with it, and only three manuscript pages appear to have survived. It is by no means clear what the story, or even the basic situation, was to have been, but apparently Hubert Semmes and his wife, Doris, are estranged, and their Negro servant, Della, takes it upon herself to bring them together again: she rides a streetcar into town (which appears to be about the size of Memphis) and sends a telegram signed "Doris" to Mr. Semmes in New Orleans, telling him to stop being a fool and to come on home. The main interest of the fragment lies in the figure of Della herself, who, though presented with a somewhat patronising humour, is recognisably a first sketch for Dilsey in *The Sound and the Fury*. As Della left the house she "adjusted the stiff black straw hat which she wore winter and summer, sun and snow and rain, with a kind of placid implacability upon her white turban"; while she was on the streetcar she saw Negroes whom she knew passing by on wagons and carts, and "these she greeted pleasurably but unostentatiously by a grave gesture of her dark sad hand."[144] Faulkner may well have wanted to write about a figure such as Della but been unable to devise an adequate narrative vehicle. Meriwether records that Faulkner soon abandoned "The Devil Beats His Wife", and that his friend Ben Wasson used the title for a novel which he published in 1929.[145]

The first substantial piece which Faulkner completed after the publication of *Soldiers' Pay* seems to have been his second novel, *Mosquitoes*. The carbon typescript of the novel bears on its final page the manuscript note "Pascagoula, Miss/1 Sept 1926", and it was apparently at Pascagoula, on the Gulf coast of Mississippi near Biloxi, that the novel was written. Faulkner spent much of his time in Pascagoula during 1926, 1927 and 1928, and he seems either to have owned or rented a beach shack there[146]—perhaps rather like the one he later described in *The Wild Palms*, a novel in which several episodes take place on the Gulf coast east of New Orleans. Faulkner's stories of working on shrimp trawlers in the Gulf of Mexico belong to this period in his life—as, perhaps, do his bootlegging experiences—and Carvel Collins has discovered an account, dating from the autumn of 1926, which speaks of Faulkner acting as golf professional at Oxford and working in a lumber mill and on a Pascagoula schooner. According to this report, Faulkner's forthcoming book, *Mosquitoes*, had been written in the evenings, after the day's work was done.[147] Boni and Liveright, who had published *Soldiers' Pay*, also took *Mosquitoes*, and the book appeared under their imprint on April 30, 1927.

After completing *Mosquitoes* in September 1926 Faulkner seems to have begun work on two quite distinct projects, both of them of great importance in the overall history of his literary career.[148] One project resulted in the composition of "Father Abraham", apparently designed as the opening chapter of a novel about the Snopes family; and we shall consider later, in discussing *The Hamlet*, the evidence for believing that Faulkner, with some assistance from Phil Stone, had by this time already conceived the Snopes family, the general outline of their history, and many of the particular incidents which were to appear in novels and stories over the next thirty years and more. In a prefatory note to *The Mansion*, published in 1959, Faulkner speaks of the book as "the final chapter of, and the summation of, a work conceived and begun in 1925." The conception may well have dated from 1925, or even earlier, but 1926 seems a more likely date for the beginning of serious work on "Father Abraham", especially in view of a report which Phil Stone wrote, apparently for publication in the *Oxford Eagle*, in late 1926 or early 1927:

> Since his return from Europe Faulkner has been here at home playing golf and writing two new novels which are already under contract. Both are Southern in setting. One is something of a saga of an extensive family connection of typical "poor white trash" and is said by those who have seen that part of the manuscript completed to be the funniest book anybody ever wrote. The other is a tale of the aristocratic, chivalrous and ill-fated Sartoris family, one of whom was even too reckless for the daring Confederate cavalry leader, Jeb Stuart. Both are laid in Mississippi.[149]

This second novel, of course, we now know as *Sartoris*, although it was first completed by Faulkner under the title *Flags in the Dust*. Faulkner seems to have got into difficulties with "Father Abraham"— the manuscript version still extant[150] breaks off unfinished—and to have put it temporarily aside while he proceeded with *Flags in the Dust*, of which the completed typescript is dated September 29, 1927.

One reason why the Sartoris material may have come rather more easily to Faulkner at this particular moment of his career is that many of the incidents derived from his own experience or from family legend and that some of the characters were based fairly directly on members of his own family circle. He told Robert Cantwell in 1938 that his knowledge of Southern and local history came not from reading but from talking to people: "When I was a boy there were a lot of people around who had lived through it, and I would pick it up—I was just saturated with it, but never read about it."[151] In the early 1950's he told Robert Linscott of the importance to his writing of these occasions in his boyhood when the house would be full of relatives talking about the past, and especially the past of the family itself.[152] In the course of the correspondence which preceded the publication of *The Portable Faulkner*, he sent Malcolm Cowley a brief biographical outline and added a comment about his family background: "I'll be glad to give you all the dope when we talk together. Some of it's very funny. I just dont like it in print except when I use it myself, like old John Sartoris and old Bayard and Mrs. Millard and Simon Strother and the other Negroes and the dead airmen."[153]

In a letter to Cowley already quoted, Faulkner states specifically that his own great-grandfather, Colonel W. C. Falkner, had been "a prototype" of John Sartoris, and there seems little doubt that old Bayard was based largely upon the Colonel's son, Faulkner's grandfather, J. W. T. Falkner, himself the founder and first president of a local bank. According to John Faulkner, the characterisation of Mrs. Millard in *The Unvanquished* as well as that of Mrs. Jenny Du Pre in *Sartoris* owed a good deal to J. W. T. Falkner's daughter Mrs. Holland Falkner Wilkins, who took over the running of her father's house after her mother's death, and whose own daughter, Sallie Murry Wilkins (subsequently Mrs. R. X. Williams, Jr.) was brought up almost as a sister to the Falkner boys.[154] It seems likely, however, that Faulkner also drew upon an aunt of an older generation, Aunt Bama (Mrs. Walter McLean of Memphis), who was a daughter of the old Colonel himself. Simon Strother, the coachman in *Sartoris*, was presumably based on one of the Negro servants who had served successive generations of the Falkner family.

Phil Stone was closely involved in the writing of *Sartoris*, and in a letter apparently written in late 1928, just before the publication of the novel, he declared: "It is a far better book than I ever thought Bill would write by now." He described it as "a sad and lonely simple book," with "none of that flip and youthful smartness of *Soldiers' Pay* and *Mosquitoes*," and added: "I invented some few parts of it and I'm quite proud of them." After commenting on some of the characters and praising the "lovely prose" of parts of the book, Stone reported: "Bill thinks it will sell. I think it's too good to sell, but I do think that it will make Bill's literary reputation and sell his future books."[155] Faulkner may have been optimistic about the prospects of *Sartoris* at this particular moment, but he had earlier been close to despair about the book. *Mosquitoes*, published in April 1927, sold poorly, despite the enthusiasm of a few reviewers, of whom the most notable was Conrad Aiken,[156] and although Boni and Liveright had a three-book contract with Faulkner they refused to take *Flags in the Dust*, as it was then called.[157] Other publishers turned the book down, and it was not until fairly late in 1928 that Harcourt, Brace accepted a shortened version of the novel for publication as *Sartoris*.

The experience was a bitter one for Faulkner, but it was indirectly responsible for some of his greatest work. As he said in the Modern Library introduction to *Sanctuary*, he began to think that his work would never again be published. In an unpublished autobiographical piece, however, he describes how, once he had stopped thinking in terms of possible publication, he experienced a quite extraordinary liberation of his creative powers:

> One day I seemed to shut a door between me and all publishers' addresses and book lists. I said to myself, Now I can write. Now I can make myself a vase like that which the old Roman kept at his bedside and wore the rim slowly away with kissing it. So I, who had never had a sister and was fated to lose my daughter in infancy, set out to make myself a beautiful and tragic little girl.[158]

The girl was Caddy, the heroine of *The Sound and the Fury*, and the moving intimacy of the passage perhaps reflects something of the personal difficulties through which, as he once told Maurice Coindreau,[159] Faulkner was passing at the time when he was engaged upon the composition of this, his first great novel. In the same autobiographical piece from which we have just quoted, Faulkner also declared that *The Sound and the Fury* was unique among the seven novels he had then (in late 1932 or early 1933) completed, in that he had written it "without any accompanying feeling of drive or effort, or any following feeling of exhaustion or relief or distaste. When I began it I had no plan at all. I wasn't even writing a book. I was thinking of books, publication, only in the reverse, in saying to myself, I wont have to worry about publishers liking or not liking this at all." Only *The Sound and the Fury* had given him "that emotion definite and physical and yet nebulous to describe: that ecstasy, that eager and joyous faith and anticipation of surprise which the yet unmarred sheet beneath my hand held inviolate and unfailing, waiting for release."[160]

Faulkner was not entirely consistent in speaking on different occasions about the length of time it took him to write *The Sound and the Fury*, but it can be said with some assurance that he finished the final typescript when he was in New York in October 1928 and that he had been engaged on the book during most, perhaps all, of the preceding months of that year. In an admirable account of the composition and publication of the novel, Meriwether records that Faulkner did the typing in the room on Macdougal Street occupied by his friend and literary agent, Ben Wasson, and that when he had completed the typescript he handed it to Wasson with the comment, "Read this, Bud.

It's a real sonofabitch."[161] Faulkner seems to have had little hope that *The Sound and the Fury* would be published,[162] and his pessimism received early justification when the book was rejected by Harcourt, Brace, who were then preparing to publish *Sartoris*. By early 1929, however, when Faulkner was back in Oxford,[163] *The Sound and the Fury* had been taken by the new publishing house of Jonathan Cape and Harrison Smith.[164]

In an article published in 1962, a former reader for Cape and Smith speaks of the book arriving there as "a severely battered manuscript" which had already been rejected by thirteen publishers,[165] but since the period between the completion of the typescript and the signing of the contract was, at most, four months, there can clearly have been no time for so much traffic to have gone on. Other evidence indicates that when Harcourt, Brace turned down *The Sound and the Fury* Harrison Smith took the initiative in getting hold of the book: he already knew Faulkner's work since he had been an editor at Harcourt, Brace at the time of the decision about *Sartoris* and, indeed, had himself influenced that decision.[166] According to Faulkner's introduction to the Modern Library *Sanctuary*, Smith told him that *The Sound and the Fury* would not sell; at the same time, Faulkner recalled, the acceptance encouraged him to "think of myself again as a printed object. I began to think of books in terms of possible money. I decided I might just as well make some of it myself." In January 1929, just at the time when *The Sound and the Fury* was accepted by Cape and Smith, and when *Sartoris* was published by Harcourt, Brace, Faulkner began work on the first version of *Sanctuary*. He said in the Modern Library introduction that the writing took him "about three weeks"; to judge from the dates on both the manuscript and the carbon typescript of the novel it took him the best part of five months and was not completed until May 25, 1929.[167]

The work was done in Oxford, where, with the exception of his New York trip, Faulkner seems to have stayed more or less continuously since the autumn of 1927. John Faulkner spoke of his brother's frequent attendance during this period at country dances, where he would sit quietly by the whiskey tub, drinking, watching, and listening,[168] and Faulkner may also have been involved, in late 1928 and early 1929, in the unsuccessful campaign of his uncle J. W. T. Falkner II, to be elected District Attorney.[169] Faulkner himself spoke in 1958 of the valuable experience of country people, their lives and their talk, which he obtained from accompanying his uncle on political campaigns: "I would go around with him and sit on the front galleries of country stores and listen to the talk that would go on."[170] According to John Faulkner, it was on one such trip, presumably during an earlier campaign, that Faulkner actually witnessed the incident on which he based the anecdote of the spotted horses.[171]

In the summer of 1929 Faulkner was married. Estelle Oldham

Franklin had divorced her husband and returned to Oxford with the two children of the marriage, Malcolm and Victoria (known as Cho-Cho). She and Faulkner seem quickly to have resumed, and then deepened, their relationship of earlier days, and on June 20, 1929, they were married just outside Oxford in the old slave-built Presbyterian Church at College Hill.[172] They spent their honeymoon at Pascagoula, and it was there that Faulkner corrected the galleys of *The Sound and the Fury* and wrote Ben Wasson a remarkable letter in which he explained what he had been trying to do in the first section of the novel and why he was dissatisfied with the way that section had been set up in the galleys.[173]

When Faulkner and his wife returned to Oxford they rented an apartment from Miss Elma Meek, to whom Faulkner later gave a page of the manuscript of *Pylon*.[174] That autumn he wrote *As I Lay Dying*—while working night-shift at the University power-plant, according to his own account[175]—and by January 12, 1930, he had completed the final typescript.[176] Meanwhile, on October 7, 1929, *The Sound and the Fury* had been published. It sold poorly, at a time when Faulkner was urgently in need of money to support his new family, but the warm critical reception must have contributed to the interest shown by the editors of national magazines in the short stories which Faulkner began sending them by the early months of 1930. From the record of submissions which Faulkner kept for about two years from January 1930, we can see that he succeeded in placing no less than thirty of the forty-two stories which he tried to sell to magazines during that period.[177]

Many of the stories had probably been written in the 1920's; even so, as Meriwether observes, the sheer number of them is impressive, as is the proportion of acceptances, while the fact that five stories had been accepted by the high-paying *Saturday Evening Post* before the publication of *Sanctuary* on February 9, 1931, tends to undermine Phil Stone's statement that it was only after *Sanctuary* that editors began taking Faulkner's work.[178] In a note dated January 1, 1931, which appears on the back of a page from a carbon typescript of "The Brooch,"[179] Faulkner jotted down some of the money he had earned in 1930. From *Scribner's*, presumably as an advance payment for "Dry September," published January 1931, he had received $200; from the *Saturday Evening Post* he had had two payments of $750 each, for "Thrift," published in September 1930, and "Red Leaves," published the following month. Thus these last two stories each brought Faulkner more money than either of his first two novels, for which he apparently received advances of $200 and $400 respectively,[180] and it seems extremely unlikely that he received anything like $750 for *Sartoris* or *The Sound and the Fury*.

The financial rewards of short-story writing were of great importance to Faulkner at this time, and indeed at later periods as well. His early success in placing stories, especially with the *Saturday Evening Post*, may have been one of the factors which encouraged Faulkner, in April 1930,[181] to purchase Rowanoak, one of several similar houses built in Oxford shortly before the Civil War. The house, which stands at the end of a curving, cedar-lined drive, is of two stories, with a few steps leading up to the verandah and the front door, and four columns supporting the central pediment; it was in poor condition when Faulkner bought it, and he seems to have carried out with his own hands, skilfully and proudly, much of the necessary work of renovation and modernisation.[182] One of Faulkner's visitors in the early autumn of 1931 later described the house as "gray and rotting"; another, early in 1932, found the house "in the process of a gentle renovation."[183] The purchase of such a house appears in retrospect to have been an event of both practical and symbolic importance, reaffirming in concrete terms that decision to stay in the South which Faulkner had made long before, and perhaps reflecting a desire to sustain a particular mode of Southern existence. In this respect it is perhaps relevant to note that of the books in his library which Faulkner took the trouble to inscribe, a large number bear dates from 1930, 1931, and 1932; most of them also carry the name of the house. He put his name at about this time in books which had previously belonged to other members of the family, and in 1932 he systematically inscribed with his name, the year, and the name of the house each of the fourteen volumes of a library edition of the Bible.[184] It is almost as though such actions were for Faulkner part of the ritual essential to setting up a permanent home.

In October 1930, about four months after Faulkner and his wife had moved into Rowanoak, *As I Lay Dying* was published. Some reviewers spoke of the unpleasantness of its subject-matter, a comment made with even greater frequency and force about its successor, *Sanctuary*, which appeared in February 1931—not in the form in which Faulkner had originally written it in the early months of 1929, but in a much revised version which he had produced by tearing down the galleys and extensively rewriting them. Though this revision greatly improved the novel, we shall see[185] that it did nothing to reduce the violence of the action, and the reception of *Sanctuary*, which was to set an unhappy pattern for American criticism of Faulkner for many years to come, concentrated almost exclusively upon this aspect of the book. Some critics admired it, but after *Sanctuary* it became commonplace to speak of Faulkner as the leading representative of a school or "cult" of cruelty and violence; other critics, equally missing the point, attacked Faulkner for his lack of social conscience.[186] Despite the general incomprehension displayed by the reviewers, or perhaps because of the rather lurid reputation they had given the book, *Sanctuary* was a modest commercial success, and Faulkner himself became a minor celebrity.

The mild notoriety created by *Sanctuary*, together with the general awareness among contemporary writers of the technical achievement represented by *The Sound and the Fury*, made Faulkner the centre of a good deal of attention when he appeared at the conference of Southern writers held at Charlottesville, Virginia, in October 1931, just after the publication of *These 13*, his first volume of short stories. He seems not, however, to have created a good impression. Sherwood Anderson, who was present, wrote to his future mother-in-law on October 24, at the end of the two-day meeting: "Bill Faulkner had arrived and got drunk. From time to time he appeared, got drunk again immediately, & disappeared. He kept asking everyone for drinks. If they didn't give him any, he drank his own."[187] Allen Tate, who was also at the conference, recalls Faulkner's behaviour in somewhat similar terms and says that Faulkner especially disgraced himself during a visit to Princess Troubetzkoy (Amelie Rives Troubetzkoy, the novelist), who lived just outside Charlottesville.[188]

There are plenty of stories about Faulkner's drinking, and although many such accounts have become greatly exaggerated through retelling, others seem too circumstantial to be dismissed. Phil Stone, in 1931, could speak of Faulkner as "the most normal, the sanest man I have ever known. He has less tendency to any sort of excess ... than any man I have ever known."[189] Marshall Smith, calling on Faulkner in the summer of 1931, found him happily making, and quietly drinking, home-brewed beer.[190] Yet Faulkner apparently had some reputation as a drinker in New Orleans,[191] and there is no doubt that he was drinking heavily later that autumn of 1931, and that he drank too much again in the 1950's. He also got drunk on numerous occasions in the intervening years, especially in Hollywood and New York, but much more rarely than popular legend would suggest. The drinking bouts referred to by Robert Coughlan in *The Private World of William Faulkner* apparently belong to the 1950's phase. According to Coughlan, who had talked with several of Faulkner's relations and friends, these bouts sometimes produced violence but were generally unobtrusive: "He would supply himself with whiskey and, after a period of elation, retire to his own bed, drinking until sleep or coma set in, drinking again when consciousness returned, until days and nights had passed and slowly he returned to the world."[192] Robert N. Linscott, a former editor at Random House, recently published an account of encounters with Faulkner in New York in the early 1950's; on one occasion, according to Linscott, Faulkner talked about his own drinking:

His grandfather used to give him heeltaps (the last drops left in the glass), he said. Then later he drank a lot to ease the pain when he was in an airplane crack-up. But mostly, he thought, his drinking was a matter of chemistry. He'd go along for weeks or months at a normal gait—two bourbons at luncheon, two more after five, a Martini before dinner, and half a bottle of wine with it, and maybe another bourbon or two to nurse along during the evening. And then the craving would come. Most often he'd fight it off. But once in a while something would happen that would "get me all of a turmoil inside," and liquor seemed the only escape. It was only when he was caught in a situation he couldn't easily cope with that he'd give in to what he called the chemistry of craving and go over-board. You would be aware of the symptoms of increasing tension—drumming fingers, evasive looks, monosyllabic replies to questions—then he'd disappear, and, when you next heard of him, he'd be out cold.[193]

John Faulkner, like Coughlan and Linscott, spoke of his brother's drinking as a relief from reality, but he also produced some evidence to suggest that Faulkner himself often exaggerated the extent of his drunkenness, that he would "play drunk" simply to "excuse himself from going to work for a while."[194] John Cullen, who had been hunting with Faulkner, reckoned that Faulkner could usually "control his drinking, take it or leave it alone,"[195] and this comment touches upon what seems to have been an essential characteristic of Faulkner's drinking. He drank heavily at times, with disastrous results which occasionally necessitated hospital treatment. But these unhappy periods apparently represented the occasional surrenders of a man who was otherwise possessed of tremendous powers of will, determination, and endurance—qualities which alone enabled him to survive the extraordinary personal and practical pressures to which he was subjected for most of his adult life. Faulkner stayed with Malcolm Cowley in the early autumn of 1948, at a time when he was recovering from a bad drinking bout, and Cowley recalls with admiration the sheer will-power with which Faulkner gradually brought himself back to normal, enduring evident agony in obeying to the letter the instructions of his doctor, taking his drinks at ever more widely spaced intervals until he was capable of taking just one Martini with his lunch and nothing further.[196] Above all, when Faulkner was writing he drank only very occasionally, or not at all, and there is much shrewdness in John Faulkner's remark that "no man could turn out the amount of work Bill did and drink as much as people claimed he did."[197]

Many stories of Faulkner's drinking come from those who met him at publishers' parties and similar social gatherings. Carl Van Vechten, for example, recalls several meetings with Faulkner in New York from the late 1930's onwards and says that apart from one occasion in December 1954, at Van Vechten's own apartment, when he agreed to be photographed, Faulkner had always had too much to drink and had withdrawn as a result into taciturnity or even into complete silence.[198] On the other hand, it seems clear that Faulkner had early adopted taciturnity and silence, with or without the drinking, as a deliberate defence against the intrusions of the world, specifically the social and literary world. He had no literary small-talk and disliked talking to literary people: as he often said, he didn't want to discuss his own books and had never read theirs.

This is not to say that Faulkner did not enjoy his first taste of fame during his visit to New York in the autumn of 1931. He seems to have gone on there shortly after attending the Southern Writers' Meeting at the University of Virginia on October 23rd and 24th, although he also spent a day or two in Chapel Hill at this time. Faulkner arrived in New York early in November and stayed on into early December.[199] At the very beginning of December, Mrs. Faulkner joined him in New York for a short visit. Interviewed in Memphis on November 30, she said: "The reason I'm going to New York is to keep people away from him. He has an apartment on the 28th floor of a building and his last letter said that he liked it better, for he could forget the noise and see the sun and sky."[200] While in New York, Faulkner went to a good many parties and made a number of new acquaintances: it was apparently at this time that he first encountered Nathanael West, whom he was later to meet again in Hollywood,[201] and among the books he had at the time of his death were signed copies of Philip Barry's *Hotel Universe*, dated December 17, 1931, and of Marc Connelly's *The Green Pastures*, which Faulkner himself had also inscribed in New York on November 20, 1931.[202] But although Faulkner seems always to have enjoyed his visits to New York as a temporary release from the special tension of life in Oxford, he was never tempted by the attractions of literary centres as such. His early flirtations with New York, New Orleans, and Paris were all short-lived, and he never forgot that his real business was the writing of books, a job he could best do in his own part of the world and in the relative seclusion of his own home. This attitude was largely responsible for his behaviour at social and literary gatherings, where he conserved his energies and his emotional expenditure, choosing silence rather than chit-chat, making little effort to conceal his impatience with both the frivolous and the over-earnest, with the hangers-on of the literary and publishing world, or, for that matter, with some of its most powerful figures.

Faulkner's withdrawals, however, were sometimes more apparent than real. As he had listened quietly in the past to the daily talk of country people, so he listened now to the party talk of urban sophisticates. Sometimes he even heard something that he could make use of in an immediate and practical way. Ben Wasson recalls one party during this particular visit of Faulkner's to New York at which someone talked about British torpedo boats during the First World War, about the young men who crewed them and who drank desperately when they were ashore. As Wasson and Faulkner walked home from the party, Faulkner kept repeating, over and over, "Those pore fellows, those pore fellows"; a few weeks later, after Faulkner had returned to Mississippi, Wasson received the completed typescript of "Turn About".[203] From Faulkner's short story sending schedule it appears that he sent "Turn About" to Wasson on January 9, 1932;[204] since he was still in New York at the beginning of December, and may even have stayed on for the publication of *Idyll in the Desert* on December 10, he must have written the story at considerable speed. Wasson must also have acted promptly, since on March 5, 1932, "Turn About" was published in the *Saturday Evening Post*.

Anthony Buttitta published in 1938 an account of the few October days which Faulkner had spent in Chapel Hill, North Carolina, seven years earlier as the guest of Buttitta himself and Milton A. Abernethy, who were editing from Chapel Hill the little magazine, *Contempo*. During most of the visit, Buttitta recalled,

> [Faulkner] stayed in bed, resting and drinking an occasional spot, even eating his meals in bed. He did venture out after three days, and we took him to a movie at Durham, twelve miles away; but the movie irritated him, and as soon as we were comfortably seated, he was ready to go. "Don't want to hear talk," he said. "Would rather talk myself. Let's go out and talk." He started talking the moment we got outside; he told us of his new book, "Light in August," the manuscript of which he had brought to Chapel Hill; and later he recited, over and over, a poem by James Joyce.

In January 1932 Buttitta received a letter from Faulkner, inviting him to stay at Rowanoak: " 'I will warn you,' he wrote, 'that I am trying to finish my novel, and so I am going to let you entertain yourself during the forenoons. But in the afternoons and evenings we can get together.' "[205]

The novel, of course, was still *Light in August*, which he had begun in Oxford the previous August and which he now seems to have succeeded in completing fairly rapidly, since the final page of the manuscript is dated "Oxford, Miss./19 Feb. 1932".[206] In the unpublished autobiographical piece from which we have already quoted his comments about the writing of *The Sound and the Fury*, Faulkner said that the ecstasy he had then experienced did not recur when he wrote *As I Lay Dying* because he knew all about the book before he began, but that he had hoped to recapture it in writing *Light in August* which he began "knowing no more about it than a young woman, pregnant, walking along a strange country road." He continued:

The book was almost finished before I acquiesced to the fact

that it would not recur, since I was now aware before each word
was written down just what the people would do, since now I was
deliberately choosing among possibilities and probabilities of behaviour and weighing and measuring each choice by the scale of
the Jameses and Conrads and Balzacs. I knew that I had read too
much, that I had reached that stage which all young writers must
pass through, in which he believes that he has learned too much
about his trade. I received a copy of the printed book and found
that I didn't even want to see what kind of jacket Smith had put
on it.[207]

He believed at that time "that in *The Sound and the Fury* I
had already put perhaps the only thing in literature which would
ever move me very much: Caddy climbing the pear tree to look in the
window at her grandmother's funeral while Quentin and Jason and
Benjy and the negroes looked up at the muddy seat of her drawers."[208]
It was just at this time, however, and particularly during the period
between the completion of the manuscript of *Light in August* on
February 19, 1932, and the publication of the book the following
October, that several important acknowledgments of Faulkner's major
stature were being published. In February 1932 appeared a special
Faulkner issue of *Contempo*, and it was presumably as a result of the
Chapel Hill visit that Faulkner's name appears alongside those of
Lewis Mumford, Ezra Pound, and Langston Hughes as one of the
magazine's six "contributing editors." In printing nine poems and
one short story by Faulkner, all previously unpublished, the magazine
hailed him as "America's most creative living writer,"[209] while a
similar enthusiasm was shown by Paul Romaine somewhat later in the
year when introducing *Salmagundi*, a little volume containing poems
and essays by Faulkner which had previously appeared in magazines.
Also in 1932, six of the poems first published in the February issue of
Contempo reappeared in a volume entitled *An Anthology of the
Younger Poets*.[210] There is ample evidence here of the kind of reputation which Faulkner was gradually establishing in his own country.
In France, meanwhile, serious interest in Faulkner had begun with
Maurice Coindreau's translations of "A Rose for Emily" and "Dry
September" and his article, "William Faulkner", in the June 1931
issue of the *Nouvelle revue française*: Coindreau, who had a remark-
ably full and clear appreciation of the intelligence and technical
virtuosity of Faulkner's work, did not hesitate to introduce him to
French readers as "une des figures les plus intéressantes de la jeune
littérature américaine."[211]
The popular success of *Sanctuary* had won Faulkner another and
rather different kind of reputation, and it was not altogether surprising that he should soon receive an approach from Hollywood.[212]
Faulkner accepted an offer from Metro-Goldwyn-Mayer and began

work in Hollywood on May 16, 1932.[213] In the year which followed he worked on nine "properties," only two of which were actually produced : *Lazy River*, released on March 7, 1934, and *Today We Live*, released April 28, 1933. The latter, based on Faulkner's own story "Turn About," was the only MGM production for which he received screen credit, but two weeks after its release, on May 12, 1933, Paramount released their production *The Story of Temple Drake*, based on Faulkner's *Sanctuary*. Despite the appearance of these two films MGM did not renew Faulkner's contract when it expired on May 13, 1933.[214] Faulkner had not been especially happy in Hollywood, and he seems to have spent only part of the year working there. Joseph L. Blotner lists books inscribed as at Rowanoak in September and October 1932, thus offering strong, if not conclusive, evidence that Faulkner was in Oxford during those months, and Faulkner himself told several times the story of how he continued to draw pay from MGM while living at home from the autumn of 1932 until the spring of 1933, and of how his contract was eventually terminated while he was working in New Orleans, apparently on the film which eventually became *Lazy River*.[215] According to a newspaper article of December 1932, Faulkner had "engineered an abrupt and mysterious disappearance" on the day after his arrival at the MGM studios; there was even a "vague report" that he was on his way home; but a week later he reappeared, "as mysteriously as he had vanished." The article continued :

"The truth is that I was scared," commented the writer in his Mississippi drawl, after he had been acclimated. "I was scared by the hullabaloo over my arrival, and when they took me into a projection room to see a picture and kept assuring me that it was all going to be very easy, I got flustered."[216]

The same article mentions work in progress on two short stories by Faulkner, and it appears that the properties on which Faulkner worked but which were never produced included "Honor," based on his short story of that title, and "War Birds," based on parts of *Sartoris* and of the stories "Ad Astra" and "All the Dead Pilots."[217]

On April 20, 1933, shortly before Faulkner's contract with MGM came to an end, his second and final book of poems, *A Green Bough*, was published. Faulkner, who often spoke of himself as a frustrated poet, set a good deal of store by his verse, but he seems to have written few, if any, poems after the middle 1920's. Many of the poems in *A Green Bough* are extant in versions dating from 1924 and 1925, and although Faulkner continued to revise the poems included in the volume—it was at the galley stage that he added, or perhaps replaced, the sixth stanza of poem VIII[218]—few of the revisions seem to have been extensive or specially significant. A volume of Faulkner's poems, to be entitled "A Greening Bough," was already in prospect early in 1925[219] and the main reason for delay seems to have been Faulkner's difficulty in finding a publisher for a book of his verse. The only poem of Faulkner's to have its first publication after the appearance of *A Green Bough* was "The Flowers That Died", published in *Contempo* in June 1933. One of four published poems by Faulkner which have never been collected, its characteristic features can be seen from the opening stanza:

> The flowers that died last year again are growing,
> Pale flames kindle on the hearth of day;
> And faint horns of the morning, faintly blowing,
> Lighten the bannered path for dawn to stray.[220]

It might be tempting to read some special significance into this last poem which Faulkner ever published, were it not that the imagery and cadences are so Swinburnian, suggesting that this may be a very early example of Faulkner's verse rather than a very late one.[221]

The great occasion of Faulkner's personal life in 1933 was the birth, on June 24, of his daughter Jill.[222] A daughter, Alabama, born to Mrs. Faulkner in 1931, had lived only a few days—John Faulkner told a pathetic story of his brother going out to the cemetery alone to bury the child—and the birth of another child was deeply important to Faulkner.[223]

It was apparently also in 1933 that Faulkner purchased a private aircraft. When Henry Nash Smith visited him early in 1932, Faulkner showed great interest in the information that Smith had travelled from Dallas to Jackson in a tri-motored cabin aircraft: "I've never ridden in a cabin plane ... I'd like to have a chance to fly one."[224] Following the success of *Sanctuary* and his year with MGM, Faulkner was able to buy a cabin aircraft, a Waco, of his own, and it was presumably in the Waco, and in company with his friend, Vernon Omlie of Memphis, that Faulkner flew to attend the dedication ceremonies of Shushan Airport, New Orleans, in February 1934.[225] As we shall see, Faulkner's experiences during this trip provided him with much of the material for *Pylon*, and, as with "Turn About," he must have worked rapidly, since *Pylon* was actually published in March 1935, scarcely more than a year later. It was in the Waco, too, that Dean Swift Falkner, the youngest of the Falkner brothers, was killed at Thaxton, Mississippi, during the afternoon of Sunday, November 10, 1935. According to newspaper reports, Dean Falkner had been in Pontotoc, Mississippi, for two days, taking up passengers for short flights, and the three passengers who were killed with him when the Waco crashed—an eye-witness said that a wing fell off and dropped into a cemetery a mile from the spot where the aircraft itself came down—were local farmers who had gone up to look at their farms from the air.[226] Faulkner, as the owner of the aircraft and the one who had encouraged Dean in his flying activities, felt largely responsible for what had happened; in later years he expressed this feeling in very practical terms by taking a great interest in Dean's daughter, also called Dean, who had not been born at the time of her father's death, and by paying for her education.[227]

In the month of Dean's death, November 1935, Faulkner returned to Hollywood. His employers on this occasion were Twentieth Century-Fox, and his first assignment was *Road to Glory* (released September 4, 1936); the director was Howard Hawks, who had been both producer and director of *Today We Live*, and who seems to have been largely responsible for persuading Twentieth Century-Fox to employ Faulkner, despite the fact that Faulkner's earlier work for MGM had not made much of an impression in Hollywood.[228] Faulkner received screen credit for *Road to Glory* and *Slave Ship*, and of his work on the latter he once said: "I'm a motion picture doctor. When they find a section of a script they don't like I rewrite it and continue to rewrite it until they are satisfied. I reworked sections in this picture. I don't write scripts. I don't know enough about it."[229] During the two years he was employed by Twentieth Century-Fox, Faulkner also worked on a number of pictures for which he did not receive screen credit. During that time, too, legends about him continued to accumulate, and some of these were mentioned as early as August 1936 by Nunnally Johnson, himself a Southerner, in an interview with a newspaper columnist. As well as telling the story about Faulkner working in Oxford when the studio thought he was in Beverly Hills, Johnson spoke of

an early conference in which Faulkner sat for three hours without opening his mouth. Toward the close Mr. Zanuck, presiding, inquired: "Are there any further questions?" Mr. Faulkner sat up and cleared his throat. "Yes, sir."

"What did you have in mind, Mr. Faulkner?" asked Mr. Zanuck, hopeful of some great creative suggestion. "Please," answered Faulkner, "may I have an office?"[230]

While Faulkner was in Hollywood in late 1935 and early 1936 he seems to have continued working on *Absalom, Absalom!*, which he had begun before writing *Pylon*, and which he completed back in Oxford in the spring of 1936.[231] Later in 1936 he returned to Hollywood and was apparently working there when *Absalom, Absalom!* was published that October.[232] During the first seven months of 1937 he seems to have been in Hollywood more or less continuously: Maurice Coindreau, to whom Faulkner had written from Beverly Hills on February 26, stayed with him there in late June in order to discuss the translation of *The Sound and the Fury* on which Coindreau was at that time engaged, and it was one evening during this visit that Faulkner read aloud the story, "Afternoon of a Cow," pretending that it was by a man called Ernest V. Trueblood.[233] Later that summer Faulkner was back in Oxford[234] and in an interview given to the Memphis *Commercial Appeal* on November 17 he compared Hollywood to "a very wealthy, over-grown country town. In fact, it reminds me very much of a town that has sprung up as the result of an oil boom." He continued, "I knew very few actors, but the ones with whom I did come into contact were normal, hard-working people, leading much saner lives than we are led to believe." He told the reporter that he did not intend to return to Hollywood and that he disliked scenario writing "because I don't know enough about it. I feel as though I can't do myself justice in that type of work, and I don't contemplate any more of it in the near future." Announcing that *The Unvanquished*, which the reporter calls "a collection of short stories," would appear in February, Faulkner also said that he was working on a new novel. He hoped to finish it by the following summer but it might take longer: although he had written books in six weeks, "sometimes it takes as long as a year and a half, time depending on the amount of concentration." In any case, he intended to stay in Oxford until the book was finished.

The Unvanquished did appear in February 1938, and *The Wild Palms*, presumably the novel on which Faulkner was working at the time of interview,[235] was published in January 1939. Faulkner seems, moreover, to have spent most of 1938 in Oxford: Blotner lists books dated there in April, September, and October, and Robert Cantwell found Faulkner there towards the end of the year when he went in search of material for an article scheduled to coincide with the publication of *The Wild Palms*. Faulkner seems to have spoken freely to Cantwell about his great-grandfather, Colonel Falkner, perhaps because the material of *The Unvanquished* was still fresh in his mind. Certainly his observations reveal how closely certain aspects of "An Odor of Verbena," in particular, were taken from Colonel Falkner's character and career. Colonel Falkner, said his great-grandson, had probably been an overbearing man, and no doubt largely responsible for the quarrel with Thurmond which led to his death; moreover, "he had killed two or three men. And I suppose when you've killed men something happens inside you—something happens to your character. He said he was tired of killing people. And he wasn't armed the day Thurmond shot him, although he always carried a pistol."[236] Faulkner also spoke of his own childhood, of hearing about the Civil War from the old people who had lived through it, and of playing Civil War games with a Negro boy rather like Ringo in *The Unvanquished*. On the second day of his visit Cantwell was taken to see Aunt Caroline Barr, the Falkner family's Negro mammy, to whom Faulkner later dedicated *Go Down, Moses*, and driven out to Faulkner's farm, where he met Uncle Ned, the elderly Negro who later appeared under his own name in the piece on Mississippi which Faulkner wrote for *Holiday* magazine and in *The Reivers*.

Faulkner had bought the farm outside Oxford in 1938,[237] not long before Cantwell's visit, and he continued to run it, apparently with little concern for financial success, until the end of his life. John Faulkner had little patience with his brother's ideas about farming,[238] and Faulkner himself, once the first enthusiasm had worn off, appears to have regarded the farm as a kind of occasional hobby and relaxation. From time to time he did some writing at a kind of summerhouse on the farm, but its main importance was that it gave him an opportunity to acquire the kind of knowledge about farming—about the crops, the animals, the seasons, the weather, the land, and, not least, the tenants—without which he could scarcely have written such books as *The Hamlet* and *Go Down, Moses*. It also provided minimal justification for one of his favourite tongue-in-cheek remarks, that he was not a literary man at all, but a farmer. In a characteristically down-to-earth passage, John Cullen, Faulkner's one-time hunting companion, describes Faulkner's farming activities during the last years of his life:

> He owns a 320-acre farm, the old Joe Parks place, which is located in Beat Two on Highway 30 several miles from Oxford and four or five miles from the county line. On the bottom land he raises corn and hay to feed his stock, but he keeps very little stock on his farm. Mainly he feeds the corn and hay to his two jumping horses, which he keeps at his home in town. The hills of his farm are planted in pine trees. Faulkner and his Negro farm manager, Rinsy, grow no money crops, and apparently the farm is an expense instead of an income. ... He keeps the farm because he likes the country, because he likes to see things grow and wishes to think of himself as a farmer. For him, farming is actually a hobby.[239]

Cullen's book, *Old Times in the Faulkner Country*, is primarily concerned with Faulkner's participation in the expeditions which every autumn went out from Oxford and Lafayette County to hunt in the Mississippi Delta country. It is not clear from the book just when Faulkner began taking part in the hunts in which Cullen himself was involved. At one point Cullen remarks: "William Faulkner did not go with our camp when he was a young man. But he did hunt with Colonel Stone's camp even while he was still just a boy, and he killed a deer when he was only fifteen or sixteen years old."[240] John Faulkner spoke of his brother's taking up hunting again as a member of the Stone hunt, apparently in about 1930,[241] and it seems from the publication of "Lion" in 1935 that Faulkner must certainly have done a good deal of hunting by the early 1930's. At the same time, as Cullen usefully reminds us, Faulkner "never saw many of the things he has written about. The stories of the old hunters are often the sources of his tales."[242] Cullen mentions possible sources in fact or legend for various characters and incidents in Faulkner's novels and stories, and makes some interesting comments about Faulkner's behaviour in camp:

> Faulkner is never gloomy. He is always cheerful, quiet, and willing to do his part of the hardest, dirtiest work in camp. I have never heard him grumble about any hardships we ever had, and sometimes it has been pretty rough in the Delta.... As a woodsman, Faulkner is as good as any of us. If he is on a stand, he stays there until it is time to go in to camp. He is as good with a compass as anyone I know. In five thousand acres a man must have a compass to avoid getting lost. When no one will go with Faulkner, he takes his flashlight and goes coon hunting by himself at twelve o'clock at night in the lonely bottoms.[243]

Faulkner's interest in farming and hunting, like his love of horses, was an essential facet of his personality. If there was a certain self-consciousness about some aspects of his behaviour, and even about his insistence on calling himself a farmer, there can be no serious doubt of the depth of his feeling for the land and for the animal life, wild and domestic, which it sustained.

The visit by Robert Cantwell, as a representative of *Time*, was an indication that Faulkner, in the late 1930's, still retained much of his reputation of a few years earlier, and on January 18, 1939, the day before the publication of *The Wild Palms*, he was formally elected—along with Marjorie Kinnan Rawlings, John Steinbeck, and others—to the National Institute of Arts and Letters.[244] The year 1939 was also notable for Conrad Aiken's article on Faulkner's style in the November *Atlantic Monthly*,[245] one of the first deeply considered appreciative pieces—in English, at least—to reach a wide audience. Faulkner himself seems to have spent most of 1939 in Oxford, working on *The Hamlet*, which he had begun to pull together out of a mass of old and new Snopes material towards the end of 1938.[246] At this point in his career Faulkner was probably writing as hard and as fruitfully as he had ever done. Once *The Hamlet* had been organised into its final form some time late in 1939 and published in April 1940, Faulkner seems to have turned his attention to the rich material which he eventually shaped into *Go Down, Moses*. Dan Brennan, who later published novels himself, called on Faulkner in July of 1940 and found him working on two stories subsequently incorporated into *Go Down, Moses*, "Was" and "Go Down, Moses". When Brennan asked Faulkner where he had got the idea for the latter story, he said: "I was down to the station last week and a coffin came in off the train." To a question as to whether he thought his work was improving. Faulkner replied: "Ten years ago I was much better. Used to take more chances. Maybe I'm tired. I've had insomnia lately."[247]

It is hard, in fact, to detect any falling off of Faulkner's work in *The Hamlet* or *Go Down, Moses*, but there seems little doubt that the early 1940's were troubled years for Faulkner. The fact that he volunteered for service as an air raid warden[248] gives a very inadequate indication of the degree to which he was moved and troubled by the outbreak of the Second World War; more suggestive, perhaps, is his later statement that the idea of *A Fable* first came to him shortly after Pearl Harbor.[249] He was also experiencing many personal difficulties, one of the worst of which was a renewed and desperate shortage of money.[250] This pressure rather than any other was apparently responsible for driving him back to Hollywood in the summer of 1942, and it is some measure of his desperation that, as he later told Malcolm Cowley, he was forced to accept not a short-term job such as he had previously undertaken but a seven-year contract with Warner Brothers on not especially favourable terms: Henry Miller, writing from Hollywood on September 15, 1942, remarks that Faulkner "only gets three hundred [dollars] a week at Warner Brothers Studios."[251] With the help of Random House, Faulkner subsequently succeeded in extricating himself from this contract;[252] even so, his overall period of employment, from July 27, 1942, to September 19, 1945, made this much the most extended of his Hollywood experiences. During this time Faulkner probably worked on a total of seventeen screenplays, of which eleven were actually produced, but the only films for which he received screen credit were *To Have and Have Not* (released January 20, 1945) and *The Big Sleep* (released August 31, 1946), based on the novels by Ernest Hemingway and Raymond Chandler. Both films were directed by Faulkner's old collaborator Howard Hawks, and both starred Humphrey Bogart, of whom Faulkner spoke admiringly in a later interview.[253]

Faulkner did not stay continuously in Hollywood during these years. As he wrote to Malcolm Cowley late in 1944: "I can work at Hollywood 6 months, stay home 6, am used to it now an[d] have movie work locked off into another room."[254] The first period of active work for Warner Brothers apparently lasted from July 27, 1942, until August 18 of the following year; one of the things Faulkner did at this time was collaborate with Dudley Murphy on a treatment, provisionally entitled "Revolt in the Earth," of his own novel *Absalom, Absalom!*. In 1944 Faulkner worked on *To Have and Have Not* from February 14 to May 13, and he seems to have stayed on in Hollywood until beginning a further stint, mostly on *The Big Sleep*, running from June 12 to December 12:[255] in his first letter to Malcolm Cowley, written from the Warner Brothers studios at Burbank on May 7, Faulkner says that he is expecting his family to arrive on July 1 and that he will be returning to Oxford sometime in the fall. He adds that he can now rarely afford to go to New York since "I try to save what I earn here to stay at home as long as possible on."[256] Faulkner's final stint for Warner Brothers lasted from June 7 to September 19, 1945;[257] he expected to have to go back to Hollywood by March 16, 1946, when six months were up, but that April he told Cowley that Random House had won him a reprieve and made it financially possible for him to stay at home at least until September.[258] In fact, he never returned to Warner Brothers, and his subsequent screen-writing activities were of a limited and short-term nature: in 1948, for example, he worked on a science fiction idea for Howard Hawks; in 1951, again for Hawks, he apparently wrote a screenplay based on William E. Barrett's novel, *The Left Hand of God* (the film was eventually released in September 1955 but Faulkner's screenplay was not used).[259] A few years later he collaborated on the screenplay of *Land of the Pharaohs*, produced and directed by Howard Hawks and released in July 1955.[260] Faulkner joined Hawks on location in Egypt during the early months of 1954,[261] and according to one account he said he was doing the job as a favour to Hawks, who had helped him in the past, rather than for any other reason.[262] It was presumably to Hawks that Faulkner was alluding when he spoke, in 1955, of the film director with whom he had an understanding: "When I need money I call him, and when he needs a script he calls me."[263]

Faulkner's interest in Hollywood, from start to finish, was primarily financial. He rarely went to the cinema for pleasure, and had little enthusiasm for Hollywood itself. A newspaper article of February 1947 reported some remarks which Faulkner was said to have made to a companion as they stood on a Los Angeles street: "I'll be glad when I get back home ... Nobody here does anything. There's nobody here with any roots. Even the houses are built out of mud and chicken wire. Nothin' ever happens an' after a while a couple of leaves fall off a tree and then it'll be another year."[264] In a letter to Cowley written in the autumn of 1945, Faulkner speaks of "that damned west coast place" and of his relief that it "has not cheapened my soul as much as I probably believed it was going to do."[265] Yet Faulkner did not despise his own work in Hollywood, nor screen-writing as such. Asked by Jean Stein whether working for the movies could be injurious to a writer, he replied: "Nothing can injure a man's writing if he's a first-rate writer. If a man is not a first-rate writer, there's not anything can help it much."[266] The weakness of screen writing, he explained to his audience in Japan, was that it had to be a compromise, with "no chance for the individual to make something as he himself thinks it should be made";[267] at the same time, as he said to Jean Stein, "If I didn't take, or feel I was capable of taking, motion-picture work seriously, out of simple honesty to motion pictures and myself too, I would not have tried. But I know now that I will never be a good motion-picture writer; so that work will never have the urgency for me which my own medium has."[268] For Faulkner, screen-writing was one of the ways by which he made his living, one of the profitable opportunities available to an American writer in the middle of the twentieth century. His pride, his sense of craftsmanship, would not allow him to do a shoddy or unprofessional piece of work, and Faulkner's professionalism was the quality which Howard Hawks valued so highly: "He has inventiveness, taste, [Hawks told Coughlan] and great ability to characterize and the visual imagination to translate those qualities into the medium of the screen. He is intelligent and obliging—a master of his work who does it without fuss."[269]

Faulkner's rather bitter comments about Hollywood in 1944 and 1945 no doubt sprang largely from his irritation at having to engage in long periods of film work at a time when he was anxious to continue work on A Fable, of which he had completed a first draft, somewhat unhappily entitled "Who?", by the beginning of 1944.[270] The date December 1944 which appears on the final page of A Fable presumably refers to the commencement of work not on the original version but on the subsequent version which eventually became the published book. Writing to Malcolm Cowley in an undated letter which apparently belongs to the late spring of 1945, Faulkner said that he had already sent Random House about seventy pages of the new book; in April 1946 he spoke of "working on what seems now to me to be my magnum o."[271]

The correspondence between Faulkner and Cowley was primarily concerned with the preparation of The Portable Faulkner, which was published by Viking Press on April 29, 1946, and had an important effect on Faulkner's contemporary reputation; Cowley's editing of the volume, together with his introduction, has had a continuing influence upon the course of Faulkner criticism. By the early 1940's, Faulkner's work had begun to receive a certain amount of serious critical attention, still chiefly in France, but increasingly in America itself—notably from Conrad Aiken and Warren Beck.[272] With the general reading public, however, Faulkner had lost much of the rather limited popularity he had achieved in the early 1930's, his books (partly because of the war) had nearly all gone out of print, and in July 1944 Cowley was able to write:

> Do you want to hear a New York market report on your standing as a literary figure? It's about what I suggested in my other letter— very funny, and a great credit to you, but bad for your pocketbook. First, in publishing circles your name is mud. They are all convinced your books won't ever sell, and it's a pity, isn't it? they say, with a sort of pleased look on their faces . . . The second-rate bright boys among the critics did a swell job of incomprehending and

unselling you ... Now, when you talk to writers instead of publishers or publishers' pet critics about the *oeuvre* of William
Faulkner, it's quite a different story; there you hear almost nothing
but admiration, and the better the writer the greater the admiration
is likely to be. Conrad Aiken, for example, puts you at the top of
the heap....[273]

A year later, on August 9, 1945, Cowley wrote reporting the decision
to publish *The Portable Faulkner* and added: "the reason the book
pleases me is that it gives me a chance to present your work as a whole,
at a time when every one of your books except 'Sanctuary'—and I'm
not even sure about that—is out of print."

Writing to Cowley on May 7, 1944, Faulkner had revealed his own
dissatisfied awareness of the low state of his American reputation:

> I would like very much to have the piece done. I think (at 46)
> that I have worked too hard at my (elected or doomed, I dont know
> which) trade, with pride but I believe not vanity, with plenty of
> ego but with humility too (being a poet, of course I give no fart for
> glory) to leave no better mark on this our pointless chronicle than
> I seem to be about to leave.[274]

Faulkner gave Cowley his co-operation in the project, supplied a
certain amount of biographical information, gave explanations of
what he had been trying to do in a number of his stories and novels,
and did his best to help with various difficulties which Cowley encountered as a result of his choice of method—the arrangement of
excerpts from Faulkner's work in such a way as to present a chronological survey of Yoknapatawpha County. At one level, the precision
of Faulkner's replies shows the imaginative depth of his conception
of the county and its history. When Cowley raised a question as to
whether Sutpen bought his land from Issetibbeha or from Ikkemo-
tubbe, Faulkner's answer was clear and concise:

> Sutpen's deed would derive from Issetibbeha's grant, since Issetib-
> beha as the chief granted all the land, that is, made treaty to
> surrender the patent, though the white purchaser's deed from the
> govt. might be dated years later. Ikkemotubbe, (Doom) as Issetib-
> beha's inheritor, would have sold land still under his uncle's patent.

In the same letter, on the other hand, Faulkner confessed that he
had pitied Cowley in anticipation of the various inconsistencies he
would discover: "I never made a genealogical or chronological chart,
perhaps because I knew I would take liberties with both—which I
have."[275]

The idea of such a chart, however, was very much in Faulkner's mind at this time. In the summer of 1945, replying to Cowley's letter of August 9, Faulkner welcomed the decision to publish *The Portable Faulkner* with the words: "By all means let us make a Golden Book out of my apocryphal county. I have thought of spending my old age doing something of that nature: an alphabetical, rambling genealogy of the people, father to son to son."[276] That autumn, in a reply to Cowley's letter of September 17, Faulkner followed up his own suggestion that Cowley might include the final section of *The Sound and the Fury*—rather than the Jason section, which Faulkner had previously suggested—with the offer to write over the coming weekend a page or two of prefatory synopsis, summarising the three preceding sections and explaining the situation. Not surprisingly, the piece grew far beyond the length which Faulkner had originally intended for it. His imagination was seized afresh by the characters, themes, and situations of the book which had moved him more than anything else he had written, and what Cowley received that October, and eventually printed as an Appendix to *The Portable Faulkner*, was in the nature of an extended genealogy of the Compson family. "Here it is," Faulkner wrote. "I should have done this when I wrote the book. Then the whole thing would have fallen into pattern like a jigsaw puzzle when the magician's wand touched it." And in the same letter: "Let me know what you think of this. I think it is really pretty good, to stand as it is, as a piece without implications."[277] When Cowley pointed out a number of inconsistencies between the appendix and the original novel, Faulkner's first response was to speak of the genealogy as giving "a sort of bloodless bibliophile's point of view. I was a sort of Garter King-at-Arms, heatless, not very moved, cleaning up 'Compson' before going on to the next 'C-o' or 'C-r'."[278] Since Faulkner clearly had been moved when writing the piece, this answer was perhaps a little disingenuous, and some months later he offered a more convincing justification of his reluctance to check the appendix against the original:

> I dont want to read TSAF again. Would rather let the appendix stand with inconsistencies, perhaps make a statement (quotable) at the end of the introduction, viz: the inconsistencies in the appendix prove that to me the book is still alive after 15 years, and being still alive is still growing, changing; the appendix was done at the same heat as the book, even though 15 years later, and so it is the book itself which is inconsistent: not the appendix. That is, at the age of 30 I did not know these people as at 45 I now do; that I was even wrong now and then in the very conclusions I drew from watching them, and the information in which I once believed. (I believe I was 28 when I wrote the book, that's almost 20 years.)[279]

Faulkner seems not to have shared all of Cowley's ideas about his

work or, in particular, about his attitude to the Southern past.[280]
Whatever his reservations, however, Faulkner seems to have thought
Cowley had done a good job, and in April 1946, after receiving a copy
of the published book, he wrote in terms of warm congratulation:
"The job is splendid. Damn you to hell anyway. But even if I had
beaten you to the idea, mine wouldn't have been this good. By God, I
didn't know myself what I had tried to do, and how much I had succeeded."[281] Faulkner had cause to be grateful to Cowley for promot-
ing and carrying through *The Portable Faulkner* at a time when the
name of William Faulkner had faded into comparative obscurity, at
least in America. The book did a good deal to start people reading
Faulkner again. It afforded an opportunity for readers to come to his
work afresh, or for the first time, and a challenge to reviewers and
critics to make up their minds about him: thus Robert Penn Warren's
review in the *New Republic* has itself become a point of departure for
much subsequent Faulkner criticism.[282] Faulkner himself may have
gained something from the opportunity to review in a fresh light the
whole body of his work; he may also have gained valuable encouragement from the reception of the book in America and from the various
reminders, in Cowley's previous letters to him, of the kind of esteem
in which his work was held by some of those best competent to judge.
On September 17, 1945, Cowley wrote:

Did I tell you about the story I heard from Sartre, about
Hemingway drunk in Paris insisting that Faulkner was better than
he was? ... He said about you [on another occasion], "Faulkner
has the most talent of anybody but hard to depend on because he
goes on writing after he is tired and seems as though he never threw
away the worthless. I would have been happy just to have managed
him." Hemingway would be a good manager, too—he knows how
to say exactly what he feels and set a high price on it.

"Did I tell you what Jean-Paul Sartre said about your work?" Cowley
had asked Faulkner a few weeks earlier. "What he said about you
was, 'Pour les jeunes en France, Faulkner c'est un dieu.' Roll that over
on your tongue."[283]
    During 1945, 1946 and 1947 Faulkner worked hard, if intermit-
tently, on *A Fable*. As late as March 1946, Harold Ober, Faulkner's
agent, was still referring to it as "Who?", but on April 18, 1946, he
received a letter in which Faulkner said that the book would have a
different title, that it was a big book of a kind he had not previously
attempted, and that it must be done right, even though it might take
another two years to complete. In July 1947 Faulkner told Ober that
he had done about four hundred pages of the book and expected it to
run to a thousand when finished. By the end of 1947, however, he
had apparently run into serious difficulties with *A Fable* and turned

his attention, temporarily at least, to other projects. In January 1948 he began writing *Intruder in the Dust*,[284] and the publication of the book, in September of the same year, was an event of considerable historical importance in his career. *Intruder in the Dust* was the first novel of Faulkner's to have appeared since *Go Down, Moses*, more than six years earlier; it seemed to speak out with a new directness and explicitness upon a burning issue of the day, and it sold more copies (about 18,000 in the first year) than any of his previous books had done.[285] *Intruder in the Dust*, indeed, completed what *The Portable Faulkner* had begun, the re-establishment of Faulkner as a literary nobility. In an interview given while he was in New York in the autumn of 1948, Faulkner complained of popular curiosity about his personal life and spoke nostalgically of the days in New Orleans when he was a "free man," with "one pair of pants, one pair of shoes, and an old trenchcoat with a pocket big enough for a whisky bottle." During the same interview he remarked :

> I write about the people around Oxford. I know them, and they know me. They don't much care what I write. "Why, look here," they'll say. "Bill Faulkner's gone and got his picture in the New York paper. It says here he's written a book." So they come around and try to borrow money, figuring I've made a million dollars. Or else they look twice and figure I couldn't make a thousand.[286]

When Metro-Goldwyn-Mayer bought *Intruder in the Dust* and proceeded, in 1949, to make the film in Oxford itself, the resultant local excitement seems for the first time to have awakened Faulkner's fellow-townsmen to the realisation that he was a figure to be reckoned with.[287]

The publication of a collection of Faulkner's stories was authorised by Random House in 1948, and that autumn, flying home after visiting New York for the publication of *Intruder in the Dust* on September 27 and staying with Malcolm Cowley at his home in Connecticut, Faulkner amused himself by working out a scheme for such a volume.[288] The plan which Faulkner then devised was incorporated, with the addition of a few more stories, into the published *Collected Stories* of 1950. Omitted from the list were the Gavin Stevens "detective" stories which by this time Faulkner had already decided to publish in a separate collection—the *Knight's Gambit* volume of November 1949.

In November 1948 Faulkner was elected to membership of the American Academy of Arts and Letters;[289] in the early summer of 1950 he was awarded the Academy's Howells Medal for Fiction. In a letter apologising for not appearing to receive the award in person and make the customary brief speech of acceptance Faulkner explained that he was "a farmer this time of year" and that "up until he sells crops, no Mississippi farmer has the time, or money either, to travel anywhere on. Also I doubt if I know anything worth talking two minutes about."[290] It can at least be said of these remarks that Faulkner was genuinely involved that summer, if not in farming, at least in local events. In early September, for example, he issued the "Beer Broadside," one of his anti-prohibitionist contributions to the battle then raging in Oxford for and against the legalisation of the sale of beer. To the argument that Oxford should prohibit beer sales because the neighbouring town of Starkville and Water Valley had done so, Faulkner replied with an ironic, and hilarious, demonstration of the irrelevance of such reasoning:

> Since Starkville is the home of Mississippi State, and Mississippi State beat the University of Mississippi at football, maybe Oxford, which is the home of the University of Mississippi, is right in taking Starkville for a model. But why must we imitate Water Valley? Our high school team beat theirs, didn't it?[291]

Faulkner's continuing involvement with the life of his town and region is also suggested by his participation in one of the annual hunting trips to the Delta, in company with John Cullen, Uncle Ike Roberts, and other regular members of the hunt, in November 1950, the month in which he heard that he was to receive the Nobel Prize.[292]

The award to Faulkner of the 1949 Nobel Prize for Literature—the Academy had not been able to agree on a candidate the previous year—was announced in Stockholm on November 10, 1950. It followed the publication of *Collected Stories* the previous August but seems to have been even more immediately influenced by Faulkner's general European reputation, which at that time was still much higher than his American reputation. Continuing American doubts about Faulkner's work, and some apprehension as to the reasons why he had been awarded the prize, were well summed up in a *New York Times* editorial the following day:

> His field of vision is concentrated on a society that is too often vicious, depraved, decadent, corrupt. Americans must fervently hope that the award by a Swedish jury and the enormous vogue of Faulkner's works in Latin America and on the European Continent, especially in France, does not mean that foreigners admire him because he gives them the picture of American life they believe to be typical and true. There has been too much of that feeling lately, again especially in France. Incest and rape may be common pastimes in Faulkner's "Jefferson, Miss." but they are not elsewhere in the United States.[293]

There was at first some doubt as to whether Faulkner would go to Stockholm to receive the prize, but at the end of November Mrs. Faulkner announced that her husband would certainly make the trip. Faulkner himself was said to be "in bed with a severe cold. He became ill after a hunting trip in northern Mississippi." According to Coughlan's fairly circumstantial account, Faulkner's indisposition had been caused by excessive drinking.[294] On December 7, Faulkner was in New York with his daughter, Jill, who was then still at school and who had undertaken to write reports of the trip for a local newspaper. The following day they flew together to Stockholm, where on December 10 Faulkner received his medal and scroll at the hands of King Gustav. Before leaving New York Faulkner said that he would take Jill to Paris before they returned home: "Seeing Paris seems to be in the mind of every young female." He also said that he had not yet decided what to do with the $30,000 prize money: "This prize has been won by thirty years of my life that are passed [sic], and what's left doesn't need that money."[295] In the event, the prize money became the basis of the funds now administered by the William Faulkner Foundation, a body established in January 1961 and charged by Faulkner himself with the aims of encouraging writers in Latin America and of awarding scholarships to Mississippi Negroes seeking higher education.[296]

In 1951 Faulkner received other honours: in March his editor, Saxe Commins, accepted on his behalf the National Book Award for the *Collected Stories*, and in October he went himself to New Orleans to be made an officer of the Legion of Honour by the French Consul-General.[297] That September saw the publication of *Requiem for a Nun* and during the summer Faulkner seems to have spent several weeks in Cambridge, Massachusetts, where the Brattle Theatre Group planned to produce a stage version of the book. Faulkner, in collaboration with Albert Marre, and with some assistance from Ruth Ford, tried to complete such a version, but the Brattle Theatre production never materialised.[298] The producer, Lemuel Ayers, who in July had sent Faulkner a list of suggestions for adapting the book to the stage, remained interested in the possibility of presenting *Requiem for a Nun* in New York, and it was not until March 1952 that he finally abandoned the idea, at least for that season.[299]

When he had finished working on *Requiem for a Nun*, Faulkner seems to have turned his attention once again to *A Fable*, in a determined effort to finish a book on which he had already been working, on and off, for nine years, and of which one section had already appeared in print, as *Notes on a Horsethief*, in February 1951. Faulkner was apparently in Oxford for the better part of 1952, although he made a trip to Paris in the spring,[300] and according to one account he was still working on the stage version of *Requiem for a Nun*.[301] That winter, however, Faulkner was in Princeton and New

York and working steadily at A Fable. When Loïc Bouvard interviewed him in Princeton on November 30, 1952, Faulkner was staying at the Princeton Inn;[302] later he apparently stayed with Saxe Commins at his home in Princeton and on weekdays commuted with Commins to New York, where he worked at the offices of Random House, at least part of the time in the room where Commins was conducting business.[303]

Early in 1953 Faulkner, who was still doing occasional screen-writing jobs for Howard Hawks, for the first time tried his hand at writing for television, collaborating in an adaptation of his short story, "The Brooch."[304] The performance, on April 2, 1953, was severely criticised in the New York Times by Jack Gould, who accused Faulkner of turning "a bitter story of a man caught in a fatal mother complex" into "a soap opera that dutifully met all the provisions of television's purity code." Since Gould felt that Faulkner had betrayed his responsibility to sustain high standards, he was extremely un-impressed by advance publicity which claimed that Faulkner had completed the adaptation in forty-eight hours and quoted him as saying: "Television is a stimulating medium for the writer, and I'll probably feel more at home in it when I know more about it."[305] Faulkner did at least two other pieces of writing for television: in 1954 he adapted another of his short stories, "Shall Not Perish," and in 1960 his original television play, The Graduation Dress, was broadcast. These were both shown by CBS, who also presented be-tween 1954 and 1960 nine other adaptations from Faulkner's writ-ings, including, in 1954, versions of "Smoke" and "Barn Burning" by Gore Vidal and, in 1956, a version of As I Lay Dying; NBC's only Faulkner production during the same period was of The Sound and the Fury, in December 1955.[306]

In June 1953 Faulkner gave the commencement address at Pine Manor College, Wellesley, Massachusetts, where his daughter Jill was graduating at the top of her class. Two years earlier, in May 1951, he had given the commencement address when Jill graduated from the University High School in Oxford; a year later, in August 1954, he hurried back to Oxford from an International Writers Conference at São Paulo, Brazil, which he and Robert Frost had both been attending, in order to give Jill away at her wedding, on August 21;[307] A Fable was published on August 2, and it must have been a source of satis-faction to Faulkner that the publication of the book over which he had anguished for so long had so nearly coincided with the twenty-first birthday (in June) and wedding of the daughter to whom he was so deeply attached and to whom the book itself was dedicated. Faulkner spoke of this dedication to his audience in Japan the follow-ing year:

Why, that was the year she was twenty-one years old, she had been the youngest of the children and she had inherited lots of my traits. That is, she liked horses, too, and she spent a lot of time with me for that reason. With horses and with farmwork. And when she was little, she was more or less under my feet all the time 'cause she just liked the land, she liked dirt, she liked animals, and she listened to me for advice more than the others did, and for that reason I was more interested in watching her development because I had a chance to see, "Am I any good at this business of leading a child's development of character?" and this was just a gesture toward her when she became of age and was no longer under my thumb. It was just a way of saying, "Good-bye to your childhood, you are grown now and you are on your own." That's all.[308]

A *Fable* had for Faulkner the significance of a cumulative statement and affirmation, and it seems to have been no accident that the completion and publication of the book closely coincided with a number of important speeches and other public statements which Faulkner made during the early and middle 1950's. The Pine Manor commencement address, published in the *Atlantic Monthly* two months later as "Faith or Fear," and the Foreword to *The Faulkner Reader*, dated from New York in November 1953 (the month when A *Fable* was completed), were two such statements. Even earlier, in May 1952, speaking in Cleveland, Mississippi, at the annual meeting of the Delta Council, Faulkner had attacked what he considered the demoralising effects of governmental paternalism, especially as experienced by the farmers of the Delta:

What we need is not fewer people but more room between them, where those who would stand on their own feet, could, and those who won't, might have to. Then the welfare, the relief, the compensation, instead of being nationally sponsored cash prizes for idleness and ineptitude, could go where the old independent uncompromising fathers themselves would have intended it and blessed it: to those who still cannot, until the day when even the last of them except the sick and the old, would also be among them who not only can, but will.[309]

Faulkner's most forceful public statements, however, were made in 1955 and 1956. In January 1955, when A *Fable* had won him a second National Book Award (it later won him a Pulitzer Prize as well), Faulkner began his address of thanks by defining the artist in the simple humanist terms which were to become familiar from many subsequent statements and interviews:

By artist I mean of course everyone who has tried to create something which was not here before him, with no other tools and materials than the uncommerciable ones of the human spirit; who has tried to carve, no matter how crudely, on the wall of that final oblivion, beyond which he will have to pass, in the tongue of the human spirit, "Kilroy was here."[310]

The artist, he said, must always fail in his attempt to attain ultimate perfection, but "even failure is worth while and admirable, provided only that the failure is splendid enough, the dream splendid enough, unattainable enough yet forever valuable enough, since it was of perfection." What troubled him, Faulkner concluded, was that success in America had become too readily attainable: "Perhaps what we need is a dedicated handful of pioneer-martyrs who, between success and humility, are capable of choosing the second one."[311] In statements made later in 1955 Faulkner's remarks on the condition of contemporary American society became even more astringent. In April, for instance, he gave at the University of Oregon a speech entitled "Freedom American Style," of which a revised version was published the following July as "On Privacy: The American Dream: What Happened to It." Provoked by what he considered intrusions upon his own privacy, Faulkner declared:

> The American sky which was once the topless empyrean of freedom, the American air which was once the living breath of liberty, are now become one vast down-crowding pressure to abolish them both, by destroying man's individuality as a man by (in that turn) destroying the last vestige of privacy without which man cannot be an individual.[312]

Meanwhile, in the spring of 1955, Faulkner wrote from Oxford a series of letters to the Memphis *Commercial Appeal* on the integration question. As Hodding Carter remarked in 1957, in an article which conveniently reprints the most important sections of these letters, by making these and subsequent statements about integration "William Faulkner ventured beyond the ultimate Southern pale; and nothing, not even the initial Oxford reaction to *Sanctuary*, could match what has happened to him since."[313] In November 1955, after his return from a series of overseas visits on behalf of the State Department, Faulkner spoke out even more plainly. At a meeting of the Southern Historical Association in Memphis on November 10, he spoke on "American Segregation and the World Crisis," insisting firmly on the shame of segregation and showing his new awareness of the effect which segregation had upon the conception of America held by people overseas.[314]

The following year he addressed an article in a national magazine to each of the three main groups involved in the integration issue. The first of these, published in *Life* in March 1956, was "A Letter to the North," a plea to Northerners to take a moderate stand and not to exert too great or too hasty pressure upon the South. The intention of the article was to warn; its message, though more carefully and happily phrased, was essentially that of the notorious and obviously unsatisfactory interview of the same month, in which Faulkner was quoted as saying that if a fresh Civil War were to break out—as he thought it might if the North pushed too hard—then he would "fight for Mississippi against the United States even if it meant going out into the street and shooting Negroes."[315] "On Fear: The South in Labor," published in *Harper's* in June 1956 (and incorporating a revised version of the speech to the Southern Historical Association), was another plea for moderation, but one addressed primarily to the South: it urged Southerners to see the necessity and inevitability of integration, to rid themselves of the largely irrational fear of what Negro economic advancement would imply, and to learn to accept change peacefully while time yet remained. Finally, in September 1956, Faulkner contributed to the Negro magazine, *Ebony*, a piece entitled "If I Were a Negro." He began by disowning the remark about shooting Negroes in defence of Mississippi, and then went on to quote from his article, "A Letter to the North", a paragraph which summed up his advice to Northern liberals and to the officers of the National Association for the Advancement of Colored People. "Go slow, pause for a moment," Faulkner had said in that earlier article; he now explained that he had been afraid at that time that violence and bloodshed would follow any attempt to force the readmittance of the Negro girl, Autherine Lucy, to the University of Alabama, and that the gist of his advice was really "Be flexible":

Not the individual Negro to abandon or lower one jot his hope and will for equality, but his leaders and organizations to be always flexible and adaptable to circumstance and locality in their methods of gaining it. If I were a Negro in America today, that is the course I would advise the leaders of my race to follow: to send every day to the white school to which he was entitled by his ability and capacity to go, a student of my race, fresh and cleanly dressed, courteous, without threat or violence, to seek admission; when he was refused I would forget about him as an individual, but tomorrow I would send another one, still fresh and clean and courteous, to be refused in his turn, until at last the white man himself must recognize that there will be no peace for him until he himself has solved the dilemma.[316]

In the statements he made at this time Faulkner's main hope and intention was to speak for the small but significant group of Southern moderates—people like himself who loved their land and believed in it to the extent that they were "willing to face the contempt of the Northern radicals who believe we don't do enough, and the contumely and threats of our own Southern reactionaries who are convinced that anything we do is already too much."[317] In the event, Faulkner received in abundance both the contempt on the one hand and the contumely and threats on the other, since none of the embattled groups was prepared to listen with patience to his pleas. In Oxford itself, as Hodding Carter remarked, the outrage was immediate and personal. John Faulkner recalled that Faulkner's attitude towards integration "did not set well with the rest of us," although the family was prepared to let him go his own way without interference. Of the general reaction, John Faulkner said: "Of course, as soon as Bill started talking integration he became subject to anonymous phone calls at odd hours. Mysterious voices cursed him, and his mail was filled with abusive anonymous letters. Since none of us agreed with Bill's views we said, 'It serves him right. He ought to have known this would happen.' "[318] The Negroes in Oxford itself seem always to have regarded Faulkner as one of their best friends, but national Negro leaders joined in attacking him and W. E. B. DuBois once challenged him to a public debate.[319] Among Northern liberals Faulkner's views on integration were almost totally misunderstood, and the degree of his emotional and intellectual identification with traditional Southern attitudes was consistently exaggerated. It may be true that Faulkner always held to the view that neither whites nor Negroes really wanted integration in any practical social sense;[320] yet it could be argued that even this assessment might contain elements of uncomfortable truth, and certainly no one who now reads with care the formal statements which Faulkner made between 1955 and 1957 can fail to acknowledge the courage of his stand or the strong sense of duty on which it was based.

Faulkner's concern with the racial issue in America seems clearly to have been increased by his experience, in the summer and early autumn of 1955, of a round-the-world trip made under the auspices of the State Department. In August he was in Japan, where he took part in the Summer Seminar in American Literature held at Nagano; there were some fifty Japanese participants, and the record of their questions and Faulkner's answers was published in 1956 as *Faulkner at Nagano*. As the editor of the volume observed, the questions "ranged from the nature of Truth to the nature of Japanese mothers-in-law," but one of the participants recalls with admiration and affection Faulkner's unfailing courtesy and patience: "However silly the questions were, he never let us see that he thought them foolish."[321] After brief visits to other countries in the Far East, Faulkner moved on to Europe. He arrived in Rome on August 28, declaring to reporters, "I am not a writer, I am a peasant—even if I do write books and people read them."[322] On September 17 he was in Munich,[323] and later that month he arrived in Paris, where he was much feted and interviewed.[324] In mid-October, after a brief visit to England, he went on to Iceland for a week before returning to the United States.[325]

Shortly after his return Faulkner began work on *The Town*, and he seems to have stayed mainly in Oxford during the period of writing the book, which was also a time when he was deeply engaged in the integration controversy. The final stages of *The Town* were completed in September 1956, partly in Charlottesville, Virginia, where Jill and her husband now lived, and in October it was announced that Faulkner would be writer-in-residence at the University of Virginia, in Charlottesville, during the following Spring semester.[326] He took up his appointment in February 1957 and seems to have spent most of his time in Charlottesville until the following June, with two important exceptions. In late March and early April he was away on another State Department trip, this time to Greece. On March 28 he was presented with the 1957 Silver Medal of the Athens Academy, and on March 30 he attended a gala performance of the Greek production of *Requiem for a Nun*.[327] An American production of the play was still almost two years off, but in Europe there had already been several productions, the first in Zürich in October 1955, the most recent in Paris, in an adaptation by Albert Camus, in September 1956.[328] Faulkner was also away from Charlottesville in late May, the month which saw the publication of *The Town*, when he was in New York for the presentation of the Howells Medal of the American Academy of Arts and Letters to John Dos Passos.[329]

From February to June 1958 Faulkner was again writer-in-residence at the University of Virginia, and he and Mrs. Faulkner were now spending so much of their time in Charlottesville, even when he was not actually engaged by the University of Virginia, that in June 1958 they bought a house there.[330] No doubt the chief attraction of Charlottesville continued to be the presence of Jill and her husband, and now their children, Faulkner's grandsons. But Faulkner apparently found fewer intrusions upon his privacy in Charlottesville than he had done in Oxford—he once said that he liked Virginians because they were snobs and so did not have time to bother him—and he also liked the riding and foxhunting which Charlottesville offered; there are photographs of him in full hunting kit of the traditional English type, and in 1962 he told an interviewer: "There is something about jumping a horse over a fence, something that makes you feel good. Perhaps it's the risk, the gamble. In any event it's a thing I need."[331] Faulkner did not cut himself off from Oxford, however. He retained possession of Rowanoak and the farm, and returned to Mississippi at fairly frequent intervals. His mother, Mrs. Maud Butler Falkner, was still living in Oxford until her death in October 1960, and Faulkner liked to visit her as often as possible: when he was staying in Oxford he is said to have called on her nearly every day. For many years Faulkner had helped to meet his mother's household and other expenses, and he had also paid much of the cost of the various illnesses from which she had suffered in her old age. John Faulkner pays tribute to Faulkner's generosity towards other members of his family and towards the family's Negro dependants; John Cullen also speaks of Faulkner's unostentatious generosity to his neighbours, and there is a story that in the 1930's Faulkner sold some of his property in order to help Phil Stone, who was then in financial difficulties.[332]

During his last years Faulkner was busy not only with the publication of *The Mansion* (in November 1959) and the completion of *The Reivers*, but also with some of the public activities which had become a familiar part of his life: in March and November 1958, for example, two brief periods of residence at Princeton University; in October 1959, an address in Denver, Colorado, to a conference of the United States National Commission for UNESCO; in April 1961, a State Department trip to Venezuela; in April 1962, a brief visit to the United States Military Academy at West Point, where he talked informally with the cadets and with a group of visiting women students from Vassar. Back in Charlottesville that same month of April 1962, however, he declined an invitation to the White House on the grounds that it was too far to go to eat with people he didn't know.[333]

That summer Faulkner and his wife were in Oxford. On June 4 *The Reivers* was published, to almost universal acclaim. And then, on Friday, July 6, Faulkner was dead. According to John Faulkner, his brother was in the hospital for a check-up when he suddenly suffered a heart-attack. Three weeks previously he had had a bad fall from a horse, one of several during his last years, and W. M. ("Mac") Reed, of the Gathright-Reed drugstore in Oxford, recalled that when Faulkner paid his last visit to the store on the Tuesday he was still wearing the brace necessitated by injury to his back.[334]

Faulkner was not an old man, and he was still writing with great vigour, as *The Reivers* had shown only a month before. To the world at large, therefore, his death brought both a sense of shock and a sense of waste. In Oxford itself, except among the few people who knew Faulkner well, it seems to have made relatively little impact: there was a curiously minimal quality about the fifteen-minute closure observed by Oxford shopkeepers, at the instigation of the local newspaper, while Faulkner's funeral was taking place on July 8,[335] and one account of the funeral noted: "Few of the shoppers standing in the blazing sun on the sidewalks turned to watch as the procession rolled past."[336] It was "Mac" Reed, one of the few constant friends that Faulkner had had in Oxford and now on the board of the William Faulkner Foundation, who spoke of Oxford's sad failure to appreciate either Faulkner's greatness as a writer or his quality as a man: the people of Oxford, he said, "never really understood that Bill was their closest friend who was trying to show them in his own peculiar way that they must appreciate the good life better. He told me that many times."[337] This might serve in some respects as Faulkner's epitaph, certainly with no less appropriateness than the rather sentimental lines of "My Epitaph," the last poem of A *Green Bough*, which were naturally seized upon by reporters and subsequently by John Faulkner. Better than either—perhaps even better, because more precisely relevant, than the Nobel Prize address—might be the letter which Faulkner wrote from Oxford in June 1950 to thank the American Academy of Arts and Letters for awarding him the Howells Medal for Fiction :

The medal received, also the transcription of Mr. MacLeish. It's very fine indeed to have these concrete evidences—the gold and the voice—of the considered judgment of one's peers. A man works for a fairly simple—limited—range of things : money, women, glory; all nice to have, but glory's best, and the best of glory is from his peers, like the soldier who has the good opinion not of man but of other soldiers, themselves experts in it, who are themselves brave too.

Though it still seems to me impossible to evaluate a man's work. None of mine ever quite suited me, each time I wrote the last word I would think, if I could just do it over, I would do it better, maybe even right. But I was too busy; there was always another one. I would tell myself, maybe I'm too young or too busy to decide; when I reach fifty, I will be able to decide how good or not. Then one day I was fifty and I looked back at it, and I decided that it was all pretty good—and then in the same instant I realised that that was the worst of all since that meant only that a little nearer now was the moment, instant, night: dark: sleep: when I would put it all away forever that I anguished and sweated over, and it would never trouble me anymore.[338]

THE WORK

SOLDIERS' PAY

UNTIL he wrote *Soldiers' Pay* Faulkner seems to have thought of himself primarily as a poet, though with some potentialities as a graphic artist. It is therefore not surprising that in writing the novel he should have drawn heavily upon the verse he had already written and upon the kind of painting and illustration which interested him as an artist. In the poem "The Lilacs" Faulkner had already portrayed the figure of the terribly wounded airman for whom death would have been preferable,[1] and in the course of the novel itself he quotes from his own poems several times: the epigraph is the final stanza of a poem subsequently published as poem XXX of *A Green Bough*, and when Januarius Jones explains to Cecily Saunders why he has called her "Atthis" (p. 227) he quotes from poem XVII of *A Green Bough* and uses an image which appears in poem XV. When Margaret Powers makes her first appearance in *Soldiers' Pay* she is specifically described as a Beardsley figure, and we are reminded of the influence of Aubrey Beardsley on Faulkner's own drawings, although Faulkner lacked Beardsley's fascination with the grotesque and his most immediate model was probably the American artist, John Held, Jr. These highly mannered drawings of Faulkner's, particularly those in the copies of *Marionettes* which he produced for his friends, depict highly formal and vaguely symbolic landscapes, with slim figures in attitudes of repose or of graceful arrested movement, the whole composed into a patterned relationship of bold and precisely defined forms.[2] He seems to be seeking something of this same quality—which is almost that of the *commedia dell' arte*—in *Soldiers' Pay*, not only in the working out of the action but in some of the descriptions as well:

Mahon was asleep on the veranda and the other three sat beneath the tree on the lawn, watching the sun go down. At last the reddened edge of the disc was sliced like a cheese by the wistaria-covered lattice wall and the neutral buds were a pale agitation against the dead afternoon. Soon the evening star would be there above the poplar tip, perplexing it, immaculate and ineffable, and the poplar was vain as a girl darkly in an arrested passionate ecstasy. Half of the moon was a coin broken palely near the zenith and at the end of the lawn the first fireflies were like lazily blown sparks from cool fires. A negro woman passing crooned a religious song, mellow and passionless and sad. (p. 286)

61

Again:

> The road gashed across the land, stretched silent and empty before him, and below the east was a rumorous promise of moonlight. He trod in dust between dark trees like spilled ink upon the pale clear page of the sky, and soon the moon was more than a promise. He saw the rim of it sharpening the tips of trees, saw soon the whole disc, bland as a saucer. Whippoorwills were like lost coins among the trees and one blundered awkwardly from the dust almost under his feet. (p. 312)

Throughout the book the descriptions tend always in the direction of artificiality: in Chapter III, for example, the rain is described in terms of "assaulting gray battalions" (p. 119): it is compared to "cavalry with silver lances" (p. 119); it "galloped" over Mr. Saunders and his son (p. 120); Emmy watches it "surge by like a gray yet silver ship" (p. 121); others hear it "like a million little feet" (p. 121); as it dies down, it appears "with an occasional gust running in long white lines like elves holding hands across the grass" (p. 121). It is characteristic of the formal manner of *Soldiers' Pay* that it should be rich—one might say, obsessively rich—in similes but relatively lacking in metaphor, and later in the novel (pp. 298-299) military images are again used both to describe the rain and to bolster Faulkner's attempt to create an effect of simultaneity, to overcome the limitations of spatial form and give the sense of several events taking place at the same moment in time.

Faulkner also appears to be fascinated with the symbolic possibilities—it may be, not always very clearly apprehended—of natural phenomena: the Rector's garden, for instance, private and highly formal, with its ancient and highly prized rose-bush, and the swirling silver tree, image of motion in stasis, which also appears in such unpublished works as "Mayday" and "The Wishing-Tree," where it figures as the "wishing-tree" itself, attended by the figure of St. Francis.[3] Description becomes thematic and emblematic rather than imitative. Thus sexual desire and sexual experience are repeatedly evoked in terms of water imagery, and a deliberate consistency appears in the images used to describe certain of the characters: Januarius Jones, with his fat body and yellow eyes, is several times referred to as a satyr; Donald Mahon, as a youth, had been like a faun; while Cecily Saunders is persistently evoked in terms of plants, and especially of trees. On her first appearance, in Chapter Two, she bends "sweetly as a young tree," (p. 70) and a few pages later she is more elaborately described:

> She was like a flower stalk or a young tree relaxed against the table: there was something fragile, so impermanent since robustness and

strength were unnecessary, yet strong withal as a poplar is strong through very absence of strength, about her; you knew that she lived, that her clear delicate being was nourished by sunlight and honey until even digestion was a beautiful function ... (p. 80)

The image of a poplar frequently recurs, other tree images abound, and early in their relationship Jones identifies Cecily as a "hamadryad" (p. 77).

Faulkner's presentation of Cecily as a kind of tree-spirit or wood-nymph raises some interesting questions. It may simply have been his intention to define her as a kind of wild thing, a creature not to be confined within established bounds, and certainly not within the limits represented by the Rector's deeply loved and carefully cultivated garden, itself an image of his withdrawal into illusion. But other possibilities suggest themselves. On page 67 of the book we read:

Jones' morale rose balloon-like. "I will try any drink once," he said, like Jurgen.

Faulkner had apparently been reading James Branch Cabell's *Jurgen* (1919), and when, ten pages later, Jones calls Cecily a hamadryad, it is perhaps relevant to recall that one of Jurgen's more sustained amatory relationships was with the hamadryad, Chloris, in the land of Leûke. There are several other aspects of Faulkner's presentation of Jones which suggest a possible association with the figure of Jurgen: both are sexually aggressive and immensely self-satisfied, both make arrogant displays of erudition and have a fondness for ponderous reflections on human existence. At the first appearance of Jones in Chapter II of *Soldiers' Pay* there are several things which recall *Jurgen*, and particularly the beginning of that book: Jones's fascination with the church-spire recalls the remark in *Jurgen* about all steeples being "of phallic origin"; the Rector shows Jones his garden, as Nessus shows Jurgen the "garden between dawn and sunrise"; the rose-tree the Rector has so carefully cultivated, and which Jones finds so unimpressive, is faintly reminiscent of Jurgen's irritation, in the land of Cocaigne, with the female nature-myths and "their mystic roses that change colour and require continual gardening"; Jones's host gives him an ill-fitting cast-off garment of his own to wear, rather as Nessus gives Jurgen his shirt, and this unusual garment is later remarked by Cecily and Margaret Powers, rather as Jurgen's shirt elicits comment from those who meet him; Jones on first meeting Cecily speculates whether her eyes are "gray or blue or green?" (p. 72), just as Jurgen never knows whether the eyes of Dorothy la Desirée are "grey, blue or green."[4]

The resemblances between *Soldiers' Pay* and *Jurgen* are of so detailed a nature as to suggest that Faulkner intended the presentation of

Januarius Jones as a kind of parody of Cabell's presentation of Jurgen —even the coincidence of the initials may not be accidental. If this was in fact the intention, he does not seem to have sustained it with any care in the later chapters of the book, except insofar as Jones continues in his career of erudite pomposity and indiscriminate lechery, and it remains unclear just how this element in the book was designed to correlate with the material centering on Donald Mahon. Donald's pre-war activities seem to have been somewhat similar to Jones's, at least so far as women were concerned, and in the final chapter Jones eventually manages to substitute himself for Donald in Emmy's mind, unconsciously echoing the words which Donald had used in his earlier seduction. However, despite these somewhat ambiguous similarities, Faulkner's principal aim seems to have been to set off Mahon, the figure representing the terrible realities of war, against the fantasy figure of Jones. The two men represent a polarity within the novel, and Jones's effective avoidance of Mahon emphasises this opposition and at the same time appears as characteristic of his entirely irresponsible and amoral attitude to the world.

Yet the basically non-realistic presentation of Jones makes the application to him of such terms as "irresponsible" and "amoral" ultimately irrelevant. If we feel that this use of fantasy is incompatible with the Mahon material and disruptive of the book's overall seriousness, we must nevertheless recognise that this is just the effect which Faulkner seems to have calculated. We should perhaps be cautious, therefore, in insisting on the novel's realistic elements. The Rector is continually spoken of as being in a dream, and all the characters seem ultimately to operate on a level that is by no means wholly realistic. Objections have been made to the presentation of Donald Mahon in that he is too shadowy, too ill-defined, too appallingly absent, to operate as an effective centre of the action or as an adequate counterpoise to Jones. It was of course a figure of a similar inarticulate and uncomprehending kind, for whom time is a fluid quantity and the present has little if any meaning, that Faulkner, with great technical adventurousness, was to use as the point of view in the first section of The Sound and the Fury; in Soldiers' Pay, however, we never know just how much Mahon sees, feels, or comprehends, although other characters are judged in terms of their behaviour towards him much as the characters in the later novel are judged by their treatment of Benjy. The point about Mahon seems to be that he is in large measure conceived in abstract terms as the Wounded Hero, a figure of myth. In Soldiers' Pay Faulkner appears not to have attempted any systematic working out of the situation, but Margaret Powers seems almost to become a priestess of the cult—there may be some significance in the reason she gives for refusing to marry Gilligan at the end of the book : "If I married you you'd be dead in a year, Joe. All the men that marry me die, you know." (p. 306)—while Cecily is apparently the virgin who is to restore the hero to health. It is perhaps in terms of this pattern that we should read the scene in Chapter VII in which Cecily, having given herself to George, rushes in to tell the Rector that she "cannot" marry Donald because "I am not a good woman any more." (p. 276) In this context, too, Cecily's identification as a wood-spirit seems to take on additional meaning, as does the insistence—especially through the sequence of Lowe's letters to Margaret Powers—on the steady, inevitable progress of the spring from April into May.[5]

At the same time, it seems important that none of these elements should be particularly stressed. The book is full of mythological allusions, of literary references, and of hints of the symbolic significances lurking in natural phenomena. Most of these allusions, however, seem designed to enrich the suggestiveness of the book in a general way— as when Jones refers to Cecily as Atthis—rather than to fit into any organised overall pattern. Soldiers' Pay, we must always remember, was Faulkner's first novel, the work of a man who still thought of himself primarily as a poet, and who had just published The Marble Faun, a pastoral cycle which one critic has described as Faulkner's attempt "to make a mythological poem, composed in a language of echoes and innuendoes and arranged in a kind of musical order. This was fixed in the formal context of traditional conventions of the English eclogue, using the cycle of the four seasons and the hours of the day to establish a relationship between separate poems. The effect gained by joining the evocative method of symbolist poetry with the highly developed patterns of the English pastoral is a unique conjunction."[6]

In writing his first novel Faulkner seems to have adopted a somewhat similar structural technique in an effort to give unity to a highly heterogeneous body of material. The technique is intimately related to the richness of allusion that we have already noted, the emphasis on the progress of the seasons, the recurrent images and symbols, the associations established between particular characters and particular natural objects or phenomena, the elaborately "poetic" nature of much of the language, the almost Spenserian obsession with similes. It is in terms of this technique that we can understand the lack of direct chronological progression in the narrative and the reliance instead on what appears at first to be a series of excessively fragmented scenes: incidents are placed in abrupt succession in an attempt to suggest simultaneity; characters appear and reappear with apparent inconsequentiality; moments of comedy and pathos meet and merge; at times we are given merely the disembodied voices of many different characters, or evocations of the mood of particular hours of the day. Faulkner's intention, it would seem, was that these brief scenes, interrelated by a pattern of recurring imagery and allusion, should finally be integrated into a single "poetic" whole, and that the disparate thematic elements of the novel would similarly blend and cohere. That he was not wholly successful in this attempt is clear; what is also evident, however, is that the endeavour was immensely ambitious and that it was pursued by Faulkner with a competence and consistency quite astonishing in a first novel.

In stressing the poetic element in *Soldiers' Pay*, however, it is important not to undervalue its success at a more conventional level. The opening scenes in the train, though slightly out of tune with the remainder of the book, are done with sophistication and wit, and throughout the novel Faulkner successfully sustains narrative interest and displays considerable shrewdness in characterisation. Some of the minor characters are crudely drawn—the Negroes, for example—but Gilligan is a remarkably successful attempt at a type Faulkner was not to portray again in his novels, the sufferings of the Rector are movingly evoked, and there are moments of direct and simple human experience—Mr. Saunders holding his son in his arms after his visit to Mahon, Gilligan telling Margaret Powers that Mahon is dying. Technically, too, it is remarkable that in this first novel Faulkner should have found his way to the technique of juxtaposition which, in a variety of forms, was to be central to so many of his major works. Already in *Soldiers' Pay* the quick succession of scenes permits a wide range of effects, from the comic to the pathetic, and the presence of Januarius Jones casts an ironic light over much of the book, as if the action were being regarded with a kind of double vision, alternating the tragic mask with the comic. One may here suspect that the young author has deliberately assumed an attitude of pseudo-sophisticated bitterness, self-consciously enrolling himself among the wastelanders, but elsewhere in the book he creates an almost Hardyesque sense of life's ironies. Coincidence is a frequent device, and although this is often effective at a merely comic level, as in the night encounters of Januarius Jones with George Farr, there are also more ambiguous moments, as when Cecily embraces Jones, mistaking him for Donald, and when Jones is able to substitute himself for Donald in the grief-stricken mind of Emmy. There are, too, a few moments of deliberate agony: Margaret Powers failing to repeat to Emmy the suggestion that she should marry Donald; Gilligan missing Margaret Powers on the train at the end of the novel.

These ironies are effective at a certain level. But they often seem gratuitously painful and too obviously contrived. The whole book, indeed, affects us in formal, almost balletic, terms, rather than as a direct presentation of human experience.[7] For all the evocations of a Southern town which are offered at various points in the novel, the action remains curiously unlocalised in time or space: the local inhabitants are a composite chorus rather than individuals; the Rectory itself could be in England almost as convincingly as in Georgia; and the class-structure of the novel seems at times to be quite specifically English. Realism is sacrificed to thematic continuity, pattern dominates plot, and it often appears that more attention is being devoted to the establishment of a *leit-motif* than to the exploration of the incident which justifies its existence. In *Soldiers' Pay*, rich and remarkable achievement though it was, Faulkner had not yet learned to fuse technique with experience, and he had not yet discovered his subject.

MOSQUITOES

THE basic situation of *Mosquitoes*, the isolation of a group of New Orleans intellectuals, artists, and socialites aboard a motor yacht on Lake Pontchartrain, may have had some parallel in Faulkner's own experience: Carvel Collins speaks of Faulkner's friendship with Colonel Charles Glenn Collins, a colourful character of Scottish origin who entertained his friends aboard a chartered yacht,[1] and Faulkner himself in the article on Anderson which he contributed to the *Dallas Morning News* on April 26, 1925, recalls spending a weekend with Anderson on a "river boat."[2] Many of the characters in the book were based, wholly or in part, on figures prominent in the New Orleans literary and social world at the time when Faulkner knew it best, early in 1925: the identification of Dawson Fairchild as Sherwood Anderson is clear beyond doubt, and among other people whose characteristics Faulkner is said to have drawn upon are Sam Gilmore and Julius Friend, one of the editors of the *Double Dealer*; according to Carvel Collins, a local bootlegger named Slim may have provided ideas for the character of Pete, or at least for his brother Joe.[3]

That the book was in part a *roman à clef* may have a significance beyond that of simple historical interest. Undoubtedly the book contained humorous notes to which only the ears of the initiated would be attuned, and in this sense Faulkner might seem to have been expressing a certain solidarity with the literary world of New Orleans. On the other hand, *Mosquitoes* is very largely a satirical novel—it is hard to think that many of those who recognised themselves among the characters can have been especially pleased—and constitutes in its overall effect a repudiation of New Orleans and of all such literary milieux. One of the most persistent themes in the novel is the sterility of talk, of the mere proliferation of words:

> Talk, talk, talk: the utter and heartbreaking stupidity of words. It seemed endless, as though it might go on forever. Ideas, thoughts, became mere sounds to be bandied about until they were dead. (p. 186)

As Olga Vickery has shown,[4] such passages as this are related to the opposition between words and actions which Faulkner explores in various ways in the course of the novel; they must also be regarded as Faulkner's verdict on the literary life of New Orleans. Those who remember Faulkner in New Orleans speak of him with remarkable consistency as rather silent and withdrawn—Mark Frost, the taciturn, strenuously gnomic poet of the novel, with his slim literary achievement and his grandiose assessment of his own literary importance, may well be Faulkner's attempt at a satirical self-portrait—and the shortness of his stay in New Orleans and his subsequent decision to live permanently in Oxford seem almost certainly to have been related to his impatience with the long, inconclusive, and creatively wasteful discussions which went on in the Vieux Carré and in the offices of the *Double Dealer* during that brief period when New Orleans could, with some justification, think of itself as a literary centre. If *Mosquitoes* was a *roman à clef*, its ultimate significance was that Faulkner was shaking the dust of New Orleans from his shoes, determined to strike out on new and more adventurous paths of his own.

The recipe for the book was simple. Faulkner took a representative selection of artists and hangers-on from the "art-world" of New Orleans, added to this group of obsessive verbalisers two young people (Jenny and Pete) who come from a completely different social situation and operate on a simple level of unreflective, unverbalised action, put them all aboard a yacht, and set the yacht afloat on Lake Pontchartrain. Once afloat and in motion, which for most of them consists simply in drinking and talking, the characters tend to fall into three main groups, with some overlapping. There are the older men : Fairchild, Julius (the Semitic man), Gordon, Major Ayers and Mark Frost. There are the older women : Mrs. Maurier, Mrs. Wiseman, Miss Jameson—and Mr. Talliaferro. Finally, there are the young people : the niece (Patricia), her brother (apparently called Theodore, although his sister also refers to him as Gus and Josh), and Jenny and Pete. To the older passengers these young people seem unmistakably and impregnably bound together by their very youthfulness :

> Forward, Jenny, the niece, her brother come temporarily out of his scientific shell, and Pete stood in a group; Pete in his straw hat and the nephew with his lean young body and the two girls in their little scanty dresses and awkward with a sort of terrible grace. So flagrantly young they were that it served as a barrier between them and the others, causing even Mr. Talliaferro to lurk nearby without the courage to join them. (p. 239)

Faulkner does not appear to be especially sympathetic towards these young people, despite the interest in Patricia which he suggests by way of Gordon's attraction to her and the awareness of the sexual desirability of Jenny which he confesses autobiographically : Jenny remembers meeting the "little kind of black man" called Faulkner who said he was "a liar by profession" and who said he could dance with Jenny's friends but not with Jenny herself "because he said he didn't dance very well, and so he had to keep his mind on the music while he danced." (pp. 144-145) Nevertheless, the young people are individually more independent and self-assured than most of their elders, much more certain of their role in the world and much less disposed to discuss that role with others. Pete has his concern for his hat and for Jenny; Jenny, mindless and beautiful, simply exists; the nephew is completely absorbed in his gadgetry; Patricia, though in some ways more complex, is dominated by her simple, unquestioning commitment to experience, and persistently acts with no premeditation other than that of a day-dream. Patricia is one of the main agents in creating such activity as the novel has to offer: her search for experience brings her into close relationships with several members of the party and with David, the steward, who is outside the group altogether. The other principal activating agents are also women: Mrs. Maurier, desperately determined to make the expedition a success; Miss Jameson, implacably searching for a man; and Jenny, most disruptive of all through the simple fact of her infinitely disturbing presence, "her sheer passive appeal to the senses." (p. 104)

Faulkner uses this situation and these agents as a means of exploring a wide variety of sexual relationships, bringing into constantly shifting juxtaposition his group of men and women of different ages and from widely divergent backgrounds. Thus we see Jenny and Pete together, Jenny and the young nephew, Jenny and Mr. Talliaferro, Pete and Miss Jameson, Miss Jameson and Mark Frost, Miss Jameson and Gordon, Gordon and Patricia, Patricia and David, and so on. We see the sad grotesquerie of Mrs. Maurier's entrapment of Mr. Talliaferro, and the possessive feeling of Patricia for her brother—they are twins, and she has something masculine about her, we are told, her brother something feminine. There is also the brutal sexuality of the swamper who takes David and Patricia back to the boat in a curiously disturbing episode which clashes violently with the prevailing artificiality of the book; in another such episode, devoted to an evocation of Pete's background, we encounter the world of prostitution. Throughout the book there are the many discussions of sex, and a number of anecdotes touching on the subject, notably Fairchild's story of his childhood experience in the lavatory, and further extensions of the theme appear in the descriptions of Gordon's statue and in the quotation and discussion of the poem "Hermaphroditus."

That Faulkner at one time intended an even broader exploration of sexual relationships is made clear by the typescript of *Mosquitoes* now in the Alderman Library. Though there are many differences between the typescript and the published book, most of these are of minor importance and there is nothing to suggest any major process of revision between the completion of the typescript in the summer of 1926 (the final page bears the manuscript note: "Pascagoula, Miss/1 Sept 1926") and the publication of the book on April 30, 1927.

What did happen, however, was that certain fairly extensive deletions were made from the typescript, apparently with a view to removing or modifying some of the passages dealing with sex. Some mildly bawdy remarks by Fairchild have been excised from the dialogue appearing on pages 97-98 of the published book, and there is a similar, though longer, deletion of approximately one and a quarter typescript pages from the dialogue on page 185, at the point immediately following Fairchild's observation that the population would certainly decline "if a man were twins and had to stand around and watch himself making love." In the typescript Fairchild goes on to suggest that a mechanical contrivance might be devised to perform the task of procreation, although there would always be some reactionaries who preferred to do things the old way.[5] The most extensive and most interesting of the deletions, however, involves the removal of a whole subsection of more than three pages of the typescript at a point immediately preceding the heading "Twelve O'clock" on page 156 of the book. The deleted material represents a continuation of the scene between Jenny and Patricia which appears on pages 136 to 151 : after they have been in bed for some time Patricia makes tentative approaches to Jenny, who, still not properly awake, responds with a kiss. Patricia is shocked at the kind of kiss Jenny gives her, and is on the point of showing her how to kiss in a "refined" manner when Mrs. Wiseman opens the door and switches on the light.[6] This cut apparently made necessary another a little later in the book : the scene between Jenny and Pete which ends on page 177 is considerably longer in the typescript, where it transpires that the reason Jenny is dissatisfied with Pete's kissing is that he does not do it in the refined way that she has recently learned from Patricia.[7] The exchange of confidences and kisses between Patricia and Jenny does not develop any further; nonetheless, it does represent a notable extension of the sexual theme in the novel. In view of the range of presentations Faulkner offers, we may even find it slightly curious that neither novel nor typescript contains any unmistakable allusions to male homosexuality, although it is possible that David, the steward, has tendencies in that direction.[8]

The treatment of sexual themes in Mosquitoes has been discussed at some length, because it has perhaps been insufficiently emphasised in the past, and because it shows Faulkner's early attempt to tackle problems which he dealt with much more successfully in later novels : especially interesting in this respect is his return to a Gulf coast setting in The Wild Palms for a story, that of Charlotte Rittenmeyer and Harry Wilbourne, which has certain affinities with the episode of Patricia's frustrated elopement with David. At the same time, it would be wrong to suggest that the book is wholly taken up with Faulkner's exploration of the possible varieties of sexual attraction and repulsion among his characters. The other major topics of conversation are art, creativity, and the opposition between words and action. The whole book becomes, in a sense, a demonstration of the futility of talk, of words, and we have already seen that this may be related to Faulkner's growing awareness of his own needs as a writer—an awareness also reflected in the statements on art and literature made at various points in the book. Indeed, the various themes continually merge and inter-relate. The sexual contrast between the powerful Gordon and the pathetic Talliaferro is at the same time a contrast between the dedi-cated artist and the essentially uncreative dilettante, between the man who prefers to act and do rather than speak and the man who talks out all his dilemmas and is totally ineffectual in action.

Dawson Fairchild makes in the course of the novel a number of down-to-earth comments on sex, and he becomes, as a figure in the pattern of the discussions, an example of profuse verbalisation; but his presence in the book seems to be primarily an outcome of Faulk-ner's own situation as a writer. Faulkner owed much to Anderson, and his awareness of the debt—and at the same time, his complete assurance as to the value of his own work—is made clear in the dedication to *Sartoris* in 1929: "To Sherwood Anderson through whose kindness I was first published, with the belief that this book will give him no reason to regret that fact." The debt is acknowledged once more in the appreciative article on Anderson published in the *Atlantic Monthly* in 1958; Faulkner also spoke warmly of Anderson in various interviews. But in 1926 it was apparently necessary for Faulkner, as an artist, to shake off Anderson's influence, and it may also have been necessary to him as a man to shake off Anderson's patronage. Certainly the presentation of Anderson in the character of Fairchild is not especially generous. The bemused, struggling earnestness of Fairchild, his perpetual groping towards final compre-hension and adequate expression, his painstaking accounts of child-hood experiences whose importance he believes to be enormous but whose meaning he cannot quite grasp—all this was extremely accurate as an evocation of Anderson, and must have been painfully so for Anderson himself. What does not appear so clearly in *Mosqui-toes* is the positive side of Anderson's talent, the side to which Faulkner himself had earlier paid tribute in the *Dallas Morning News* article, praising "I'm A Fool," for example, as the best short story in America.[9] The greatest compliment he pays Anderson in the novel, ironically enough, is in attributing to Fairchild the splendid Al Jackson tall tales which provide the liveliest episodes in the whole book. The Al Jackson material had been worked up in an exchange of letters between Faulkner and Anderson;[10] the irony lies in the fact that Faulkner's treatment of the material was superior in ingenuity to Anderson's, and considerably better written. Indeed, Faulkner's per-ception of this, his realisation that he had nothing further to learn from Anderson, may have been one of the factors prompting him to the repudiation which Mosquitoes undoubtedly represents.

That Faulkner should have incorporated the Al Jackson material into Mosquitoes at all is an indication of the extent to which the novel was for him a kind of rag-bag into which he could gather up all the usable odds-and-ends of his brief literary past. This is one of the reasons for the novel's comparative failure. The book nevertheless possesses a great and continuing interest deriving largely from the fact that it gave Faulkner an opportunity to try out a variety of stylistic and structural devices, thus pointing the way to his expansive literary future. "I'm not ashamed of it," Faulkner said of Mosquitoes during one of the class-sessions at the University of Virginia, "because that was the chips, the badly sawn planks that the carpenter produces while he's learning to be a first-rate carpenter . . ."[11] In conception, as we have seen, Mosquitoes was an "idea" book, rather as Soldiers' Pay had been, and the idea was the not especially original one of enforcing intimacy between a varied group of people for a period long enough to exhaust the resources of mere politeness. The novel was also an "ideas" book, in the sense in which Aldous Huxley spoke of the "novel of ideas," and in this respect it appears as a young man's audacious and even arrogant attempt to display his intellectual and stylistic virtuousity both by a series of extended discussions on such issues as sex and art and by a pattern of dramatic incident in which the debaters would appear in roles corresponding, directly or ironically, to the positions they had taken in discussion.

The book seems to have changed as it grew, however, and towards the end, particularly following the return of the Nausikaa and its passengers to New Orleans, it develops into a fairly elaborate series of technical experiments of a kind only very occasionally foreshadowed in earlier pages:

> Three gray, softfooted priests had passed on, but in an interval hushed by windowless old walls there lingers yet a thin celibate despair. Beneath a high stone gate with a crest and a device in carven stone, a beggar lies, nursing in his hand a crust of bread.
>
> (Gordon, Fairchild and the Semitic man walked in the dark city. Above them, the sky: a heavy, voluptuous night and huge, hot stars like wilting gardenias. About them, streets: narrow, shallow canyons of shadow rich with decay and laced with delicate ironwork, scarcely seen.)
>
> Spring is in the world somewhere, like a blown keen reed, high and fiery cold—he does not yet see it; a shape which he will know —he does not yet see it. The three priests pass on: the walls have hushed their gray and unshod feet.
>
> (In a doorway slightly ajar were women, their faces in the star-

light flat and pallid and rife, odorous and exciting and unchaste. Gordon hello dempsey loomed hatless above his two companions. He strode on, paying the women no heed. Fairchild lagged, the Semitic man perforce also. A woman laughed, rife and hushed and rich in the odorous dark come in boys lots of girls cool you off come in boys. The Semitic man drew Fairchild onward, babbling excitedly.)

That's it, that's it! You walk along a dark street, in the dark. The dark is close and intimate about you, holding all things, any-thing—you need only put out your hand to touch life, to feel the beating heart of life. Beauty: a thing unseen, suggested: natural and fecund and foul—you don't stop for it; you pass on. (p. 335)

This is the part of the novel which, while recalling certain aspects of *Soldiers' Pay*, looks forward, however hesitantly, to Faulkner's future work. Here appear the traces of Joycean influence that later developed into the complexities of the Quentin section of *The Sound and the Fury*, and it is at this later stage of the book that we see the final growth of Mr. Talliaferro into a pathetic and potentially tragic Prufrock figure, a shadowy anticipation of the Reporter in *Pylon*.[12] Here, too, we find the statements of artistic principle and belief which seem most fully to embody Faulkner's own position—almost as if the book, with its exploration and exposition of many different view-points, had been the means by which he had argued out his own un-certainties and arrived eventually at a clearer conception of his role as an artist. Faulkner's presence is felt throughout the book, possibly through Mark Frost, certainly through the figure of Gordon, the dedicated artist, and, more lightheartedly, through the autobio-graphical sketch of the man who was "a liar by profession." But it is in the reflections of Fairchild and of Julius, the Semitic man and chief representative of disenchanted reason, as they walk through the night streets of New Orleans, that something like a firm statement finally emerges; Fairchild speaks of genius as "that Passion Week of the heart," (p. 339) and Julius declares again and again: "I love three things: gold, marble and purple ... form solidity color." (p. 340) The "Wealthy Jew" in Faulkner's sketch of that name, published in the New Orleans *Times-Picayune* in 1925, had affirmed his love of "gold; marble and purple; splendor, solidity, color," and the substitu-tion of "form" for "splendor" is perhaps a mark of Faulkner's rapidly growing maturity.[13] The intoxication with the sheer splendour of language, everywhere evident in *Soldiers' Pay* and in the pieces written in New Orleans, is still present in *Mosquitoes*, and Faulkner was never to lose it entirely, but there is also in this second novel a much greater sense of the need to match language to character, to situation, and to emotional temperature. The heightened stylistic effects in the final pages are justifiable in terms of the movements of intoxicated, quasi-visionary experience which they embody; earlier in the novel the characters, though not always very fully drawn, have had sufficient individuality to mark most of their speeches as peculiarly their own, and the more or less consistent parody of Anderson's style in the speeches of Fairchild has had its part to play in this pattern.

The importance of *Mosquitoes* in Faulkner's career has not yet been properly estimated. It is not a good novel, but it was an essential step in Faulkner's progress towards the great achievements of the late 'twenties and early 'thirties. In writing *Mosquitoes* he shed a whole layer of literary pseudo-sophistication which he had picked up from the kind of writing currently in vogue. He escaped from the influence of Scott Fitzgerald: the presence of *This Side of Paradise* and *The Beautiful and Damned*, also the novels of a young man, full of clever talk and literary miscellanea, is strongly felt in the book.[14] He shook off, once and for all, the influence of Huxley and George Moore, and, not least, that of James Branch Cabell, who had influenced *Soldiers' Pay*, as well as the unpublished "Elmer" and "Mayday," and traces of whose characteristic phallic imagery can perhaps be seen in the descriptions of the pipe which the nephew is making and in Mr. Talliaferro's vision of himself as an unloaded gun. *Soldiers' Pay* and *Mosquitoes* are two of the most obviously and deliberately "contemporary" of Faulkner's novels. He wrote them at a time when he had already been seized by the literary ambition, the need to write, but when he had not yet found his proper material. In this situation he turned naturally to the literary modes fashionable with the contemporary public and with the literary group with whom he had mingled in New Orleans. There was a final irony in his using a form so characteristic and expressive of that milieu to deliver his pronouncement upon it.

SARTORIS

Sartoris occupies a curious position in Faulkner's career : certainly the last work of his apprenticeship, it is arguably the first work of his maturity. If there seems to be an extraordinary gulf between the book and its great successor, *The Sound and the Fury*, it nevertheless represents a very considerable advance over its two predecessors, *Soldiers' Pay* and *Mosquitoes*. *Mosquitoes*, however, was something of a sport, a deliberate exercise in a particular contemporary mode, and the major line of development seems to run directly from *Soldiers' Pay* to *Sartoris*. Several elements of the central situation in *Soldiers' Pay* reappear in *Sartoris*, though in a greatly modified form : Bayard Sartoris, like Donald Mahon, is a young Southerner home from flying in the First World War; Mahon's physical wounds have their counterpart in Bayard's psychic wounds, and Bayard's experiences serve almost as effectively as Mahon's injuries to isolate him from his family and friends. There are other resemblances : the assumption on the part of relations and friends that a settled relationship with a young woman may be the best treatment for the wounded hero; the action of a particular young woman (Margaret Powers, Narcissa Benbow) in marrying a sick man whom she believes she can help as a kind of substitute for what might have been a fuller relationship with a man now dead (Dick Powers, John Sartoris); and the evocation of the settled domestic background of the man now so torn by war in terms of the dedicated cultivation of gardens.

We also see in *Sartoris* that concern with the natural setting of human life, with the regular and ceaseless procession of the seasons, which we have already noted in *Soldiers' Pay*, and earlier in *The Marble Faun*. We are constantly made aware of the movement of time and the seasons from the beginning of the novel in the early spring of 1919, as old Bayard drives home past the newly tilled fields; the later stages of the spring are traced as one plant after another comes into bloom; the book then moves into high summer with its heat, into late summer, with its last rose, into the fall, when young Bayard and his bride watch the Negroes making sorghum molasses, and so into the winter, when young Bayard escapes to the simplicities of life with the MacCallums and hunts with Buddy MacCallum in the cold December rain. The final pages of the novel pass quickly through the winter, spring and early summer of 1920, until the twin accomplishment of young Bayard's death and his son's birth on June 11, and it is notable that despite the brevity with which this period of time is treated the seasonal movement is still precisely insisted upon :

> Then it was definitely spring again. Miss Jenny's and Isom's annual vernal altercation began, pursued its violent but harmless course in the garden beneath her window. They brought the tulip bulbs up from the cellar and set them out, Narcissa helping, and spaded up the other beds and unswaddled the roses and the transplanted jasmine. Narcissa drove into town, saw the first jonquils on the deserted lawn blooming as though she and Horace were still there, and she sent Horace a box of them, and later, of narcissi. But when the gladioli bloomed she was not going out any more save in the late afternoon or early evening, when with Miss Jenny she walked in the garden among burgeoning bloom and mocking-birds and belated thrushes where the long avenues of gloaming twilight reluctant leaned, Miss Jenny still talking of Johnny, confusing the unborn with the dead. (p. 358)

The inevitable movement of the seasons, with their associated human activities, is seen as possessing an almost ritualistic significance and Faulkner uses it to evoke a paradoxical sense both of the permanency of human life and experience and of the passing of the generations.

It is perhaps a mark of immaturity that Faulkner should have returned so deliberately to some of the thematic materials of his first novel, but it is undoubtedly a mark of his growing assurance and skill that in *Sartoris* these materials are much more closely integrated with each other and with the narrative pattern and social setting. Whereas in *Soldiers' Pay* the insistence on seasonal motifs was little more than a formal and self-consciously "literary" counterpoint to the central narrative and thematic pattern, in *Sartoris* the land, the weather, the seasons, and all aspects of the natural world function as essential elements in the conditioning environment of the characters. They also serve as powerful reminders of those temporal perspectives in which Faulkner forces us to view the lives and actions of succeeding generations of the Sartoris family and of those other families, Negro and white, which revolve about it and inhabit the same corner of the world. The spirit of place is evoked with a power and a deliberateness which recalls the novels of Hardy, and, as in a book like *The Mayor of Casterbridge*, the place is very specifically a small town, compact in itself, even a little self-consciously urban in its social life, but gripped in an intimate and inescapable relationship with the surrounding countryside upon which it depends.

In developing a social context for the central action of the novel, Faulkner seems to have set out quite consciously to present a portait, as full and as varied as possible, of the life of the South, or at least of his particular part of it. "Beginning with *Sartoris*," Faulkner told Jean

Stein in 1956, "I discovered that my own little postage stamp of native soil was worth writing about and that I would never live long enough to exhaust it."[1] The greater assurance of the characterisation in this book as compared with its predecessors undoubtedly resulted, in large measure, from the fact that Faulkner was here drawing, and virtually for the first time, on his own childhood, on his personal memories of older members of his family, and on the store of family legend which had grown up about the figure of Colonel W. C. Falkner, and it was this same immersion in his own background which gave such strength and richness to his presentation of the environment in which the characters move. Faulkner's technique in this respect is sometimes a little crude, and a number of set-pieces—of which the apostrophe to the mule, a deliberate exercise in the mock-heroic, is only the best-known—seem to have been rather arbitrarily introduced. Generally speaking, however, the total impression of a particular town, a particular countryside, and a particular way of life is built up gradually and fairly unobtrusively in terms of the characters and their movements—as Horace Benbow, returning from the war, drives through the town on his way from the railway station to his home, as young Bayard and his companions drive out into the country in search of whiskey or across country to serenade college students, as the ladies of the various families meet at one another's houses to exchange visits and gossip. Faulkner introduces us in this manner to a remarkably broad and varied segment of Mississippi life, providing glimpses not only of the town families with their relatively dense social life, but also of the country people: the Negro family with whom young Bayard stays the night of Christmas Eve; Hub and his pathetic mother (or wife), forerunner of Mrs. Armstid, living on their dilapidated farm; and the MacCallums, the simple, vigorous hill-folk whom Faulkner so greatly admires. Moreover, in his fascinated preoccupation with the delineation of Mississippi life in all its richness and variety, his sheer evocative detailing of buildings, furniture, flowers, clothes, Faulkner displays an interest in the décor of life that is quite as intense as that shown by Twain or Howells or any of the local-colourists of the Realist school. Dr. Peabody's consulting room, for example:

> Besides the desk, the room contained three or four miscellaneous chairs in various stages of decrepitude, a rusty stove in a sawdust-filled box, and a leather sofa holding mutely amid its broken springs the outline of Dr. Peabody's recumbent shape; beside it and slowly gathering successive layers of dust, was a stack of lurid, paper-covered nickel novels. This was Dr. Peabody's library, and on this sofa he passed his office hours, reading them over and over. Other books there were none.
> But the waste-basket beside the desk and the desk itself and the

mantel above the trash-filled fireplace, and the window-ledges too, were cluttered with circular mail matter and mail order catalogues and government bulletins of all kinds. In one corner, on an up-ended packing-box, sat a water cooler of stained oxidized glass, in another corner leaned a clump of cane fishing-poles warping slowly of their own weight; and on every horizontal surface rested a collection of objects not to be found outside of a second-hand store—old garments, bottles, a kerosene lamp, a wooden box of tins of axle grease, lacking one; a clock in the shape of a bland china morning-glory supported by four garlanded maidens who had suffered sundry astonishing anatomical mishaps, and here and there among the dusty indiscrimination, various instruments pertaining to the occupant's profession. (p. 102)

Sartoris is one of the most directly and explicitly "Southern" of all Faulkner's novels, and the sense of the Southern past, represented primarily by the old Colonel and other dead Sartorises, becomes the strongest of the presences which dominate to an extraordinary degree both the atmosphere and the action. These presences—they include time, the land, and the seasons as well as the past—often make themselves physically felt through the sense of smell, and throughout the book there are references not only to the scent of flowers and plants but to the spirit of a dead or absent person filling a room "like an odor"; the "odor" (p. 181) of Aunt Sally Wyatt still lingers in the Benbows' house long after the old lady has left, so that their imaginations often trick them into thinking her actually present, and at the very beginning of the novel Will Falls brings with him the spirit of old John Sartoris, "like an odor, like the clean dusty smell of his faded overalls." (p. 1) Colonel Sartoris, though dead, is "a far more palpable presence than either of the two old men." (p. 1) Young Bayard, lying with his wife, had thought not of her but of his absent brother, and now that both are dead it is still of his brother that he thinks:

Nor was he thinking of her now, although the walls held, like a withered flower in a casket, something of that magical chaos in which they had lived for two months, tragic and transient as a blooming of honeysuckle and sharp as the odor of mint. He was thinking of his dead brother; the spirit of their violent complementing days lay like dust everywhere in the room, obliterating that other presence, stopping his breathing, and he went to the window and flung the sash crashing upward and leaned there, gulping air into his lungs like a man who has been submerged and who still cannot believe that he has reached the surface again. (p. 48)

This sense of the presence of the past and of the power and palpability of the unseen is so strong throughout the book that at times it tends almost to overwhelm the ostensible human action, or at least to cast over it a certain air of unreality :

> But behind these dun bulks and in all the corners of the room there waited, as actors stand within the wings beside the waiting stage, figures in crinoline and hooped muslin and silk; in stocks and flowing coats, in gray too, with crimson sashes and sabers in gallant, sheathed repose; Jeb Stuart himself, perhaps, on his glittering garlanded bay or with his sunny hair falling upon fine broadcloth beneath the mistletoe and holly boughs of Baltimore in '58. Miss Jenny sat with her uncompromising grenadier's back and held her hat upon her knees and fixed herself to look on as her guest touched chords from the keyboard and wove them together, and rolled the curtain back upon the scene. (pp. 60-61)

The Unvanquished offers a fuller treatment of the Southern past at its most dramatic moment, the period of the Civil War and its immediate aftermath, but the particular time-perspective of Sartoris, the fact that the events of the Civil War are recorded not as they happen but as they are recalled over a lapse of more than fifty years, makes it possible for those events to be recounted romantically, in all their legendary glory, at the same time as they are criticised and revalued within the context of the novel as a whole—explicitly by Miss Jenny, with her affectionate scorn for the folly of all male Sartorises, implicitly, and more radically, by the presentation of young Bayard, his dilemmas, and his fate.

This presentation reveals, however, an element of unresolved conflict. In part, Bayard is a Sartoris, doomed by his birth, by the death of a beloved brother, and by his personal amalgam of courage and folly, to a restless life and violent death. But Bayard is also a lost-generation figure, one of the pilots who "died" when the war ended, one of those of whom the subadar speaks in the story "Ad Astra" :

> "What is your destiny except to be dead? It is unfortunate that your generation had to be the one. It is unfortunate that for the better part of your days you will walk the earth a spirit. But that was your destiny."[2]

Bayard Sartoris himself appears in the story—which can be read, indeed, as a kind of commentary on Sartoris—and it is interesting that in "Ad Astra," in which a special point seems to be made of the mixture of nationalities involved in the war, Bayard appears to be essentially the same character as he is in the specifically Southern context of Sartoris. What this suggests, and what a reading of the novel tends to confirm, is that in Sartoris Faulkner has attempted to place a "Twenties" hero, a type who had appeared in the work of other novelists (in John Dos Passos's *Three Soldiers*, for example) and whom he himself had already hinted at in *Soldiers' Pay*, within the context of an intensely localised Southern setting. In large measure, his attempt was successful, and especially his dramatisation of Bayard's efforts to find a solution, or at least solace, through hunting, work in the fields, or other forms of relationship to the land. But a certain tension remains, a sense of some inadequacy and imprecision in Faulkner's presentation of Bayard and his relationships, and this unease is increased by the curious juxtapositions Faulkner seems deliberately to engineer between Bayard's acts of desperation and humorous scenes involving Negroes.

From a consideration of the text of *Sartoris* as published it would appear that Faulkner has failed to portray Bayard in sufficient depth. His relationship with Narcissa Benbow remains somewhat obscure; so does the precise relevance to the Bayard material of the relationship between Narcissa and her brother, let alone the further relationship between Horace and Belle Mitchell. In attempting to arrive at a final assessment of *Sartoris*, however, it is important to remember that the published novel differs greatly from the book which Faulkner originally wrote. A manuscript and a loosely-bound typescript of this book, both bearing the title *Flags in the Dust*, are now on deposit at the Alderman Library. The manuscript opens with a description of Evelyn—later John—Sartoris on war service with the Royal Air Force in France:

One June dusk in 1918 a tender drove up to an aerodrome up toward Arras and stopped before the squadron office. It contained a single passenger who was talking to the driver in a loud steady voice. The driver descended first and assisted him to dismount unsteadily —a huge young giant with a bleak ruddy face beneath the casual slant of his cap, who bade the driver a florid farewell and crossed the empty 'drome toward the sheet-iron edifice which housed the officers' mess.

The room was lighted by kerosene lamps with tin reflectors and and [sic] it was occupied by several lounging men. The newcomer slammed the door behind him and raised his voice in a shout and tugged his trench-coat off and flung it to the floor. An orderly appeared at another door.

"Yes, Sir."

"Whiskey," the newcomer said. "Whiskey for everyone. My chit. I am Comyn, of the Irish nation, and its bloody dry driving up from Wing," he stated, looking about. "Oh, I say, Sartoris," he said to a tall lean youth with reckless blue eyes and tawny hair, "One of those new Camel squadrons came through Wing today, replacing 65. There's a Sartoris in it. Any of your people?"

"It's Bayard," Evelyn Sartoris said, springing to his feet. "Hell, I'm going up there." He too raised his voice, but at that moment the orderly returned with a tray of bottles and glasses. "Nip over and tell the Flight Sergeant of B to get Mr. Sartoris' machine out," he directed.

"Dont be a pukka fool," his flight-commander said from his chair, without raising his head from the French pictorial magazine he perused, "You cant fly up there at this hour."

"Why not? It aint dark yet, is it?" Sartoris demanded . . .[3]

After this opening indication of the relationship between the two Sartoris brothers, the manuscript version moves to old Bayard in his study at home, going through the chest of family relics. This is essentially the same material as on pages 89-93 of the published book, but in the manuscript each relic is used by Faulkner as the occasion for an evocation of some moment in the Sartoris past—the time when the Yankees came to Colonel Sartoris's house, the building of the railroad, the shooting of the carpet-baggers, and so on. At the end of the section we learn that the reason for Bayard's going to the chest has been the death of young Bayard's wife, Carolyn, and her son. The next section opens with Simon coming to the bank for Bayard, corresponding to pages 2-3 of the published book, and from this point onwards the manuscript runs roughly parallel to the later typescript, which incorporates, however, a great many changes and additions. The typescript opens with material corresponding to that on pages 20-23 of the published book, although part of the present opening is also included here. From the moment when Simon comes for old Bayard at the bank, the typescript (like the manuscript) begins to follow essentially the same narrative and structural pattern as the published book, although it retains a very substantial amount of material which was deleted before the publication of the book as *Sartoris* in 1929.

It is obvious that extensive changes were made, by Faulkner or by someone else, between the completion of the typescript on September 29, 1927, and the publication of the book on January 31, 1929, and the job was apparently done by Faulkner's friend Ben Wasson, then acting as his literary agent, at the time when Faulkner was typing the final version of *The Sound and the Fury* in Wasson's New York room in the early autumn of 1928.[4] Most of the changes involve Horace Benbow and his sister, Narcissa: as with *Sanctuary*, the earlier version of the novel was much more the story of the Benbows than was the version which finally appeared in print. At the point where a break occurs on page 75 of the published text, for example, the typescript has several pages devoted to an analysis of Narcissa's feelings about John and Bayard Sartoris and to an account of Narcissa's activities at home during the years of the First World War. A long paragraph further analysing Narcissa's reactions to Bayard appears in the typescript at a point corresponding to the break on page 151 of the published book—we learn, for example, that "All of her instincts were antipathetic towards him" but that, despite all the defences she erected against him, he "thundered at the very inmost citadel of her being"[5]—and the typescript version of the succeeding dialogue gives considerably more information about Narcissa's inner feelings. From page 398 of the typescript,[6] we can see that the line of four periods near the top of page 245 in the book represents the deletion of another long description of Narcissa's emotions as she sits by the sleeping Bayard:

> and she realized that today, for the first time since the day of his injury, that old paradox of shrinking and fascination and dread had returned; and for the moment she believed that though Horace was her cross and her derision, Bayard was a curse put upon her because of her love and jealousy and selfishness toward Horace, and that there would be peace for her only in a world where there were no men.

In the parts of the typescript which correspond to pages 176-182 of the published book we find that the order of the scenes has been changed in the process of revision and that a great deal has been cut out, including a description of Belle Mitchell and her way of life and an extended portrait of Horace which devotes much attention to his regret at leaving Oxford (England) for the last time. In the published book, on pages 186-87, Horace plays tennis with a young girl called Frankie; in the typescript this episode is treated at much greater length and we are given Horace's inner thoughts as he plays with Frankie and "watches the taut revelations of her speeding body in a sort of ecstasy."[7] The long account of Little Belle's recital which occupies pages 314-322 of the typescript is condensed in the book to a single paragraph on pages 196-197. These are only a few of the many deletions of material relating to Horace: most such deletions are only one or two paragraphs in length, but some of them are more substantial—notably the removal of the whole account on pages 490-503 of the typescript of Horace's affair with Belle's sister, Mrs. Joan Heppleton, while Belle is away getting a divorce, and the omission, at a point following the end of the first section of Part Five of the published book, of a further description of Horace's life with Belle, and, in particular, of his being forced to carry a dripping box of shrimps home from the railroad station once a week.

The other major deletions are of material relating to Byron Snopes.

Some pages relating to Byron are present in the book but not in the typescript, and there appear to be some pages of typescript missing; these would contain material approximately corresponding to pages 109-111 of the published book.[8] With this apparently accidental exception, the process of revision seems to have involved deletion of Snopes material, as of Benbow material, wherever possible. The brief scene involving Byron Snopes and Virgil Beard on pages 228-229 of the book is a condensation of a much longer scene in the typescript, in the course of which Byron tries to escape from Virgil Beard by going to live with I. O. Snopes, despite the deterrent provided by "the hulking but catlike presence of I.O.'s son Clarence."[9] Byron's thoughts and activities on the day he robs the bank and disappears are dealt with at much greater length in the typescript, where it becomes clear that he is mainly prompted by the news that Narcissa is to marry Bayard Sartoris. Most notable here is the complete deletion of a scene in which Byron, after robbing the bank, drives out to Frenchman's Bend, calls on Minnie Sue Turpin, to whom he is apparently engaged to be married, and tries to make violent love to her, "babbling a name not hers." The girl fights him off and the scene ends with a moving evocation of his despair:

> He sat where she had left him for a long time, with his half-insane face between his knees and madness and helpless rage and thwarted desire coiling within him. The owl hooted again from the black river bottom; its cry faded mournfully across the land, beneath the chill stars and the hound came silently through the dust and sniffed at him, and went away. After a time he rose and limped to the car and started the engine.[10]

The corrected typescript of *Flags in the Dust* is approximately a fourth longer than the published novel *Sartoris*.[1] It seems clear that although *Flags in the Dust* was an imperfect novel, with a number of episodes treated at unnecessary length, it was in many ways a more satisfying book than *Sartoris*. *Flags in the Dust* was a novel in which two young men returned from the war, Bayard Sartoris and Horace Benbow, were played off against each other—through their very different relationships with Narcissa, wife of one, sister of the other; through their contrasted attitudes to life and to love; and through the utterly opposed paths they follow to very similar ends, both in effect embracing self-destruction without delusion or attempt to retreat, Bayard by crashing the experimental plane, Horace by marrying Belle. The original title of the novel was one which referred to both the Benbow and the Sartoris sides of the story, and in the context of the whole book such moments as Narcissa's decision to call her child Benbow Sartoris had a wide range of reverberation. The cutting down of *Flags in the Dust* to make the novel we know as *Sartoris* involved the abandonment of this internal balance: the Sartoris material remained virtually intact, apart from the passages describing Narcissa's relationship with John, but the Benbow material underwent a drastic reduction. Something was no doubt gained in abbreviating or even removing some of this material, but it seems clear that more was lost. Much of the Sartoris material itself, especially Narcissa's relationship with Bayard, cannot be properly understood except in relation to a full presentation of the Benbow material, and the somewhat puzzling and indeterminate role which Horace plays in *Sartoris* is due not simply to his personal ineffectiveness but very largely to the fact that we are not being told everything about him that we need to know. We are told enough about Horace's relationships with various women to be puzzled by them; we are not told enough to see how his weak and untidy involvement with every woman he meets is intended to afford a stark contrast with Bayard's cold and rigid independence.

The book as we have it seems segmented and fragmented even to the extent that characters exist in isolation rather than in interaction. We so rarely see Narcissa and Horace together that we do not fully understand the relationship between them, nor are we given an adequate opportunity to assess the validity of their judgments of each other. We never appreciate the precise quality of what Horace calls Narcissa's "calm," any more than we come fully to grips with what Narcissa calls Bayard's "coldness." Thus, although *Flags in the Dust* might not have been a markedly better novel than *Sartoris*, the published book is open to a number of criticisms which could not have been made if the work had appeared as originally written; and the fact that Faulkner seems to have resisted any temptation to make alternative use, in a short story or in another novel, of material deleted from *Flags in the Dust*, perhaps suggests that he may always have retained the hope that the novel would eventually appear in a form approximating more closely to the *Flags in the Dust* typescript.[12]

Sartoris, the novel as published in 1929, is not one of Faulkner's major works, but when all reservations have been made, it remains a much better novel than most critics have been willing to allow. Its special richness derives from its evocation of the spirit of place and of certain aspects of the Southern past, and from its humour, although this is too much on one level and often rather facile in its reliance on the comic Negro. *Sartoris* is also of great significance as a source-book for Faulkner's future development: it is the work in which he for the first time discovered and explored the geographical, historical, social and imaginative world of his mature fiction, in which he embodied his original and remarkably comprehensive conception of what we now know as Yoknapatawpha County. Faulkner himself recognised this significance in 1958 when recommending *Sartoris* as the novel which people should read first, the book which "has the germ of my apocrypha in it."[13]

THE SOUND AND THE FURY

PERHAPS the single most arresting fact about the manuscript of *The Sound and the Fury* is that the first page bears the undeleted title "Twilight."[1] Clearly the title was no more than tentative: it may, indeed, have been the title of the original short story from which the novel grew, and it is worth noting in this respect its closeness to "That Evening Sun Go Down," the quotation from W. C. Handy's "St. Louis Blues" used as the title of another story of the Compson children on its first publication. But it is interesting to speculate whether the title was intended to apply to the one section or to the work as a whole and on its possible breadth of reference in either case. As a title for the first section alone, "Twilight" would presumably refer to the half-world of Benjy himself, held in a state of timeless suspension between the light and the dark, comprehension and incomprehension, between the human and the animal. As a title for the whole book, the word immediately suggests the decay of the Compson family caught at the moment when the dimmed glory of its eminent past is about to fade into ultimate extinction.

In Quentin's section, in particular, twilight, as a condition of light and a moment in time, takes on very considerable importance. In his most agonising recollections of Caddy, he sees her at twilight, sitting in the cleansing waters of the branch and surrounded by the scent of honeysuckle, and these three elements of the scene—the twilight, the water and the honeysuckle—take on an obsessive significance for Quentin himself and operate as recurrent symbols throughout this section of the novel. As water is associated with cleansing, redemption, peace and death, and the honeysuckle with warm Southern nights and Caddy's passionate sexuality, so twilight, "that quality of light as if time really had stopped for a while," (pp. 209-210) becomes inextricably confused in Quentin's mind with the scents of water and of honeysuckle until "the whole thing came to symbolise night and unrest." (p. 211) Quentin continues:

> I seemed to be lying neither asleep nor awake looking down a long corridor of grey halflight where all stable things had become shadowy paradoxical all I had done shadows all I had felt suffered taking visible form antic and perverse mocking without relevance inherent themselves with the denial of the significance they should

86

have affirmed thinking I was I was not who was not was not who.
(p. 211)[2]

This passage would seem to be central to the meaning both of the
particular section and of the book as a whole. There has just been a
momentary anticipation of Quentin's carefully planned final release
through death by water—travelling back into Cambridge he becomes
aware of "the road going on under the twilight, into twilight and the
sense of water peaceful and swift beyond" (p.210)—and we realise
that Quentin himself is at this moment not merely mid-way between
sanity and madness but precisely poised between waking and sleeping,
between life and death.[3] His world has become in fact "shadowy
paradoxical"—we have just seen his actual fight with Gerald Bland
overlaid in his consciousness by his remembered fight with Dalton
Ames—and, for all the apparent orderliness of his actions, he has
finally lost his sense of personal identity ("thinking I was I was not
who was not was not who"). The passage, in this respect, seems also
to relate directly to the passage in *Macbeth* from which Faulkner took
his final title for the book, and specifically to its descriptions of life
as "a walking shadow," a tale "signifying nothing."

The phrase about "all stable things" becoming "shadowy paradoxical" aptly defines the hallucinatory world of the Quentin section,
but it is also relevant to the treatment of "fact," of "truth," throughout the novel. Like *Absalom, Absalom!, The Sound and the Fury* is
in part concerned with the elusiveness, the multivalence, of truth,
or at least with man's persistent and perhaps necessary tendency to
make of truth a personal thing: each man, apprehending some fragment of the truth, seizes upon that fragment as though it were the
whole truth and elaborates it into a total vision of the world, rigidly
exclusive and hence utterly fallacious. This forms an essential part of
the conception which Faulkner dramatised through the interior monologues of the first three sections of *The Sound and the Fury*, and the
novel might thus be considered as in some sense a development, much
richer than anything of which Anderson himself was capable, of the
"theory of the grotesque" propounded at the beginning of *Winesburg,
Ohio*:

The old man had listed hundreds of the truths in his book....
There was the truth of virginity and the truth of passion, the truth
of wealth and of poverty, of thrift and of profligacy, of carelessness
and abandon. Hundreds and hundreds were the truths and they
were all beautiful.

And then the people came along. Each as he appeared snatched
up one of the truths and some who were quite strong snatched up a
dozen of them.

It was the truths that made the people grotesques. The old man had quite an elaborate theory concerning the matter. It was his notion that the moment one of the people took one of the truths to himself, called it his truth, and tried to live his life by it, he became a grotesque and the truth he embraced became a falsehood.[4]

Faulkner admired Winesburg, Ohio, and there is a discernible similarity between Anderson's conception of Winesburg and Faulkner's creation of Jefferson, the town which he had begun somewhat painstakingly to lay out in Sartoris and which in The Sound and the Fury is for the first time integrated into the structure and action of the novel. In 1925 Faulkner especially praised Winesburg, Ohio for its "ground of fecund earth and corn in the green spring and the slow, full hot summer and the rigorous masculine winter that hurts it not, but makes it stronger";[5] he praised it, that is to say, for just that recurrent evocation of the land and the moving seasons which he himself achieved in Soldiers' Pay and Sartoris and which is also present, though less persistently and much less obviously, in The Sound and the Fury. Some of the time-levels in the Benjy section can be identified by their allusions to the cold, the rain, and so on, while Quentin, in his section, is intensely aware, with the heightened sensitivity of a man about to die, of the countryside through which he walks:

In the orchard the bees sounded like a wind getting up, a sound caught by a spell just under crescendo and sustained. The lane went along the wall, arched over, shattered with bloom, dissolving into trees. Sunlight slanted into it, sparse and eager. Yellow butterflies flickered along the shade like flecks of sun. (p. 151)

Jason, as might be expected, shows no such sensitivity, but in the final section both the settings of the action and the changing weather of that particular day are very precisely described, and throughout the novel such evocations of place, of climate, of seasonal change are among the many elements which anchor action and meaning firmly to the human level.

The notation of manners in the novel is not especially rich, nor is any particular attention given to the detailed creation of scene and setting, but in the third and fourth sections, at least, there exists a sense of a social and physical environment that is more than adequate to counteract the metaphysical elements in the novel's thematic material, to prevent its explorations of human grotesquerie from wandering into the fantastic, as so often happens in the work of Carson McCullers, Flannery O'Connor and other Southern writers. No account of The Sound and the Fury can afford to undervalue those elements for which, primarily, we read the book and which seem clearly to have been most important to Faulkner himself—its powerful image of a family in disunion and decay, its presentation of the tragedy of "two lost women," of Caddy and her daughter. "Art is simpler than people think," wrote Faulkner to Cowley[6] and, highly sophisticated literary craftsman though he was, he never lost sight of the essential fact that technique alone is meaningless, that it achieves value only insofar as it serves to evoke, define and illuminate the human situation.

It was at the Nagano Seminar in 1955 that Faulkner gave his fullest account of how *The Sound and the Fury* came to be written :

That began as a short story, it was a story without plot, of some children being sent away from the house during the grandmother's funeral. They were too young to be told what was going on and they saw things only incidentally to the childish games they were playing, which was the lugubrious matter of removing the corpse from the house, etc., and then the idea struck me to see how much more I could have got out of the idea of the blind, self-centeredness of innocence, typified by children, if one of those children had been truly innocent, that is, an idiot. So the idiot was born and then I became interested in the relationship of the idiot to the world that he was in but would never be able to cope with and just where could he get the tenderness, the help, to shield him in his innocence. I mean 'innocence' in the sense that God had stricken him blind at birth, that is, mindless at birth, there was nothing he could ever do about it. And so the character of his sister began to emerge, then the brother, who, that Jason (who to me represented complete evil. He's the most vicious character in my opinion I ever thought of), then he appeared. Then it needs the protagonist, someone to tell the story, so Quentin appeared. By that time I found out I couldn't possibly tell that in a short story. And so I told the idiot's experience of that day, and that was incomprehensible, even I could not have told what was going on then, so I had to write another chapter. Then I decided to let Quentin tell his version of that same day, or that same occasion, so he told it. Then there had to be the counterpoint, which was the other brother, Jason. By that time it was completely confusing. I knew that it was not anywhere near finished and then I had to write another section from the outside with an outsider, which was the writer, to tell what had happened on that particular day. And that's how that book grew. That is, I wrote that same story four times. None of them were right, but I had anguished so much that I could not throw any of it away and start over, so I printed it in the four sections. That was not a deliberate *tour de force* at all, the book just grew that way. That I was still trying to tell one story which moved me very much and each time I failed, but I had put so much anguish into it that I couldn't throw it away, like the mother that had four bad children, that she would have been better off if they all had been eliminated, but she couldn't relinquish any of them. And that's the reason I have the most tenderness for that book, because it failed four times.[7]

A number of points here demand discussion. In the first place, there is a good deal of evidence to support Faulkner's statement that the novel began as a short story. Maurice Coindreau recalls Faulkner telling him:

> "Ce roman, à l'origine, ne devait être qu'une nouvelle, me dit, un jour, William Faulkner. J'avais songé qu'il serait intéressant d'imaginer les pensées d'un groupe d'enfants, le jour de l'enterrement de leur grand'mère dont on leur a caché la mort, leur curiosité devant l'agitation de la maison, leurs efforts pour percer le mystère, les suppositions qui leur viennent à l'esprit."[8]

It was to be a story, therefore, similar in conception to "That Evening Sun," in which the Compson children are again placed in a situation whose adult significance they do not fully comprehend; Faulkner published the story in March 1931, and he had written it, at the very latest, by October 1930.[9] With this in mind we can quite readily disentangle from the opening section of *The Sound and the Fury*, where they occur in chronological and logical sequence, the sometimes quite widely separated fragments of a short story, "without plot," describing the experiences of the Compson children on the night of their grandmother's funeral; it is in the course of this material, moreover, that we first meet the image of Caddy's muddy drawers—seen from below as she clambers up the tree outside the Compson house in order to see what is happening inside—which, on other occasions, Faulkner spoke of as the basic image from which the whole book originated.

Faulkner told his Japanese audience that he used no notes in writing *The Sound and the Fury*, and certainly none seem to have survived. It is astounding that the complexities of the Benjy section should have been accomplished without recourse to notes, but Faulkner was clearly capable of such feats: the whole of *As I Lay Dying*, for instance, was apparently written without notes and with little subsequent revision, the whole thing completely pre-conceived and then written out in a single creative burst, while the appearance in *Sartoris* of embryonic versions of many scenes and episodes not fully developed, so far as we can tell, until many years afterwards, is sufficient evidence of the clarity and ambitiousness of Faulkner's conceptualising powers. The Benjy section, however, seems to have been evolved under creative pressure, not conceived beforehand. All Faulkner's accounts of the creation of *The Sound and the Fury* agree in stressing the extent to which the novel grew as his imagination worked upon it, its scope and meaning expanding irresistibly outwards, and the degree to which he allowed it to develop—giving no thought to its commercial pros-

pects—in the directions which the themes and the material seemed
to demand. Faulkner was hardly accurate in speaking of Quentin as
telling "his version of that day, or that same occasion," but there is
some overlapping of the events which Benjy and Quentin experience
or recall, and their interior monologues certainly illuminate the same
fundamental situation—the plight of the Compson family, with its
vigorous past, its pathetically inadequate present, and its manifest
lack of any future.

The pattern established by Faulkner's disposition of the novel's four
sections can be viewed in a number of different ways, and they have
been seen, for example, as exemplifying different levels of consciousness, different modes of apprehension or cognition, contrasted states
of innocence and experience; M. Coindreau speaks of them as four
movements of a symphony.[10] All these elements are present, and
there is an overall movement outwards from Benjy's intensely private
world to the fully public and social world of the fourth section. The
pattern, however, is not solely progressive: despite the superficial
affinities between the first and second sections on the one hand and
the third and fourth sections on the other, the most fundamental
relationships would seem to be those between the first and last sections,
which offer a high degree of objectivity, and between the second and
third, which are both intensely subjective. Benjy is a first-person
narrator, as are Quentin and Jason, but his observations do not pass
through an intelligence which is capable of ordering, and hence dis-
torting, them; he reports the events of which he is a spectator, and
even those in which he is himself a participator, with a camera-like
fidelity. His view of Caddy, it is true, is highly personal, but we infer
this view from the scenes which his camera-mind records; Benjy does
not himself interpret this or other situations and events; still less does
he attempt to impose a biassed interpretation upon the reader, as,
in effect, do Quentin and Jason. Nor does he himself judge people,
although he becomes the instrument by which the other characters are
judged, their behaviour towards him serving as a touchstone of their
humanity.

Faulkner seems to have worked gradually towards the convention
of pure objectivity which he follows in the Benjy section, and it is
interesting to see the trend of his revisions, between manuscript and
published work, to the well-known scene in which Benjy burns his
hand. The incident begins in the manuscript as follows:

"Ow, mammy," Luster said. "Ow, mammy." I put my hand out to
the firedoor.
"Dont let him!" Dilsey said, "Catch him back." My hand jerked
back and I put it in my mouth, and Dilsey caught me. I could still
hear the clock between the times when my voice was going. Dilsey
reached back and hit Luster on the head.

"Git that soda," she said. She took my hand out of my mouth. My voice went louder then. I tried to put it back, but Dilsey held it. She sprinkled soda on it. "Look in the pantry . . ."[11]

The published text reads as follows:

"Ow, mammy." Luster said. "Ow, mammy."
I put my hand out to where the fire had been.
"Catch him." Dilsey said. "Catch him back."
My hand jerked back and I put it in my mouth and Dilsey caught me. I could still hear the clock between my voice. Dilsey reached back and hit Luster on the head. My voice was going loud every time.
"Get that soda." Dilsey said. She took my hand out of my mouth. My voice went louder then and my hand tried to go back to my mouth, but Dilsey held it. My voice went loud. She sprinkled soda on my hand.
"Look in the pantry . . ." (p. 72)

A similar process of revision can be seen in the last paragraph of the section, which opens on page 33 of the manuscript as follows:

Father went to the door and stood with his hand on the light button. He looked at us again, and the light went off and he turned black in the door. Then the door turned black. Caddy held me . . .

Benjy would scarcely have been capable of the linking of cause and effect implicit in "light button," and in the book this passage becomes:

Father went to the door and looked at us again. Then the dark came back, and he stood black in the door, and then the door turned black again. Caddy held me . . . (p. 22)

Such changes, though interesting, are of a minor kind, and they are typical in this of many of the revisions which Faulkner made to the original manuscript version of the first section.

Some of the revisions are more substantial, however, and it will be useful to look more closely at the changes made between the manuscript of the novel and the bound carbon typescript, both now in the Alderman Library. Several of the discrepancies between these two versions reveal Faulkner working towards what was to prove at once an elaboration and a simplification of his technique in the opening section of the book. Thus the first page of the manuscript lacks all the references to Luster's hunting in the grass for his lost quarter and to the fact that the day is Benjy's birthday which appear in the typescript and on pages 1 and 2 of the published text, and in the manuscript version as a whole there is an almost total absence of material relating to Luster's search for the quarter, to his desire to go to the show, to Benjy's birthday or to Benjy's age. Faulkner presumably realised before or during the process of reworking the first section that the allusions to Benjy's birthday and, still more, to Luster's search for the missing quarter, could be made to serve as a kind of motif or signal of present time in the section and thus assist the reader in keeping his bearings among the shifting and merging time-planes. At a later stage still, in correcting the proofs of the book, Faulkner attempted to provide another kind of assistance to the reader by the addition of further italicisation to indicate points at which a shift of scene was taking place.

In both manuscript and typescript Faulkner had indicated by means of underlining that he wished the breaks in time sequence within the Benjy section to be suggested by changes back and forth between roman and italic type: it seems not to have been his intention that all such breaks should be accompanied by a type change, but rather that occasional italicisation should alert the reader to the kind of process going on in Benjy's mind.[12] In his admirable article on the textual history of the novel, James B. Meriwether has shown that when Faulkner received the galley proofs from Cape and Smith he found that considerable editorial changes had been made in the first section, apparently by his friend and literary agent, Ben Wasson, whom Cape and Smith had recently appointed as an assistant editor. In particular, the device of italicisation had been abandoned and replaced by the insertion of breaks in the text (i.e. wider spaces between lines) at points where breaks in the time sequence occurred.[18] Wasson had presumably defended his action on the grounds that italicisation permitted the differentiation of only two dates, whereas at least four distinct times were actually involved. Faulkner replied, rejecting these arguments and explaining why he had restored the italics as they had appeared in his typescript and even added a few more in order to avoid obscurity; his letter, forcefully phrased, reveals beyond all question the absolute self-confidence and intellectual clarity with which he regarded the finished novel and the technical experimentation which it embodied:

I received the proof. It seemed pretty tough to me, so I corrected it as written, adding a few more italics where the original seemed obscure on second reading. Your reason for the change, i.e., that with italics only 2 different dates were indicated I do not think sound for 2 reasons. First, I do not see that the use of breaks clarifies it any more; Second, there are more than 4 dates involved. The ones I recall off-hand are: Damuddy dies. Benjy is 3. (2) His name is changed. He is 5. (3) Caddy's wedding. He is 14. (4) He tries to rape a young girl and is castrated. 15. (5) Quentin's death. (6) His father's death. (7) A visit to the cemetary [sic] at 18. (7) [sic] The day of the anecdote, he is 33. These are just a few I recall, so your reason explodes itself.

But the main reason is, a break indicates an objective change in tempo, while the objective picture here should be a continuous whole, since the thought transference is subjective; i.e., in Ben's mind and not in the reader's eye. I think italics are necessary to establish for the reader Benjy's confusion; that unbroken-surfaced confusion of an idiot which is outwardly a dynamic and logical coherence. To gain this, by using breaks it will be necessary to write an induction for each transference. I wish publishing was advanced enough to use colored ink for such, as I argued with you and Hal [Harrison Smith] in the speak-easy that day. But the form in which you now have it is pretty tough. It presents a most dull and poorly articulated picture to my eye. If something must be done, it were better to re-write this whole section objectively, like the 4th section. I think it is rotten, as is. But if you wont have it so, I'll just have to save the idea until publishing grows up to it. Anyway, change all the italics. You overlooked one of them. Also, the parts written in italics will all have to be punctuated again. You'd better see to that, since you're all for coherence. And dont make any more additions to the script, bud. I know you mean well, but so do I. I effaced the 2 or 3 you made.

*   *   *

I hope you will think better of this. Your reason above disproves itself. I purposely used italics for both actual scenes and remembered scenes for the reason, not to indicate the different dates of happenings, but merely to permit the reader to anticipate a thought-transference, letting the recollection postulate its own date. Surely you see this.[14]

In reworking the manuscript version of the second section Faulkner made far more extensive additions and revisions than in the preceding section. This becomes immediately clear from a comparison between the opening paragraph of the manuscript and the corresponding passage in the published book. The manuscript reads:

The shadow of the sash fell across the curtains between 7 and 8 oclock, and then I was hearing the watch. [sic] again, and I lay there looking at the sinister bar across the rosy and motionless curtains, listening to the watch. Hearing it, that is. I dont suppose anybody deliberately listens to a watch or a clock. You dont have to. You can be oblivious to the sound for a long while, then in a second of ticking it can create in the mind unbroken the long diminishing parade of time you did not hear. Where up the long and lonely arrowing of light rays you might see Jesus walking, like.

The true Son of Man : he had no sister. Nazarene and Roman and Virginian, they had no sister one minute she was

Beyond the wall Shreve's bedsprings complained thinly, . . .[15]

Here for comparison, are the opening paragraphs of section two in the published book :

> When the shadow of the sash appeared on the curtains it was between seven and eight oclock and then I was in time again, hearing the watch. It was Grandfather's and when Father gave it to me he said, Quentin, I give you the mausoleum of all hope and desire; it's rather excrutiating-ly apt that you will use it to gain the reducto absurdum of all human experience which can fit your individual needs no better than it fitted his or his father's. I give it to you not that you may remember time, but that you might forget it now and then for a moment and not spend all your breath trying to conquer it. Because no battle is ever won he said. They are not even fought. The field only reveals to man his own folly and despair, and victory is an illusion of philosophers and fools.
>
> It was propped against the collar box and I lay listening to it. Hearing it, that is. I dont suppose anybody ever deliberately listens to a watch or a clock. You dont have to. You can be oblivious to the sound for a long while, then in a second of ticking it can create in the mind unbroken the long diminishing parade of time you didn't hear. Like Father said down the long and lonely light-rays you might see Jesus walking, like. And the good Saint Francis that said Little Sister Death, that never had a sister.
>
> Through the wall I heard Shreve's bed-springs . . . (pp. 93-94)

Faulkner's alterations achieve certain improvements in phrasing and elaborate the insistence on time, but perhaps the most interesting of the new elements are the references to Mr. Compson. Throughout the section, as revised in the carbon typescript and the published book, Quentin's mind runs on his father almost as much as it does on Caddy. Quentin is, of course, very much like his father in many ways, and in his obsession with family tradition and honour it is understandable that he should refer to his father, the head of the family, as a transmitter of that tradition and as a source of authority and advice. The irony of this situation, however, and a major cause of Quentin's tragedy, is that just as his mother has failed him as a source of love so his father fails him utterly in all his roles of progenitor, confessor and counsellor. He has become, indeed, Quentin's principal enemy, his cold and even cynical logic persistently undermining the very basis of all those idealistic concepts to which Quentin so passionately holds. Throughout the section there is a battle in progress between Quentin's romantic idealism and Mr. Compson's somewhat cynical realism, a battle which is not finally resolved in *The Sound and the Fury* and which is resumed on an even larger scale in *Absalom, Absalom!*. Indeed, if we are to understand that the discussion between Quentin and his father at the end of the section is purely a figment of Quentin's imagination and never actually took place, then it has to be said that in *The Sound and the Fury* the battle is never properly joined—as, according to Mr. Compson himself, no battle ever is—and that it is, rather, a series of skirmishes in which Quentin suffers a progressive erosion of his position and a steady depletion of his reserves. Father and son are, in any case, too much alike in their fondness for words, for abstractions, and in choosing to evade life—the one in drink, the other in suicide—rather than actively confront it.

Whenever Quentin acts, his concern is for the act's significance as a gesture rather than for its practical efficacy. He seeks pertinaciously for occasions to fight in defence of his sister's honour, knowing in advance that he will be beaten and concerned in retrospect only that he has performed the act in its ritualistic and symbolic aspects. It is the fight with Gerald Bland which reveals most clearly the degree to which Quentin's obsessions have divorced him from actuality, since throughout the struggle it is the remembered fight with Dalton Ames which remains for Quentin the superior reality. Throughout a whole day of quite extraordinary incident—with two fights, an arrest, a court hearing, much movement and many encounters—Quentin's mind remains preoccupied with the past. It is almost as though Faulkner were playing on the idea that a drowning man sees his whole life pass before him, and we come to realise that this last day of Quentin's is a kind of suspended moment before death.

Quentin's own obsession with time derives primarily from his recognition of it as the dimension in which change occurs and in which Caddy's actions have efficacy and significance. His search is for a means of arresting time at a moment of achieved perfection, a moment when he and Caddy could be eternally together in the simplicity of their childhood relationship; his idea of announcing that he and Caddy had committed incest was, paradoxically, a scheme for regaining lost innocence :

> it was to isolate her out of the loud world so that it would have to flee us of necessity and then the sound of it would be as though it had never been ... if i could tell you we did it would have been so and then the others wouldnt be so and then the world would roar away ... (p. 220)

The similarity between this conception and the image of motion in stasis which haunted Faulkner throughout his life, especially as embodied in Keats's "Ode to a Grecian Urn," suggests—as do the echoes of Joyce—that Quentin is in some measure a version of the artist, or at least the aesthete, as hero. But Quentin's conception is artificial, rigid, life-denying: as Mr. Compson observes, "Purity is a negative state and therefore contrary to nature. It's nature is hurting you not Caddy . . ." (p. 143) The inadequacy of Quentin's position is exposed in terms of Caddy and her vitality and humanity. In the Benjy section we recognise Caddy as the principal sustainer of such family unity as survives: we glimpse her as the liveliest spirit among the children and their natural leader, as the protector and comforter of Benjy, and even as the pacifier of her mother, and it is highly significant for us as well as for Benjy that she is persistently associated with such elemental things as the fire, the pasture, the smell of trees, and sleep. Her sexual freedom appears as the expression of a natural rebellion against the repressive, contradictory, and essentially self-centred demands made upon her by the different members of her family; it certainly seems spontaneous and affirmative by the side of Quentin's fastidious or even impotent avoidance of sexual experience—we note, for example, his revulsion at his childish experiments with Natalie and the fact that he is known at Harvard for his indifference to women —or Jason's rigid compartmentalisation of his sexual life and strict subordination of it to his financial interests.

Caddy finds an outlet from family repression in sexual activity, but she is also both a principle and a symbol of social disruption. Her assertion of individuality is much less positive and urgent than that of such a character as Ursula Brangwen in D. H. Lawrence's *The Rainbow*; even so, she is brought, like Ursula, to break with traditional patterns and, in so doing, to demonstrate just how moribund those patterns have become, how irrelevant both to modern conditions and to the needs of the human psyche. It is possible to feel, however, that although Caddy is the core of the book she is not herself a wholly successful creation. Faulkner often spoke of Caddy, outside the novel, with an intensely passionate devotion : "To me she was the beautiful one," he said at the University of Virginia, "she was my heart's darling. That's what I wrote the book about and I used the tools which seemed to me the proper tools to try to tell, try to draw the picture of Caddy."[16] The original image of the little girl with the muddy drawers grew into the rich and complex conception of Caddy, beautiful and tragic both as child and as woman, but although this conception is already present in the first section of the novel it is evoked, necessarily, in somewhat fragmentary fashion, as we glimpse Caddy in various family situations, as we sense how much she means to Benjy, as we come to associate her, through Benjy, with images of brightness, comfort and loss. In the second section Caddy is more clearly visible, and there are passages of remembered dialogue as revealing of Caddy's character as of Quentin's, but the world of Quentin's section is so unstable, so hallucinatory, that the figure of

Caddy, like so much else, is enveloped in uncertainty. In Jason's section Caddy's agony is most movingly evoked, but only briefly so, while in the final section of the book she is no more than a memory.

It was an essential element in Faulkner's overall conception of the novel that Caddy never be seen directly but only through the eyes of her three brothers, each with his own self-centred demands to make upon her, each with his own limitations and obsessions. Asked at Virginia why he did not give a section to Caddy herself, Faulkner replied that it seemed more "passionate" to do it through her brothers, and one is reminded of his remarks at Nagano about the beauty of description by understatement and indirection: "Remember, all Tolstoy said about Anna Karenina was that she was beautiful and could see in the dark like a cat. That's all he ever said to describe her. And every man has a different idea of what's beautiful. And it's best to take the gesture, the shadow of the branch, and let the mind create the tree."[17] It certainly seems likely that to have made Caddy a "voice" in the novel would have diminished her importance as a central, focal figure. As the book stands, however, Caddy emerges incompletely from the first two sections, and in the last two attention shifts progressively from her to her daughter, Quentin. The different limitations in the viewpoints of Benjy, Quentin and Jason make unavoidable the shadowiness, the imprecision, of Caddy's presentation: because the mind of each is so closed upon its own obsessions it is scarcely true to speak of their interior monologues as throwing light upon Caddy from a variety of angles; it is rather as though a series of photographs in differing focus were superimposed one upon the other, blurring all clarity of outline or detail. The novel revolves upon Caddy, but Caddy herself escapes satisfactory definition, and her daughter's tragedy, simply because it is more directly presented, is in some ways more moving.

It is characteristic that Jason should be the only member of the Compson family who is able to cope with the practical and social implications of Caddy's defection. Where Mrs. Compson can only moistly complain, Benjy bellow his incomprehending grief, Quentin commit suicide, Jason can adjust himself to the situation and turn it to his own advantage and profit. Jason—the one Compson who was capable of meeting Snopes on his own ground, as Faulkner wrote to Malcolm Cowley[18]—becomes in this way the representative of the new commercial South, and his section strikes a specifically contemporary note in its evocation of the petty business man, with Jason himself appearing, in this role, as a typical figure, sharing the fundamental characteristics of a legion of other small businessmen in North and South alike. It is perhaps for this reason that Jason's seems much the least "Southern" of the sections. If it also seems the most readily detachable section—it was the one which Faulkner first suggested for inclusion in *The Portable Faulkner*[19]—that is a measure of the degree to which Jason's singleminded and ruthless pursuit of material self-interest serves to isolate him not only from his family but from the community as a whole. The attitude of Jefferson towards Jason is sufficiently revealed through the reactions of such characters as Earl, Job, and, in the final section, the sheriff, while Jason's opinion of Jefferson is amply expressed in statements such as the following: "Like I say if all the businesses in a town are run like country businesses, you're going to have a country town." His contempt for the town is only exceeded by his contempt for his own family, its history and its pretensions:

> Blood, I says, governors and generals. It's a damn good thing we never had any kings and presidents; we'd all be down there at Jackson chasing butterflies. (p. 286)[20]

Since Jason's instincts are commercial and materialistic, they are also anti-rural and anti-traditional: his is a willed deracination from the community in which he continues to live. As we have seen, however, it is this very materialism and deracination which makes Jason the one male Compson with any practical competence.

The progression from Benjy's section through Quentin's to Jason's is accompanied by an increasing sense of social reality: Benjy is remote in his idiocy and innocence, Quentin moves from the isolation of his half-mad idealism into the total withdrawal of suicide, but Jason is wholly in the world, acutely sensitive to social values, swimming with the contemporary commercial current. The action of the novel is thus presented increasingly in terms of social, economic and political perspectives; it is Jason who first refers, however ironically, to the family's more distinguished past, and it is not until the last section of the novel that we are first given an image of the Compson house in all its decrepitude. To interpret *The Sound and the Fury* simply as a socio-economic study of the decline of a Southern family is obviously inadequate; what can be said is that this is one of the novel's many aspects, and one which becomes increasingly important as the book proceeds. It seems possible that Faulkner felt that he had created the social context of the action in insufficient detail, that the book did not clearly evoke the patterns of manners and customs within which his characters moved: the Compson "Appendix" he wrote for *The Portable Faulkner* is devoted partly to clarifying the meaning of the novel at certain points but primarily to the elaboration of the Compsons' family history and to the further definition of their place in the social and economic life of Jefferson. It is in the Appendix, too, that we find the abundantly particularised description of the farmers' supply store which Jason now owns and which Miss Melissa Meek valiantly enters,

> striding on through that gloomy cavern which only men ever

entered—a cavern cluttered and walled and stalagmite-hung with plows and discs and loops of tracechain and singletrees and mule-collars and sidemeat and cheap shoes and horse liniment and flour and molasses, gloomy because the goods it contained were not shown but hidden rather since those who supplied Mississippi farmers, or at least Negro Mississippi farmers, for a share of the crop did not wish, until that crop was made and its value approximately computable, to show them what they could learn to want, but only to supply them on specific demand with what they could not help but need—and strode on back to Jason's particular domain in the rear: a railed enclosure cluttered with shelves and pigeon-holes bearing spiked dust-and-lint-gathering gin receipts and ledgers and cotton samples and rank with the blended smell of cheese and kerosene and harness oil and the tremendous iron stove against which chewed tobacco had been spat for almost a hundred years, . . .[21]

This was the kind of thing which Faulkner had done superbly in *The Hamlet* and *Go Down, Moses*, and it is possible to think that *The Sound and the Fury* would have been strengthened by some such stiffening, by a richer notation of setting and social context. Faulkner wrote the book from within the comprehensive conception of the world of Jefferson which he had already achieved and amply demonstrated in *Sartoris*, and he may have underestimated the extent to which it was desirable to recreate this world for the reader of *The Sound and the Fury*. It is noteworthy, at any rate, that in subsequent novels such as *As I Lay Dying, Light in August, Absalom Absalom!, The Hamlet*, and *Go Down, Moses*, Faulkner seems quite deliberately to create setting and context, in both physical and social terms, at a very early stage of the book, evoking and defining the situation almost in the manner of Balzac or Hardy before proceeding to the main action.

It must be admitted that each of the first three sections of *The Sound and the Fury* has about it some suggestion of the *tour de force*: the Quentin section seems a deliberate exercise in the Joycean mode, while the Jason section raises to the level of art the nakedly self-revelatory monologue of the unimaginative man which Sinclair Lewis had developed in *Babbitt* and *The Man Who Knew Coolidge*, published in 1922 and 1928 respectively. The Benjy section seems to have been more exclusively Faulkner's invention, a deliberate attempt to extend the boundaries of the novel beyond the point to which Joyce had already pushed them. Yet Faulkner never regarded the book as a *tour de force*; unlike *As I Lay Dying, The Sound and the Fury* was a book which grew and developed as he worked upon it, and his adoption in the final section of the point of view of the omniscient author seems to have been forced upon him not by the demands of a deliberate design but by the more immediate pressures stemming from an urgent need for self-expression.

In various accounts of the writing of *The Sound and the Fury* Faulkner says that having failed in three attempts to tell the story, to rid himself of the "dream," he had tried in the final section to pull the whole novel together, retelling the central story more directly and clearly.[22] In fact, the section contributes relatively little to our understanding of the narrative events touched upon in earlier sections; rather it forces us to view some aspects of those earlier sections in a radically different way. Simply by giving us for the first time detailed physical descriptions of Dilsey, Benjy, Jason and Mrs. Compson, Faulkner—playing on some of the most fundamental of human responses to storytelling—effectively modifies our feelings towards them. Simply by recreating in such detail the routine of Dilsey's day, evoking the qualities demanded in performing such duties in a household such as that of the Compsons', Faulkner allows her to emerge for the first time both as a fully-drawn character and as a powerful positive presence. When the action shifts to Jason and his vain pursuit of Quentin we notice that many of his experiences have something in common with Quentin's experiences during the last day of his life—there are, for example, the journeyings back and forth, the moments of violence, the unsatisfactory brushes with the representatives of the law—and we come finally to recognise that, for all the differences between them, both brothers display a similar obsessiveness and fundamental irrationality.

We read the fourth section in the emotional, as well as thematic and narrative, context of its three predecessors. The last of these, Jason's section, has been sustained on a scarcely varied note of savage bitterness, and imbedded within it have been some of the most painful incidents in the book, notably those in which Jason frustrates Caddy's frantic attempts to see her child; only the flashes of brilliantly sardonic humour have prevented its final effect from being one of total negation. It is therefore tempting, in the final section, to see in the immensely positive figure of Dilsey, and the importance given to her, a certain overall reassurance and even serenity; but although the section does contain positives which to some extent off-set the negations of the previous sections it would be too much to say that the novel closes on a note of unqualified affirmation. Dilsey "endures," but her endurance is tested not in acts of spectacular heroism but in her submission to the tedious, trivial and wilfully inconsiderate demands made upon her by the Compson family, as when Mrs. Compson allows her to make her painful way upstairs to tend to Benjy before telling her that he is not yet awake:

Mrs Compson stood watching her as she mounted, steadying herself against the wall with one hand, holding her skirts up with the other.

"Are you going to wake him up just to dress him?" she said.

Dilsey stopped. With her foot lifted to the next step she stood there, her hand against the wall and the grey splash of the window behind her, motionless and shapeless she loomed.

"He aint awake den?" she said.

"He wasn't when I looked in," Mrs Compson said. "But it's past his time. He never does sleep after half past seven. You know he doesn't."

Dilsey said nothing. She made no further move, but though she could not see her save as a blobby shape without depth, Mrs Compson knew that she had lowered her face a little and that she stood now like a cow in the rain, as she held the empty water bottle by its neck.

"You're not the one who has to bear it," Mrs Compson said. "It's not your responsibility. You can go away. You dont have to bear the brunt of it day in and day out. You owe nothing to them, to Mr Compson's memory. I know you have never had any tenderness for Jason. You've never tried to conceal it."

Dilsey said nothing. She turned slowly and descended, lowering her body from step to step, as a small child does, her hand against the wall. "You go on and let him alone," she said. "Dont go in dar no mo, now. I'll send Luster up soon as I find him. Let him alone, now." (pp. 338-339)

The Easter Sunday service in the Negro church is immensely moving, an apotheosis of simplicity, innocence, and love, with Dilsey and Benjy as the central figures:

> In the midst of the voices and the hands Ben sat, rapt in his sweet blue gaze. Dilsey sat bolt upright beside, crying rigidly and quietly in the annealment and the blood of the remembered Lamb. (pp. 370-371)

But the moment passes; the sense of human communion rapidly dissolves as they move into the world of "white folks" (p. 371) and return to the Compson house, described now for the first time and seen as a symbol of decay:

> They reached the gate and entered. Immediately Ben began to whimper again, and for a while all of them looked up the drive at the square, paintless house with its rotting portico. (p.372)

It is clear, however, that Faulkner does not intend any simple moral division between the Negroes and their white employers. Luster in particular has been less impressed by the service than by the performance on the musical saw he had witnessed the previous night, and in his treatment of Benjy he displays a streak of mischievous cruelty. Dilsey tries to comfort Ben, but she is forced to rely upon the treacherous Luster to take him to the cemetery and it is with a note of pathetic resignation that she says, "I does de bes I kin." (p. 396) On the final pages of the novel it is pride, the sin which has been the downfall of the Compson family, which induces Luster to drive to the left at the monument instead of to the right, and if the final restoration of Benjy's sense of order seems at first to offer a positive conclusion to the novel we must also remember that the order thus invoked is one purely of habit, entirely lacking in inherent justification, and that it is restored by Jason, whose concern is not with humanity or morality or justice but only with social appearances. As so often in this novel, such meaning as at first sight the incidents appear to possess proves on closer inspection to dissolve into uncertainty and paradox.

In Shakespeare's play, Macbeth's "sound and fury" soliloquy is spoken as death approaches, and by the end of Faulkner's novel the doom of the Compson family seems about to be finally accomplished. In *Macbeth* the forces of good, embodied in Malcolm and Macduff, are gathering strength and it is perhaps characteristic of the desperate mood of *The Sound and the Fury* that the forces of good are not so readily identifiable, nor seen as ultimately triumphant. Yet in *Macbeth* the forces of good are external to Macbeth and Lady Macbeth, whereas in *The Sound and the Fury* some of the elements making for life do appear within the Compson family group, most notably in Dilsey but also in Caddy and her daughter. It is Quentin who gives Luster the quarter he so desires, it is Quentin who struggles in the last section to maintain at least some semblance of family harmony and order but who finally breaks down under Jason's verbal torture, and it is perhaps to be taken as a sign of hope—especially in view of the resurrection images which some critics have perceived in the description of her empty room—that Quentin finally makes good her escape and that, unlike her mother, she leaves no hostage behind. In the Compson genealogy Faulkner speaks of Quentin in pessimistic terms, yet the suggestion that Faulkner wanted to write a novel about Quentin after her departure from Jefferson[23] at least indicates that he felt the Compsons were not yet finished with, that there was more to be said —or perhaps only more to be suffered.

AS I LAY DYING

SEVERAL attempts have been made to establish specific relationships between *The Sound and the Fury* and *As I Lay Dying*, to "pair" the two books,[1] and they do invite comparison as products of the same immensely creative period in Faulkner's career, as two of his most ambitious stylistic experiments, and as his only substantial adventures in "stream of consciousness" techniques. It is arguable, too, that *As I Lay Dying* follows up *The Sound and the Fury* in its treatment of a tightly-knit family situation revolving upon a single female figure. Here the central figure is Addie, the mother, instead of Caddy, the sister, and Faulkner seems to have attempted to avoid repeating whatever inadequacies there may have been in his presentation of Caddy, at least to the extent of giving Addie one of the fifty-nine sections of interior monologue into which the novel is divided. *As I Lay Dying* might also be said to mark a development from *The Sound and the Fury* in that Faulkner is now at pains to establish the setting and social context of the novel from the beginning:

> Jewel and I come up from the field, following the path in single file. Although I am fifteen feet ahead of him, anyone watching us from the cottonhouse can see Jewel's frayed and broken straw hat a full head above my own.
>
> The path runs straight as a plumb-line, worn smooth by feet and baked brick-hard by July, between the green rows of laid-by cotton, to the cottonhouse in the center of the field, where it turns and circles the cottonhouse at four soft right angles and goes on across the field again, worn so by feet in fading precision.
>
> The cottonhouse is of rough logs, from between which the chinking has long fallen. Square, with a broken roof set at a single pitch, it leans in empty and shimmering dilapidation in the sunlight, a single broad window in two opposite walls giving onto the approaches of the path. When we reach it I turn and follow the path which circles the house. Jewel, fifteen feet behind me, looking straight ahead, steps in a single stride through the window. (p. 1)

The geometrical and diagrammatic precision of this passage operates on a number of levels: as already suggested, the description carefully establishes scene and setting; but it also represents our first insight into the mind of Darl, creating that initial impression of absolute

rationality and clarity of vision which is progressively dissoived as
the book proceeds. It establishes, moreover, the basic terms of that
conflict between Darl and Jewel which provides the major source of
tension in this family novel, and which proves, in the end, to be the
rock on which the family splits. The rigidity of Jewel is here opposed
to the flexibility and circuitousness of Darl, and there is already a
suggestion of the contrast between Jewel's fierce masculinity and that
feminity of Darl's which is associated with his powers of intuition
and which thus provokes the anger and enmity of Dewey Dell.[2]

The associated drama of Darl's personal breakdown recalls that
of Quentin Compson in *The Sound and the Fury*, and Darl's vision,
his perception of the world and of himself, undoubtedly has something in common with Quentin's state of mind on the day of his
suicide :

> In a strange room you must empty yourself for sleep. And before
> you are emptied for sleep, what are you. And when you are emptied
> for sleep, you are not. And when you are filled with sleep, you
> never were. I dont know what I am. I dont know if I am or not.
> Jewel knows he is, because he does not know that he does not know
> whether he is or not. He cannot empty himself for sleep because he
> is not what he is and he is what he is not. Beyond the unlamped
> wall I can hear the rain shaping the wagon that is ours, the load
> that is no longer theirs that felled and sawed it nor yet theirs that
> bought it and which is not ours either, lie on our wagon though
> it does, since only the wind and the rain shape it only to Jewel and
> me, that are not asleep. And since sleep is is-not and rain and wind
> are *was*, it is not. Yet the wagon *is*, because when the wagon is
> *was*, Addie Bundren will not be. And Jewel *is*, so Addie Bundren
> must be. And then I must be, or I could not empty myself for sleep
> in a strange room. And so if I am not emptied yet, I am *is*.
> How often have I lain beneath rain on a strange roof, thinking
> of home. (pp. 75-76)

This expression of Darl's uncertainty as to his personal identity—an
uncertainty which leads eventually to a total disassociation of his
personality and to madness—can appropriately be set against the
central statement of Quentin's disordered perception :

> I seemed to be lying neither asleep nor awake looking down a long
> corridor of grey halflight where all stable things had become
> shadowy paradoxical all I had done shadows all I had felt suffered
> taking visible form antic and perverse mocking without relevance
> inherent themselves with the denial of the significance they should
> have affirmed thinking I was I was not who was not was not who.

These passages also suggest certain thematic similarities between the two books. The idea of "twilight," for example, whose significance in *The Sound and the Fury* we have already discussed, is also important in *As I Lay Dying*: Addie Bundren is herself at the twilight point, the poised moment, between life and death; it is at the hour of twilight that she dies; and throughout the early part of the book the dying of the day and of the daylight is persistently linked with the moment of her death, somewhat in the manner of Shakespeare's Sonnet LXXIII.

More important, however, is the extent to which the whole journey to Jefferson with Addie's body becomes for Darl, and for the reader, an outrageous "denial of the significance [it] should have affirmed." We are challenged throughout the book, as throughout *The Sound and the Fury*, to confront and, so far as possible, to bridge the gulf that divides our personal systems of value from those adhered to by the characters; we are equally challenged to perceive and resolve the contradictions that necessarily follow from the use of multiple points of view. A major source of ironic, and often comic, effects in *As I Lay Dying* is the frequency with which characters are completely mistaken in their judgments of each other, and of themselves. We quickly realise, for example, that Cora Tull is utterly wrong about the kind and quality of the relationships within the Bundren family, while her own obsession with the cakes she has made prepares the way for the throw-away humour of Addie's brief but shattering reference to "Cora, who could never even cook." (p. 165) Of a similar order is the recurrent association of Jewel with images of rigidity— the description of him in Darl's opening section, quoted above, is reinforced by many subsequent allusions to his wooden face and eyes, his wooden back, and so on—in direct contrast to the inward passion and fury of his nature.

In *As I Lay Dying*, then, as in *The Sound and the Fury*, we are confronted with the problems of the elusiveness of truth, the subjectivity of what individuals call fact, and there is a sense in which these two novels together with the later *Absalom, Absalom!* can be regarded as a trilogy on this theme. In *Absalom, Absalom!*, as in the two earlier novels, the narrative is assembled from fragments; the central situation is progressively illuminated by the light thrown upon it from a number of different viewpoints, none of them possessing final authority. *As I Lay Dying* represents a development from *The Sound and the Fury* in that the authorial voice is entirely dispensed with, but *Absalom, Absalom!* goes a step further than *As I Lay Dying* in that we ultimately remain in doubt as to what has "really" happened, something which is not seriously at issue in *As I Lay Dying*. Here the concern with the many faces of truth merges with, and is eventually superseded by, the examination of the many meanings of experience—specifically, of the widely divergent purposes which the various members of the Bundren family hope to achieve in the course of their joint expedition to Jefferson. Regarded in this light, the multiplicity of viewpoints, which is much more marked than in *The Sound and the Fury* or *Absalom, Absalom!* and which may give an initial appearance of fragmentation, begins to appear rather as a means both of dramatising diversity and of focusing it upon a single course of action. A further focusing effect is achieved by the way in which the relationships within the Bundren family radiate about Addie, the mother, as both their physical and their symbolic core. Addie's powerful personality and the principle of family unity which she embodies have long held the family together and continue so to hold it at least until her body has been buried, and it is entirely natural that she should not only occupy the foreground of the novel throughout but become, in effect, the battlefield on which her husband and her children—especially Jewel and Darl—fight out their personal rivalries and antagonisms. What finally gives the technique its unifying force is the way in which the successive segments not only advance the action, the progress towards Jefferson, but continually cast light inwards upon the central situation, deepening our understanding of the characters and intensifying our awareness of their often violent interrelationships.

It has sometimes been suggested that the sheer profusion of points of view in *As I Lay Dying* is self-defeating, and there is perhaps a sense in which the *tour de force* draws attention to itself by its very brilliance. But Faulkner succeeds marvellously in catching the tone of voice of such characters as Anse—it is the skills evident in the Jason section of *The Sound and the Fury* which are being exploited here—and the use of a wide range of viewpoints gives moral as well as narrative perspective, offers scope for rich ironic effects, and broadens the sense of social reality. A clear distinction must be made, however, between viewpoints, such as those of Darl, Cash, and other members of the Bundren family, which display a developing internal drama, a progression from one segment to the next, and those, such as MacGowan's and Samson's, which are single expressions of an outside view. The technique of the novel represents, of course, a *tour de force* of conception as well as of execution, and in his determination to avoid any authorial intrusion Faulkner perhaps allowed a certain dilution of the tensions arising from the internal psychological dramas of his major characters. The centripetal effect of the technique might have proved still more powerfully cohesive if the segmentation had been less radical, if the points of view had been fewer, if they had been identified from the start, and if each one had recurred more frequently. On the other hand, the book as it stands offers a vivid evocation of the widening circle of impact of the Bundrens' adventure, an effect which harmonises with the circular and radiating techniques of the book as a whole and with its recurring images of the circle, from the circling buzzards to the wheels of the wagon itself.

It seems possible to speak freely of *As I lay Dying* as a *tour de force* not only because of its obvious technical brilliance but because Faulkner himself often referred to it in those terms. He also said on more than one occasion that the book had been conceived in its totality before a word was written and that he had actually composed it in a period of six weeks.[3] These remarks have sometimes been misunderstood and are worth a brief examination. There is no doubt that the book was written very rapidly: the first page of the manuscript bears the date "25 October 1929" and the last page the date "11 December 1929," while the carbon typescript is dated "January 12, 1930,"[4] indicating that Faulkner had not only written the book in less than seven weeks but had completed the typing up—usually, for Faulkner, a process of revision as well—in a further month. What does need some qualification is the suggestion that the book was written "without changing a word" and the further assumption, frequently made, that it went to the printer virtually unchanged. In fact, as George P. Garrett has shown,[5] the manuscript provides ample evidence of the way in which Faulkner reworked his material even as he wrote the manuscript itself, and further study of the manuscript reveals even more extensive revision at this stage in the writing of the book—for instance, in the Cash section on page 77 of the book. In the manuscript each of the separate sections is begun on a fresh page, and there is evidence that in at least once instance, that of the Darl section and the following Cash section, beginning respectively on pages 147 and 156 of the published book, Faulkner reversed the order of sections from what he had originally intended. There are also a few places where revised or additional material has been stuck on to the manuscript page: in the reproduction of the final manuscript page which appears as Plate V in the Faulkner number of the *Princeton University Library Chronicle*, the lines formed by the edges of two such passages can be faintly discerned. Faulkner made many more alterations and a few additions to the book at a later stage, presumably in the process of making the typescript, which is itself almost identical with the published book. The Vardaman section beginning on page 61 of the book and the Dewey Dell section beginning on page 110 are both considerably changed from the manuscript version, while the episode on pages 221-223 in which Jewel attempts to fight the man on the passing wagon who had commented on the smell from Addie's coffin is present in the manuscript only in rudimentary form.[6]

Clearly, Faulkner's remarks about the writing of *As I Lay Dying*, and of other books as well, are not always to be interpreted in a strictly literal manner. As he said to one of his last interviewers, speaking of interviews generally: "I'm liable to say anything on these occasions, and often contradict myself."[7] Writing *As I Lay Dying* he said in 1955, was "easy, real easy.... I could write a book like that with both hands tied behind my back. It just came all of a piece with no work on my part."[8] Early in 1956, however, he mentioned *As I Lay Dying* in the context of a discussion about techniques:

> Sometimes technique charges in and takes command of the dream before the writer himself can get his hands on it. That is *tour de force* and the finished work is simply a matter of fitting bricks neatly together, since the writer knows probably every single word right to the end before he puts the first one down. This happened with *As I Lay Dying*. It was not easy. No honest work is. It was simple in that all the material was already at hand. It took me just about six weeks in the spare time from a twelve-hour-a-day job at manual labor.[9]

Faulkner wrote *As I Lay Dying* with unusual swiftness, writing at the very height of his powers; but he did not write it without effort, nor did he hesitate to make whatever subsequent alterations, additions, or deletions he thought desirable.

In both of the interviews just mentioned Faulkner went on to explain the essential simplicity of the conception underlying *As I Lay Dying*. "I just thought of all the natural catastrophes that could happen to a family and let them all happen," he said in 1955.[10] And in 1956: "I simply imagined a group of people and subjected them to the simple universal natural catastrophes, which are flood and fire, with a simple natural motive to give direction to their progress."[11] In essentials, it seems fair to say, *As I Lay Dying* is a simple anecdote recounted with a dazzling apparatus of techniques and in a manner that sometimes verges on the epic, resonant with biblical echoes of the Old Testament and of all the famous journeys of history, myth and legend: Odysseus, Jason, King Edward I and his dead Queen Eleanor. This aspect of the novel was early recognised by Valery Larbaud, one of those French critics to whom belongs the distinction of first taking the full measure of Faulkner's genius:

> Du reste nous pouvons, sans aucune intention de parodier le sujet de ce roman, le transposer en un épisode de caractère épique: l'épisode des Obsèques de la reine (homérique) Addie Bundren, conduites selon ses dernières volontés par son époux Anse et par les princes leurs enfants: l'aîné, Cash, le très habile charpentier, boiteux comme Héphaïstos; Darl en qui un esprit de démence et de prophétie habite; Jewel, cru fils d'Anse, en réalité le "vivant mensonge", le fils adultérin d'Addie et du Devin (entendez le Révérend) Whitfield; et le dernier né, Vardaman, un enfant, et la princesse Dewey Dell, âgée de dix-sept ans, qui porte en ses flancs le fruit de ses amours clandestines avec un bel

"étranger", Lafe, ouvrier venu de la ville pour aider à la récolte du coton (son prénom semblerait indiquer une origine scandinave: Leif?)[12]

What emerges even more clearly is that this simple story of poor farmers in the remote hill-country of northern Mississippi is deliberately presented as being played out against a background of cosmic scale. The atmosphere at the beginning of the book is repeatedly described as sulphurous and brooding:

> The sun, an hour above the horizon, is poised like a bloody egg upon a crest of thunderheads; the light has turned copper: in the eye portentous, in the nose sulphurous, smelling of lightning. (pp. 35-36)

When at last it begins to rain, "The first harsh, sparse, swift drops rush through the leaves and across the ground in a long sigh, as though of relief from intolerable suspense. They are big as buckshot, warm as though fired from a gun." (p. 71) Mood and setting are continually evoked on this grandiose scale, and there is a persistent invocation, in the description and in the imagery, of the elements of earth, air, fire and water: Addie, for example, declares that Jewel will save her "from the water and from the fire," (p. 159) while Dewey Dell compares herself to "a wet seed wild in the hot blind earth," (p. 60) and thinks of Darl's eyes as being "full of the land dug out of his skull and the holes filled with distance beyond the land." (p. 23)

There does not appear to be any consistent pattern designed to associate particular characters with particular elements: Faulkner's principal purpose seems rather to have been to enforce a reading of the novel, an interpretation of the Bundren family and its adventures, at a much higher and more universal level than either the characters or the action would seem at first sight to require or even to deserve. And, despite the outrageousness of the story, its frequent air of macabre fantasy, it gradually dawns upon us that this is in some sense a primitive fable of human endurance, an image of the tragi-comedy of all human experience. The family name, Bundren, even suggests a possible allusion to the burden which Bunyan's Christian carries with him on his journey to the Celestial City: Anse is specifically referred to as a man who has no burden but himself (p. 68), and he and his family can perhaps be regarded as making an ironic pilgrim's progress to the celestial city, the promised land, of Jefferson, where Anse at least receives his reward, in the shape of new teeth, a new wife, and a gramophone, while Darl discovers the path to Hell that leads even from the very gates of the celestial city.

With the brilliance of the writing and the immense centripetal force generated by the technique, *A I Lay Dying* is supremely all of a piece. Like *The Sound and the Fury*, it is written in a variety of styles, and certain passages seem over-written, or at least over-extended, as if the creative exuberance that informs the whole work had here overflowed into effects that were in excess of the needs of this particular book. Yet even in set-pieces such as the following, the distinguishing strength of the book is everywhere apparent:

> A-laying there, [says Anse] right up to my door, where every bad luck that comes and goes is bound to find it. I told Addie it wasnt any luck living on a road when it come by here, and she said, for the world like a woman, "Get up and move, then." But I told her it wasnt no luck in it, because the Lord put roads for travelling: why He laid them down flat on the earth. When He aims for something to be always a-moving, He makes it long ways, like a road or a horse or a wagon, but when He aims for something to stay put, He makes it up-and-down ways, like a tree or a man. And so He never aimed for folks to live on a road, because which gets there first, I says, the road or the house? Did you ever know Him to set a road down by a house? I says. No you never, I says, because it's always men cant rest till they gets the house set where everybody that passes in a wagon can spit in the doorway, keeping the folks restless and wanting to get up and go somewheres else when He aimed for them to stay put like a tree or a stand of corn. Because if He'd aimed for a man to be always a-moving and going somewheres else, wouldn't He a put him longways on his belly, like a snake? It stands to reason He would. (pp. 31-32)

Allen Tate recalls Faulkner telling him that this passage embodied the idea—apparently based upon a remembered anecdote—from which the whole book grew,[13] and it is tempting to think that the actual plot of the book, the story of the slow journeying with the decaying corpse, was also based on anecdotal material of this kind. Its apparent predecessor among Faulkner's own works was the short story, "The Liar," first published in the New Orleans *Times-Picayune* on July 26, 1925. As Carvel Collins has pointed out, "The Liar" was Faulkner's first published story with a rural setting;[1] both "The Liar" and *As I Lay Dying* deal with the Mississippi hill-country and its people, both are concerned with the relationship between fiction and reality, and, as the manuscript of *As I Lay Dying* reveals, Faulkner at one time intended to use in the novel some of the same names for his characters as he had used in the story: Armstid's section beginning on page 175 was originally given to Stannes, while the MacCallum who appears on pages 102-103 was previously Mitchell.[15] When Faulkner said in the *Paris Review* interview that the speed with which he wrote *As I Lay Dying* was largely due to the fact that "all the material was already at hand,"[16] he may have meant, among other things, that he had been thinking about characters such as the Bundrens and their neighbours for many years, that he knew these people and their ways, and that he had a fund of anecdote and observation on which to draw.

In this, perhaps the most important, aspect of the book it seems fair to speak of Faulkner as having achieved something comparable to the Irish folk-dramas of Synge: there is much the same vigour of language, the same humorous realism, the same identification with a particular region and its way of life. Certainly Faulkner knew and admired *The Playboy of the Western World*,[17] and there is a passage in Synge's preface to that play which would apply with almost equal accuracy to *As I Lay Dying*. Synge has been paying tribute to the rich language of the Irish peasantry, and he continues:

> This matter, I think, is of importance, for in countries where the imagination of the people, and the language they use, is rich and living, it is possible for a writer to be rich and copious in his words, and at the same time to give the reality, which is the root of all poetry, in a comprehensive and natural form.[18]

A rich and copious language in combination with a natural and comprehensive presentation of reality: this seems a just summary of Faulkner's achievement in *As I Lay Dying*, and it is the multiplicity of stylistic variation as well as of viewpoint which is primarily responsible for the book's extraordinary success in holding in balanced and reconciled suspension its wide range of radically diverse elements.

SANCTUARY

PROBABLY the best known of all the sentences written by William Faulkner occurs not in one of his novels, nor in the Nobel Prize speech, but in the Introduction to the Modern Library issue of *Sanctuary*: "To me it is a cheap idea, because it was deliberately conceived to make money." (p. v) Early critics of Faulkner often seized on the remark as offering justification of their own dislike of the book, and Ellen Glasgow, quoting the sentence in a letter to a friend, commented: "That covers a good deal of that kind of writing nowadays in the South. If anything is too vile and too degenerate to exist anywhere else it is assigned to the 'honest' school of Southern fiction, and swallowed whole, bait and all, by Northern readers, who have never been below Washington, but have a strong appetite."[1] Recent Faulkner criticism, however, has tended to put a higher valuation on *Sanctuary*, and several writers have emphasised the significance of the concluding sentences of the same Introduction, in which Faulkner makes it clear that in speaking of the book as a "cheap idea" he had in mind the first, unrevised version which he wrote in the first half of 1929, and that before the book was actually published in 1931 he had completely revised it—paying part of the cost of the extensive resetting of type which this involved—in an attempt to make the final work something which would not disgrace the books of which he was most proud. "I made a fair job," Faulkner concluded (p. viii), and in 1955 he told a questioner in Japan:

> Remember, the one you read was the second version. At that time I had done the best I could with it. The one that you didn't see was the base and cheap one, which I went to what sacrifice I could in more money than I could afford, rather than to let it pass. The one you saw was one that I did everything possible to make it as honest and as moving and to have as much significance as I could put into it.[2]

In serious Faulkner criticism the ghost of the *Sanctuary* Introduction has for some time been satisfactorily exorcised. Yet even those who have recognised that the first and not the final version was "the cheap idea" have tended to assume that Faulkner's rejection of the original, his determination to rewrite it, stemmed largely from his dissatisfaction with that deliberately "horrific" quality which he also mentions in the Introduction:

I took a little time out, and speculated what a person in Mississippi would believe to be current trends, chose what I thought was the right answer and invented the most horrific tale I could imagine and wrote it in about three weeks and sent it to [Harrison] Smith, ... who wrote me immediately, "Good God, I can't publish this. We'd both be in jail." (p. vi)

It is natural to assume from this account that *Sanctuary* as published was considerably less horrific than the original, and in approaching the novel we have continued to be haunted by the disturbing image of an *Ur-Sanctuary* which presumably demonstrated to an even greater degree those characteristics of violence, physical realism and sexual perversion for which the book itself was once notorious. For this reason we have perhaps found it difficult to view the book in proper perspective, tending to lay stress on certain elements rather than on others which may conceivably be of at least equal importance in Faulkner's overall conception of the work. Fortunately sets of the original galleys of *Sanctuary* have survived, and by studying these we may be led to rather different assessments both of the book as first written and of the kind of revisions which Faulkner made before publication.

At the Alderman Library there is the complete 138-page manuscript of the original version, a bound carbon typescript of this version, and, in the Massey Collection, a set of the unrevised galleys.[3] The University of Texas has another set of the unrevised galleys which Faulkner himself prepared for the printer. Despite the great interest of these revised galleys, they appear to be of relatively little textual importance: in doing the job of revision Faulkner tried to save as much of the original as he could without compromising the integrity of the whole revision process; thus he tended either to retain passages from the original galleys intact, except for changes in the naming of characters, or to do a complete job of rewriting, subsequently typing up this new material and linking it with the surviving material from the original galleys to constitute what amounted to a fresh set of galleys.[4]

The manuscript and the carbon typescript of *Sanctuary* in the Alderman Library both precede the unrevised galleys. The typescript, which bears on the title page the manuscript note "Oxford, Miss./ January-May, 1929," displays many differences of textual detail from the unrevised galleys, but the sequence of the material, the narrative structure, is precisely the same in both. The same is true of the manuscript, which is also dated "January, 1929-May, 1929," except that the order of Chapters III and IV is here reversed and there are traces of different openings to the novel with which Faulkner must have experimented at one time or another. One of these corresponds closely to the opening of Chapter IV of the published work, where there

appears the description of Temple Drake running across the campus
to keep her dates with the town boys in their cars.[5] Another begins
with a description, subsequently excised, of Temple's appearance at
Goodwin's trial, corresponding to the description of her on page 341
of the published book, and continues with a second, undeleted, paragraph corresponding to the account of the entrance of Temple's father
into the courtroom on pages 346-7.[6] Again, these early versions are
of great interest, but it seems clear that the most fruitful texts for
comparison, the ones most likely to reveal Faulkner's attitudes towards
what we have called the Ur-Sanctuary on the one hand and the published Sanctuary on the other, are the unrevised galleys and the book
itself. All students of Faulkner must here be greatly indebted to Mr.
Linton R. Massey, whose valuable study of the unrevised galleys
concludes with two sets of tables, one comparing the galleys against
the published book, the other comparing the published book against
the galleys.[5]

An attempted reconstruction of the unrevised text, based on the
tables supplied by Mr. Massey, might well suggest at first sight that
the usual assumptions about the unrevised Sanctuary were in fact
correct: the scenes presenting Temple's experiences at the Old Frenchman Place, culminating in her rape by Popeye with the corn-cob, and
the much more explicit accounts of the bizarre triangular relationship
between Popeye, Temple and Red in the Memphis brothel—these
famous episodes in the published book have all been taken over
from the original, generally with very little alteration.[8] Closer study,
however, reveals the remarkable fact that Sanctuary as published is in
certain ways notably more violent than the version which Faulkner
rejected. Chapter XXIX of the book, for example, contains only newly
written material, and it is in this chapter that Horace Benbow witnesses the savage lynching of Goodwin and is himself threatened
with a similar fate. In the unrevised galleys a rumour that Goodwin
may be lynched is mentioned in a letter from Narcissa to Horace, but
the lynching itself is nowhere described or even mentioned.

Further study of the unrevised galleys reveals that the extensive
deletions made by Faulkner in no instance included anything that
might be described as especially violent or "horrific." The main
direction of these deletions was greatly to reduce the emphasis on the
relationship between Horace Benbow and his various relations and
friends. Faulkner retained Horace as a central figure but jettisoned
much of the material which had originally surrounded him. His sister,
Narcissa, remains a fairly important figure, and so does his step-
daughter Little Belle, but they are now seen more clearly in their
relation to Temple Drake and to a particular conception of Southern
womanhood; there is no longer the same interest in the Benbow-
Sartoris family complex for its own sake. It is, to borrow the title of
the Paramount film which was subsequently made from the book, the

story of Temple Drake,[9] with the consequences it brings and the moral issues it invokes, which forms the narrative and thematic core of *Sanctuary* as published, and much of the cutting and rewriting was apparently designed to allow this central line to emerge much more clearly.

Yet these were by no means the only, or even the most radical, changes which Faulkner made. What must strike the reader of *Sanctuary* in any of its unrevised states is how badly it is put together. Ironically enough, it seems probable that either of the rejected openings we have already noted in the manuscript of *Sanctuary* would have served Faulkner better than the opening he eventually decided upon—a scene closely corresponding to the beginning of Chapter XVI of the published book, with Horace visiting Goodwin in jail at a moment in time after the murder, the rape, and most of the other crucial narrative events in the novel have already taken place. The scene contains many allusions to people and events of which the reader knows nothing, and it is only with great difficulty that he is able to reconstruct what has happened. Throughout the first six chapters of the unrevised text our attention is directed solely at or through Horace; his personal relationships are explored at considerably greater length than in the novel as we now have it, and these explorations are allowed to intrude, with bewildering shifts in time-sequence and point of view, upon what thus becomes a highly disconnected and confusing account of his adventures at the Old Frenchman place. It is not until Chapter VII that Temple Drake makes her appearance, in a scene that is almost identical with Chapter IV of the published book. The events which follow Temple's arrival at the Old Frenchman place are also narrated with many apparently arbitrary shifts of time, scene, and viewpoint, and much that Faulkner dramatises in the final version is here somewhat awkwardly narrated in the first person by Ruby Lamar. The later sections of the early version run rather more smoothly, and the episode of Virgil and Fonzo visiting Miss Reba's brothel in the belief that it is an hotel actually assumes additional ironic point from being immediately juxtaposed with the account of Temple's introduction to the same establishment, but the great failure at the end of this version, as Mr. Massey points out,[10] is that at what should have been the culminating moment of the action there is merely an anti-climactic tidying-up accomplished by an exchange of letters between Horace and Narcissa and a brief final chapter recording the death of Popeye.

It is impossible to say how far the fatal "cheapness" inherent in Faulkner's original conception of *Sanctuary* corresponded to his account of it in the Modern Library Introduction. The impulse which initiated the book seems to have come in some measure from the occasion when Faulkner met a girl in a New Orleans night club and heard from her the astonishing tale of her abduction by a Memphis gangster. The girl's story gave Faulkner some of the narrative material of *Sanctuary* and several of the most notable characteristics of Popeye, but Carvel Collins, who records the incident, notes: "In dealing with the startling real events Faulkner by no means exaggerated them for cheap effect—quite to the contrary he reduced their horror."[11] We have already seen that the cheap idea cannot have been simply that of writing a "tough" story of gangsterism and sexual violence, for the sections of the unrevised galleys which deal with Popeye and Temple Drake were allowed to stand, almost unchanged and almost in their entirety, in the published book; Collins's evidence further suggests that *Sanctuary* was by no means a wholly abstract or arbitrary conception, since in writing the novel Faulkner drew upon material which was already available to him and which he may already have been mulling over in his mind. When Faulkner spoke of a cheap idea the abruptness and forcefulness of his condemnation was an index of the imperiousness of his artistic integrity rather than of the actual value of his original intentions in writing *Sanctuary*. Speaking in Japan in 1955, Faulkner said that on receiving the unrevised galleys he told Harrison Smith, his publisher: "You can't print it like this; it's just a bad book."[12] There was undoubtedly a large element of deliberate sensationalism in the original conception of *Sanctuary*, and something of this survives in the published book, but the crucial fault may have lain in the combination of these sensational intentions with a too casual conception of the overall structure of the novel, an ill-considered assumption on Faulkner's part that the Temple Drake material could be readily wedded to a development of the Horace Benbow material with which he had already worked in *Sartoris*. Faulkner perhaps had in mind a crude juxtaposition of Horace's superficially humdrum but obsessively internalised emotional life with the much more violent experiences undergone by Temple Drake. The principal weakness of the original version was consequently one of balance and structure: the slackness and loose proliferation of the Benbow material had produced narrative confusion in the opening chapters and a persistent failure of dramatic tension culminating, as we have seen, in the clumsy exchange of letters at the point where the published book has the climactic scene of the lynching of Goodwin and the threatened lynching of Horace himself.

In revising the galleys, then, Faulkner used the Temple Drake material as the core around which the remainder of the novel could accrete, but at the same time he retained Horace Benbow as the central intelligence and, indeed, tied him much more firmly and specifically to that function. Horace is one of Faulkner's well-meaning failures, the intellectual of generous impulses but inadequate courage or will to action, tending always to dissipate his energies in talk: "I lack courage: that was left out of me," Horace tells Ruby. "The

machinery is all here, but it wont run." (p. 18) The type appears again
in such characters as Mr. Compson—especially in the Quentin section
of *The Sound and the Fury* and in "That Evening Sun"—and Ike
McCaslin, and it reaches its fullest development in Gavin Stevens. In
The Town Stevens even takes over some of Benbow's specific attributes: like Benbow in *Sartoris*, he is a Y.M.C.A. official in France
during the First World War and takes Montgomery Ward Snopes
with him on his staff. Benbow's failure as a man of action, however,
is a consequence not only of his personality but of his membership
of a particular social class, with inherited attitudes and privileges
which prevent him from achieving genuine understanding of people
lower down the social scale.

Thus the first two chapters of the published *Sanctuary* establish,
among many other things, the character of the relationship between
Benbow and Goodwin's woman, Ruby Lamar, and the contrast drawn
between Horace's pampered ineffectuality and Ruby's tough acceptance of hardship is central to the book as a whole. While he is at the
Old Frenchman place Horace, ironically anticipating Gowan Stevens,
both talks and drinks too much, and Ruby's judgment of him at this
time is subsequently proved to be all too accurate:

> "That fool," the woman said. "What does he want. . . ." She list-
> ened to the stranger's voice; a quick, faintly outlandish voice, the
> voice of a man given to much talk and not much else. "Not to
> drinking, anyway," the woman said, quiet inside the door. "He
> better get on to where he's going, where his women folks can take
> care of him." (p. 13)

The isolated world of the Old Frenchman place is harsh and violent
in many ways, but it is a world which Ruby, left undisturbed by outsiders, is sufficiently able to sustain and control. Unfortunately, the
next intruders, Gowan and Temple, prove to be even more alien to
that world than Horace had been and they are not merely foolish
but dangerous: Gowan's drunken aggressiveness and Temple's automatic coquetry provoke an atmosphere of rising tension which eventually explodes with the accomplishment of Temple's rape and Tommy's
murder, acts anticipated, recognised as foredoomed, by some of the
leading participants. The sense of tragic inevitability surrounding
these and other actions must have been one of the factors which
prompted André Malraux's famous remark that *Sanctuary*
demonstrates the intrusion of Greek tragedy into the detective
story.[13]

When Goodwin is arrested for the murder of Tommy, Horace sets
out with knightly zeal to see justice done and to save Ruby, the
distressed damsel. Essentially it is she rather than Goodwin who moves
Horace's interest and compassion, as he makes clear in answering

Narcissa's accusation that he has deliberately involved himself with "a street-walker, a murderer's woman":

> "I cant help it. She has nothing, no one. . . . Asking nothing of anyone except to be let alone, trying to make something out of her life when all you sheltered chaste women—" (p. 139)

As the novel proceeds, however, Horace has occasion to measure the gulf that divides his palely chivalric idealism from the unpalatable realities of a society which he discovers to be corrupt at every level, especially the highest, intricately criss-crossed by soiled bonds tying the brothel to the State capital, the jail to the courthouse (the symbolic scene-setting of *Requiem for a Nun* is already foreshadowed in *Sanctuary*). Horace, initially embattled in virtue, is forced to a recognition of his own inadequacy and guilt, though it is a guilt incurred less by his own actions than by his inescapable association with Narcissa and Temple and other members of his family and class. He realises that he has no moral right to advise, and no skill to help, people like Goodwin and Ruby who have long been inured to living with situations more desperate than any which he, in his sheltered life, has even contemplated, and who have lived out through suffering a devotion and integrity more real than anything approached by the messy self-indulgence of his own multifarious emotional involvements with his sister, his wife, his step-daughter, and even with Ruby herself.

For all Horace's earnest endeavours, events sweep on past him. While the tragic farce of Goodwin's trial is being played out he speaks scarcely a word: he is forced to watch helplessly the corrupt manipulations of Eustace Graham, the District Attorney, and their ratification by that other representative of law and order, Judge Drake.[14] Faulkner inexorably brings the reader to contemplate with Horace not only the rottenness of the whole social fabric, with the righteous revealed in all their inhumanity, and law and justice proved all too susceptible to perversion, but also a total inversion of official values ironically underlined by the fact that Lee Goodwin and Ruby Lamar, those victims of Southern society, bear two such highly honoured Southern names.[15] In part, of course, Horace's failure is a failure of character, an inevitable consequence of his own ineffectuality and of that disabling obsession with Little Belle which prevents him from entertaining such possibilities as that Little Belle's close counterpart, Temple Drake, might prove unreliable in the witness-box. Yet the social criticism, the condemnation of "the free Democratico-Protestant atmosphere of Yoknapatawpha County," (p. 151) is so firmly and unequivocally made that one can, perhaps, speak of *Sanctuary* as Faulkner's *Measure for Measure*.

There are, indeed, many points of similarity between the novel and Shakespeare's play: the same counterpointing of tragedy and comedy, the same presentation of a "low" world which constantly parallels and revalues the "high" world by which it is morally condemned, the same settings of brothel, prison, and place of justice, the same insistence on themes of guilt and injustice and of the corruption of the most egregiously virtuous. There are even possible parallels between the role of Lucio in the play and that of Senator Clarence Snopes in the novel, between Mistress Overdone and Miss Reba, and between Barnardine's indifference to impending execution and the similar indifference displayed by Popeye (whose name closely recalls that of Pompey, the pimp, in the play). Bearing in mind Faulkner's fondness for using quotations as titles for his novels—as in *The Sound and the Fury, Absalom, Absalom!, Go Down, Moses,* and *As I Lay Dying,* which Carvel Collins identifies as coming from a translation of the *Odyssey*[16]—it even seems possible that Faulkner may have taken the title of *Sanctuary* from the speech in which Angelo explores the conflict between his desire for Isabella and his sense of the virtue and justice which he embodies both through the office he holds and through his own reputation:

> Is this her fault or mine?
> The tempter or the tempted, who sins most?
> Ha!
> Not she; nor doth she tempt: but it is I,
> That, lying by the violet in the sun,
> Do as the carrion does, not as the flower,
> Corrupt with virtuous season. Can it be
> That modesty may more betray our sense
> Than woman's lightness? Having waste ground enough,
> Shall we desire to raze the sanctuary,
> And pitch our evils there? O, fie, fie, fie!
> What dost thou, or what art thou, Angelo?
> Dost thou desire her foully for those things
> That make her good? O, let her brother live!
> Thieves for their robbery have authority
> When judges steal themselves.[17]

Apart from the obvious relevance of the last line to the corruption of Eustace Graham and other representatives of the law,[18] the lines which most suggest *Sanctuary* are those containing the title-word itself: "Having waste ground enough,/Shall we desire to raze the sanctuary,/ And pitch our evils there?" This fits perfectly the rape of Temple Drake, that flower of Southern womanhood, and her subsequent corruption in the Memphis brothel, where indeed there was "waste ground enough" in the persons of Miss Reba's accommodating girls: the closeness of Temple's name to the meaning of "sanctuary" here hardly needs emphasis. If Faulkner did in fact have *Measure for Measure* to some extent in mind during the writing of *Sanctuary* he may also have seen a connection between Angelo's Isabella and Horace Benbow's wife, Belle—or, more especially, his obsessively desired but sexually inaccessible step-daughter, Little Belle.

Technically the novel is of considerable brilliance, and much of its strength derives from Faulkner's precise and economical presentation of specific and highly charged images, his vivid evocation of momentary sense-impressions. One thinks, for example, of the superbly staged opening—the technique is, here, essentially theatrical—and especially of Horace's sudden glimpse of Popeye's reflection in the settling waters; of Temple and the rat, their faces "not twelve inches apart"; of Temple's sensations during the crash of Gowan's car, where Faulkner, as so often in this novel, works towards a fidelity to experiential data that seems reminiscent of Hemingway in its intentions, although it is very different from Hemingway in manner; of the fragmentary glimpses of Memphis life caught by Popeye and Temple as they drive into town on a Sunday afternoon:

> They reached Memphis in midafternoon. At the foot of the bluff below Main Street Popeye turned into a narrow street of smoke-grimed frame houses with tiers of wooden galleries, set a little back in grassless plots, with now and then a forlorn and hardy tree of some shabby species—gaunt, lopbranched magnolias, a stunted elm or a locust in grayish, cadaverous bloom—interspersed by rear ends of garages; a scrap-heap in a vacant lot; a low doored cavern of an equivocal appearance where an oilcloth-covered counter and a row of backless stools, a metal coffee-urn and a fat man in a dirty apron with a toothpick in his mouth, stood for an instant out of the gloom with an effect as of a sinister and meaningless photograph poorly made. From the bluff, beyond a line of office buildings terraced sharply against the sunfilled sky, came a sound of traffic— motor horns, trolleys—passing high overhead on the river breeze; at the end of the street a trolley materialised in the narrow gap with an effect as of magic and vanished with a stupendous clatter. On a second storey gallery a young negress in her underclothes smoked a cigarette sullenly, her arms on the balustrade. (pp. 169-170)

Such a passage, though undoubtedly effective in its evocation of time and place, may nevertheless seem a little too mechanically contrived, relying as it too often does on such formulae as : "with an effect of." One notes a certain over-strenuousness, too, about the extraordinary emphasis throughout the novel on descriptions of the characters' eyes: the "rubber knobs" (p. 4) of Popeye, for example, the glowing eyes of Tommy, with their "pale irises," (p. 119) and the eyes of Dr. Quinn, which looked, behind his spectacles, "like little bicycle wheels at dizzy speed; a metallic hazel." (p. 179) There is a slightly arbitrary extravagance about the imagery here and throughout the book : from beneath the shade in Temple's room "the smoke-colored twilight emerged in slow puffs like signal smoke from a blanket," (p. 179) while the clock with its one hand stood on the mantelpiece "one-armed like a veteran from the wars." (p. 180) A similar audacity—deliberate, self-conscious—is perhaps to be recognised in the way Faulkner more than once abruptly juxtaposes a scene of violence or pathos with a scene of farcical comedy. *Sanctuary*, indeed, is a novel in which the reader is continually shocked, not only, or even primarily, by the violence of the narrative events, but also by the startling nature of the language, the imagery, and even the structural devices. This is, in part, an effect which Faulkner must deliberately have sought : it certainly works to evoke the rapt outrage of Temple's experience; it also serves, perhaps, as a disruption of normal linguistic expectations corresponding to the radical distortion of official moral and ethical standards which is continually occurring at the narrative level.

Sanctuary, however, though written after *The Sound and the Fury*, is still an early novel, only three years away from *Mosquitoes*. Faulkner may therefore have still been consciously experimenting with the application of Imagist techniques to the novel, or he may still have felt a need to enter into artistic competition with writers like Anderson, Hemingway and Fitzgerald. Such a sense of competition may have encouraged Faulkner in writing such splendid set-pieces as the scene of Red's funeral and the chapter in which Virgil and Fonzo put up at Miss Reba's brothel. These episodes are the product of the kind of comic vitality which found expression throughout Faulkner's career, right up to his last novel, *The Reivers*, in which he uses some of the same Memphis settings as appear in *Sanctuary*; they are sheer *tours de force*, executed with great energy and brilliance and un-questionably enriching the novel as a whole. Faulkner was still a young writer, but the composition of *The Sound and the Fury* must have given him a new-found creative assurance. The original version of *Sanctuary* was written in the aftermath of *The Sound and the Fury*; there was a certain slackening of creative energy, but the technical and verbal adventurousness which distinguishes the best scenes, the scenes contained in the final text, was the product of the same expansive mood—the mood of a great writer who discovers his right material at the same moment as he realises the full range and strength of his creative powers—which found its fullest expression in the more sustained *tour de force* of *As I Lay Dying*.

Sanctuary is not one of Faulkner's great novels—despite the judg-ment of Albert Camus that, with *Pylon*, it represents the height of his achievement.[19] If it had been published in its original form it would undoubtedly have been one of his worst books, although it would still have contained within it the brilliant scenes that constitute the present

Chapters XVIII, XXI, XXIII and XXV. There can be no doubt, however, of the care and determination with which Faulkner carried out his revision of the galleys, and although it is impossible to prove any special relationship between the novel and *Measure for Measure* it is tempting to posit such a relationship as an index of the seriousness of the thematic material which Faulkner had embodied in the book from the first. We have seen that even the phrase "cheap idea" needs to be read in the context of the extraordinarily high artistic standards to which Faulkner had adhered in theory from the first, and which, in *The Sound and the Fury* and *As I Lay Dying* (completed before the revision of *Sanctuary*) he had so recently set himself in practice. Faulkner could not make of *Sanctuary* a work to equal his achievement in *The Sound and the Fury* and *As I Lay Dying*, but he certainly reworked it into something which justified his own judgment—a characteristic blend of modesty and superbly assured self-knowledge—that he had "made a fair job."

LIGHT IN AUGUST

BY comparison with *The Sound and the Fury* and *As I Lay Dying* the opening pages of *Light in August* display a much closer approximation to the techniques and progressions of "conventional" fiction. The first chapter, with its image of Lena Grove pursuing her tranquil way steadily across the face of Mississippi, immediately recalls the opening of such Hardy novels as *The Mayor of Casterbridge* or *The Return of the Native*, and even the abrupt transitions to apparently unrelated material in the second and third chapters will not disturb anyone familiar with Dickens— with, say, *Bleak House*, or *Our Mutual Friend*. Throughout *Light in August*, indeed, we are aware of an essential affinity with the major traditions of the nineteenth-century novel and especially with the work of Hardy and Dickens, and the initial impression of the relative conventionality of *Light in August* to some degree remains to the end of the book. But the demands the novel makes of its readers are by no means of a wholly conventional nature; this is especially true of the kind of moral and emotional engagement which Faulkner extorts, but it is also true of the narrative technique, which is much less straightforward than might appear at first sight.

The "time present" of the novel, as defined by the opening account of Lena's meeting with Armstid, begins on a Friday afternoon. In a sense, however, Lena's relationship with Armstid and his wife lies outside the action of the novel proper; it is a framing episode, a prelude, linked with the epilogue or coda provided in the final chapter of the book. The point at which the main action of the novel is engaged is at the very end of the first chapter, when Lena arrives on the outskirts of Jefferson and sees the smoke rising from the ruins of Miss Burden's home. This is about midday on the Saturday, and it is important to note that, for all the novel's abundance of narrative incident, many of the major events have by this time already taken place. One major event—indeed, it is one of the three crucial events in the immediate action of the novel—has taken place during the night which Lena spent at the Armstid's: this is the death of Joanna Burden. The two other crucial events both take place on the ninth day following Lena's arrival in Jefferson; that Monday morning Lena gives birth to her child, and that afternoon Percy Grimm hunts down Joe Christmas and kills him. A very considerable proportion of the novel is taken up with extended "flashbacks" which recount the history of various characters up to the point at which they become involved in the present action. The longest of these retrospections, telling the story of Christmas himself, occupies Chapters six to twelve inclusive, and the others, though much shorter, may even so occupy several pages or almost the whole of a chapter. These passages are introduced and deployed very much as the long sentences in later novels such as *Go Down, Moses* and *Intruder in the Dust*: the immediate action is quite simply held in suspension for the duration of the flashback, rather as the action in *Moby Dick* is sometimes arrested while some essential point of background information is supplied. Faulkner practises no particular subtlety or concealment in introducing these flashbacks, and there even seems to be a touch of deliberate crudeness in the introduction at a late stage of the novel of characters who are to play an important part in its events, or in our interpretation of these events: "In the town on that day lived a young man named Percy Grimm" (p. 425); "Gavin Stevens though had a different theory. He is the District Attorney, ..." (p. 419)

It is almost as though, in his passionate need to tell the tragic story of Christmas, Faulkner scorned mere literary finesse, and in answer to a question about the style of *Light in August* he once said:

I don't know anything about style. I don't—I think a writer with a lot to—pushing inside him to get out hasn't got time to bother with style. If he just likes to write and hasn't got anything urging him, then he can become a stylist, but the ones with a great deal pushing to get out don't have time to be anything but clumsy, like Balzac, for instance.[1]

Faulkner had a great deal "pushing inside him" when he wrote *Light in August*, but he was himself a much more deliberate writer than these remarks might seem to imply, and, despite the apparent crudity, he undoubtedly achieves powerful emotional effects by his techniques of delayed revelation and delayed introduction of characters. We first see Christmas, for example, as he appears to Mooney, the foreman at the planing mill, to Byron Bunch, and to the people of Jefferson generally: only later are we given those details of Christmas's birth and upbringing which force us radically to amend our judgment of a man whom we, like the people of Jefferson, have already condemned on sight as inherently vicious and worthless. Similarly, it is only at a very late stage in the book that we are allowed to see Hightower's situation to some extent from his own point of view. If, on the other hand, we are given Lena Grove's history the moment she appears, that is primarily because she and her background are so simple and so easily explained, and because she seems not so much a character in the book, with possibilities of development and unanticipated variety, as a kind of impersonalised catalytic force, effecting change but itself unchanging. She provides a steady imperturbable groundnote, an onward linear progression that offers a constant contrast to the desperate contortions—moral, emotional, and physical—of the other characters.

It seems possible to speak almost in diagrammatic terms of this novel, rich as it is in symbolic potentialities, disposed in large and readily distinguishable blocks of material, and with whole scenes presented almost in the form of tableaux, as formalised, even frozen, action:[2] Lena traversing the face of Mississippi "like something moving forever and without progress across an urn" (p. 5); Christmas and McEachern waiting in rigid immobility during the intervals of their hourly ritual of command, refusal, and punishment; Percy Grimm pursuing Christmas "with that lean, swift, blind obedience to whatever Player moved him on the Board." (p. 437) It is remarkable that a great deal even of the present action of the novel is not directly recounted but reflected in the minds and memories of witnesses who were not themselves involved in the action : Gavin Stevens giving his interpretation of the events leading to Christmas's death; the furniture dealer telling his wife of his encounter with Lena and Byron Bunch; the impersonal "they" of the latter part of Chapter 15, recounting "about supper tables in electrically lighted rooms and in remote hill cabins with kerosene lamps" (p. 330) the story of Christmas's arrest in Mottstown and the curious behaviour of Doc Hines and his wife. It is almost as though Faulkner were seeking to "domesticate," to incorporate within the structure of a conventional novel, the technique of multiple reflection which he had earlier employed in As I Lay Dying, and it is certainly clear that in Light in August he is concerned not merely to tell the stories of Joe Christmas, Lena Grove and Gail Hightower but also, and perhaps primarily, to show the impact of these stories upon the people of Jefferson.

One cannot avoid speaking in the plural of the stories of Christmas, Lena and Hightower, for there are quite unmistakably three distinct strands in the novel. They are not, however, entirely separable strands, and critics have become steadily more aware of the essential unity of the novel, a unity secured through various forms of thematic interrelation and ironic reflection rather than through the more familiar kinds of narrative link—though even these links are stronger and more numerous than has often been allowed, as Malcolm Cowley discovered when he attempted to separate one of the strands for inclusion in The Portable Faulkner.[3] Joanna Burden, in the corruption of a sensuality discovered too late and pursued too far, offers an obvious contrast to the healthy animality of Lena Grove; Lena herself, travelling down her "peaceful corridor paved with unflagging and tranquil faith and peopled with kind and nameless faces and voices," (p. 4) is at the opposite pole from Joe Christmas, who for fifteen years has travelled down a street which "ran on in its moods and phases, always empty : he might have seen himself as in numberless avatars, in silence, doomed with motion, driven by the courage of flagged and spurred despair." (p. 213) Faulkner himself spoke of Hightower as the antithesis of Christmas, in that he "escaped into his past,"[4] presumably an allusion to the way in which Christmas, bereft of all certainty about his past, cannot rest from his passionate engagement with the present. On a more comic level, there is the utter dichotomy between the conscientious Byron Bunch and his shiftless "rival" and near-name-sake, Lucas Burch. There are also subsidiary patterns of contrast between these characters and among the minor characters, as well as patterns of irony operating through the recurrence of similar acts in different contexts: when Byron Bunch fights with Lucas Burch, for example, we may remember Joe Christmas's similar defeat following his final chivalric gesture towards Bobbie Allen, the prostitute; in view of Byron's pathetic adventures in the final chapter, we ought perhaps to think also of Joe's earlier experience with the Negro girl and Faulkner's comment about "that spontaneous compulsion of the male to fight with or because or over the partner with which he has recently or is about to copulate." (p. 148) There is irony of a more bitter kind in that Percy Grimm and Hightower, the one ruthlessly pursuing Christmas, the other in a supreme though belated moment of abnegation trying to defend him, are essentially akin in their obsessive allegiance to a dead past.

Running throughout the book is that fundamental irony which Faulkner explores to a greater or lesser degree in almost all of his novels: the gulf between appearance and actuality, the contrast between the public and the private self. We have already noted the contrast between the outward face of Joe Christmas and the inner reality with which the reader becomes increasingly familiar as the book progresses. Another character whom we apprehend on two levels in this way is Joanna Burden, inwardly a chaos of sensuality, outwardly a woman of mature wisdom, dispensing "advice, business, financial and religious, to the presidents and faculties and trustees, and advice personal and practical to young girl students and even alumnae, of a dozen negro schools and colleges through the south." (p. 20) Hightower and Byron Bunch are other characters in whom we become aware of such a duality, while again and again we realise that the characters themselves are seeing their fellow men and women not as they actually are but as they wish them to be: so Miss Burden sees Christmas as "negro"; so Hightower discerns in his wife, as Joe Christmas discerns in Bobbie Allen, a non-existent quality of love.

These ironic patterns are clearly related to that theme in the novel which critics have often, and rightly, identified as being of major significance: the demand of organised society and organised religion that the human individual act in strict accordance with prescribed abstract patterns. At the hands of religious authoritarians such as Hines and McEachern, Christmas has suffered all his life from this demand, and it is in response to the same rigid requirement that he is finally hunted down according to the rules prescribed in Jefferson for the treatment of "nigger murderers." There are, too, several passages in the novel which seem to imply a general social denunciation. After the death of Miss Burden, for instance, the people of Jefferson refused to let her body lie in peace but preferred to believe that it "cried out for vengeance":

> Because the other made nice believing. Better than the shelves and the counters filled with long familiar objects bought, not because the owner desired them or admired them, could take any pleasure in the owning of them, but in order to cajole or trick other men into buying them at a profit; and who must now and then contemplate both the objects which had not yet sold and the men who could buy them but had not yet done so, with anger and maybe outrage and maybe despair too. Better than the musty offices where the lawyers waited lurking among ghosts of old lusts and lies, or where the doctors waited with sharp knives and sharp drugs, telling man, believing that he should believe, without resorting to printed admonishments, that they labored for that end whose ultimate attainment would leave them with nothing whatever to do. And the women came too, the idle ones in bright and sometimes hurried garments, with secret and passionate and glittering looks and with secret frustrated breasts (who have ever loved death better than peace) to print with a myriad small hard heels to the constant murmur *Who did it? Who did it?* periods such as perhaps *Is he still free? Ah. Is he? Is he?*[5] (p. 273)

It is interesting, however, that Faulkner's criticism of Jefferson is relatively mild. After the arrest of Christmas it is the peace and quiet of the town which is insisted upon: Percy Grimm walks across "the quiet square empty of people peacefully at suppertables about that peaceful town and that peaceful country," (p. 430) and Faulkner makes it entirely clear in this deeply imagined and superbly evoked episode that it is Percy Grimm alone who provokes the town to that course of ritual action of which he himself inevitably becomes the final instrument. The men who share Grimm's pursuit of Christmas do not necessarily share his savagery, for one of them vomits at the sight of the castration, and it is clear that, in his presentation of Grimm, Faulkner was not especially concerned to portray a specifically Southern type of violence: years later he wrote to Malcolm Cowley of having created a Nazi before Hitler did.[6] Although it would be an exaggeration to say that in its conduct towards Christmas the society of Jefferson appears at its collective worst, it might at least be said that the occasion permitted the worst elements in Jefferson to emerge and take command. But in any case a counterbalance is supplied by Lena Grove: she brings out—not always readily, but eventually—the best in Jefferson, and it is with Lena, in her familiar role as the calm recipient of kindness, that the book begins and ends.

There is, however, little qualification or amelioration of the book's rejection of organised religion and religious fanatacism. The bigotry of several characters, in the past as well as the present, is closely examined and shown to be self-condemned by its own rigidity and inhumanity, and it is a final astringent touch in Faulkner's treatment of this theme that as Percy Grimm hunts down Joe Christmas his face displays "that serene, unearthly luminousness of angels in church windows," (p. 437) and his voice sounds "clear and outraged like that of a young priest." (p. 439) All these characters, so assured in their narrow faith, are in contrast to Joe Christmas himself, a man engaged in unceasing introspection, a persistent and desperate search for personal identity and for a meaning in life.[7] He is several times likened to a monk, and Faulkner, answering a question put to him at the University of Virginia, spoke revealingly of Christmas's self-isolation from the world:

> I think that was his tragedy—he didn't know what he was [i.e. white or Negro], and so he was nothing. He deliberately evicted himself from the human race because he didn't know which he was. That was his tragedy, that to me was the tragic, central idea of the story—that he didn't know what he was, and there was no way possible in life for him to find out. Which to me is the most tragic condition a man could find himself in—not to know what he is and to know that he will never know. [8]

For all his confusion, however, it is Christmas who discovers one of the two forms of religious and moral experience which Faulkner appears to offer as valid. Christmas, who becomes godlike in his last agony, discovers the way of suffering, of passive acceptance, the path of crucifixion. The opposite but complementary figure in the novel is Lena Grove, who, in her simple and unquestioning acceptance of a kind of natural religion, seems to embody those simple and permanent values which Faulkner so frequently and so powerfully affirmed, the values of endurance, patience, fecundity, and simple faith. "That will be her life, her destiny," Hightower recognises: "The good stock peopling in tranquil obedience to it the good earth; from these hearty loins without hurry or haste descending mother and daughter." (p. 384)

The opposition, and indeed counterpoint, of Lena Grove and Joe Christmas is clear and apparent throughout the novel, and its validity is readily acceptable. The disturbing figure, morally and structurally, is that of Hightower. He has seemed to many critics a shadowy and indeterminate figure, lacking a sufficiently substantial stake in the plot or an adequately defined role in the moral or symbolic patterns of the book as a whole. But such a judgment may result from a failure to distinguish Hightower's functions from Faulkner's deliberate characterisation of him as a non-participator, a man withdrawn from life and its sufferings. He is clearly a character with a special significance for Faulkner, a type who had long haunted his imagination. No clearly identifiable forerunner of Hightower appears in any of Faulkner's published works, though we may detect several points of similarity with Mr. Compson, but in the unpublished story "Rose of Lebanon" he is directly prefigured in the central character, Gavin Blount, a bachelor doctor with a run-down Memphis practice, of whom his friend Randolph Gordon thinks "with tolerance and a right smart of affection and a little contempt. Because the life he led was no life for a man, ... He had inherited from his father what practice he had. Or rather, he had inherited from his father a practice which, by 20 odd years of unflagging endeavour, he had reduced to the absolute minimum."[9] Blount is utterly devoted to a local social organisation, the Guards, of which he has been chairman for seventeen years, inheriting the post ultimately from his great-uncle, also called Gavin Blount, who had died on the field of Chickamauga, and his obsession with this Civil War past leads him to consider marriage with a survivor of that period. When Gordon asks Blount why, at the age of 43, he has not married, Blount replies :

"... She wouldn't have me."
"Who wouldn't have you?"
"Lewis Randolph."
Lewis Randolph is my mother, she is 82 years old.

The second section of the story ends at that point. In the third section Blount himself tells the story of Lewis Randolph, who had kissed all one hundred and four men of her husband's regiment in December 1861, just before the battle of Shiloh, and whose husband, Charley Gordon, had eventually been killed the night Van Dorn burned Grant's stores at Holly Springs, shot at point-blank range by someone with a shotgun during the raiding of a chicken-roost. The story has a comic ending and the treatment of Blount is quite different from the presentation of Hightower in *Light in August*, but the death of Charley Gordon has clearly been taken over into the novel, as have many aspects of Blount, the man to whom Randolph Gordon says, "You cant live then and now too," and who replies, "I can die trying."

Blount reappears in another unpublished story, "The Big Shot," in which he becomes a representative of "the old sense of honor dead everywhere else in America except in the south and kept alive here by a few old ladies who acquiesced in '65 but never surrendered."[10] Dal Martin, the "big shot," has social pretensions for his daughter and persuades Dr. Blount to allow her name to be included on the list for the Guards ball, bribing him by the offer of an art gallery to be named after his grandfather who had died in Forrest's cavalry in 1864. Blount later feels he has betrayed his honour and begs Martin to release him from their agreement, offering to find the money for the art gallery himself; Martin refuses, and Blount commits suicide. In addition to the appearance of a Hightower type in these two unpublished stories, there exist at the University of Texas a few pages of what appears to be an early draft of *Light in August*; this version opens with a description of Hightower in his study and continues with material that was eventually absorbed into the published novel, partly into the third chapter, where Hightower first appears, and partly into the penultimate chapter, in which Hightower's life story is told.[11]

Hightower appears in *Light in August* as the final expression of a conception which had long been present in Faulkner's mind. What is wrong with Hightower, the source of the general uneasiness about him, is that he has remained in the novel the haunting conception which Faulkner tried unsatisfactorily to embody in the unpublished stories. The actions and obsessions of Gavin Blount in "Rose of Lebanon" and "The Big Shot" are grotesquely in excess of the conceivable demands of the human situation in which Faulkner presents him. So, we may well feel, are the actions and obsessions of Gail Hightower. The "idea" informing Faulkner's presentation of Hightower is clear; it is, indeed, sufficiently implied in the obvious symbolism of his name.[12] But Hightower is not a fully realised character, though he might have become so if Faulkner had told the story of his life at an earlier stage in the novel and had treated that story with a higher degree of dramatisation. On the other hand, it may in one sense be very much to the point that Hightower is not completely realised— obsessed with the past, he does not live in the present where realisation can occur—and he is, in any case, more closely integrated into the novel than critics have sometimes suggested. In that rich opening chapter the way is prepared for him in the elaborate image of discarded machinery:

> ... gaunt, staring, motionless wheels rising from mounds of brick rubble and ragged weeds with a quality profoundly astonishing, and gutted boilers lifting their rusting and unsmoking stacks with an air stubborn, baffled and bemused upon a stumppocked scene of profound and peaceful desolation, unplowed, untilled, gutting slowly into red and choked ravines beneath the long quiet rains of autumn and the galloping fury of vernal equinoxes. (pp. 2-3)

Almost all the images associated with Hightower in succeeding chapters are already present in this passage.

Hightower has, too, more than a merely narrative connection with the Byron Bunch-Lena Grove relationship. He is more than once described as an eastern idol, and for Byron Bunch he is initially a repository of wisdom; it is Byron who interprets the stale smell of Hightower's house as the odour of goodness. Byron at the opening of the book is Hightower's disciple, his imitator in silence, withdrawal, isolation from life; but Byron is converted by his love for Lena to a new concern for humanity which soon extends beyond his relationship with Lena herself and overflows into a compassionate if hopeless attempt to aid Joe Christmas. What vitiates so many of the relationships in the novel—between Joanna Burden and Joe Christmas, for example, between Christmas and his various women, between Hightower and his wife—is their selfishness and lack of generosity: the partners use those whom they claim to love primarily as a means of attacking some personal problem. As Hightower comes eventually to realise of his own married life, such relationships remain on an abstract level rather than a human one, and they are effectively criticised in terms of the warm, humane, and outward-going quality of Byron's love for Lena. Byron not only breaks with his earlier discipleship but actually becomes his master's teacher, showing him the way to that recognition of value in life, in human involvement, which Hightower finally achieves. It is, however, too late for Hightower to be effectively reborn. Lena does not name her baby after him, and his mind cannot rest in the vision of human solidarity and interdependence which he has with such agony achieved but returns ineluctably to that obsessive image of his grandfather which has haunted him throughout his life —though Faulkner himself reminded us that this image was not in itself an ignoble one: "[Hightower] had to endure, to live, but that was one thing that was pure and fine that he had—was the memory of his grandfather, who had been brave."[13]

Faulkner said more than once that he began *Light in August* with nothing clearly in mind save the image of Lena Grove—"knowing no more about it than a young woman, pregnant, walking along a strange country road."[14] The Hightower image presumably became associated with this basic image at a fairly early stage in the writing of the book, although it is just conceivable that the manuscript pages at Texas represent the remains of an attempt on Faulkner's part to write a novel with Hightower as its central figure. The suggestion that "Light in August" is a countryman's expression used of a cow or mare due to drop her calf or foal in that month might tend to confirm the primacy of the Lena Grove element, but it seems unlikely that in choosing a title for so various a novel Faulkner would have such a narrow range of relevance in mind.[15] In any case, discussion of this point has to some extent diverted attention from other substantial

justifications for the title which appear within the book itself. Many
critics have noticed the frequency in the novel of images of light and
dark, for example, and Faulkner spoke very interestingly of a special
quality of light which he had in mind:

> [I]n August in Mississippi there's a few days somewhere about
> the middle of the month when suddenly there's a foretaste of fall,
> it's cool, there's a lambence, a luminous quality to the light, as
> though it came not from just today but from back in the old classic
> times. It might have fauns and satyrs and the gods and—from
> Greece, from Olympus in it somewhere. It lasts just for a day or
> two, then it's gone, but every year in August that occurs in my
> country, and that's all that title meant, it was just to me a pleasant
> evocative title because it reminded me of that time, of a luminosity
> older than our Christian civilization.[16]

It is this light which shines on the day of Christmas's death and at
the moment when Hightower finally recognises the truth about himself and the extent of his responsibility both for his own suffering and
for that of his dead wife: "In the lambent suspension of August into
which night is about to fully come, it [the wheel of his thinking]
seems to engender and surround itself with a faint glow like a halo."
(p. 465) But Faulkner seems to hint at some wider meaning in his
references to "the old classic times . . . fauns and satyrs and the gods"
and the "pagan quality" of Lena Grove. The "earth-mother" qualities
in Lena Grove are clearly hinted at in her name, and have long been
recognised. But given Faulkner's undoubted familiarity with the
stories of classical mythology and with the works of Joyce and Eliot,
and his probable acquaintance with Frazer's *The Golden Bough*, it
would not be surprising if he had further analogies in mind: not
necessarily a complex and carefully articulated pattern of analogy
such as Joyce evolved in *Ulysses*, but perhaps some slightly opportunistic exploitation of an available source such as he had shown in
his allocation of three sections of *The Sound and the Fury* to the dates
of Easter 1929 or in the various hinted analogies in *Light in August*
itself between Joe Christmas and Jesus Christ, between Lena Grove
and the Virgin Mary, and between Byron Bunch and Mary's husband,
Joseph.[17]

Any search for underlying patterns in *Light in August* might well
begin with a consideration of the extensive series of parallels and
substitutions which appear in the course of the novel and which again
and again establish thematic and even narrative links between its
different strands. An obvious example is Mrs. Hine's confused identification of Lena's baby with Joe Christmas when he was a child, and
her further reference to the baby as being actually Christmas's son.[18]
One thinks also of the similarities between the apparently opposed

backgrounds of Hightower and Miss Burden, fanatics of the South and of the North; of the parallelism between the tragic encounter of Joe Christmas with Percy Grimm and the primarily comic encounter of Byron Bunch with Lucas Burch, which takes place at the same moment in time; of the reverberations set up in the reader's mind by the incident of Christmas breaking into a Negro church like an impersonation of the devil, recalling as it does both the mad forays into Negro churches made by his grandfather, Doc Hines, and the moment of Satanic glee caught by the camera as Hightower leaves his empty church.

Most important of all, however, is the relationship between Miss Burden and Lena Grove and Lena's replacement of Miss Burden at the plantation after the latter's death, and there are reasons for thinking that Faulkner may have intended a series of allusions to the goddess Diana and to the sacred groves where she was worshipped. Lena Grove's name is an obvious hint leading in this direction, and the Burden house itself is several times described as standing almost hidden among a grove of trees, a grove which still stands even when the house itself has gone; the place, too, is one to which Negro women have come for many years as to a shrine or to a "wise woman"—"approaching the house in a manner not exactly secret, yet purposeful, ... emerging again and returning down the radiating paths not fast and yet not loitering." (p. 243) Miss Burden, the original mistress of the grove, is not on the face of it an especially Diana-like character, but she has certain characteristics in common with the Roman Diana— notably her masculinity, her reputation for virginity, and her moon-like ebb and flow of passion as she and Christmas pass through all the different phrases of their relationship—and it is she whom the Negro women have consulted in their troubles, especially, it appears (p. 251), in those troubles of pregnancy and childbirth which were Diana's special province. Lena Grove, on the other hand, with her name, her air of timeless permanence, and her fecundity, has much in common with that Ephesian Diana who was specifically an earth-mother, fertility figure.

Is there, perhaps, some sense in which Faulkner intended the ritualistic murder of Joanna Burden, carried out as Lena Grove pauses overnight on the outskirts of the town, to be an act preparatory to the replacement of Miss Burden's alien, outmoded, and sterile influence by the natural vitality and fecundity embodied in Lena? Certainly something more than the mere establishment of a weak narrative link seems to be involved in Lena's occupation of the cabin on the Burden estate and the birth there of her child. Hightower, in particular, makes it clear that new life has come to the run-down plantation, the "ruined garden," (p. 264) that some kind of symbolic rebirth has been enacted:

He emerges from the woods at the far side of the pasture behind the cabin. Beyond the cabin he can see the clump of trees in which the house had stood and burned, though from here he cannot see the charred and mute embers of what were once planks and beams. 'Poor woman,' he thinks. 'Poor, barren woman. To have not lived only a week longer, until luck returned to this place. Until luck and life returned to these barren and ruined acres.' It seems to him that he can see, feel, about him the ghosts of rich fields, and of the rich fecund black life of the quarters, the mellow shouts, the presence of fecund women, the prolific naked children in the dust before the doors; and the big house again, noisy, loud with the treble shouts of the generations. (p. 385)

Hightower sees the pathos of Miss Burden's passing, but the reader may sense that her death has in some way been a precondition of the rebirth which is here so eloquently evoked. The death seems fated, like so much else in the novel, and, like the death of Joe Christmas nine days later, it is certainly executed in ritualistic fashion: Miss Burden herself prepares for it in prayer and Christmas prepares for it by performing what can perhaps be best described as the quasi-rituals of stripping himself of the last woman-sewn button and showing himself naked in the lights of a passing car, by shaving at the spring, and by temporarily immersing himself in the "thick black pit" (p. 107) of the Negro district.

Immediately before Christmas goes in to kill Miss Burden, at midnight on the Friday, we are given this insight into his thoughts:

Now it was still, quiet, the fecund earth now coolly suspirant. The dark was filled with the voices, myriad, out of all time that he had known, as though all the past was a flat pattern. And going on: tomorrow night, all the tomorrows, to be a part of the flat pattern, going on. He thought of that with quiet astonishment: going on, myriad, familiar, since all that had ever been was the same as all that was to be, since tomorrow to-be and had-been would be the same. Then it was time. (p. 266)

This is as precise a verbal definition as can be found in the novel of the kind of representative significance embodied by Lena Grove: Christmas here realises, in a flash of insight, the fundamental permanence of the earth and of human experience which lies beneath and beyond the immediate present of agonised searching and violent experience in which he is himself so inextricably engaged. Also significant, however, is the final statement: "Then it was time." This is the moment on which, in a very real sense, the whole novel turns, the moment of midnight on the Friday night which Lena spends at the Armstids'. It is on this point of time that the entire long flashback recounting Christmas's previous experiences is poised, and since the flashback begins on page 111 and occupies only a few pages short of a third of the novel, it must be considered one of Faulkner's most extended experiments in suspended time.

The statement, "Then it was time," may thus be in the nature of an announcement that the moment has been released from its suspension, that the action is henceforward immersed once more in the flow of time. This is, however, a novel in which the course of present events is very carefully charted and in which many of the characters display an extraordinary awareness of time: Byron meticulously keeps his own time when working alone; Hightower always knows the time although he has no clock; while Christmas is being pursued he is driven to speak to people not by any need for food but by his need to know what day it is. It seems probable that Faulkner had some kind of deliberate time scheme in mind as he wrote the book, and since the ancient festival of Diana used to be celebrated in August it is conceivable that he intended some allusion to it.[19] The fact that fire was especially important in the celebration of the festival would then give additional significance to the fire at the Burden house and to the title of the novel itself. There are several more hints of this kind, and there are even a number of features in the account of Christmas's pursuit and murder by Percy Grimm—most notably, the comparison of Grimm to a young priest—which tempt one to wonder whether Faulkner's imagination may not initially have been seized by Frazer's description in the opening pages of *The Golden Bough* of the "barbarous custom" followed in Roman times to decide the succession to the priesthood of Diana's sacred grove and sanctuary at Nemi.[20]

These suggested correspondences between *Light in August* and the mythology and anthropology surrounding the figure of Diana may be entirely accidental. Alternatively, such correspondences, like those linking characters in the book with the members of the Holy Family, may represent only one among several patterns of analogy which Faulkner pursued in the course of the novel, and it is possible that he intended a symbolic substitution of Lena as a Holy Mother figure (an aspect in her presentation which is particularly stressed in the final chapter) for the barren Diana figure of Miss Burden.[21] But one thing is clear: the structure of *Light in August* cannot be adequately defined as a loose combination and conflation of three separate stories. As other critics have argued, there are in effect three quite distinct conclusions to the novel, each containing a bare minimum of references to the other two, and it would have been extremely simple for Faulkner, had he so wished, to establish a much closer texture of purely narrative links between the three strands. He did not so choose, however, and the structure of *Light in August* which we have already remarked as harking back in certain important respects to *As I Lay Dying* may also be said to look forward to the divided "double-novel" structure of *The Wild Palms*. But in reading *Light in August* we are not especially aware of the discreteness of the different narrative strands. Much of the novel's cohesion derives from its interconnecting patterns of reflection, repetition, substitution, and contrast. Something is also gained by Faulkner's use of recurrent images, such as that of the circle, and of analogical patterns. But the great and unifying strength of the book remains its most obvious one: the sheer force and passion of its presentation of Joe Christmas, the quintessential victim, and the way in which we, like all the characters in the book, are irresistibly swept into the vortex of Christmas's restless life and agonising death.

PYLON

Pylon, as a novel about the air, may seem at first sight to be something of a sport among Faulkner's works. Yet it is not surprising that Faulkner should have wanted to write on a subject in which he was himself so intensely interested. He had spent some time at the Royal Air Force training school in Canada in 1918, and after the war he continued to fly whenever possible; he seems at least to have tried his hand at the kind of performance put on by the groups of barnstorming fliers who travelled around the countryside, and he certainly encouraged his brother, Dean, in his activities as an exhibition flier and flying instructor until Dean's death in November 1935, not quite eight months after the publication of *Pylon*. Flying provided the subject-matter of Faulkner's earliest published story, of one or two of his early poems, and of several of the short stories he began publishing in national magazines from 1930 onwards. Two of these stories were specifically concerned with barnstorming fliers : "Honor," which has several narrative elements in common with *Pylon*, and "Death Drag," which indicated something of Faulkner's attitude towards the kind of people with which *Pylon* is primarily concerned—an incredulous amazement, compounded equally of admiration and horror, at the cold courage of these men and at their readiness to risk their lives, on a daily basis, for such trivial and uncertain rewards. Both these stories, however, had been written and published well before the events which seem not only to have impelled Faulkner to write an entire novel about flying but also to have provided him with much of the thematic and narrative material for such a book.

In *My Brother Bill*, John Faulkner says that Faulkner attended the opening of Shushan Airport, New Orleans, in 1933, and that *Pylon* was based largely on his experiences there.[1] The airport was in fact opened in February 1934, not in 1933, but that Faulkner was present, and that he was deeply affected by what he saw, there can be no doubt. Even the physical features of Feinman Airport, as Faulkner describes it in *Pylon*, bear many points of resemblance to Shushan Airport : both are built on land reclaimed from a lake, both have administration buildings flanked by two large hangars, and the design of each is characterised as "modernistic."[2] The rotunda of the administration building at Feinman Airport is described as "spacious, suave, sonorous and monastic, wherein relief or murallimning or bronze and chromium skilfully shadowlurked presented the furious, still, and legendary tale of what man has come to call his conquering of the infinite and impervious air" (pp. 37-38); the tower of the actual airport carried historical murals inside and, on the outside, reliefs of aircraft and symbolic figures representative of great flying exploits.[3] All over the airport in *Pylon* appears the initial "F," commemorating Colonel H. I. Feinman, chairman of the Sewage Board, after whom the airport has been named; the New Orleans Airport was named after the president of the Levee Board, Colonel A. L. Shushan, of whom it is reported that he "put the word 'Shushan,' or the letter 'S', in every available spot, repeating it literally scores of times in metal and stone. Once he boasted that it would cost not less than $50,000 to remove his trademark."[4]

Even more significant for the overall meaning of *Pylon* are the similarities between the events of the novel and the actual happenings which accompanied the opening ceremonies and subsequent air races and displays at Shushan Airport in February 1934. The ceremony of dedication, attended by Colonel Shushan himself, was held on the afternoon of Friday, February 9. Speeches were made, and the band of Louisiana State University played, but the scheduled flying display had to be greatly curtailed owing to bad weather, although Milo Burcham, "world champion upside down flier," flew inverted through the rain.[5] The Saturday and Sunday flying programmes were abandoned because of continuing bad weather, and on the Monday, February 12, it was announced that the stunts and races planned to coincide with the Mardi Gras festivities would be postponed *en bloc* until the following Wednesday, Thursday and Friday, and that all the entrants would stay on in New Orleans in order to take part. During the first full day of flying, Wednesday, February 14, there was a performance by the French pilot, Michel De Troyat, "European acrobatic [sic] champion," and a delayed opening parachute drop by Clem Sohn, who left his aircraft at 10,000 feet, carrying with him "a sack from which he released flour to make a trail through the sky," and did not release his parachute until he was 2,000 feet from the ground.[6] Competitors in the various spot parachute jumping competitions held during the meet included Jack Monahan, who was injured on the first day when he was caught in a cross-current of wind and blown against the sea-wall, and a woman named Eris Daniels, who, two days later, made an unintended landing in Lake Pontchartrain. To judge from the photograph of Miss Daniels which appeared in the New Orleans *Times-Picayune*,[7] she wore breeches and knee-length boots for her descent, but her participation in the jumping event suggests a possible source for certain aspects of Faulkner's presentation of Laverne in *Pylon*. Jack, the parachute jumper in *Pylon*, does a jump like Sohn's carrying just such a bag of flour, and he has an accident rather like Monahan's,[8] while Faulkner seems to have combined both De Troyat and Milo Burcham in the figure of the French pilot,

Jules Despleins, who apparently does most of his stunts upside down.[9] Even more striking is the similarity between the crash of Lieut. Frank Burnham's rocket plane in *Pylon* and the actual crash of Captain W. Merle Nelson, who was burned to death in the evening of the opening day of the Shushan meet "when his small comet plane crashed to earth and was destroyed by fire."[10]

On the second day of the air meet, the major race was won by James R. ("Jimmy") Wedell, who came from New Orleans and was one of the leading racing pilots of the day. In a race for aircraft of 550 cubic-inch capacity, Roger Donrae (his name is spelled DonRae in some reports), a flier from Wisconsin who also took part in spot parachute jumping competitions, had trouble with his engine when rounding the home pylon on the fifth lap: it stalled, started, then stalled again, and Donrae "shot up into the air near the lake" before gliding safely to earth. In another race one of the pilots was nearly forced down into the lake when, as he rounded the second pylon, two miles from the shore, "the crankcase of his engine cracked open,"[11] while the following day Harold Neuman of Kansas City, flying in the race for aircraft with 1,000 cu. inch capacity, was brought down by engine failure after having just reached the home pylon. His aircraft missed the runway and rolled into a pool of water; Neuman himself was at first trapped in his cockpit, but quickly freed. Mrs. Neuman, running out from the grandstands when her husband crashed, was one of the first to reach the scene, and Neuman was able to walk off the field carrying his baby and with his wife's arm around him.[12] There are various details here which Faulkner made use of in *Pylon*, but the incident which seems most to have impressed itself upon his imagination was one which occurred on the Saturday (February 17), the air meet having been extended for a further two days owing to continued interruptions caused by bad weather.

During the Saturday display, Ben Grew, a parachute jumper whose parachute had opened very late on the Thursday,[13] this time opened it too soon, so that the lines became entangled with the tail of the aircraft from which he had jumped. The pilot, Charles N. Kenily, aged 27, of Marion, Ohio, tried to free Grew, but before he could do so the aircraft crashed into Lake Ponchartrain, about 100 yards from the airport. Small boats went out and Grew's crushed body was brought ashore, but Kenily, who had jumped or fallen from the aircraft at a height of between 500 and 1,000 feet, and whose parachute had not opened, could not be found. Kenily, it was reported, "was a barnstorming pilot, having brought his plane here for any flying which he might be employed to do, without any official place on the race program"; his wife, with their infant child in her arms, was watching from the grandstands.[14] Faulkner must have used these events, considerably altering them in the process, as the basis for the description of Roger Shumann's death in *Pylon*: the elements of the crash into the lake and the unrecovered body are present in both the actual death and the fictional one, and so is the element of self-sacrifice, for it appears from some newspaper reports that Kenily could have saved himself if he had jumped at once instead of trying to save Grew.[15] The incident of the wreath dropped from the air, mentioned in the final pages of *Pylon*, seems to have been taken over from Nelson's death rather than from Kenily's: on the same page as the *Times-Picayune* reported Kenily's crash, it also mentioned that Nelson's ashes were to be scattered over the lake from the air early the following morning (Monday, February 19).[16] The Monday issue of the *Times-Picayune* reported that Kenily's body had still not been found; it also spoke of Ben Grew in a sentence which might well have struck Faulkner, if he read it, as an epitomisation of the flier's deracination: "Officials of the Pan-American races were without information Sunday as to whether Grew has any relatives, and no plans had been made Sunday night for his funeral."[17]

Faulkner's fascination with the lives of such fliers is a principal source of the energy of *Pylon*, as well as of the book's continuing interest, and the nature of this fascination emerges clearly from the answer which Faulkner gave to a question about *Pylon* at the University of Virginia in 1957:

> To me they were a fantastic and bizarre phenomenon on the face of a contemporary scene, of our culture at a particular time. I wrote that book because I'd got in trouble with *Absalom, Absalom!* and I had to get away from it for a while so I thought a good way to get away from it was to write another book, so I wrote *Pylon*. They were ephemera and phenomena on the face of a contemporary scene. That is, there was really no place for them in the culture, in the economy, yet they were there, at that time, and everyone knew that they wouldn't last very long, which they didn't. That time of those frantic little aeroplanes which dashed around the country and people wanted just enough money to live, to get to the next place to race again. Something frenetic and in a way almost immoral about it. That they were outside the range of God, not only of respectability, of love, but of God too. That they had escaped the compulsion of accepting a past and a future, that they were—they had no past. They were as ephemeral as the butter-fly that's born this morning with no stomach and will be gone to-morrow. It seemed to me interesting enough to make a story about, but that was just to get away from a book that wasn't going too well, till I could get back at it.[18]

This is a convincing account of the inception of *Pylon*, of how and why it came to be written, and before considering the nature and meaning of Faulkner's treatment of the fliers and their world it may be useful to consider a little further what he says about having written *Pylon* as a kind of relief or respite from the larger task of writing *Absalom, Absalom!*. Faulkner's statements of this kind cannot always be taken at face value—his very pride tempted him to self-deprecation in discussing his own work—but there are indications that *Pylon* may in fact have been written rather hurriedly and perhaps at a relatively low intensity. The typescript setting copy, for instance, bears a number of abruptly phrased editorial comments—e.g., "Don't understand," "This sentence is cockeyed," "Can't we have a paragraph in the next four pages"[19]—but there is nothing to show that Faulkner made any response to these comments or even that he actually looked at the copy again after the editors had been through it. On a spot check, indeed, it appears that most of the numerous deletions and alterations made by the editors were carried through into the final text, and since the few manuscript corrections which are certainly in Faulkner's hand bear no relation to any editorial remarks they may well have been made before the submission of the typescript to Smith and Haas. The corrected galleys of the book show evidence of Faulkner having gone through them, but there is very little rewriting or rearrangement of material, simply some revision of punctuation (mainly the substitution of dashes for lines of periods at moments of excited description, as on pages 31 and 233 of the book) and occasional straight cutting of short passages with the insertion of a few words where these are necessary to ensure continuity. The general tendency of Faulkner's revisions was somewhat to tone down extravagances of style, but all the indications are that he went through the galleys impatiently rather than systematically.[20]

It may also be a sign of haste or lack of total engagement that Faulkner, in writing *Pylon*, seems to have drawn heavily on themes and even characters which he had used in his previous book, *Light in August*: Dr. Shumann and his wife, for example, are in some ways curiously similar to Doc Hines and Mrs. Hines, while the policeman who pursues Laverne after her descent from the air has interesting affinities with Percy Grimm. Perhaps the most important debt to *Light in August* is the close correspondence between Laverne and Lena Grove: like Eula Varner in *The Hamlet* they are "earth-mother" figures, symbols of continuity, permanence, and rebirth, and it may not be an accident that the names of the three women are near-anagrams of each other. Lena's steady progression through *Light in August*, her unworried poverty, her confidence in her own resilience, her apparent indifference to the identity of her male companions, her fecundity—these all find some echo in the character and career of Laverne, despite the distortions and inversions implicit in Laverne's involvement in the world of aviation. This involvement suggests, in a very literal sense, deracination, divorcement from the earth, and its consequences appear in Laverne's affectation of male clothes, her virulence of language, her aggressiveness, her role of servant to the machine; at the same time her sexual desirability, her corn-coloured hair, and her pregnancy all affirm her essential kinship with Lena Grove, and her departure at the end of the novel with Jack and their unborn child may carry something of the same connotations as Lena's departure at the end of *Light in August*.[21] Faulkner seems to insist, in both cases, on the indomitability of woman, of the life-principle, and of the basic family unit. The unconventional relationship between Laverne, her two "husbands," and the joint son, appears to function smoothly only in the service of the machine; on other occasions, in other situations, tension and divisions arise, and when the group is broken by Shumann's death it cannot close its ranks: Jackie, the boy, must be left with Shumann's father, allowing Laverne and Jack to begin afresh with the child that they know to be exclusively theirs.

It should be said that Faulkner may have been engaged not in "borrowing" ideas from *Light in August* but in a deliberate attempt to rework similar ideas from a different point of view. The correspondences between the Reporter and Byron Bunch, for example, are obvious, but they appear to be largely of an ironic nature. The Reporter brings together the two worlds of the fliers and of New Valois rather as Byron brings together the different strands of *Light in August*, and like Byron he moves from detachment to passionate involvement; but whereas Byron's activities are for the most part positive and valuable in their results, for others and for himself, those of the Reporter culminate in a series of disasters. The worst of those disasters, the death of Shumann, distantly echoes the death of Joe Christmas. Shumann, flying the tight, deadly course around the pylons, is driven on to do what he must, and, like Joe Christmas caught in the inescapable circle of his fate, he is given no freedom of choice until the very moment of his death when, as Christmas chooses to turn and face his pursuers, he chooses to crash into the lake instead of on to the crowded airport. The arguments for regarding Shumann as a Christ-figure[22] are not especially convincing, yet in so far as they can be advanced they tend to support the analogy with Christmas.

There are too, and less surprisingly, certain structural similarities between *Pylon* and *Light in August*. In both novels the actual time present is strictly limited, much of the previous action is recounted in flashback or spoken narrative—the single voice of the Reporter assuming the role occupied by various commentators in *Light in August*—and the narrative as a whole is built up in a series of blocks instead of being presented as a continuous stream. In *Light in August* these blocks often coincided with chapter divisions; in *Pylon* this tendency is maintained, and what is especially notable is the increased solidity of the chapter unit itself. There are shifts of scene within the chapter, but the chapter itself tends to have a firm internal structure and to close crisply on a final sentence that would not have been inappropriate as the ending of a short story. Each chapter has a separate title, a feature then unique in a Faulkner novel, and the second chapter in particular, "An Evening in New Valois," has just the kind of internal structure—spoken narrative within a setting and situation which serves primarily to provide the oral recital with a plausible context—which we find in many of the short stories Faulkner was publishing at about this time.

Some of the most characteristic features of *Pylon* appear to owe less to *Light in August* than to Eliot's *The Waste Land*. The main techniques of the novel are primarily poetic both in intention and in effect, aiming at the establishment of a total pattern of imagery through an almost obsessive recurrence of significant phrases, symbols, places, objects. Again and again in *Pylon* the characters are forced to circumvent the barrier of Grandlieu Street, the city's clotted artery, and there are repeated references to the carnival litter of confetti and serpentine strewn about the streets, to the unreality of the city of New Valois, to the disembodied voice of the airport announcer. The aircraft are described as insects, as mosquitoes, wasps, gnats, and dragonflies; Jiggs is a "manpony," looking and even walking like a horse, though he is also compared to a dog; Jack, the parachutist, is always "bleak" and handsome. The Reporter himself is consistently associated with images of death and decay: he is the "skeleton," the "cadaver," the "scarecrow," the "ghost"; other characters identify him as Lazarus, as a refugee from the cemetery, as an inhabitant of hell, an habitué of the eternal shades.

This cluster of associations about the figure of the Reporter is so obvious and sustained that it is tempting to see him as the figure of Death stalking Roger Shumann, until Shumann becomes the sacrificial victim of the Shrovetide rites enacted during the course of the novel. Faulkner may well have made some play with such thematic material, in much the same way as he hints at Christian imagery in *The Sound and the Fury* and *Light in August*. Some critics have spoken of Shumann's final crash into the waters of the lake as a redemptive "death by water," similar to that in *The Waste Land*, and there can be no doubt that the novel draws heavily on this and other poems of Eliot's for much of its imagery: by entitling the penultimate chapter "Lovesong of J. A. Prufrock," for example, Faulkner himself draws attention to the similarities between the figure of Prufrock, in all his ineffectuality and incapacity for life, and that of the Reporter. Donald T. Torchiana has suggested that Faulkner's use of Eliot's imagery gives rise to an unresolved and undesirable ambiguity:

Faulkner is so decidedly anti-modern in *Pylon* that he seems to have accepted Eliot's prescriptive, now classical image of the modern city, a waste land, at almost secondhand. In this case, his ani-

modernity is *a priori*, when it ought to have been a discovery.
Indeed, his real discovery seems to have been the essential humanity
of the flyers, despite their "half-metallic" appearance, and the
essential inhumanity of the ordinary human being in New Valois.[23]

Torchiana has undoubtedly located one of the main points of difficulty in the novel, but the difficulty can perhaps be resolved. Faulkner
is primarily interested in the fliers; they are the book's point of
concentration. The city and the airport exist largely as a setting for
the fliers and, through the connection with Feinman and his business
associates, as an economic context. If the writing of *Pylon* did not
engage Faulkner's creative energies to the full, it would not be surprising that he should accept Eliot's imagery "at almost secondhand."
In attempting a novel of the poetic, thematic type he may well have
taken over Eliot's images as a convenient and generally acceptable
poetic shorthand for evoking and defining those aspects of his novel,
those elements in his equation, with which he was not at that
moment especially concerned.

But the modernity of which the fliers partake seems to be quite
different in kind from that of the corrupt city. There is a profound
irony in the Reporter's initial outrage at the deracination of the fliers
and their disregard for conventional morality, since, as we later discover, no one could be more deracinated and many-fathered than himself. Torchiana takes up William Van O'Connor's suggestion that the
presentation of the fliers should perhaps lead us to doubt the absolute-
ness of Faulkner's anti-modernity,[24] but he does not go on to point
out that modernity is not the central issue of the book. There is no
conflict between modern and traditional values because the latter are
simply not represented in the novel, unless obliquely in the images
surrounding Shumann's death. Faulkner, in any case, is never dog-
matically anti-modern. He is, however, consistently "pro-life," and it
is with the opposition between the life of the fliers, however paradoxically evinced, and the death of the city that the book is principally
concerned. One of the ironies which Faulkner must have perceived in
the sequence of violent events which he witnessed at the opening of
Shushan Airport was the way in which the fliers were being
indirectly exploited for self-seeking political and financial ends:
Shushan himself was a leading supporter of Huey Long, and
Faulkner's presentation of Feinman and his city associates is somewhat
reminiscent of John Dos Passos's characterisation of the cynical
financiers, unconcerned with the fate of the men who fly the aircraft,
in his play, *Airways, Inc.*[25]

An even more direct and specific source of irony, in February 1934,
was the fact that the theme of that year's Mardi Gras parade was "The
Conquest of the Air." Wednesday, February 14, the first day of the
postponed air meet, the day of Captain Nelson's death in his burning

rocket plane, was Ash Wednesday; that morning the *Times-Picayune* reported the celebrations of the previous night:

> It was an air-minded Mardi Gras. Rex's chosen subject for his parade was the "Conquest of the Air," and the floats merrily depicted every conceivable flight, from the ill-fated nonstop "flop" of Daedalus and Icarus to the "Lone Eagle's" triumph, represented by the final float.[26]

Faulkner makes no direct allusion to this aspect of the Mardi Gras, though he uses the phrase "conquering ... of the air" (pp. 37-38) in his description of Feinman airport. At the same time, some of the book's most strenuous stylistic effects are devoted to the evocation of the empty and meaningless frivolity of the festivities, which serve as a constant contrast and counterpoint to the lives of the fliers and to the events at the airport in which they are involved. The refuse of the parade is described as "spent tinseldung of Momus' Nilebarge clatterfalque," (p. 77) and this violent image of disgust, of an utterly hollow splendour, depends upon the combination and concentration of mutually incompatible elements and upon the fact that Momus, the god of ridicule, is one of the deities traditionally celebrated during the New Orleans Mardi Gras festivities. In thus exploiting the symbolic potentialities of the Mardi Gras, Faulkner's main intention was further to emphasise his presentation of the city itself. New Valois is the unreal city; its inhabitants are dead; Faulkner's description of it is an exercise on the theme, "I had not thought death had undone so many."[27]

We have seen the Reporter repeatedly associated with images of death; we are told more than once that he lives in Noyades Street, which Hagood translates as "The Drowned," and Faulkner presumably intended an allusion here to the final lines of "The Love Song of J. Alfred Prufrock":

> We have lingered in the chambers of the sea
> By sea-girls wreathed with seaweed red and brown
> Till human voices wake us, and we drown.[28]

The Reporter's metaphorical drowning links him with the actual drowning of Shumann, and there is a discernible parallel between these two intensely opposed characters who have both, in their entirely different ways, been "woken" from their rapt absorption in a non-human world—the Reporter in the totally artificial world of the newspaper, Shumann in the mechanised world of flying, in which he and his companions had become little more than servants of the aircraft themselves. Both of them break from their old patterns. The Reporter achieves a quasi-involvement in life, an involvement by proxy as it were, through his well-intentioned but ultimately disastrous intrusions into the lives of the fliers; he also becomes so much at odds with his former role as a newspaperman that by the end of the novel he is capable of composing the two contradictory interpretations of Shumann's death. Shumann, for his part, allows the needs of the human situation—specifically, the financial requirements consequent upon Laverne's pregnancy—to persuade him into unprofessional action : he flies too close to the pylons at speeds he knows to be dangerous. Both the Reporter and Shumann act unprofessionally, but they both do so in what they conceive to be the interests of other human beings; Shumann, however, acts with complete unselfishness, since the child Laverne carries is not his; the Reporter, on the other hand, is ultimately selfish, because of his obsession with Laverne, and his activities, pursued so loquaciously and so incompetently (that he is so easily cheated over the absinthe shows that he does not even know his own world of New Valois), offer a kind of ironic counter-point to the silent, efficient abnegation and sacrifice of Shumann. There are two worlds opposed in *Pylon*, the world of New Valois and that of the fliers. The Reporter and Shumann are the chief representa-tives of their respective worlds; they are ironically parallel and they come together in uneasy alliance in their common concern for Laverne, about whom the action of the novel ultimately revolves.

It is important to emphasise the Reporter's active role in the overall pattern of the novel. He is not merely the point of view from which the world of flying is observed, but himself the vehicle of much of the novel's meaning. What brings him increasingly into conflict with the demands of his job is his ever-growing awareness of the elements of falseness and unreality in the city and public which he nominally serves and, more especially, his consciousness of the many faces of truth. He becomes obsessed with the fact that he cannot be "the Reporter" without also being an interpreter, and with the knowledge that the act of interpretation necessarily involves distortion : the two accounts of Shumann's death are deliberately contradictory, but they are equally false. Since his viewpoint dominates the novel, the much-criticised style, with its peculiarly clotted, congested effect, may well represent Faulkner's attempt to mirror both the Reporter's personal unreality—his corpse-like appearance and his incapacity for life— and his unceasing outrage not only at the exploits of the fliers but at the elusiveness of those facts which in theory constitute the basic materials of his trade.

When, in 1957, Faulkner spoke of the fliers as "ephemera and phenomena on the face of a contemporary scene," he undoubtedly seized upon a fundamental aspect of *Pylon's* structure and imagery; but in referring to them further as "outside the range of God, not merely of respectability, of love, but of God too," he defined only the attitude held by the Reporter at the beginning of the novel. The effect of the book as a whole, especially in its treatment of Shumann's death, is somewhat different, and the Reporter's initial conception of the fliers' dehumanisation is progressively undermined. In his review of Jimmy Collins's autobiographical book, *Test Pilot*—a review which appeared after the publication of *Pylon* and in the month of Dean's death—Faulkner suggested that there must be something unnatural and inhuman about racing and test pilots, and he predicted the appearance of a new race of beings specially bred from childhood to high-speed flying: "These would be a species and in time a race and in time they would produce a folklore." In *Test Pilot* itself, he said, he had hoped to find a folklore not of the future but of the present, "not of the age of speed nor of the men who perform it, but of the speed itself."[29] Interesting as these remarks are, there seems no grounds for thinking that Faulkner had been concerned in *Pylon* with the themes for which he had looked in *Test Pilot* or that he had himself deliberately sought to create a contemporary folklore of any kind. If *Pylon* has not become a seminal source of symbols and legends which have reverberated down the succeeding years of ever-increasing speed, if it has not achieved, in the literature of flying, the classic status of, say, the writings of Saint-Exupèry, that is largely because Faulkner did not attempt to write a book which would have that kind of significance and because he was not especially concerned to define the experience of those like Captain Warren in "Death Drag," the man who "had himself seen his own lonely and scudding shadow upon the face of the puny and remote earth."[30] The novel does not explore at all fully the actual business of flying particular aircraft under a particular set of conditions; it gives us no insight into Shumann's mind as he flies too close to the pylons, as he pushes his machine beyond the limit of safety, as his machine finally breaks up in mid-air and takes him on his last dive into the lake. For the airman to see himself in relation to the earth implies a certain measure of introspection, and it seems to have been essential to Faulkner's conception of the men of speed with whom he was concerned in *Pylon* that they were incapable of introspection, or rather that they had deliberately denied themselves that obsolescent and subversive luxury. The fliers in *Pylon* are therefore presented almost entirely from the outside, usually through the appalled eyes of the Reporter—an enthusiast, an aficionado, of aviation, but utterly an outsider. Faulkner sought to emphasise the isolation of these people, their remoteness from the earth-bound remainder of mankind, and it seems to have been part of his purpose that the reader should be kept, with the Reporter, and perhaps with himself, in a state of permanent outrage. This need to outrage was again incompatible with any importance the novel might have had as a repository of folklore: the copulation in the aircraft cockpit and the subsequent semi-nude descent of Laverne into the lusting mob below is only the most notable example of a series of incidents and relationships which, while they serve to establish the gulf between the fliers and the customs and values of the conventional world, are at the same time so extreme, so apparently arbitrary, that they forgo any possible claims to archetypal status.

It was suggested earlier that the style of *Pylon* might be thought of as a reflection of the Reporter's outrage; perhaps we can now speak of the whole novel as Faulkner's bold attempt to find the language, the imagery, and the narrative vehicle in which to embody his conception of the strange, deracinated lives of the fliers, and of the violent contrast between their world and the world of twentieth-century urban society—a world apparently more "normal," but actually more corrupt and moribund, because demonstrating a much lesser capacity for life, self-sacrifice, and renewal. *Pylon*, indeed, can be best seen as an experiment in the primarily poetic mode which was soon to produce *Absalom, Absalom!*, and while altogether less ambitious than its great successor, it is not so dissimilar in kind: in both novels tension and meaning are alike sustained by calculated effects of imagery and style. *Pylon* sometimes seems over-extended and over-written; Faulkner may have composed it while his mind was still partly engaged with the problem of *Absalom, Absalom!*; and it is certainly a minor work—one, moreover, which takes its setting and characters from beyond the boundaries of Yoknapatawpha County. Yet the novel cannot be written off either as a failure or as a sport. It has obvious technical and thematic affinities with other works of Faulkner's and, at its own level and within its own limits, it is an assured and unmistakable success, a powerful demonstration not of Faulkner's eccentricity but of his extraordinary diversity and range.

ABSALOM, ABSALOM!

THE galleys of *Pylon* carry dates from early January 1935; the manuscript of *Absalom, Absalom!* is dated "March 30, 1935" on the first page and "31 January 1936" on the last.[1] On returning to *Absalom, Absalom!* after the period of respite or detour which had produced *Pylon* Faulkner must have begun his task virtually afresh, and in 1957 he said, "I don't remember at what point I put it [*Absalom, Absalom!*] down. Though when I took it up again I almost rewrote the whole thing. I think that what I put down were inchoate fragments that wouldn't coalesce and then when I took it up again, as I remember, I rewrote it."[2]

Some information as to the actual process of Faulkner's composition of *Absalom, Absalom!*, the steps by which he arrived at the intricate structure of the published book, may one day be gained from a closer study of the complete manuscript, which is now at the University of Texas. The first page of this manuscript is close to the published text,[3] but the manuscript as a whole is a composite, made up of material written at different times over what may have been a fairly long period. Many sections, some brief, some of one or more paragraphs in length, have been affixed to the base sheets, and these sections, like the base sheets themselves, are in a variety of different inks and even show minor differences in handwriting. It seems possible that careful study might reveal the outline of previous states of the manuscript material and thus throw valuable light on the construction of this most carefully articulated of Faulkner's novels.

Material representing other pre-publication stages of *Absalom, Absalom!* is now at the University of Virginia. The typescript setting copy, as corrected by Faulkner and his editors, shows only minor discrepancies from the published text, but it is interesting to see that it was only at a fairly late stage that Faulkner made up his mind about the conclusion of Chapter III. The typescript originally had Wash Jones tell Rosa to hurry out to Sutpen's Hundred, but Faulkner later added in holograph an ending similar to the present conclusion of Chapter IV, in which Wash tells Rosa that Henry has shot Charles Bond, only to opt finally for further suspension, striking the whole ending through and substituting the one which now appears on page 87 of the published book.[4] The main interest of the typescript is the evidence it provides of the extent to which Faulkner revised the book in response to editorial objections. There are also at Virginia a number of typescript pages from a version of Chapter I which preceded the version in the setting copy, and it is clear from annotations made on the first page that this version was at one time submitted as the first chapter of the final typescript. It is also clear that the pages missing from this rejected version were in fact incorporated into the final typescript, and it appears that while Faulkner was reworking the first chapter at his editors' request the printers went ahead and set up in dummy the first ten pages of Chapter II.

Comparison of the two versions of the first chapter shows that Faulkner reworked it in considerable detail. He retained many of the passages which the editors proposed to exclude, but he seems to have accepted other deletions and to have done a certain amount of re-writing, partly of passages to which the editors had raised some objection and partly of passages with which he himself was dissatis-fied in some way.[5] Even where he did alter or delete passages to which his editors had objected, it is hard to believe that Faulkner accepted the reasons they advanced: the complaint, for example, that certain paragraphs contained material which the reader would be told about in greater detail later in the book was one which revealed little under-standing of what Faulkner was trying to do in the novel as a whole. To comments about the content of the book Faulkner sometimes wrote a succinct and pointed reply. When an editor deleted a passage on the grounds that knowing Sutpen's father wouldn't have encouraged anyone to sign a note for Sutpen, Faulkner wrote: "It would in the South. If they had known who his father was, more than Compson and Coldfield would have appeared to get him out of jail. *Leave as is.*"[6] Chapter I, however, is the only one which bears indications of extensive revision by Faulkner himself. Throughout the remainder of the book there occur editorial alterations which Faulkner apparently accepted without protest, perhaps in the interests of getting the book into print with the minimum of delay and distrac-tion: it was his first novel with his new publishers, Random House, and he seems to have been prepared to make co-operative gestures which were unusual for him, at least at this stage of his career. These alterations consist mainly of minor deletions, additions of clarifying words or phrases, substitutions of proper names for pronouns, and rearrangements both of structures within sentences and of long sentences into shorter ones. There is, however, a marked decrease in the incidence of such alterations as the book proceeds, and from the latter part of Chapter VII to the end of the final chapter editorial marks of any kind are rare. A spot check revealed slight discrepancies between these portions of the setting copy and the published book, and these may represent alterations made at galley stage.

Whatever the state of the *Absalom, Absalom!* material may have been at the time Faulkner turned aside to write *Pylon*, it is clear from *Pylon* itself, and especially from its final pages, with their emphasis on the instability and malleability of fact, that the central technical and thematic problems of *Absalom, Absalom!* had continued to be very much in Faulkner's mind. The nature of these problems was well brought out in an exchange during one of the class-discussions at the University of Virginia:

Q. Mr. Faulkner, in *Absalom, Absalom!* does any one of the people who talks about Sutpen have the right view, or is it more or less a case of thirteen ways of looking at a blackbird with none of them right?
A. That's it exactly. I think that no one individual can look at truth. It blinds you. You look at it and you see one phase of it. Someone else looks at it and sees a slightly awry phase of it. But taken all together, the truth is in what they saw though nobody saw the truth intact. So these are true as far as Miss Rosa and as Quentin saw it. Quentin's father saw what he believed was truth, that was all he saw. But the old man was himself a little too big for people no greater in stature than Quentin and Miss Rosa and Mr. Compson to see all at once. It would have taken perhaps a wiser or more tolerant or more sensitive or more thoughtful person to see him as he was. It was, as you say, thirteen ways of looking at a blackbird. But the truth, I would like to think, comes out, that when the reader has read all these thirteen different ways of looking at the blackbird, the reader has his own fourteenth image of that blackbird which I would like to think is the truth.[7]

These remarks are very much to the point. We have already seen Faulkner—most notably in *The Sound and the Fury*, most recently in *Pylon*—exploring the question of the subjectivity of experience, the elusiveness of fact. From a technical point of view, the four sections of *The Sound and the Fury* might be said to represent four different modes of cognition; in *As I Lay Dying* the whole action ultimately exists in the minds of the various characters, and certainly our understanding of that action depends upon our ability to disentangle fact from bias, to apply a correction factor, as it were, and make allowance for the distortions inherent in each of the different viewpoints. But in all of Faulkner's novels which employ a multiplicity of viewpoints the "experience" of the novel includes both the fact and the bias, and also, what is especially important, the tensions we perceive in their relationship. This is particularly true of *Absalom, Absalom!*, where the explorations of the nature of truth are pursued by means of a technique which becomes itself the sustaining medium of the action and the chief vehicle of meaning. In the direct narrative sense, *Absalom, Absalom!* is Sutpen's story: it is he who dominates the action, it is his tragedy which Quentin and Shreve strive to recreate. Yet Sutpen, long dead, is reflected in such varied and usually violent shapes in so many different minds that he assumes an air of portentousness and mystery which, while fascinating Quentin and Shreve, makes him at the same time essentially unknowable. Sutpen, in fact, remains elusive both as symbol and as character. But what we do know about him is his meaning for, and effect upon, Quentin, and as the action progresses Sutpen recedes from the foreground, allowing the weight of the novel's major concerns to be subtly shifted on to Quentin's shoulders. By the end of the book the importance of arriving at a satisfactory interpretation of the Sutpen story is at least equalled by the importance of seeing the significance which this solution will carry for Quentin himself, the extent to which it will relax or tighten the rack on which he is stretched, the particular twist it will give to the knife.

It is fair to speak of the story as having three main narrators. Miss Rosa Coldfield and Mr. Compson are narrators in their own right, projecting distinct interpretations of Sutpen—interpretations deeply coloured by the relationship in which they stand to him and by their own particular qualities of character and personality. The actual method or manner of their telling is also more distinct than has usually been allowed. Rosa's account, with its "demonizing" and linguistic extravagance, suggests the violence and verbal frenzy—action larger than life-size, language pushed beyond its proper limits—of decadent Jacobean drama: [8]

> Once there was (they cannot have told you this either) a summer of wistaria. It was a pervading everywhere of wistaria (I was fourteen then) as though of all springs yet to capitulate condensed into one spring, one summer: the spring and summertime which is every female's who breathed above dust, beholden of all betrayed springs held over from all irrevocable time, repercussed, bloomed again. It was a vintage year of wistaria: vintage year being that sweet conjunction of root bloom and urge and hour and weather; and I (I was fourteen)—I will not insist on bloom, at whom no man had yet to look—nor would ever—twice, as not as child but less than even child; as not more child than woman but even as less than any female flesh. Nor do I say leaf—warped bitter pale and crimped half-fledging intimidate of any claim to green which might have drawn to it the tender mayfly childhood sweetheart games or given pause to the male predacious wasps and bees of later lust. But root and urge I do insist and claim, for had I not heired too from all the unsistered Eves since the Snake? Yes, urge I do: warped chrysalis of what blind perfect seed: for who shall say what gnarled forgotten root might not bloom yet with some globed concentrate more globed and concentrate and heady-perfect because the neglected root was planted warped and lay not dead but merely slept forgot? (pp. 143-144)

Mr. Compson, on the other hand, much less involved, much cooler and more sceptical in his assessment of Sutpen and of the world at large, concentrates his attention on different aspects of the story and treats them in quite a different manner. His rather effete disenchantment suggests another form of literary decadence, that of the late nineteenth century, the *fin de siècle*,[9] and the sources and implications of his treatment of the Sutpen material appear quite specifically in his description of the octoroon's visit to Bon's grave:

> It must have resembled a garden scene by the Irish poet, Wilde: the late afternoon, the dark cedars with the level sun in them, even the light exactly right and the graves, the three pieces of marble (your grandfather had advanced Judith the money to buy the third stone with against the price of the store) looking as though they had been cleaned and polished and arranged by scene shifters who with the passing of twilight would return, and strike them and carry them, hollow fragile and without weight, back to the warehouse until they should be needed again; the pageant, the scene, the act, entering upon the stage—the magnolia-faced woman a little plumper now, a woman created of by and for darkness whom the artist Beardsley might have dressed, in a soft flowing gown designed not to infer bereavement or widowhood but to dress some interlude of slumbrous and fatal insatiation, of passionate and inexorable hunger of the flesh, walking beneath a lace parasol and followed by a bright gigantic negress carrying a silk cushion and leading by the hand the little boy whom Beardsley might not only have dressed but drawn ... (p. 193)

The names of Wilde and Beardsley in this passage suggest that Faulkner is here making objective and dramatic use of that self-conscious aestheticism which he himself had adopted during an early stage of his career.

Miss Rosa and Mr. Compson have an essential role to play in the total narrative structure; ultimately, however, the burden of recreation, interpretation, and suffering falls inexorably on Quentin, just as, with utterly different effect, Mr. Lockwood is the final repository of the story of *Wuthering Heights*. Shreve, Quentin's Canadian roommate at Harvard, participates in the task of imaginative reconstruction, but the final responsibility remains inescapably Quentin's. The quotations from the narratives of Miss Rosa and Mr. Compson may suggest that what confronts him is, among other things, a literary task, virtually a problem of authorship, involving questions of literary technique and of the author's attitude towards his material. This task —a novelist's, perhaps, dealing in the creation of imaginative truth, rather than an historian's—was the one which Miss Rosa, herself a

"So maybe you will enter the literary profession as so many Southern gentlemen and gentlewomen too are doing now and maybe some day you will remember this and write about it. You will be married then I expect and perhaps your wife will want a new gown or a new chair for the house and you can write this and submit it to the magazines. Perhaps you will even remember kindly then the old woman who made you spend a whole afternoon sitting indoors and listening while she talked about people and events you were fortunate enough to escape yourself when you wanted to be out among young friends of your own age."

"Yessum," Quentin said. *Only she dont mean that*, he thought. *It's because she wants it told.* (pp. 9-10)

Quentin's final failure to resolve the quasi-authorial problems which confront him is closely related to his passivity, which itself has important implications for his initial and much more successful role of listener. It is the availability and apparent suitability of Quentin as an audience which at once provokes and modifies the recitals of Miss Rosa and Mr. Compson; the particular flavour of their narrations is largely determined by their awareness of who and what Quentin is. As a young, intelligent Southerner, eldest son of his family and hence destined to become "the Compson," about to leave the homeland for the foreign environment of New England and Harvard, Quentin seems an appropriate repository for a story which they both dimly recognise as embodying some quintessential and symbolic relationship to the whole Southern experience, and which they both hand on to Quentin as if it were some dark inheritance from the Southern past. At the very beginning of the novel there are already two Quentins:

Then hearing would reconcile and he would seem to listen to two separate Quentins now—the Quentin Compson preparing for Harvard in the South, the deep South dead since 1865 and peopled with garrulous outraged baffled ghosts, listening, having to listen, to one of the ghosts which had refused to lie still even longer than most had, telling him about ghost-times; and the Quentin Compson who was still too young to deserve yet to be a ghost, but nevertheless having to be one for all that, since he was born and bred in the deep South the same as she was—the two separate Quentins now talking to one another in the long silence of notpeople, in notlanguage, . . . (p. 9)

As the book proceeds, Quentin is buffeted to and fro not only between these two facets of himself but between the conflicting allegiances to differing interpretations of Sutpen and his story which seem to be demanded of him by Miss Rosa, by his father, and by the information he is able to collect for himself from other sources. His own version of the story contains, suspended in uneasy co-existence, substantial elements of all these interpretations, each of which attracts him for different reasons at different times. He never manages to free himself from these presences to the extent that would permit a radical re-interpretation of the whole Sutpen story and its Southern context, and he remains to the end that fatally divided and ghost-dominated personality to whom we are introduced at the beginning of the book :

> his very body was an empty hall echoing with sonorous defeated names; he was not a being, an entity, he was a commonwealth. He was a barracks filled with stubborn back-looking ghosts . . . (p. 12)

In the later chapters of the novel, Shreve's participation in the reconstruction of Sutpen's story serves neither to remove from Quentin any of the final responsibility for the task nor to mitigate Quentin's anguish. For the most part Quentin and Shreve are seen as two young men, of similar age and aspirations, sharing intimately in the same experience of Harvard. Shreve is not presented as wiser than Quentin, nor as fundamentally unlike him; Shreve even races ahead of Quentin at times in his eagerness to give an essentially romanticised interpretation of the relationships between Charles Bon, Henry Sutpen, and Judith (as at the end of Chapter VIII), and the two of them are caught up together in their imaginative identification with the dead figures of Henry and Charles—though it is significant that Quentin identifies more readily with Henry, the brother of Judith, and Shreve with Charles Bon, the stranger to the world of Jefferson and Sutpen's Hundred. Yet Shreve is not always precisely attuned to Quentin's mood; indeed, he often cuts directly across it. At times he reminds Quentin of Mr. Compson, and his attitude, though less cynical and world-weary, is scarcely less sceptical. Faulkner once spoke of Shreve as holding Quentin's story "to something of reality. If Quentin had been let alone to tell it, it would have become completely unreal. It had to have a solvent to keep it real, keep it believable, creditable, otherwise it would have vanished into smoke and fury."[10] This is undoubtedly one aspect of Shreve's role; another is his contribution of those moments of disenchanted humour which do something to relieve the tension and actual pain of the final chapters. Moreover, the presence of Shreve allows Faulkner to organise his material about a dialogue, his favourite device for the treatment of direct narrative. The relationship within the dialogue, however, is not simply that of speaker and listener, as it was when Quentin was hearing the accounts of Miss Rosa and Mr. Compson. Here the listener as a distinct, passive entity almost disappears; what remains is the listener as constant *provocateur*[11] and as occasional brake—" 'wait then,'

Shreve said. 'For God's sake wait.' " (p. 216) Shreve elicits from Quentin more and more details of the Sutpen story. He deploys his rather aggressive ignorance about the South in such a way as to compel Quentin to face difficulties which he might otherwise have passed over, and by his relentless questioning at the very end of the novel—" 'Why do you hate the South?' " (p. 378)—he forces Quentin to squeeze from the story, and from himself, the last drop of anguish.

Only by death, it seems, will Quentin succeed in exorcising the Southern ghosts which inhabit his body and mind, but the interrogation by the alien Shreve in the alien New England climate and situation at least brings Quentin to a fuller knowledge both of himself and of his region. Quentin had been brought up to think of Sutpen as probably a monomaniac and monster and as certainly an upstart and a danger to the established social order; but as the story develops Sutpen gradually assumes in Quentin's mind the shape and proportions of a tragic hero—a man of great personal power and splendid vision; a bold seeker after those material values which all the South, and all America, tacitly accepted as good, indeed as the essential criterion of "quality"; a brave fighter and leader in the struggle against the North; and ultimately a defeated and tragic figure only because of his rigid adherence to principles of racial and social inhumanity which many besides himself were pledged to uphold. Quentin, as Faulkner remarked in a letter to Malcolm Cowley, must have thought of Sutpen as "trash."[12] What he learns is that in vigour, in character, and in vision Sutpen far outstripped any of Quentin's own family, alive or dead, and that Sutpen's history—his somewhat suspect purchase of the land from its Indian owners, his erection of a plantation and a great house at the cost of the sweat of his Negro slaves, his determination to found a dynasty—was only an exceptionally rapid and concentrated version of the history of virtually all Southern families, including Quentin's own. The point is explicitly made in the course of Miss Rosa's narration in Chapter V:

> Judith created by circumstance (circumstance? a hundred years of careful nurturing, perhaps not by blood not even Coldfield blood, but certainly by the tradition in which Thomas Sutpen's ruthless will had carved a niche) to pass through the soft insulated and unscathed cocoon stages: bud, served prolific queen, then potent and soft-handed matriarch of old age's serene and well-lived content—Judith handicapped by what in me was a few years' ignorance but which in her was ten generations of iron prohibition, who had not learned that first principle of penury which is to scrimp and save for the sake of scrimping and saving, . . . (p. 156)

The implication for Quentin himself is clearly that those traditions and genealogies by which Southern families set such store—and not least the Compson family itself—were ultimately lacking either in substance or in value. What Quentin also learns is that the fatal flaw in Sutpen's design was precisely that flaw of man's inhumanity to man inherent in the recent history and structure of the South, a flaw represented not only by slavery itself but by other and surviving forms of racial and social intolerance.

One of the two most powerful images of such inhumanity in the novel is Sutpen's refusal to recognise Charles Bon as his son, with its bitterly ironic echo of that incident in his own childhood when he had been turned away from a door which he had counted on entering. The other image—even more vivid, perhaps, because more directly presented—is that of Sutpen's treatment of Milly Jones, the incident which directly provokes his murder at the hand of Wash Jones, Milly's grandfather. At the end of a life of devotion and unqualified admiration both of Sutpen and of those Southern values for which he appeared to stand, Wash Jones is brought to an appalled recognition :

> Better if his kind and mine too had never drawn the breath of life on this earth. Better that all who remain of us be blasted from the face of it than that another Wash Jones should see his whole life shredded from him and shrivel away like a dried shuck thrown onto the fire. (pp. 290-291)

That it is not Sutpen alone who falls under Wash's condemnation but all Southerners of the class to which he now belongs, is made clear by Wash's allusions to the men he knows will shortly come to exact vengeance for Sutpen's death :

> men of Sutpen's own kind, who used to eat at his table with him back when he (Wash) had yet to approach nearer the house than the scuppernong arbor—men who had led the way, shown the other and lesser ones how to fight in battles, who might also possess signed papers from the generals saying that they were among the first and foremost of the brave—who had galloped also in the old days arrogant and proud on the fine horses about the fine plantations—symbol also of admiration and hope, instruments too of despair and grief. (p. 289)

There are phrases here which eloquently evoke the tragic paradox of the old South as well as the agonising ambiguity of the new valuation which Quentin as well as Wash Jones is forced to make : "symbol[s] also of admiration and hope, instruments too of despair and grief." Once Sutpen's situation begins to be properly understood, however, his ardent and valiant participation in the Civil War—that element in his character which Rosa Coldfield and, at first, Quentin himself find difficult to assimilate into their total conceptions of him—becomes entirely natural and indeed inevitable. Given his "design," his determination to acquire for himself all those advantages, actual and symbolic, which he had as a child identified as the essential possession of the rich and powerful, it is wholly understandable that he should be foremost among those who fought to preserve the particular system of society which alone upheld—economically, politically, and morally —the way of life to which he aspired and which, by the outbreak of the war, he had in fact attained. It is notable, however, that after the war he finds himself at odds with the more established representatives of his new class because of his refusal to join in anti-Reconstruction activities, rejecting what he apparently regards as the negativism of such activities in favour of more positive efforts to restore the land.

Sutpen remains in many ways a characteristic type of the *nouveau-riche*. One thinks, for example, of the ostentatious extravagance of his house and its furnishings, of the grandiose memorials which he obtains for his wife and himself at a moment of such desperate crisis for the South, of the empty social posing of his wife. Ellen's attempt to secure Bon as a husband for Judith seems characteristic of the tendency of the *nouveaux-riches* to seek alliances with the old aristocracy, or at least with embodiments of the social graces which they feel themselves to lack. The story of Sutpen, considered simply as a social phenomenon, has a range of reverberation extending far beyond the limitations of its Southern setting—as does the human tragedy of Sutpen, with its suggestions of hubris and family doom on the Greek pattern.[13]

The point of departure for Sutpen's story—the image of the child being turned away from the big house, what is referred to in the novel as the "boy-symbol"—seems to have existed in Faulkner's imagination long before he began work even on his first attempt towards what eventually became *Absalom, Absalom!*. Among the Faulkner papers preserved at the University of Virginia is the typescript of an unpublished short story, "The Big Shot". The typescript is undated, but it is clear from the short story sending schedule which Faulkner kept at this time that he began sending it to magazines before January 30, 1930, and that it had already been rejected by four magazines before Faulkner sent it to the *Saturday Evening Post* on April 14, 1930.[14] In this early story there appears, as the central character, the figure of a racketeer called Dal Martin, operating in a Southern city during the Prohibition era; in the account which we are given of Martin's birth and history we see clearly, for all the disparity in time, the outlines of Thomas Sutpen, at least insofar as Sutpen spends his life "trying to get even with that man who in his youth had said, Go to the back door."[15] Martin, the narrator tells us,

> was born and raised on a Mississippi farm. Tenant farmers—you know : barefoot, the whole family, nine months in the year. He told me about one day his father sent him up to the big house, the

house of the owner, the boss, with a message. He went to the front door in his patched overalls, his bare feet: he had never been there before; perhaps he knew no better anyway, to whom a house was just where you kept the quilt pallets and the corn meal out of the rain (he said 'outen the rain'). And perhaps the boss didn't know him by sight; he probably looked exactly like a dozen others on his land and a hundred others in the neighborhood.

Anyway the boss came to the door himself. Suddenly he—the boy—looked up and there within touching distance for the first time was the being who had come to symbolise for him the ease and pleasant ways of the earth: idleness, a horse to ride all day long, shoes all the year round. And you can imagine him when the boss spoke: "Dont you ever come to my front door again. When you come here, you go around to the kitchen door and tell one of the niggers what you want." That was it, you see. There was a negro servant come to the door behind the boss, his eyeballs white in the gloom, and Martin's people and kind, although they looked upon Republicans and Catholics, having never seen either one, probably, with something of that mystical horror which European peasants of the fifteenth century were taught to regard Democrats and Protestants, the antipathy between them and negroes was an immediate and definite affair, being at once biblical, political and economic: the three compulsions—the harsh unflagging land broken into sparse intervals by spells of demagoguery and religio-neurotic hysteria—which shaped and coerced their gaunt lives. A mystical justification of the need to feel superior to someone some-where, you see.

He didn't deliver the message at all. He turned and walked back down the drive, feeling the nigger's teeth too in the gloom of the hall beyond the boss' shoulder, . . .[16]

As a result of his experience Martin conceives an "unflagging dream" which he pursues by getting into favour with the boss—whom he finds himself not hating but admiring: "his folks would think he ought to hate him and he knew he couldn't !"—and, when the boss is in his dotage, drinking and playing cards with him behind the store. He eventually gains possession of the store, by means not entirely honest, sells it, comes to town with his wife and infant daughter, and sets up as a bootlegger. By the age of forty-eight he is a millionaire, living with his daughter in a large Spanish bungalow with an over-large staff of Negroes, while his dead wife lies "beneath a marble cenotaph that cost twenty thousand dollars among the significant names in the oldest section of the oldest cemetary [sic]: he bought the lot at a bankrupt sale—. . ."[17]

The story itself has a somewhat arbitrary O. Henryesque ending and is not of especially high quality, but it is rich in elements which

Faulkner was to take up and use in other stories and novels. We have already had occasion to note the presence in "The Big Shot" of Popeye, who reappears in *Sanctuary*, and Dr. Blount, who seems to bear a fairly direct relationship to Gail Hightower in *Light in August*, and there are even hints, in the treatment of the relationship between Martin and his daughter, of the Flem-Linda situation which Faulkner was to develop many years later in *The Town*. But the novel which draws most heavily on the story is obviously *Absalom, Absalom!*, and this indebtedness may provide some insight into a characteristic feature of Faulkner's creative method. He said at the University of Virginia that for the writer the idea of a novel usually began "with the thought, the image of a character, or with an anecdote, and even in the same breath, almost like lightning, it begins to take a shape that he can see whether it's going to be a short story or a novel."[18] To such an initial image other material rapidly accreted, and in the process of writing a new novel Faulkner was very likely to absorb into it, perhaps in completely transmuted form, a good deal of diverse material which already existed in his memory or his imagination, or actually on paper—perhaps even published. It has already been suggested that some such process may have operated in bringing together the diverse strands of *Light in August*, which, according to Faulkner, began with the image of Lena Grove on her travels, and a similar accretion may have provided the material for *The Sound and the Fury* following the moment of Faulkner's realisation that he wanted to write about the image of Caddy perched in the pear-tree. According to Faulkner, the starting-point of *Absalom, Absalom!* was Sutpen—"the idea of a man who wanted sons and got sons who destroyed him. The other characters I had to get out of the attic to tell the story of Sutpen."[19] It seems clear that in localising and pinning down this somewhat abstract conception Faulkner took over several elements from the presentation of Martin in "The Big Shot," and notably the "boy-symbol" which was to become so important in the larger work.

Much of the material of "The Big Shot" is treated in a directly sociological manner, as befits the narrative point of view, which is that of an unidentified first-person narrator who is himself recording the story as it was told to him by a newspaper reporter named Don Reeves. *Absalom, Absalom!*, like all the novels of Faulkner's maturity, is grounded in a profound sense of social reality and of historical perspective, but its manner is diversified in accordance with the characterisation of the participants in its multiple-narrative, all of whom claim to be concerned with truth, but none of whom, certainly, adopts a sociological or even reportorial approach. We have already pointed to the way in which Sutpen emerges as a type figure, both in terms of the history and society of the South and, as a successful entrepreneur and *nouveau-riche*, within a far broader context. But this view of Sutpen is built up piecemeal by the reader rather than presented directly by any of the narrators. Quentin, it is true, sees something of Sutpen's significance as a Southern figure, but until a late stage in the novel the presentation of Sutpen continues on the note and at the pitch set originally by Rosa Coldfield's "demonizing." It is Rosa's narrative, reinforced by the romantic tendencies evident in the imaginative reconstructions by Quentin and Shreve, which is primarily responsible for that aspect of the novel which has often led to the whole book being characterised as "Gothic." That the term itself did not dismay Faulkner may be inferred from a remark he once made about Melville and which is also revealing of his attitudes towards his own work: "I think that the moment in the book, the story, demands its own style and seems to me just as natural as the moment in the year produces the leaves. That when Melville becomes Old Testament, Biblical, that seems natural to me. When he becomes Gothic, that seems natural to me, too, . . ."[20] The diversification of style in *Absalom, Absalom!* functions in just these terms.

The Gothic characteristics of *Absalom, Absalom!* are worth investigating a little further, however, if only because they are among those features of Faulkner's work which have led critics to claim him as the major twentieth-century representative of American romance, inheritor of the tradition of Brockden Brown, Hawthorne, and Melville.[21] The similarities between Faulkner and Hawthorne have been frequently explored, and there have even been suggestions of specific resemblances between *Absalom, Absalom!* and *The House of the Seven Gables.*[22] There is, indeed, little doubt that Faulkner knew something of Hawthorne's work, and he includes him, along with Twain, Melville, and James, among those "predecessors who were the masters from whom we learned our craft."[23] But Faulkner included in the same list a number of English writers—Dickens, Fielding, Thackeray, Conrad, and Smollett—and he many times spoke of his debt to European authors such as Cervantes, Flaubert, Balzac, Chekhov, Gogol.[24] Faulkner's familiarity with English and European literature has often been ignored or underestimated by American critics, and the result has sometimes been not simply a misunderstanding of the nature and sources of many of his images and allusions but an insufficiently generous conception of the whole scale and direction of his endeavour.

If *Absalom, Absalom!* has Gothic elements in common with *The House of Seven Gables*, it shares far more with a novel like *Jane Eyre*. In both books there are major images of male power and one man (St. John Rivers in *Jane Eyre*, Sutpen in *Absalom, Absalom!*) who is iron-willed, immensely determined, and dedicated to the fulfilment of a purpose or design which is inhumane in its implications, against "life"—a man, as Jane Eyre says of St. John Rivers, who "forgets pitilessly the failings and claims of little people, in pursuing his own large views."[25] In each book there is a man whose first wife, a dark beauty from the West Indies, brings him wealth but has later to be put away for reasons of which the husband was unaware at the time of marriage: Sutpen's wife in *Absalom, Absalom!* because of the suspicion of Negro blood, Rochester's wife in *Jane Eyre* because she goes mad, although the presence of Negro blood is perhaps hinted at in Rochester's remark that his wife's family "wished to secure me because I was of good race; and so did she."[26] In each book the rejected wife continues to haunt her husband, threatening exposure and destruction. In each book, again, an unsophisticated girl is brought into a strange household and an important scene occurs in which the same young woman refuses what she considers an improper offer: Rosa Coldfield refuses to enter into an experimental liaison with Sutpen, while in *Jane Eyre* there is Jane's refusal to live with Rochester and also her refusal to marry Rivers, realising that he does not love her but wants her only, as Sutpen wants Rosa, in order to fulfil his design. In both books there are great houses with secret inmates (Rochester's wife, Henry Sutpen) and mysterious guardians (Grace Poole, Clytie), and these houses are eventually set on fire by desperate women who themselves perish in the blaze.

This is not to suggest that Faulkner was deliberately engaged in writing an inverted *Jane Eyre*. Both novels are related to the Gothic tradition, and many elements which they have in common are common also to the Gothic pattern. Yet the resemblances are close, and it is tempting to think that Faulkner must at some time have read *Jane Eyre* and been deeply affected by it. The main point, at least, seems clear: that in so far as Faulkner resumes the Gothic tradition in the novel he must be thought of as doing so from European sources quite as much as, or even more than, from native American sources. Faulkner may have felt some influence from Hawthorne, but the Gothic of *The House of Seven Gables* is lacking in the kind of uninhibited masculine violence which dominates *Absalom, Absalom!* and *Jane Eyre*. Among nineteenth-century American novels, only *Moby Dick* stands in this particular line, and there may indeed be traces of Captain Ahab in Faulkner's presentation of Sutpen; what is lacking even in *Moby Dick*, however, is the feminine perspective on masculine violence which characterises Rosa Coldfield's narrative in *Absalom, Absalom!* and the first-person narrative of Jane herself in *Jane Eyre*.

The attractiveness of the analogy between *Absalom, Absalom!* and *Jane Eyre* is increased rather than diminished by the fact that the complex organisation of Faulkner's novel, the progressive piecing together of events and interpretations from the evidence provided by a variety of narrators, bears a certain resemblance to the structure of Emily Brontë's *Wuthering Heights*, a novel which Faulkner knew and "admired for its craftsmanship."[27] But in sheer intricacy of design *Absalom, Absalom!* goes far beyond *Wuthering Heights* or any other predecessor. One way of looking at the book's structure is to think of it as organised about a number of crucial moments of recognition, truth, disillusion: Henry and his father in the library, Henry shooting Bon, Sutpen proposing to Rosa, Wash Jones murdering Sutpen—each moment presented in a kind of tableau arrested at a particular point of time and held in suspension while it is looked at, approached from all sides, inspected as if it were itself an artifact, like that Grecian urn which Faulkner so often invoked elsewhere. The main business of the book then becomes the interpretation of these moments, the attempt to explain and make sense of them. Each moment is evoked again and again, and at each recurrence we seem to learn a little more about it and even to be moving towards a final clarification. Again and again, however, Faulkner stops us short of elucidation, constantly reinforcing in this way a suspense which, throughout the book, is created not so much by the withholding of narrative facts—almost all of these, indeed, are supplied in the opening chapter—as by the continual frustration of our desire to complete the pattern of motivation, of cause and effect. The movement of the book becomes almost wave-like—surging forward, falling back, and then surging forward again—and it is notable that most of the chapters, including the last, end on such moments of checked resolution.

Because he has spoken to Henry Sutpen,[28] Quentin possesses the vital piece of information, the fact that Charles Bon had Negro blood inherited from his mother, which "makes sense" of the most critical moment of all, the moment when Henry kills Bon. Yet for Quentin himself this rationalisation constitutes the ultimate outrage: nothing for him is more appalling than the thought that the fratricidal tragedy, the monstrous end to a friendship and love which had promised to survive even the threat of incest (the obsessive theme of Quentin's section of *The Sound and the Fury*), should have been provoked by the ancient curse of the South. Shreve, with his utterly different background, cannot begin to comprehend the horror of this revelation, which Quentin must therefore face and come to terms with alone. Haunted by this knowledge, by his memory of the death-in-life of Henry Sutpen, and by the screams of Jim Bond, Quentin has at the end of the book found no relief: he lies, "his eyes wide open upon the window, thinking 'Nevermore of peace. Nevermore of peace. Nevermore Nevermore Nevermore.'" (p. 373) For him at least the telling of the tragedy of Sutpen has brought no purgation or release.[29]

THE UNVANQUISHED

The Unvanquished is made up of seven distinct parts, six of which had previously been published as short stories. Five of these appeared in the *Saturday Evening Post*: "Ambuscade" (September 29, 1934), "Retreat" (October 13, 1934), "Raid" (November 3, 1934), "The Unvanquished," subsequently retitled "Riposte in Tertio" (November 14, 1936), and "Vendée" (December 5, 1936); the sixth, "Skirmish at Sartoris", appeared in *Scribner's Magazine* for April 1935. In revising these stories for incorporation in *The Unvanquished* Faulkner made for the most part only very minor changes, and the last three to be published—"Skirmish at Sartoris," "Riposte in Tertio," and "Vendée" —did not differ significantly between magazine and book publication, except that "Skirmish at Sartoris" contained on its first appearance an opening paragraph supplying background information about the events of "Raid." "Ambuscade" shows fairly extensive stylistic revision to the first pages, but the changes made in the three earlier stories are otherwise in the nature of additions to the originals rather than detailed revisions: the account of Buck and Buddy McCaslin which appears on pages 52 to 57 of *The Unvanquished* is one such addition; others are the humorous recital of Ringo's reasons for wanting to hear about "cokynut cake" in "Ambuscade," and the passage about the railway in "Raid."

Part of this last addition evokes the attitude of the two boys, Bayard and Ringo, to the story of the contest between the two railway engines:

> And then to have it happen, where we could have been there to see it, and were not: and this no poste and riposte of sweat-reeking cavalry which all war-telling is full of, no galloping thunder of guns to wheel up and unlimber and crash and crash into the lurid grime-glare of their own demon-served inferno which even children would recognise, no ragged lines of gaunt and shrill-yelling infantry beneath a tattered flag which is a very part of that child's make-believe. Because this was it: an interval, a space, in which the toad-squatting guns, the panting men and the trembling horses paused, amphitheatric about the embatteld land, beneath the fading fur of the smoke and the puny yelling, and permitted the sorry business which had dragged on for three years now to be congealed into an irrevocable instant and put to an irrevocable gambit, not by

two regiments or two batteries or even two generals, but by two locomotives. (pp. 108-109)

Faulkner's main intention in introducing this passage into *The Unvanquished* was apparently to heighten the significance of the events that were being described; indeed, he raises them to a level of symbolic portentousness that is perhaps somewhat at odds with the general tenor of his narrative material, his affectionate account of the exploits of Grandmother Millard and the two children. At the same time, it can be argued that in making such an addition he was attempting to develop the possible thematic links between the stories and thus give *The Unvanquished* a more cohesive structure than could be obtained from simple narrative continuity. The attempt, if such it was, cannot be said to have been very thoroughly pursued; but further indications of Faulkner's awareness that some modification of the original stories might be desirable can be found in the manuscript and typescript versions of the last, previously unpublished, story "An Odor of Verbena".

The typescript version is very close to the published text, but the manuscript lacks one or two small but significant passages which appear both in the typescript and in *The Unvanquished* itself. On pages 254-255 of *The Unvanquished*, for example, we read of Colonel Sartoris having shot a man who was

almost a neighbor, a hill man who had been in the first infantry regiment when it voted Father out of command: and we never to know if the man actually intended to rob Father or not because Father shot too quick, but only that he had a wife and several children in a dirt-floored cabin in the hills, to whom Father the next day sent some money and she (the wife) walked into the house two days later while we were sitting at the dinner table and flung the money at Father's face.

In the manuscript there appears in the place of this passage only a brief allusion to Colonel Sartoris killing one of a number of men who tried to rob him.[1] On the next page of the manuscript the discussion between Bayard and Drusilla about the dreams of Thomas Sutpen, Colonel Sartoris, and other men ends simply with Drusilla's comparison of a dream to a loaded pistol; in the typescript and in the published book the following additional passage appears:

"But if it's a good dream, it's worth it. There are not many dreams in the world, but there are a lot of human lives. And one human life or two dozen—"
    "Are not worth anything?"
    "No. Not anything.—" (p. 257)[2]

In making these particular alterations Faulkner certainly showed himself to be aware of one of the principal difficulties in the way of any integration of "An Odor of Verbena" into the pattern established by the previous stories in *The Unvanquished*. Colonel Sartoris has previously been presented, with only minor qualifications, as possessing heroic stature. Now, in the final episode, his actions are to be revalued—explicitly by the Colonel himself, in his rejection of killing, implicitly by the pattern of the whole story—and in these small additions to the original manuscript of "An Odor of Verbena" Faulkner prepares the way for this revaluation by giving greater emphasis to the unnecessary killing in which Colonel Sartoris had indulged and to the hardness and inhumanity of the code of violence as cherished by Drusilla.

The question remains of how far Faulkner succeeded, of how much unity *The Unvanquished* possesses, and of what kind. When "Ambuscade" originally appeared in the *Saturday Evening Post* the editor announced it as "the first of a series of stories by Mr. Faulkner in which these same two boys will appear,"[3] and some remarks by Faulkner himself tend to emphasise the conception of *The Unvanquished* as a story sequence rather than a novel:

> I saw them as a long series. I had never thought of it in terms of a novel, exactly. I realized that they would be too episodic to be what I considered a novel, so I thought of them as a series of stories, that when I got into the first one I could see two more, but by the time I'd finished the first one I saw that it was going further than that, and then when I'd finished the fourth one, I had postulated too many questions that I had to answer for my own satisfaction. So the others had to be—the other three or two, whichever it was, had to be written then.[4]

Yet Cleanth Brooks, Hyatt H. Waggoner, Carvel Collins, and James B. Meriwether have all made out cases for regarding *The Unvanquished* not as a sequence of stories but as a more unified work.[5] Their arguments are persuasive and Meriwether's in particular is extremely well documented: he demonstrates the persistence throughout the book of a number of themes and topics, such as the effects of slavery, the character of the "poor white" and his place in Southern society, the symbolism of the railroad, and so on. There can be no doubt that the book does present Faulkner's view of developments in Southern society at a particular period in history—although, as Meriwether shows, Faulkner to some extent manipulates the chronology of historical events in order to throw the human situation into greater relief. Moreover, our understanding of Bayard's revision of the Sartoris code in "An Odor of Verbena" depends almost entirely upon our previous exposure to various traditional manifestations of that code, just as

Bayard's action is itself a response to his own experience of the effects of the code, his own evaluation of what the code means in practice.

In the earlier novel *Sartoris*, in which several of the characters and events of *The Unvanquished* receive their first mention, Colonel John Sartoris himself is dead; his presence is felt by those still living, but essentially he remains in the background, together with the system of values which he represents. Of the surviving Sartorises, old Bayard and Miss Jenny are presented affectionately, although the latter is made the mouthpiece of mild criticisms of the Sartoris code, while the fact that young Bayard is a Sartoris is seen to be only one element in his tragedy: he is also, and perhaps more importantly, one of the "dead pilots," those whose lives ended on Armistice Day 1918, and a man who has seen his twin brother killed. Nowhere in the novel is Faulkner forced to make a final judgment of the Sartoris code, or even to subject it to close scrutiny, and he maintains to the end an attitude of unresolved ambiguity, of mingled criticism and celebration. In *The Unvanquished* Colonel Sartoris, no longer a shadowy figure, occupies a central position, and although it is not until the end of the book that the Sartoris code is directly subjected to review, Meriwether is able to demonstrate that even in "Skirmish at Sartoris," probably the weakest of the stories, there are subtleties in Faulkner's presentation of Colonel Sartoris and his actions which make it clear that something other than uncritical admiration and endorsement is involved.[6]

In the final story, "An Odor of Verbena," Colonel Sartoris, the man who has done too much killing, realises what he has become and resolves to break out of the terrible pattern of recurrent violence in which he has become involved through adherence to the traditional Sartoris code within the particular context of a bloody war and its desperate aftermath. When he confronts Redmond without drawing his pistol, Redmond kills him, but the Colonel's last courageous gesture makes it possible for his son to repudiate violence and live, sets him free to perform his own act of courage and non-violence. In himself going unarmed to Redmond's room Bayard clearly does not reject the code in which he has been brought up; he breaks with the formal pattern of revenge, symbolised by Drusilla's presentation of the duelling pistols, but he does not offend against the code's fundamental standards of bravery and personal responsibility. George Wyatt recognises this at once, although, as he says, "I wouldn't have done it that way myself." (p. 289) Drusilla also recognises it, although by her departure she also makes it clear that Bayard's way is different from her own, and at the end of the book there is a clear note of triumph in Drusilla's acknowledgement of Bayard's action by the sprig of verbena, already firmly established as a formal accolade of the Sartoris code. At the very end of the story the omission of the final expected word, "courage," is actually a way of underlining the word and, at the same time, Bayard's vindication in terms of the code and its symbols.

"An Odor of Verbena" presents us with certain difficulties, however. Not only are we confronted with a Bayard whose character seems to have greatly changed in the years that have passed since the events of "Skirmish at Sartoris," but also with a shift in the presentation of Drusilla that cannot be explained wholly in terms of Bayard's more mature viewpoint. Drusilla's speech to Bayard as she formally presents him with the duelling pistols is grotesquely and almost ludicrously overwrought in its rhetoric and in its imagery, while the description of Drusilla's reaction when she realises that Bayard is not going to shoot Redmond is full of quite specific images of disgust: the hysterical laughter bursts out of her "like vomit," (p. 275) she tries to "hold it back with her hand like a small child who has filled its mouth too full," (p. 275) and a little later it seems "to burst out all over her face like sweat does and with a dreadful and painful convulsion as when you have vomited until it hurts you yet still you must vomit again." (p. 281) It might appear that in order to revalue the code, Faulkner has first to parody it, as a means of exorcising it, of breaking its hold, and then to deprive it of its last vestiges of grandeur. We have already seen, however, that in repudiating violence Bayard does not repudiate the essentials of the code itself, and Faulkner's intention here was presumably to present Drusilla's hysteria as at once the outcome and the index of the suffering and grief to which she had been subjected during and since the Civil War, so that it becomes virtually the counterpart of Colonel Sartoris's "intolerant" (p. 265) eyes, with their terrible resemblance to "the eyes of men who have killed too much, who have killed so much that never again as long as they live will they ever be alone." (p. 266) The element of exaggeration in the presentation of Drusilla at this point remains disturbing, however, as does the marked difference in tone and attitude between "An Odor of Verbena" and the rest of the book; we may accept the reassessment of Sartoris values within the limited context of "An Odor of Verbena" itself, but it is more difficult to accept that reassessment as retroactively effective, as enforcing also a revaluation of those episodes in Bayard's childhood and youth which have been previously described. Partly this is because those earlier stories have shown few signs of a genuine development either of theme or of character and therefore tend to remain in the memory as independent units.

In 1931, in a review of Erich Maria Remarque's *The Road Back*, Faulkner wrote:

Man does not seem to be able to stand very much prosperity; least of all does a people, a nation. Defeat is good for him, for it. . . . It is the defeat which, serving him against his belief and his desire, turns him back upon that alone which can sustain him: his fellows, his racial homogeneity; himself; the earth, the implacable soil, monument and tomb of sweat.

This is beyond the talking, the hard words, the excuses and the reasons; beyond the despair. Beyond that dreadful desire and need to justify the disaster and give it significance by clinging to it, explaining it, which is the proven best way to support the inescapable. Victory requires no explanation. It is in itself sufficient: the fine screen, the shield; immediate and final: it will be contemplated only by history. While the whole contemporary world watches the defeat and the undefeated who, because of that fact, survived.[7]

The Unvanquished may perhaps be regarded as a later product of "that dreadful desire and need to justify the disaster and give it significance by clinging to it, explaining it." In other respects, our sense of what is wrong with the book may be defined in terms of its failure to match the kind of conception which Faulkner embodies in the review: the vision of moral victory created from the very fabric of physical defeat, of human misery becoming the very foundation stone of human triumph. The stories in *The Unvanquished* are not without moments of insight or of pathos—one thinks especially of the weird, tragic Negro migration in "Raid"—but for the most part they inevitably strike us as romanticised "tall tales" of heroic Southern resistance to the North. We perceive in their narrative verve and lack of serious moral complication the mark of stories skilfully and professionally created for the particular market offered by the *Saturday Evening Post*, and we are not surprised that the book was purchased by Hollywood —according to Faulkner's own story, as a potential rival to *Gone With the Wind*.[8] *The Unvanquished*, whether it is considered as a novel or as a sequence of short stories, remains distinctly a minor work. People coming to Faulkner's work for the first time are often advised to begin with *The Unvanquished*: this, indeed, was the advice which Faulkner himself gave on one occasion.[9] But the discriminating reader who begins with *The Unvanquished* is likely to find within its covers little incentive to read further in Faulkner's work and few indications of those qualities which make him a major writer.

THE WILD PALMS

THE typescript of *The Wild Palms* bears the deleted title, "If I forget thee, Jerusalem,"[1] and it seems clear that this was the title which Faulkner would have preferred. The quotation, or slight misquotation, is from Psalm 137, verse 5 : "If I forget thee, O Jerusalem, let my right hand forget her cunning," and of its many possible applications to the novel perhaps the most obvious are to the affirmation of love and loyalty which Wilbourne makes at the end of the novel and to the crucial episode involving Wilbourne's delayed decision to perform the abortion on Charlotte and the failure of his skill, or loss of his doctor's cunning, which eventually results in her death. A possible reading of the title, considered in this context, might be that Wilbourne's failure is related to his failure to hold absolutely to the ideal conception of life, the "Jerusalem," which Charlotte has set before him, and recent studies of the novel have sometimes presented Wilbourne in such an unfavourable light. The vital question, however, and one which is crucial to our whole interpretation of the book, is whether Wilbourne had been right or wrong in his reluctance to perform the abortion.

Joseph J. Moldenhauer argues that Wilbourne wanted the baby to be born because it would be "a visible sign, for all society to see, of his guilt and sin with Charlotte."[2] It seems more likely, however, particularly in view of Faulkner's use of birth and pregnancy as explicit symbols of regeneration in novels like *Light in August* and *Pylon*, that it is Charlotte who is to be criticised for demanding the abortion. Wilbourne is clearly the weaker character; he lacks Charlotte's unyielding determination and her grandeur; he speaks of her as being "a better man" (p. 133) than he is, and the remark simply reinforces the many references to Charlotte's masculinity which appear throughout the novel—at the very beginning of the book, for example, the house agent speaks of her as wearing a man's trousers, although at the same time he emphasises her sexual attractiveness, and throughout their relationship it is usually Charlotte who is the bread-winner and maker of decisions, Harry the one who cooks and looks after the house. This inversion of roles, highly significant for an understanding of Faulkner's characterisation of Harry and Charlotte, is itself only one aspect of the novel's overall insistence on the essential sterility of Charlotte's ideal. She has, rather like Thomas Sutpen, a magnificent design, but the design, like Sutpen's, has a fatal flaw, the flaw of rigidity: the assertion of the will, of the needs of the design, is made irrespective of the demands of the human situation, of humanity, of life. Because Charlotte's design demands an abortion it is seen to be, quite specifically, life-denying, and although it is characteristic of Wilbourne's weakness that he both surrenders to Charlotte's will and fatally botches the operation itself, it is at the same time indicative of his greater flexibility and humanity that he is opposed to the operation and wishes the child to be born.

It is true that Charlotte's immediate reason for not having a child is that "they hurt too much. Too damned much." (p. 217) She means by this, as Wilbourne realises, not that childbirth itself is an agony too great to be borne but that children themselves, specifically the children she has left behind with her husband, can be such a source of anguish. Yet in saying this she is in some sense betraying her own grim dictum: "that love and suffering are the same thing and that the value of love is the sum of what you have to pay for it and any time you get it cheap you have cheated yourself." (p. 48) By seeking an abortion she may herself be introducing a fatal element of cheapness, of falsity, into the relationship. At the same time, the more funda- mental element of sterility is brought out at the moment when Charlotte first tells Harry of her pregnancy: "I remember somebody telling me once, I was young then, that when people loved, hard, really loved each other, they didn't have children, the seed got burned up in the love, the passion. Maybe I believed it. Wanted to believe it ... Or maybe I just hoped." (p. 205) Like Charlotte's masculinity, this desire not to have children is not so much a perversion as the outward sign of something lacking in her make-up, in her capacity for life. She has something in common with Margaret Powers, who loses both her husbands and is childless; with Joanna Burden, who dies childless and unmarried; and even with the wilfully experimental Patricia in that other New Orleans novel, *Mosquitoes*, although Wil- bourne for his part does not display the pure passivity of David in the earlier book. Though rarely capable of initiating action, Wilbourne is often able to delay or deflect it, and—to judge especially from his long explanation to McCord about the effects of losing one's virginity at twenty-seven—there is a certain sense in which Charlotte, particularly at the beginning of their relationship, represents for him not so much a cherished object of love as a means to sexual experience. Similarly, there is a certain sense in which Wilbourne is simply an adjunct to Charlotte's design, chosen by her to play a role which another man might conceivably have filled. Yet their love is more than a quasi- marriage of emotional convenience; it becomes, for better or worse, a shared adventure, with Charlotte as the stronger partner setting the pattern of their life and of their ultimate disaster.

The disaster appears as inevitable, inherent in the very desperation and uncompromising rigidity of Charlotte's ideal. Early in their life together Harry recognises: "*There's a part of her that doesn't love anybody, anything; . . . Why, she's alone. Not lonely, alone.*" (p. 82) And a little later: "*She's worse off than I am,* he thought. *She doesn't even know what it is to hope.*" (p. 92) Charlotte is a doomed fanatic of love, savagely impatient of Wilbourne when he falls short of the ideal she has set before them:

> She grasped his hair again, hurting him again though now he knew she knew she was hurting him. "Listen: it's got to be all honeymoon, always. Forever and ever, until one of us dies. It cant be anything else. Either heaven, or hell: no comfortable safe peaceful purgatory between for you and me to wait in until good behavior or forbearance or shame or repentance overtakes us." (p. 83)

The images established in this passage recur throughout the novel. Charlotte demands of Harry total immersion in the ocean of love, but he relinquishes himself to it only with great difficulty and reluctance: "*Maybe I'm not embracing her but clinging to her because there is something in me that wont admit it cant swim or cant believe it can.*" (p. 84) That his reluctance may not be due only to his weakness and timidity but, at least in part, to his greater hold on reality, on what we come finally to recognise as life, is suggested shortly afterwards by the disturbing grotesqueness, "elegant, bizarre, fantastic and perverse," (p. 89) of the miniature figures Charlotte creates.[3] Among these figures, the last to be made, is the Bad Smell, the symbol of that decaying of love from within against which Charlotte warns Wilbourne in the passage quoted above. The figure, the objectification of the enemy, takes on something of the significance of an image in homoeopathic magic, and indeed the whole religion of love into which Wilbourne is initiated by Charlotte is highly superstitious, sustained by innumerable fetiches and tabus, from Charlotte's refusal to wear a nightgown or anything else in bed to the ultimate and fatal requirement that no third person, least of all a child of their union, must intrude upon their shared isolation.

The images of the ocean and of the bad smell which it spews up reappear in concrete terms at the end of the book, where the description of the coast town in which Charlotte dies and Wilbourne is tried thus becomes partly atmospheric and partly emblematic:

> The jail was somewhat like the hospital save that it was of two storeys, square, and there were no oleanders. But the palm was there. It was just outside his window, bigger, more shabby; when he and the officer passed beneath it to enter, with no wind to cause it, it had set up a sudden frenzied clashing as though they had startled it, and twice more during the night while he stood, shifting his hands from time to time as that portion of the bars

which they clasped grew warm and began to sweat on his palms, it clashed again in that brief sudden inexplicable flurry. Then the tide began to fall in the river and he could smell that too—the sour smell of salt flats where oyster shells and the heads of shrimps rotted, and hemp and old piling. Then dawn began (he had been hearing the shrimp boats putting out for some time) and he could see the draw bridge on which the railroad to New Orleans crossed standing suddenly against the paling sky and he heard the train from New Orleans and watched the approaching smoke then the train itself crawling across the bridge, high and toylike and pink like something bizarre to decorate a cake with, in the flat sun that was already hot. Then the train was gone, the pink smoke. The palm beyond the window began to murmur, dry and steady, and he felt the cool morning breeze from the sea, steady and filled with salt, clean and iodinic in the cell above the smell of creosote and tobacco-spit and old vomit; the sour smell of the flats went away and now there would be a glitter on the tide-chopped water, the gars roiling sluggishly up and then down again among the floating garbage. (pp. 307-308)

In the immediate present the Bad Smell, for whatever reasons, has conquered: the great love has ended in sordid disaster and in death. But the cleansing action of the ocean suggests that reassertion of the valuable and positive aspects of Charlotte's design—its courage, its idealism, its totality of commitment—which sustains Wilbourne in his refusal to accept the escapes offered him by Rittenmeyer and in that final declaration of love, that defiance of time and inevitable dissolution, to which Faulkner must surely have intended his readers to make a sympathetic response:

> But after all memory could live in the old wheezing entrails: and now it did stand to his hand, incontrovertible and plain, serene, the palm clashing and murmuring dry and wild and faint and in the night but he could face it, thinking, *Not could. Will. I want to. So it is the old meat after all, no matter how old. Because if memory exists outside of the flesh it wont be memory because it wont know what it remembers so when she became not then half of memory became not and if I become not then all of remembering will cease to be.*—*Yes,* he thought, *between grief and nothing I will take grief.* (p. 324)

The "Wild Palms" story ends with the image of the palm, which has been a recurring motif throughout, and which Faulkner must have seen as embodying so much of his conception of Charlotte: not only her grandeur, her lonely defiance, and her deep-rooted strength, but also those qualities of sterile fanaticism which ultimately destroyed

her and which he invokes through repeated insistence on the wildness
and dryness of the palms, and on the frenzied clashing of their leaves.

The "Wild Palms" story has been discussed first and at length
because that is clearly where the emphasis must lie in any interpretation of the book as a whole. "Old Man" is the more obviously
attractive story, and perhaps the better written, but all Faulkner's
accounts of the novel, as well as his final choice of title, make it clear
that he regarded the "Wild Palms" as the principal element in the
book and the chief vehicle of its meaning. At Nagano Faulkner said
that in struggling to tell the story of Charlotte and Harry he "invented
the other story, its complete antithesis, to use as counterpoint ... I
imagine as a musician would do to compose a piece of music in which
he needed a balance, a counterpoint."[4] And he concluded his rather
fuller but extremely similar account in the *Paris Review* interview with
the firm statement : "The story is that of Charlotte and Wilbourne."[5]
The form of *The Wild Palms* is so unusual that there seems no other
way of describing it than as a "double-novel," yet such a term does
not adequately indicate the primacy of the "Wild Palms" material. It
seems necessary to speak of "Old Man" as a kind of unrelated sub-
plot which provides "Wild Palms" not only with a counterpoint,
an ironic contrast and commentary, but actually with a supple-
mentary context, giving to the major strand an additional dimension
and a wider relevance.

The extent and importance of the thematic and other links between
the two stories has perhaps been somewhat exaggerated in recent
analyses of *The Wild Palms*, in a natural reaction against a tendency
among critics to dismiss the book as a crude conflation of two separate
stories and, even more, against the readiness of publishers to print the
two stories either in isolation one from the other or separated out
within the same covers—in series, so to speak, rather than in parallel.
It has been suggested that Faulkner may originally have written the
two stories separately, but none of this evidence is conclusive and
Faulkner himself specifically denied the suggestion in his remarks at
Nagano : "I did not write those two stories and then cut one into the
other. I wrote them, as you read it, as the chapters."[6] The few
manuscript pages of the novel which are now in the Alderman Library
appear to indicate that the divisions in the manuscript fell generally
at the points where they fall in the published book. The typescript
setting copy for the most part very closely resembles the published
text, but it reveals that until a late stage in the writing of the book
the first "Old Man" section and the second "Wild Palms" section were
much longer than they are at present, embracing in each case the
section which succeeds them in the published book : that is, the first
and second sections of "Old Man" were run together, as were the
second and third sections of "Wild Palms."[7]

Whatever the history of the novel, it must be discussed and interpreted as it stands, in its published form, and it is clear that Faulkner's structural method forces us to recognise certain thematic and even narrative parallels and inversions between one strand of the novel and the other. Wilbourne and the Tall Convict start out from somewhat parallel situations: both are secure and content, though not precisely happy, in the simple, spartan, ordered, almost monastic, externally controlled life of the hospital on the one hand and the prison on the other. They end in the identical situation of Parchman prison—Wilbourne arrives ten years after the events of "Old Man," but that is the very period which the Tall Convict has had added to his sentence—and even before his sentence Wilbourne begins to take on the convict's anonymity, as the deputy who arrests him casually refers to him under a variety of names, none of them his own. They are approximately the same age—Wilbourne is twenty-seven, the convict "about twenty-five" (p. 25)—and at the beginning of their stories each has abjured sex, the convict from necessity, Wilbourne from what he persuades himself to be necessity; each, however, is led by unusual circumstances (the flood, the invitation to the party) to break away from the familiar pattern of his life and to embark, in company with a strange woman, on an adventure of extraordinary violence and diversity. From this point the parallels are for the most part of that ironic kind mentioned by Faulkner himself in discussions at the University of Virginia and elsewhere. Answering a question about the woman and the convict alone in the skiff, he said:

> No, that was a definite parallel. The isolation, the solitude of the boat in that raging torrent was the solitude which Harry and Charlotte had tried so long to find, where they could be lovers—to escape from the world. They went to infinite labor and risk and sacrifice to escape from the world where this convict had been hurled out of the world against his will whether he wanted to or not. That he and the woman he saved had what Charlotte and Wilbourne had sacrificed everything to get. That's what I mean by counterpoint to the theme of the other book.[8]

A little later he said of the convict's involvement with another man's wife just before his return to prison: "It was to underline the fact that he had for free what Charlotte and Harry had given everything for. That he had the woman and the solitude but she wasn't enough—he had to go and get into trouble over somebody else's wife."[9] In giving the novel its original title, "If I forget thee, Jerusalem," Faulkner may have had in mind the convict's failure to take advantage of his situation: one significance of the title would thus be a sexual one, calling attention to the contrast between the apparently virile convict who nevertheless fails to make love to the woman he rescues, though presented with almost unlimited opportunities, and the apparently ineffectual Harry Wilbourne who nevertheless sustains a passionate affair with the extremely demanding Charlotte.

The convict is supported in his trials and adventures primarily by vanity, his simple-minded concern for his reputation and good name in the only society he knows, and by his sheer indomitability, itself the product of a monumental lack of imagination. The woman becomes an almost intolerable burden to him, yet he fulfils to the letter what he conceives to be his duty, longing all the time for a return to the security of prison: Psalm 137, from which Faulkner took his original title, embodies an affirmation of the Jews' loyalty to their homeland at the time of the Babylonish captivity, and Faulkner may have intended an ironic allusion to the situation of the convict, for whom his place of captivity is itself the only home, the only sanctuary, he knows or can imagine. The convict's experiences are inflicted upon him quite involuntarily; he has no emotional stake in the adventure nor in the woman and child whose responsibility he assumes; he accepts his sufferings, not without a sense of outrage, but with an essential passivity that is qualified only by his primitive talent for survival and by that dogged and absurdly literal pursuit of the tasks laid upon him which seems to have in it less of determination than of obsessive need, and more of stupidity than either. Wilbourne's adventure, on the other hand, is willed, or at least deliberately assented to and embarked upon, and his emotional commitment to the woman with whom he seeks to be isolated is as nearly absolute as he can make it. Charlotte has an ideal conception of love as a kind of Holy Grail which only the worthy are permitted to see and hold, and the restless journeys which she and Wilbourne make about the face of the continent are for them a dedicated search for the Grail, an increasingly desperate attempt to find, seize and perpetuate the quintessential experience and condition of love. Unhappily for them, their journey towards love inevitably becomes a flight not simply from society but from life itself, rather as the convict paddles furiously towards a Vicksburg which in fact lies far behind him.

The two stories seem to offer a number of further parallels and inter-reflections. The birth in the one is clearly set off against the abortion in the other, and they might both be said to offer ironic comments on the desert island myth—in the agony of Charlotte and Harry as they create for themselves their series of make-shift havens, and in the primarily comic horror of the convict at finding himself alone with a woman on an actual island which further conforms to the mythic pattern in being crowded with non-hostile wild life.[10] It is also possible to perceive a number of broad symbolic oppositions revolving about the water of the "Old Man" section and the wind of "Wild Palms."[11] The ultimate question to be faced is how far Faulkner's experiment succeeds, and while it is possible to feel that some violence has been used in yoking two such heterogeneous stories together, the gap between them is never too wide to prevent the imaginative, illuminating spark from jumping from one to the other. Moreover, in terms of simple emotional contrast and release "Old Man" performs an essential function in relation to the "Wild Palms" story, which is surely too painful, too agonising, too persistently on the note of near-hysteria to stand alone.

The weakness of "Old Man" when read in isolation is that it is too long, with both theme and material greatly over-extended, and it is interesting that Malcolm Cowley, in compiling *The Portable Faulkner*, should have intended at one stage to end the story at what is in the novel its penultimate chapter:

> When I took the book apart [he explained to Faulkner], it seemed to me that everything that follows is, in a sense, part of the double novel, not part of this particular episode—I mean the convict goes back to the prison farm, while the hero of the other story also goes to prison—that one goes in memory of a woman, the other because he is afraid of women, etc.; the last part of "Old Man" establishes the parallels and contrasts; but the real story ends for me with his surrender to the deputy, and I'd rather put it that way in the book.[12]

Faulkner's response to this suggestion was brief but entirely favourable: "OLD MAN. By all means. The story ends with: 'Here's your boat' etc. Stop it there."[13] Although this remark of Faulkner's could be taken as some slight indication that an "Old Man" story might have had an independent existence at some stage, it emphasises what the evidence of *The Wild Palms* itself sufficiently establishes, that the "Old Man" story as published owes its form—its length, its organisation, and the disposition of its parts—primarily to Faulkner's sense of the needs of the "Wild Palms" story and of the novel as a whole.

In attempting an overall assessment of the novel, therefore, we are brought back to a consideration of "Wild Palms." Here problems are posed by occasional uncertainties and inequalities in the writing, notably the sudden undigested shifts into the strenuous manner of *Pylon*—as when Wilbourne speaks to McCord of "the mausoleum of love, ... the stinking catafalque of the dead corpse borne between the olfactoryless walking shapes of the immortal unsentient demanding ancient meat" (p. 139)—and by the choice of settings. We may wonder why Faulkner chose, apparently so arbitrarily, to go beyond his customary range of known, familiar material. We may also wonder about such episodes as that in which Wilbourne writes love-stories for the pulp magazines—an activity which he thinks of in much the same terms as Faulkner seems to have regarded his work in Hollywood—and about Wilbourne's description of himself as a painter in the opening chapter of the book. There is much about *The Wild Palms* which does not seem wholly explicable in terms of the thematic patterns of the book or the psychology of its characters. It is, indeed, in many ways a strange and uncomfortable book, and not least in the extraordinary painfulness of the central story, the infliction upon Charlotte and, more especially, on Wilbourne of a degree of suffering that seems grossly in excess of what the situation might be thought to demand. The other novels of Faulkner's which are set wholly outside Yoknapatawpha County stand outside the main body of his work in other ways as well : A *Fable* is Faulkner's major attempt at a specifically personal statement, while *Mosquitoes* and *Pylon* clearly possess a considerable measure of direct or indirect autobiographical relevance. It is tempting to posit some kind of autobiographical or peculiarly personal significance for Faulkner's third New Orleans novel, *The Wild Palms*; for only by thinking of it in some such terms does it seem possible to account satisfactorily for the curiously personal quality of many of its incidents and allusions, or for the almost masochistic intensity of Wilbourne's agony.

THE HAMLET

FAULKNER said at the University of Virginia that he wrote *The Hamlet* "in the late twenties," mostly in the form of short stories, and that in 1940 he "got it pulled together."[1] Writing to Malcolm Cowley in 1945, he had given a fuller account of the book's history:

> THE HAMLET was incepted as a novel. When I began it, it produced Spotted Horses, went no further. About two years later suddenly I had THE HOUND, then JAMSHYD'S COURTYARD, mainly because SPOTTED HORSES had created a character I fell in love with: the itinerant sewing-machine agent named Suratt. Later a man of that name turned up at home, so I changed my man to Ratliff for the reason thag [sic] my whole town spent much of its time trying to decide just what living man I was writing about, the one literary criticism of the town being 'How in the hell did he remember all that and when did that happen anyway?' Meanwhile, my book had created Snopes and his clan, who produced stories in their saga which are to fall in later volume: MULE IN THE YARD, BRASS, etc. This over about ten years, until one day I decided I had better start on the first volume or I'd never get any of it down. So I wrote an induction toward the spotted horse story, which included BARN BURNING, AND [sic] WASH, which I discovered had no place in that book at all. Spotted Horses became a longer story, picked up the HOUND (rewritten and much longer and with the character's name changed from Cotton to Snopes), and went on with JAMSHYD'S COURTYARD.[2]

There is no doubt that Faulkner began writing a Snopes novel some time in late 1926 or early 1927. In a newspaper article written at about that time Phil Stone spoke of two novels on which Faulkner was working: one was the book we now know as *Sartoris*, the other "something of a saga of an extensive family connection of typical 'poor white trash.' "[3] Meriwether, quoting this article, also quotes from a letter which Stone wrote to him in 1957: "Bill once wrote fifteen or twenty pages on the idea of the Snopes trilogy which he entitled 'Father Abraham'. . . ."[4] These comments substantiate Faulkner's own statements about the composition of the book, and help to date the 25-page manuscript of "Father Abraham" now in the Arents Collection of the New York Public Library.

This manuscript opens with an extended description of Flem as a symbolic and legendary figure, a by-product of the democratic principle in action and successor to the Southern gentleman as the representative figure of his region and his time. There follows an account of the Old Frenchman place and its legend, and of the inhabitants of Frenchman's Bend, which bears a direct and sometimes a close relationship to the opening pages of *The Hamlet*. Once the setting has been established the "Father Abraham" manuscript goes on to describe a number of characters, notably Uncle Billy Varner and his daughter Eula, and continues with a telling of the "spotted horses" story, from the standpoint of the omniscient author, that is similar in essentials to the version which appears in Chapter I of "The Peasants", the fourth book of *The Hamlet*. A typescript of "Father Abraham," now in the Alderman Library, introduces a number of features that are absent from the manuscript and develops in particular Mrs. Littlejohn's function as a silent commentator on the follies of the male world of horse-trading. It is apparently later than the manuscript and is certainly still closer to the version used in *The Hamlet*, although it seems to have gone no further than a point shortly following the moment when the injured Henry Armstid has been carried into Mrs. Littlejohn's boarding house.[5]

The "Father Abraham" manuscript gives a more or less complete account of the whole "spotted horses" episode, but its last page, written on different paper and in different ink from the preceding pages, suddenly breaks off, as though Faulkner had abruptly abandoned an attempt to extend the material further and to develop it into the Snopes novel that he apparently had in mind. The "Father Abraham" typescript may have been completed shortly afterwards; on the other hand, it may have been a product of that later stage in the history of *The Hamlet* to which Faulkner referred in his letter to Cowley: "About two years later suddenly I had THE HOUND, then JAMSHYD'S COURTYARD." "The Hound" was first published in *Harper's* in August 1931, "Lizards in Jamshyd's Courtyard" in the *Saturday Evening Post* for February 27, 1932, but it is clear from the sending schedule which Faulkner kept for his early stories that they existed in completed form by November 17, 1930, and May 27, 1930.[6] The short story *Spotted Horses* was published in *Scribner's* in June 1931, but a version may have been finished by August 25, 1930.[7] "Centaur in Brass," a Snopes story first published in the *American Mercury* (February 1932) and later incorporated in *The Town*, also existed by August 1931.[8] All of these stories, of course, may have been written at a somewhat earlier date. Faulkner says that his first attempt to write a Snopes novel did not go any further than "Spotted Horses" (i.e. "Father Abraham"), but there is no doubt that he had already worked up a great variety of Snopes material and already had in mind the general pattern of Flem's career.

Many years later he spoke of the moment when "I thought of the whole story at once like a bolt of lightning lights up a landscape and you see everything ..."[9] The comprehensiveness of this conception is apparent from the various references to the Snopes family in *Sartoris*—brief references, to be sure, but sufficient to delineate the ground-plan of almost the whole Snopes saga :

[Montgomery Ward] Snopes was a young man, member of a seemingly inexhaustible family which for the last ten years had been moving to town in driblets from a small settlement known as Frenchman's Bend. Flem, the first Snopes, had appeared unheralded one day behind the counter of a small restaurant on a side street, patronized by country folk. With this foothold and like Abraham of old, he brought his blood and legal kin household by household, individual by individual, into town, and established them where they could gain money. Flem himself was presently manager of the city light and water plant, and for the following few years he was a sort of handy man to the municipal government; and three years ago, to old Bayard's profane astonishment and unconcealed annoyance, he became vice-president of the Sartoris bank, where already a relation of his was a bookkeeper. (*Sartoris*, p. 172)

It is presumably to *Sartoris* that Faulkner is referring when he speaks of "my book [which] had created Snopes and his clan." The novel had also created Suratt, the sewing-machine agent, whose name, as Faulkner explains, he later changed to Ratliff, and it is conceivable that Faulkner—having first abandoned "Father Abraham" in order to work on *Sartoris*—returned to the Snopes material in the latter part of 1927, after the completion of the *Sartoris* typescript at the end of September. The final typescript of *The Sound and the Fury* was completed by October 1928, however, and it seems probable that the writing of this immensely ambitious work must have engrossed most if not all of Faulkner's energies during the intervening year. By the early summer of 1930, at all events, Faulkner had taken a fresh look at the Snopes material and had begun quarrying it for short stories. From the evidence of Faulkner's letter to Cowley, and in the absence of earlier manuscripts or typescripts, it would seem that "Spotted Horses," "The Hound," "Lizards in Jamshyd's Courtyard," and "Centaur in Brass" were written at this stage. The last three may have been written virtually from scratch, although Faulkner no doubt conceived of their essential features in that original vision of the whole Snopes sequence, but there is ample evidence to show that the writing of "Spotted Horses" and the subsequent incorporation of the episode in *The Hamlet* was by no means a simple process.

When composing the version of the Texas ponies anecdote which subsequently appeared in *Scribner's* as the story "Spotted Horses",

Faulkner had a body of earlier material, including "Father Abraham," on which to draw, and in adapting this material he changed it radically. There is some evidence that at one stage—probably an early one—Faulkner may have experimented with a version of the story in which the "spotted horses" incident was divorced from any detailed account of Frenchman's Bend and its inhabitants;[10] in the *Scribner's* version actually published Faulkner did not omit this scene-setting, but he greatly reduced it in length. The most important change was in the narrative point of view, for the story is told, not in the third-person of "Father Abraham" and the novel, but in the first-person, from the point of view of a man who, although not specifically identified, is clearly the sewing-machine agent, Suratt/Ratliff. The narrator tells the story as though to a group of friends—"You-all mind the moon was nigh full that night," he says at one point—and in vigorously colloquial language: "They was colored like parrots and they was quiet as doves, and ere a one of them would kill you quick as a rattle-snake."[11] It is, in fact, essentially what the editor of *Scribner's* described it as being, "a tall tale with implications of tragedy";[12] but the point immediately to be made is that it is a by-product of the original Snopes conception, a story carved out of the material at a time when Faulkner, for whatever reason, felt unable or unwilling to work it up into a novel, and that the line of development between the original conception and *The Hamlet* does not pass through "Spotted Horses" as published in *Scribner's* but goes directly from "Father Abraham" to the novel. At the time when he was writing the version of the "spotted horses" episode which appears in the final section of *The Hamlet*, and also at the time when he was writing the present opening pages of the novel, Faulkner must certainly have had in front of him some version of the "Father Abraham" material; if he also had a copy of the *Scribner's* story he referred to it much less frequently. When adapting for incorporation into *The Hamlet* the tale of Pat Stamper's horse-trading activities which had previously been told in the *Scribner's* story, "Fool About a Horse," Faulkner again seems to have worked primarily from an earlier typescript rather than from the published story,[13] though no doubt he also had a copy of the story readily to hand.

Earlier in the letter to Cowley from which we have already quoted, Faulkner says that the *Scribner's* version of "Spotted Horses" was in the nature of a condensation of several chapters of *The Hamlet*, and it is entirely possible that Faulkner had actually got some way towards completing a Snopes novel at the time when "Spotted Horses" was written. Some day, indeed, firm evidence of this in the form of further manuscript or typescript material may become available, and in the meantime it is worth noting that Aubrey Starke, in his important article on Faulkner published in 1934, makes reference to the "the long promised, and eagerly awaited 'Snopes saga',—chief title on Mr. Faulkner's list of unpublished work."[14] Starke's further remarks on the Snopeses make clear how much material dealing with them Faulkner had already published by this time, and show that, to an intelligent reader, the whole trend of his treatment of them was already plain:

> And even if *The Snopes Saga* were not already promised we could safely predict that Mr. Faulkner would continue for some time to come the story of the Snopeses, for the rise of the class to which the Snopeses belong and the decay and disintegration of the class to which Sartorises and Compsons belong is surely the central, symbolic theme of Mr. Faulkner's comedy, as it—more than the traditional color problem—is the central problem of that part of the world in which Mr. Faulkner lives.[15]

In fact, it was not until several years later that Faulkner "pulled together" the various segments of Snopes material, although even at this stage he got no further than *The Hamlet*. It was to be another seventeen years before the publication of a further volume, *The Town*, despite the fact that the conclusion of *The Hamlet* clearly invites a sequel—the final page of the typescript setting copy actually bears the deleted words, "end Volume One."

The final composition of *The Hamlet* apparently began some time late in 1938, and a considerable amount of manuscript and typescript material has survived from this stage, including a manuscript which is practically complete up to a point corresponding to the end of the second section of Book Three, Chapter II, of the published book, a complete typescript setting copy, and many miscellaneous pages of both manuscript and typescript.[16] In the process of working towards the final version of the novel Faulkner made a great many minor additions and improvements, and the typescript setting copy is especially of interest for the evidence it provides of the many rearrangements which Faulkner made in the material of the book before eventually deciding on its final form. To take one example of many, it is clear that at one time the opening of the first new paragraph on page 128 of the published book appeared not in the first chapter of the "Eula" section but as the beginning of a proposed third chapter.[17]

The most interesting features of manuscript and typescript alike, however, are the vestiges of Faulkner's experimentation with different opening chapters. Faulkner mentions to Cowley that when he began pulling *The Hamlet* together he wrote an "induction toward the spotted horse story"; he adds that the induction included "Barn Burning" and "Wash"—"which I discovered had no place in that book at all." It seems remarkable that Faulkner should ever have thought that "Wash", much of which he had already incorporated into *Absalom, Absalom!*, might find a place in the "Snopes Saga," and one can only surmise that he may have thought of giving an historical dimension to his largely economic study of the rise of the "poor white" Flem Snopes: [18] he later used "Was" to add such a dimension to his treatment of white-Negro relationships in *Go Down, Moses*. At all events, there appears to be no clear evidence to show that "Wash" was incorporated into any of the later versions of *The Hamlet*: there is no such evidence, at least, in the manuscript and typescript versions at the University of Virginia.

The case of "Barn Burning" is different. The 17-page manuscript of the story in the Alderman Library bears the heading "BOOK ONE/ Chapter I" in addition to the deleted title "Barn Burning," while the 32-page typescript bears no title at all but simply the heading "Chapter One."[19] Deleted pagination in the typescript setting copy of *The Hamlet* shows that 32 pages have at some stage been removed and very clearly suggests that "Barn Burning" was until a fairly late stage incorporated into the novel as its opening chapter, with a version of the present first chapter as Chapter II. Sometime during the winter of 1938-1939, however, Faulkner must have changed his mind about the way the novel should open: among a group of rejected typescript pages in the Alderman Library there is a version of page 1, close to the first page (p. 3) of the published book, which bears the pencilled editorial note "Rec'd 3/20/39," while "Barn Burning" itself was published as an independent entity, and with only minor alterations from the typescript version headed "Chapter One," in *Harper's Monthly* for June 1939. Faulkner seems to have experimented with a number of other possible openings to the novel, including one which began with the first encounter between Jody Varner and Ab Snopes which now appears on page 8 of the published book. It is hard to think that this would have made a satisfactory opening, but there is no doubt that the deeply moving story of "Barn Burning" would have been in many ways an extremely effective introduction.[20] We do not know why Faulkner finally decided to take it out, but it may have been in some measure the result of a decision not to use Colonel Sartoris Snopes, the boy of "Barn Burning," as a character elsewhere in the novel, or of some feeling that the episode gave too favourable an impression of the Snopes family to serve satisfactorily as a prologue to the history of Flem. The boy is certainly absent, apart from Ratliff's reference to another little Snopes whom he remembers having once seen, from the summary of the narrative events of "Barn Burning" which appears in the present opening chapter.

The long history of *The Hamlet* reveals it clearly as a novel conceived as a single whole but written over a period of many years, with many interruptions, much revision and reworking, and a continually enriching accretion of observation, anecdote and imagery; the finished book, far from being a series of loosely connected incidents,[21] demands consideration as a carefully organised and wholly organic structure. An example of the care and deliberate artistry which went into the composition of *The Hamlet* is provided by Faulkner's extremely skilful incorporation of the "Fool About a Horse" and "Spotted Horses" episodes. As short stories "Fool About a Horse" and "Spotted Horses" are fairly straightforward and very funny tall tales of men being successfully and outrageously tricked in horse-trades.[22] The stories remain firmly within the tall tale convention, with no wider implications. When these episodes appear in the wider context of the novel, however, the characters who in the short stories are little more than conventional counters become fully known to us as individuals, as human beings capable of suffering. In these circumstances Faulkner deliberately adapts and manipulates the tall-tale convention so that while it does not control and delimit the action, as it does in the short stories, it remains as an ironic back-ground against which the events of the novel are played out, its restricted outlines providing an implicit contrast to the more fully realised characters and actions of the novel and at the same time offer-ing one possible way of viewing these events. In a sense it is another example of that multiple point of view which is fundamental to so much of Faulkner's work. The "Spotted Horses" episode as we have it in *The Hamlet* is a brilliant variation on the traditional horse-trade theme, but it also tells us a great deal about the economic and social relationships operating within the world of Frenchman's Bend and brings out with painful clarity the suffering implicit for the losers in a horse-trade and for their wives and families—something which lies wholly beyond the limits of the tall tale. The episode also places Flem Snopes among his fellows, the other traders of genius, but at the same time distinguishes him from them: he appears as absolutely predatory and unpitying in his treatment of Mrs. Armstid, he employs an agent, and we see that he never treads the same path twice, his victims being not merely fresh scalps as they would be for Pat Stamper, but further upward steps on the ladder leading to the banker's mansion in Jefferson.

The "Spotted Horses" and "Fool About a Horse" episodes thus fall into place in the total pattern of the novel as versions of the tall tale, itself an essential feature of the novel's mode, and as stages in the central narrative of the rise of Snopesism. They have an even more important function, however, as variations on the theme of greed, one of the two major themes running throughout the book. The other principal theme is that of love, and the parallel and often inter-reflecting investigations of love and greed, of men dominated by the desire for sexual or economic possession, are pursued in terms of various episodes of love and marriage, on the one hand, and of trading and barter on the other. The view that this thematic pattern provides the chief unifying factor in *The Hamlet* seems first to have been clearly

propounded by Robert Penn Warren,[23] and it is now so firmly
established that there is some danger of the novel's unity being
thought of as exclusively thematic. It is true that the linear progression of the novel is constantly interrupted and diversified by a series
of stories and episodes which are chiefly significant in terms of their
relationship to the central themes. But such apparent diversions all
possess strong narrative links with the main action, and in view of
the criticisms which have often been made of The Hamlet's "episodic"
structure it seems necessary to emphasise the strong element of
straightforward narrative continuity which runs throughout.

The theme which is the more closely tied to the narrative continuity
of the book is that of greed and self-interest, and it is perhaps worth
noting that it was this theme which seems to have dominated, almost
exclusively, the Snopes material which Faulkner wrote during the
early stages of his extended work on The Hamlet and its successors;
the counterpointed theme of love seems to have been added during
that final "pulling together" of The Hamlet in the late 1930's. In Book
One of the novel, "Flem," as we follow the rise of Flem Snopes to the
point where he is able to supplant Will Varner in his favourite flour-
barrel chair at the Old Frenchman place, it is the theme of greed which
predominates, although Book One also creates most of the characters
who are to play major roles later in the novel as well as many of the
situations through which Faulkner later develops the theme of love.
The shift of interest to this latter theme in Book Two is heralded by
its title, "Eula," but after the stories of the implacable passivity of
Eula and the passionate fury of Labove have been told, Faulkner skilfully involves them in the theme of self-interested greed and swings
the whole section into line with the central narrative by means of
Eula's marriage to Flem and Ratliff's vision of Flem taking over Hell.

Book Three, "The Long Summer," is taken up with the stories of Ike
Snopes, Houston, and Mink Snopes, each story merging smoothly into
its successor: Ike's beloved cow belongs at first to Houston, Houston
himself is murdered by Mink. These episodes relate primarily to the
theme of love, but the theme of greed irresistibly enters, generally
with tragic or ironic effects. It would be ridiculous to speak of Ike's
passion for the cow as being endorsed by Faulkner, but the heightened
language, the mythological allusions, and the sensitive evocation of
nature all work to persuade us at least of its absolute sincerity and
generosity; what finally appear as more grotesque and perverted than
Ike's own role are the attempts of his relatives to exploit his love and,
Ratliff suspects, to turn it to profit. The episode closes, however, with
a shift of mood entirely characteristic of this immensely diversified
novel, and we are given the almost unqualified humour of I.O.'s
successful trickery of Eck, who finds himself paying far more than
his fair share of the cost of buying the cow for slaughter and
so protecting the Snopes name:

"But I still dont see why I got to pay fifteen dollars, when all you got to pay is——?"

"Because you got four children. And you make five. And five times three is fifteen."

"I aint got but three yet," Eck said.

"Aint that just what I said? five times three? If that other one was already here, it would make four, and five times four is twenty dollars, and then I wouldn't have to pay anything."

"Except that somebody would owe Eck three dollars and twenty cents change," Ratliff said.

"What?" I.O. said. But he immediately turned back to his cousin or nephew. "And you got the meat and the hide," he said. "Cant you even try to keep from forgetting that?" (p. 234)[24]

Flem, absent throughout "The Long Summer," returns to Frenchman's Bend at the beginning of Book Four, "The Peasants"; his wife, Eula, has returned at the end of the previous book, bringing with her, Persephone-like, the end of that bitter winter "from which the people as they became older were to establish time and date events." (p. 296) The economic motif now again becomes dominant, first in the sale of the spotted Texas horses and finally in the defeat of Ratliff himself partly betrayed by cupidity, in the affair of the salted treasure hoard, and as Flem moves off on the last page we see that in linear terms *The Hamlet* can be simply and accurately described as the story of Flem's upward progress from near-rags to near-riches, from a dirt-farm to the ownership of a substantial bank-balance, a superbly handsome wife, and a half-share in a Jefferson restaurant. It is in the later novels of the trilogy that Faulkner completes what he must have recognised as being, among many other things, an ironic version of the American "success" myth.

Of the various episodes of the novel, it can be argued that the story of Labove is somewhat tenuously connected with the other events and characters; the others, however, are strongly bound to the central narrative line. All the episodes, including Labove's, are related in a multiplicity of ways both to the major themes of the novel and to each other. The various tales of barter and trading all throw light upon one another, and upon the whole economic and social situation of Frenchman's Bend at this particular moment in time. Similarly interrelated are the various marriages and love stories, and we can see that although the action of the novel tends to focus on the male world epitomised by the horse-swap, Faulkner also offers through his presentation of such characters as Ab's wife, Mink's wife, and Mrs. Armstid a series of comments on the role of women in this society, and especially on their capacity for sheer endurance. If we compare the short story, "The Hound," with the Mink Snopes portion of "The Long Summer," in which the same narrative material appears, we can see that although the short story is extremely powerful in its own right, the novel version has many additional qualities which it can accommodate simply because it is not a separate entity but a constituent part of a larger and intricately interrelated whole. The short story, for example, has no counterpart to the following passage in the novel:

> [Mink] watched the night emerge from the bottom and mount through the bitten corn, taking corn, taking the house itself at last and, still rising, become as two up-opening palms releasing the westward-flying ultimate bird of evening. Below him, beyond the corn, the fireflies winked and drifted against the breast of darkness; beyond, within it, the steady booming of the frogs was the steady pulse and beat of the dark heart of night, so that at last when the unvarying moment came—that moment as unvarying from one dusk to the next as the afternoon's instant when he would awake —the beat of that heart seemed to fall still too, emptying silence for the first deep cry of strong and invincible grief. He reached his hand backward and took up the gun. (p. 263)

In the limited framework of the short story such a passage would be wholly out of proportion. In the context of the novel, however, this description of the swamp lands near Mink's farm serves, at the simplest level, to extend a little further the overall description of the countryside around Frenchman's Bend, and, as such, it falls naturally into place in a larger pattern. But nature imagery is also being used here, as throughout the novel, to evoke and define the particular quality of the experiential moment and at the same time, as with a kind of visual rhetoric, to elevate moments and events to a higher, more general level of significance, and this is something of a quite different and more ambitious order. Throughout the novel Faulkner insists on the closeness to nature of the world of Frenchman's Bend, and his presentation of that world makes it possible for him to invoke nature imagery without any sense of arbitrariness or strain. This is especially, and most remarkably, true of the account of Ike Snopes's love for the cow, in which the rapturous evocation of the beauty and fecundity of nature is still further heightened by extravagant effects of rhetorical language and mythological allusion.

Stylistically, indeed, The Hamlet is one of Faulkner's greatest triumphs. Throughout the novel he exercises the utmost flexibility of style and language, ranging from direct and simple narrative to the colloquial vigour of Ratliff's telling of the "Barn Burning" and "Fool About a Horse" materials, to the baroque elevation of many of the passages describing Eula and, especially, Ike's idyll with the cow. Each episode is treated in a manner which brings out its individual quality but which also establishes its place in the structural and thematic patterns of the novel as a whole, and, where necessary, its relationship to more universal frames of reference : thus the mythological allusions in passages about Ike and Eula serve to suggest the degree to which their stories resemble those epitomisations of human experience embodied in ancient myth. This stylistic virtuosity is early established as an essential aspect of the novel's technique, and by the time Book Three has been reached it has clearly become irrelevant to wonder whether Mink himself, in the passage quoted, would have regarded the approach of darkness in quite this way. No more than in *As I Lay Dying* is Faulkner restricted to the vocabulary and manner of the characters whose attitudes and feelings he is describing : from the beginning of the novel he has established a mode which permits him to match rhetoric not so much to individuals as to emotional states and moments of crisis—of joy, agony, discovery, awareness of beauty—or, rather, to the significance of those states and moments in relation to the overall meaning of the novel.

That Faulkner is clearly aware of writing in a language foreign to his characters is evident from those moments when he skilfully plays off the richness of his formal language against the juxtaposed simplicity of colloquial speech. As Ratliff and his companions walk back to Mrs. Littlejohn's with Will Varner, who is to attend the injured Henry Armstid, we are given a description of the moonlit night :

> The moon was now high overhead, a pearled and mazy yawn in the soft sky, the ultimate ends of which rolled onward, whorl on whorl, beyond the pale stars and by pale stars surrounded. They walked in a close clump, tramping their shadows into the road's mild dust, blotting the shadows of the burgeoning trees which soared, trunk branch and twig against the pale sky, delicate and finely thinned. They passed the dark store. Then the pear tree came in sight. It rose in mazed and silver immobility like exploding snow; the mockingbird still sang in it. "Look at that tree," Varner said. "It ought to make this year, sho."
>
> "Corn'll make this year too," one said.
>
> "A moon like this is good for every growing thing outen earth," Varner said. (pp. 350-351)

Here the simple remark, "Corn'll make this year," stands in a mutually enriching relationship to the elevated description of the "burgeoning" life of the spring landscape seen by moonlight; the characters themselves are clearly incapable of speaking of nature in the terms which Faulkner employs, but by placing the countryman's ostensibly practical observation in the context of the description he suggests that the men, for all their simplicity, are not unaffected by the beauty of what they see.

In the larger context of the novel the passage just quoted is also closely related to Faulkner's presentation of Eula Varner, as her father continues his remarks on the fecundating properties of the moon with an account of how Mrs. Varner lay in the moonlight after Eula had been conceived in order to ensure that the child would be a girl. Throughout the novel Eula is associated with fertility and the forces of nature and evoked in terms of repeated allusions to the pagan deities, to Helen and Venus and Persephone, and her marriage with Flem Snopes, that forced and grotesque union of fecundity and sterility, provides *The Hamlet* with its most disturbing, most affronting, symbol. Labove, the schoolmaster, whose own love for Eula takes on almost the nature of demonic possession, forsees the marriage of this Venus, this supreme embodiment of fertility and the sexual principle, to some "crippled Vulcan . . . who would not possess her but merely own her by the single strength which power gave, the dead power of money, wealth, gewgaws, baubles, as he might own, not a picture, statue: a field, say." (p. 135) Flem is the eventual Vulcan to Eula's Venus, marrying her not from love or even desire but in exchange for a cheque and the deed to the Old Frenchman place. This coincidence of Labove's vision with subsequent narrative events serves to illustrate once again how constantly and how intricately the thematic materials of the novel interact and coalesce in terms of the narrative line: for what is significant in both the vision and its realisation is the way in which possession of Eula is linked with the ownership and exploitation of land, effecting a conjunction of the themes of love and greed and setting both against the background of the land, which with its history, and its permanence transcending history and all human concerns, constitutes one of Faulkner's major preoccupations throughout his work.

At one stage in the writing of *The Hamlet* Faulkner apparently intended to apply to the whole book the title, "The Peasants,"[25] which he eventually used for the fourth and final section. One of Balzac's novels is called *Les Paysans*, and *The Hamlet* itself opens in almost Balzacian fashion with a precise and detailed description of the historical, geographical, social, and economic setting of the novel's subsequent events. Later in the book this basic framework is extended outwards by additional descriptions of places nearby, as, for example, when Faulkner supplies vivid and often precisely detailed impressions of Mink Snopes's farm and the land round about, and of the countryside through which Ike walks with the cow. An extract will suggest the degree of Faulkner's concern, in this novel, with the historical forces, both natural and man-made, which have shaped the landscape, and especially with the sad results of man's exploitation :

A mile back he had left the rich, broad, flat river-bottom country and entered the hills—a region which topographically was the final blue and dying echo of the Appalachian mountains. Chickasaw Indians had owned it, but after the Indians it had been cleared where possible for cultivation, and after the Civil War, forgotten save by small peripatetic sawmills which had vanished too now, their sites marked only by the mounds of rotting sawdust which were not only their gravestones but the monuments of a people's heedless greed. Now it was a region of scrubby second-growth pine and oak among which dogwood bloomed until it too was cut to make cotton spindles, and old fields where not even a trace of furrow showed any more, gutted and gullied by forty years of rain and frost and heat into plateaus choked with rank sedge and briers loved of rabbits and quail coveys, and crumbling ravines striated red and white with alternate sand and clay. (p. 196)

But such passages do not stand isolated in the novel as mere historical footnotes loosely incorporated into the text. Faulkner is concerned to establish an image of a particular society in a particular place at a particular time; but the image is evoked primarily in terms of characters and their interaction, and the descriptive passages function also in terms of the human situation. The description of Mink's house, for instance, is important for its own sake, as an additional facet of the analytical portrait of the area, but it is also crucial to our understanding of Mink himself and of the reasons why he murders Houston. Thus there is obvious dramatic point in the utter poverty of the place being evoked through the eyes of Mink himself as he returns from the murder:

It was dusk. He emerged from the bottom and looked up the slope of his meagre and sorry corn and saw it—the paintless two-room cabin with an open hallway between and a lean-to kitchen, which was not his, on which he paid rent but not taxes, paying almost as much in rent in one year as the house had cost to build; not old, yet the roof of which already leaked and the weather-stripping had already begun to rot away from the wall planks and which was just like the one he had been born in which had not belonged to his father either, . . . (p. 251)

Later, when Mink goes to the Negro's cabin to find his axe, his poverty is re-emphasised in the concrete terms of a comparison with the economic position of a Negro whose cabin is "shabbier than his" but whose surrounding corn is "better than his." (p. 286) Later still, as Mink is being taken to the jail in Jefferson, his own background is implicitly evoked in terms of his awareness of "the long broad rich flatlands lush with the fine harvest" (p. 293) around Whiteleaf store and of the trim and prosperous world of Jefferson itself:

the surrey moving now beneath an ordered overarch of sunshot trees, between the clipped and tended lawns where children shrieked and played in bright small garments in the sunset and the ladies sat rocking in the fresh dresses of afternoon and the men coming home from work turned into the neat painted gates, toward plates of food and cups of coffee in the long beginning of twilight. (p. 295)

This is a world completely alien to Mink, as to the other inhabitants of Frenchman's Bend and its environs. The description at once extends, by contrast, the definition of these people's lives, and projects forward an image of the richer economic pastures to which Flem Snopes moves at the end of the novel. Nothing is wasted here. Instead of "clipped and tended lawns" the properties on which the poor whites like Mink, Ab Snopes, and Henry Armstid live have yards that are "weed-choked and grass-grown" and give an overall appearance of "cluttered desolation" (pp. 53-54); they have no "neat painted gates," for both Ab's and Mink's gates are broken and even their cabins paintless; their womenfolk wear "gray shapeless" (p. 331) garments, not "the fresh dresses of afternoon"; while their children, who are never presented as playing, have no "bright small garments" and are lucky, indeed, if they have a single pair of shoes between them.

In its sheer sociological richness *The Hamlet* recalls *Sartoris* rather than any other of Faulkner's earlier books, and it was *Sartoris* which first created in print many of the characters whose potentialities Faulkner here for the first time develops to the full. *The Hamlet* also demonstrates that sense of the slow inevitable procession of the seasons which provides an especially powerful undercurrent in *Sartoris*, but which figures to some degree in almost all of Faulkner's books from *The Marble Faun* and *Soldiers' Pay* onwards. The advance which *The Hamlet* marks over earlier novels, however, is in its wholly organic incorporation of themes and materials which had often appeared either sporadically, in set pieces, or in direct and usually ironic juxtaposition or counterpoint to the main action. One of the features of the novel which stays longest in the mind is the grouping, usually the pairing, of characters which emerges from Faulkner's thematic method. The opposition of Eula and Flem is one obvious example, but Flem's coldness and impotence is implicitly commented upon by Ike's yearning love for his cow, while the anti- or non-Snopesism of Ike is itself contrasted with the quintessential Snopesism of the other family idiot, St. Elmo. It is easy, too, to see intricate cross-references, particularly in view of Faulkner's early insistence on Eula's somewhat bovine placidity, between the Labove-Eula and Ike-cow situations. In a more direct confrontation, that between Houston and Mink Snopes, his murderer, we come to see that in large measure the very things they have in common—their fierce pride, their bitter isolation, their absolute capitulation to the women they marry—are those which most inflame their antagonism, although it should be added that Mink's principal motive for the murder seems to have been his fundamental anger at his ill-luck, especially in comparison with that of a relative like Flem or a neighbour like Houston. Even the greater attractiveness of Will Varner as compared with his son Jody—it is significant, in terms of the novel's particular scale of values, that Will Varner's sexual lustiness is not matched by his son—is also to some extent paralleled by the far greater condemnation which is reserved for Flem Snopes in comparison with his father. It has already been suggested that Faulkner may have abandoned "Barn Burning" as an opening chapter because of the extent to which it might generate undue sympathy for the Snopes family; even so, considerable sympathy for Ab's desperate economic plight is aroused in the present first chapter both by the version of the barn burning episode which Ratliff relates to Jody and by Jody's own mean calculations of how the maximum profit may be extorted from Ab's situation, while Ratliff's further recital of the Pat Stamper episode, in a version of the material first used in published form in the story, "Fool About a Horse," also evokes an Ab Snopes who is by no means a wholly unattractive figure, although Ratliff repeatedly stresses that these events date from a period before Ab "soured." (p. 30)

The most important paired opposition in the novel, and the one upon which the action as well as the morality of the book largely turns, is that between Flem and Ratliff. The whole pattern of Flem's action is set by the early episode in which Jody, as the result of his own greed and over-confidence, has put himself in the position of having to bribe Flem with a job in the store in return for a protection against Ab's barn-burning tendencies which Flem does not even promise to provide:

> Once more Varner expelled his breath through his nose. This time it was a sigh. "All right," he said. "Next week then. You'll give me that long, wont you? But you got to guarantee it." The other spat.
> "Guarantee what?" he said. (p. 27)

It is characteristic of Flem that he puts nothing into words, that the blackmail is never stated, only implied, and that he exchanges nothing of value in return for the position which is to give him his first foothold in Frenchman's Bend. Throughout the novel Flem's silence is scarcely broken: his longest speech consists of 25 words, and he speaks only 244 words in all, with a further 33 in the Hell scene created in Ratliff's imagination. For long portions of the novel he is out of sight. He is never long out of mind, however, and usually another Snopes is present to remind us of his influence. In the second chapter of "The Long Summer," for instance, Flem is represented by one of his chief henchmen, Lump Snopes, his successor as the clerk in Varner's store. In his attempts to get his hands on the money which Houston carried, and in his complete disregard for all considerations of loyalty, humanity, or simple decency, Lump offers a concrete exemplification of greed in action which is simply a crude outward manifestation of qualities embodied more subtly but not less firmly by Flem himself. Here, as elsewhere in the novel, Faulkner uses Lump to demonstrate quite clearly the evil which Snopesism represents without needing to compromise his consistent presentation of Flem himself as a silent tactician and master strategist. The account of the sale of the spotted Texas horses which occupied most of the first chapter of "The Peasants" again shows Flem operating through substitutes, himself a silent witness or—during most of the auction and the whole of the subsequent court hearings—actually absent. Lump acts as his representative on this occasion, but not even Lump, it seems, is present to lend comfort to Mink Snopes at his trial in the County Courthouse in Jefferson.

It is Ratliff, in a passage of bitter understatement, who links Mink's situation with that of Mrs. Armstid, the chief victim in the affair of the spotted horses. After describing the dreary round of Mrs. Armstid's life as she waits for her husband's leg to heal and for Flem Snopes to return the money paid for the horse, Ratliff continues:

> And after that, not nothing to do until morning except to stay close enough where Henry can call her until it's light enough to chop the wood to cook breakfast and then help Mrs Littlejohn wash the dishes and make the beds and sweep while watching the road. Because likely any time now Flem Snopes will get back from wherever he has been since the auction, which of course is to town naturally to see about his cousin that's got into a little legal trouble, and so get that five dollars. (p. 359)

This linking of the two people who are vainly waiting for Flem to rescue them reveals in miniature the pattern of the whole novel, its establishment of a composite picture of Flem, his activities, their effect, and their significance. The heavily ironic diminutive, "a little legal trouble," as a description of the brutal murder for which Mink is to be tried, precisely catches the note of Ratliff's strenuous efforts to maintain that detachment which at this point still distinguishes him from the other actual and potential victims of Flem's machinations.

The final accolade of Flem's success in *The Hamlet* is a comment spoken by an unidentified local inhabitant, representative in his anonymity of the whole world of Frenchman's Bend:

> "Couldn't no other man have done it. Anybody might have fooled

Henry Armstid. But couldn't nobody but Flem Snopes have fooled Ratliff." (p. 420)

It is characteristic of the ironies implicit in Faulkner's working out of the book's thematic patterns that it should be Ratliff, the chief and most redoubtable opponent of Snopesism, who sells Flem the share in the restaurant which gives him his first foothold in Jefferson, just as it should have been Jody, who had most to lose from his coming, who had supplied Flem with his original opening in Frenchman's Bend. Ratliff had clearly recognised Jody's folly in the opening chapter of the novel, and throughout the book he remains almost entirely uninvolved in the activities of Flem and his relations: there is no danger of his buying one of the spotted horses, and in his one direct exchange with Flem, over the contract for the goats and the signed notes he accepts from Mink, he emerges with a clear, though not unqualified, victory. He is thus presented as a worthy opponent of Flem, and it is this which makes his final downfall so triumphant a conclusion to Flem's career in Frenchman's Bend. At the same time, the fact that one of Ratliff's motives is greed, and the cause of his defeat his over-confidence in his own reading of the situation and in his own understanding of Flem's character, fits precisely into the overall pattern of greed and self-delusion established by Jody Varner at the beginning of the novel.

Ratliff was clearly a character whom Faulkner regarded as being especially important, both for what he did and for what he represented. In the early short stories in which the sewing-machine agent appears—in "Lizards in Jamshyd's Courtyard," for example, in which he is still called Suratt—he remains essentially the same loquacious, dialect-speaking character with the "shrewd plausible face" whom Faulkner first presented in Sartoris. In The Hamlet the dialect element in Ratliff's speech has been greatly reduced, and he himself is no longer simply an engaging teller of tall tales. In an interview in 1955 Faulkner named Dilsey and Ratliff as his favourite characters in his own work: "Ratliff is wonderful," he said. "He's done more things than any man I know."[26] In one of the discussions at Charlottesville in 1957 Faulkner developed his belief that man will prevail in terms of the human instinct to fight against Snopesism: "When the battle comes it always produces a Roland. It doesn't mean that they will get rid of Snopes or the impulse which produces Snopes, but always there's something in man that don't like Snopes and objects to Snopes and if necessary will step in to keep Snopes from doing some irreparable harm."[27]

That Faulkner saw Ratliff as occupying a central and representative position in the battle against Snopesism, itself a microcosm of mankind's determined struggle to prevail, is clear from The Hamlet itself. Both as a character and as a representative figure, however, Ratliff is more complex than has generally been realised. He is, in the first place, very similar to Flem in many ways. He is a trader, making his living by buying and selling, and he has done well: starting from exactly the same background as Flem himself—"My pap and Ab were both renting from Old Man Anse Holland then," (p. 34) says Ratliff of the "Fool About a Horse" episode—he has, while still a comparatively young man, gained a steady economic position, a house in Jefferson, and a half-share in a restaurant there. In so far as Ratliff and Flem are both traders, there is a natural economic rivalry between them; on the moral plane it is Ratliff's practised skill at Flem's economic game which gives him at once the confidence and the capacity to challenge Flem on his own ground. Although he seems voluble where Flem is silent, we are specifically told that Ratliff always did "a good deal more listening than anybody believed until afterward." (p. 15). He is also like Flem in being something of an outsider to the world of Frenchman's Bend, different from its inhabitants in a way of which they themselves are a little antagonistically aware: "I thought something was wrong all day," says one of them when Ratliff appears after the finish of the horse auction. "Ratliff wasn't there to give nobody advice." (p. 342)

Ratliff, as he appears in *The Hamlet*, is *in* the world of Frenchman's Bend but by no means entirely *of* it. His detachment is insisted on throughout, and like Flem, though for different reasons, he tends to be absent from the scene at crucial moments, and especially when the local farmers are being cheated of what little money they have. The reasons for Ratliff's apparent withdrawal are worth examining in some detail. His detachment from Frenchman's Bend must be related to his powers of inner detachment, his gift for viewing himself and his own actions with the disenchanted eye of reason. Nowhere does this gift appear more clearly than in the exchange with Mrs. Littlejohn in which Ratliff plainly acknowledges the puritanical streak in himself which is urging him to stop the exploitation of Ike's love for the cow, and then as firmly declares his determination to act nonetheless, not ignoring what self-knowledge has told him, but embracing that awareness as part of the personal price to be paid:

"I aint never disputed I'm a pharisee," he said. "You dont need to tell me he aint got nothing else. I know that. Or that I can sholy leave him have at least this much. I know that too. Or that besides, it aint any of my business. I know that too, just as I know that the reason I aint going to leave him have what he does have is simply because I am strong enough to keep him from it. I am stronger than him. Not righter. Not any better, maybe. But just stronger.

"How are you going to stop it?"

"I dont know. Maybe I even cant. Maybe I dont even want to.

Maybe all I want is just to have been righteouser, so I can tell myself I done the right thing and my conscience is clear now and at
least I can go to sleep tonight." (p. 227)

This intellectual quality of Ratliff's, which marks him off from the
inhabitants of Frenchman's Bend, is both his strength and his weakness. As a trader, making his living by barter, Ratliff must operate
within the established trading conventions as they are understood in
the world of Frenchman's Bend. But his intelligence and his humanity
will not allow him to remain blind to the implications of privation
and suffering which the processes of trade, especially in their quintessential form of the horse-swap, may often carry for the defeated, and
especially for their womenfolk. Ratliff is well aware of the traditional
limits of the code, and especially of its principles of respect for the
most skilful, of unconcern for the defeated, and, at all times, of non-
interference in other men's trading: "He done all he could to warn
me," thinks Ratliff of Bookwright early in the novel. "He went as far
and even further than a man can let his self go in another man's
trade." (p. 94) The crucial question for Ratliff is whether he shall go
outside the limits of the convention in order to try and combat
Snopesism.

The clearest statement of Ratliff's position comes in answer to Bookwright's query as to whether he gave Henry Armstid the five dollars
he lost to Flem in trading for one of the spotted horses:

"I could have," he said. "But I didn't. I might have if I could
just been sho he would buy something this time that would sho
enough kill him, like Mrs Littlejohn said. Besides, I wasn't protecting a Snopes from Snopeses; I wasn't even protecting a people
from a Snopes. I was protecting something that wasn't even
a people, that wasn't nothing but something that dont want
nothing but to walk and feel the sun and wouldn't know how to
hurt no man even if it would and wouldn't want to even if it could,
just like I wouldn't stand by and see you steal a meat-bone from a
dog. I never made them Snopeses and I never made the folks that
cant wait to bare their backsides to them. I could do more, but I
wont. I wont, I tell you!" (p. 367)

The final cry recalls the agony of Quentin Compson at the end
of Absalom, Absalom! when Shreve asks him why he hates the South:
"I dont. I dont! I dont hate it! I dont hate it!" (p. 378) Ratliff longs
for a continuation of the detachment he has practised, with only
minor deviations, up to this point: he has, it is true, pitted his wits
against Flem's over the matter of the goats, but this was a direct test
of skill in the game of barter, with nothing seriously at issue. He
knows that to intervene in "another man's trade," and especially to

enquire what that trading means for the man's dependents, for women like Mrs. Armstid, inevitably brings pain to a man of his intelligence and humanity. He knows, in short, that involvement hurts, and that in detachment lies not merely discretion but self-protection. Yet he knows, too, that he must take action, become involved, and his "I wont. I wont, I tell you!" evokes the agony of his dilemma. Ratliff's hesitation, his reluctance to act, is presented as the inevitable concomitant of his personal intelligence and self-awareness, and, hence, as essential to Faulkner's conception of him. Equally essential, of course, is the courage, the moral commitment, which Ratliff displays when he decides nevertheless—again, not ignoring but accepting without self-deception what self-knowledge tells him—to abandon detachment and actively challenge Flem in a bid to stop his progress by the infliction of a resounding economic defeat.

In the event, of course, it is Ratliff who is defeated—partly because of the impetuousness which overcomes him in his eagerness to act, partly because of his disabling unfamiliarity with the nature and magnitude of the operation on which he embarks, and partly, it seems, because he too has been self-betrayed by some measure of that greed and over-confidence which had earlier brought defeat to Jody Varner and to so many others who thought themselves smarter than Flem. Once Ratliff acts, abandoning his customary devices of self-protection and stepping outside the accustomed bounds of his trader's experience to do so, it becomes inevitable not only that he should be defeated by Flem, but that he should be defeated on a scale exceeding any of Flem's previous conquests. It is essential to realise, however, that Ratliff's economic defeat is not accompanied by any defeat in human terms. The strength of Ratliff appears in the very moment of his realisation of Flem's victory, as he lingers luxuriously over his break-fast before resuming the digging which he already knows to be fruitless—"We even got a new place to dig," (p. 412) he thinks, with a humour which is not destroyed by its own wryness—and, a little later, as he bets Bookwright that he himself will have in his sack the oldest of the coins by which they have both been deluded. Once again, it is this capacity for combining decency and moral solicitude with clear-eyed intellectual detachment which gives Ratliff the ability to survive defeat and to continue, not merely the struggle against Snopesism, but the perpetual affirmation of life. Ratliff's opposition to Flem Snopes is obviously of great importance, but still more important is what he represents in himself, irrespective of the particular demands of the anti-Snopes campaign. It is extremely significant that Ratliff should be able to challenge Flem at his own game, but it is even more significant that Ratliff should continually demonstrate his aptitude for another and finer game than Flem's and thus affirm the persistence, whatever triumphs Snopesism may achieve, of those qualities by which, Faulkner believed, man will ultimately prevail. As Faulkner wrote to Warren Beck in 1941 :

> I have been writing all the time about honor, truth, pity, considera-tion, the capacity to endure well grief and misfortune and injustice and then endure again, in terms of individuals who ob-served and adhered to them not for reward but for virtue's own sake, not even merely because they are admirable in themselves, but in order to live with oneself and die peacefully with oneself when the time comes. I don't mean that the devil will snatch every liar and rogue and hypocrite shrieking from his deathbed. I think liars and hypocrites and rogues die peacefully every day in the odor of what he calls sanctity. I'm not talking about him. I'm not writing for him. But I believe there are some, not necessarily many, who do and will continue to read Faulkner and say, "Yes. It's all right. I'd rather be Ratliff than Flem Snopes. And I'd still rather be Ratliff without any Snopes to measure by even."[28]

GO DOWN, MOSES

THE publication of Go Down, Moses in May 1942 appears in retrospect as a moment of culmination in Faulkner's career. It marked the end of that supremely creative period which had begun with the writing of The Sound and the Fury; it was followed by six years of virtual silence during which Faulkner published only four short stories, none of them among his best. These were not years of inactivity for Faulkner, since he spent a good deal of time in Hollywood and was largely engaged with the writing of A Fable, but they were years during which his reputation reached a low ebb, and from which he emerged, with the publication in 1948 of Intruder in the Dust, as apparently a different kind of novelist, much more ready to commit himself to specific statements on contemporary issues. But Go Down, Moses also represented a culmination in thematic terms, as the book in which Faulkner finally achieved the conjunction, and in some measure the fusion, of a number of apparently disparate ideas which had long occupied his imagination. The exploration of the history and society of his own region had been one of Faulkner's major concerns in books like Sartoris, Light in August, Absalom, Absalom! and The Unvanquished, and in the last three of these he had in different degrees engaged the problem of white-Negro relationships. The Hamlet, foreshadowed in this respect by Sartoris and other early works, had revealed Faulkner's deep and almost religious sense of the permanence and richness of the land and his preoccupation with the problem of its ownership, while a number of short stories, from "Red Leaves" (1930) onwards, had demonstrated his fascination with the wilderness and with the narrative and symbolic potentialities of the hunt.

It is not altogether clear in what way or at what moment Faulkner first clearly recognised the possibility of treating these ideas in terms of a single work, a single novelistic structure, but the conception must in some way have involved the realisation that he would need a central character whose combination of sensitivity and long life would afford scope for the two complementary strategies of innocent childhood and retrospective old age, and that he would also need to create a new family, or greatly extend an existing one, in order to provide sufficient genealogical complications to allow a full exploitation of the white-Negro theme. His answers to these needs were Isaac (Ike) McCaslin and the numerous other members, black and white, of the McCaslin family; and the fact that there exists a McCaslin family tree, drawn by Faulkner himself, is perhaps suggestive of the degree to which the family was created for a specific purpose, not evolved slowly from Faulkner's original conception of the world of Yoknapatawpha County.[1]

Because its crucial importance as an expression of Faulkner's ideas has been generally recognised, Go Down, Moses has attracted an unusual amount of critical attention. More often than not, however, this attention has been focused not on the book itself, but on "The Bear," a single segment of the whole. Again and again the five sections of "The Bear" as it appears in Go Down, Moses have been reprinted, anthologised, and discussed as if they constituted an independent entity, capable of being considered in isolation from the context of the whole book. The story, "The Bear," which appeared in the Saturday Evening Post a few days before the publication of the book, obviously possesses independent existence, as does the earlier story "Lion," from which "The Bear" must be considered to have grown, but Faulkner himself several times made it plain that he considered Go Down, Moses to be a novel, and that the five-section version of "The Bear" was essentially "part of the novel, just as a chapter in the novel," to be neither printed nor discussed out of that context:

> That story was part of a novel. It was—the pursuit of the bear was simply what you might call a dangling clause in the description of that man when he was a young boy. When it was taken from the book and printed as a short story, the publisher, who is very considerate, has a great respect for all work and for mine in particular, he would not have altered one word of that without asking me, and he didn't ask me. If he had told me he was going to print it separately, I would have said, Take this [i.e., section four] out, this doesn't belong in this as a short story, it's a part of the novel but not part of the story. But rather than to go ahead and do that without asking me—and I wasn't available at that time—he printed it as it was. It [section four] doesn't belong with the short story. The way to read that is to skip that when you come to it.[2]

Many critics intent on interpreting "The Bear" have nevertheless persisted in the assumption that Go Down, Moses is simply a collection of short stories, lacking even the narrative consistency of The Unvanquished, and apparent support for this position might be derived from the fact that in the first printing of the first edition (May 1942) the book was entitled Go Down, Moses and Other Stories. Although the English edition still retains this title, the last three words were removed from later printings of the first American edition and from the Modern Library issue (from the plates of the first edition) of 1955.

The alteration was made at Faulkner's request,[3] and there are grounds for believing that the original title may not have been entirely of his own choosing. Some light is thrown on the problem by the typescript setting copy of Go Down, Moses, now in the Alderman Library, from which it is clear that the fly-titles for the various chapters were not only inserted after the original preparation of the typescript but written and inserted not by Faulkner but by one of his editors. The title page itself is in a hand other than Faulkner's and it seems that the so-called "chapters" of "The Fire and the Hearth" were also an editorial innovation: Faulkner had distinguished them by Roman numerals with sub-divisions headed by Arabic numerals, and it was an editorial hand which altered the I, II, and III to Chapter One, Chapter Two, and Chapter Three. It is possible, of course, that the editor was acting on Faulkner's instructions, but some evidence to the contrary is provided by a copy of an unsigned letter from Random House which is now among Faulkner's papers at Charlottesville. Dated January 10, 1949, it mentions plans for re-issuing Go Down, Moses, recalls that Faulkner had emphasised in conversation the fact that he considered it a novel rather than a group of stories, and asks whether, when the book was re-issued, he would like to insert chapter numbers in addition to the titles of the individual sections. That Faulkner did not accept this suggestion may have been due in part to his familiar reluctance to return to work which was behind him, preferring always to move forward with the work he had in hand or in prospect; but he may also have recognised the force of the observation, also made in the letter, that it might be a mistake to eliminate the section titles altogether because of the way in which they had become accepted as part of the text.[4]

To establish that Faulkner thought of Go Down, Moses as a novel is not, of course, to resolve the critical problem of whether the book is a novel, whether it possesses the organic unity we are accustomed to require of the books we agree to call novels. The fact that the volume consists largely of apparently separable units, and that versions of several of these had previously been published in the form of short stories, undoubtedly encourages the assumption that it is simply a short story collection or, at most, a sequence of related short stories. And some of the shifts in period, setting, theme, and personnel which occur in the course of the book may seem disturbing at a first reading: for example, the abrupt transition between the end of "Pantaloon in Black" and the beginning of "The Old People," the first of the hunting stories; the gulf dividing the grotesquely comic presentation of Miss Sophonsiba in "Was" from our subsequent realisation that she is Ike McCaslin's mother; the apparent inconsistency between the characterisation of Roth Edmonds in "Delta Autumn" and in "The Fire and the Hearth"; and, again in "The Fire and the Hearth," the placing of the crucial confrontation between

Lucas Beauchamp and Zack Edmonds, Roth's father, within a context of primarily comic incident.

Difficulties of this kind tend to disappear with a closer reading. The introduction of the hunting episodes at the beginning of "The Old People" has already been ironically foreshadowed in "Was" by the pursuit of old Carothers McCaslin's Negro son, Tomey's Turl, by his white half-brother, Buck McCaslin, and this episode, together with the whole theme of white-Negro relationships, is further called to mind in "The Old People," as in "The Bear," by the presence of Tennie's Jim, child of Tomey's Turl and Tennie Beauchamp, brother of Lucas and Fonsiba, grandfather of the girl in "Delta Autumn," himself a concrete embodiment of the McCaslin miscegenation. One of the important factors in Ike's upbringing is precisely his remoteness from his parents and the degree to which he is consequently "many-fathered" by his cousin McCaslin (Cass) Edmonds and by Sam Fathers, as well as by that real father, Theophilus (Buck) McCaslin, whom he had never known. In "Delta Autumn" it is the very uneasiness of Roth Edmonds, the savageness of a man whom we have previously seen as quick-tempered but essentially well-meaning, which points to the guilt from which he is suffering, while the presentation of Lucas in his relationship with Roth Edmonds in the comic episodes of "The Fire and the Hearth" does help to establish the pride and independence of Lucas's character, and this relationship, dominated by the fact that Lucas is a McCaslin and by the outcome of Lucas's fight with Zack many years previously, has important implications for Roth's own attitudes and actions.

Throughout *Go Down, Moses*, indeed, the various narrative strands are rarely treated in isolation, and there are few characters who are not related in some way to more than one of the major themes. The chief and most obvious themes are those which centre upon white-Negro relationships and upon the destruction of the wilderness. It is primarily in terms of the former that the episode entitled "Pantaloon in Black" is satisfactorily integrated into the novel, despite its lack of narrative links with other chapters: indeed, Faulkner's refusal to make the few minor changes in names and relationships which would have made Rider a McCaslin has the effect not of isolating the episode in which Rider is the major character but actually of expanding, beyond the limits of the single McCaslin family, the whole scope and relevance of the book. Related to these major themes, however, are a number of minor ones, of which the most fundamental is that of love. In the hunting episodes the love is mainly that of the man for the beast he hunts and kills, and for the animal which assists and accompanies him in the hunt: Faulkner insists repeatedly, for example, on the utter selflessness of Boon's love for Lion. Elsewhere in the novel the theme is explored partly in terms of the brotherly love between successive generations of white and

Negro children, especially between Lucas and Zack and between their sons, Henry and Roth, but primarily through the presentation of a series of marriages. In "Pantaloon in Black," Rider's agony at the death of his wife is immediately contrasted with the meaninglessness of the deputy's marriage, making it plain that the deputy's incomprehension of Rider's actions springs in part from his utter unfamiliarity with the kind of love which Rider had known. But these marriages connect thematically with others in the novel, principally with that of Lucas and Molly, a union sustained over long years by loyalty and by love and itself contrasted with the marriage of Ike McCaslin, a union begun in love and passion but allowed to founder on a question of principle. The materialism of Ike's wife, her greed for possession of the plantation, is the root cause of the failure of their marriage, but Ike's refusal to compromise in this matter contrasts unfavourably with Lucas's decision to abandon the search for gold when his activities provoke Molly to seek a divorce. In this as in so many other ways the opposition between Ike and Lucas, who are first cousins, supplies a focus for the whole pattern and meaning of the book.

A number of symbols also run through the novel, and several of these are especially associated with Ike: the hunt, General Compson's hunting horn, the tainted legacy, the commissary books, with their record of "the slow outward trickle of food and supplies and equipment which returned each fall as cotton made and ginned and sold (two threads frail as truth and impalpable as equators yet cable-strong to bind for life them who made the cotton to the land their sweat fell on)." (pp. 255-256) It is, however, through Lucas and the account of his marriage that one of the novel's most positive symbols, that of the fire on the hearth, is first established. When Lucas marries Molly he lights a fire "which was to burn on the hearth until neither he nor Molly were left to feed it," (p. 47) and it is by this fire that he sits alone during the months which Molly spends in Zack Edmonds's house. At the very depth of his despair Lucas suddenly catches himself standing over the fire, "furious, bursting, blind, the cedar water bucket already poised until he caught himself and set the bucket back on the shelf, still shaking, unable to remember taking the bucket up even." (p. 47) The crisis of Lucas's fears is here expressed in concrete terms, and the fact that he stops short of extinguishing the fire is a clear indication that he does not intend passively to accept the destruction of his marriage. The symbol recurs in "Pantaloon in Black," where there is a specific reference to the fire which Lucas Beauchamp had lit on his wedding night, and it is hinted at in the final chapter, "Go Down, Moses," when Gavin Stevens goes to Miss Worsham's house and finds Molly grieving for her grandson "beside the hearth on which even tonight a few ashes smoldered faintly." (p. 379) Molly's concern for a murderer's burial may have its comic side, but it is another aspect of that intensity and longevity of family loyalty and love in which the Negroes of the novel show themselves to be so much the superiors of their white relatives and neighbours. And it is, in part, this contrast between the two races which brings to bear such a weight of anguish and bitter irony upon the moment when Roth's Negro mistress speaks to Ike the terrible words which underline more clearly than anything else the ultimate failure of his life and his endeavour: " 'Old man,' she said, 'have you lived so long and forgotten so much that you dont remember anything you ever knew or felt or even heard about love?' " (p. 363)

Ike's failure as a man is in question here, not simply his failure as a white man, but it is with this encounter between Ike and the granddaughter of Tennie's Jim that Faulkner gives the final twist to that tragic interrelationship between the white and Negro branches of the McCaslin family which he deploys as the chief vehicle for his exploration of the racial theme. The revelation of the nature and full extent of this interrelationship has been delayed until the fourth section of "The Bear," that portion of the novel which not only contains, in the discussion between Ike and Cass, the most extended account of Ike's reasons for repudiating his inheritance, but which also displays, in Ike's recollections of his inspection of the commissary books, what Malcolm Cowley rightly seizes upon as an extreme instance of Faulkner's exhaustive exploration of a moment of time held suspended within a single extended sentence.[5] Undoubtedly the fourth section of "The Bear" is a *locus classicus* for an understanding of Faulkner's views on man and society, but the fact that these views have been given such widely divergent interpretations by different critics seems to be due not only to the inherent difficulty of the ideas themselves and of the language in which they are expressed but to the frequency with which "The Bear," in its five-section version, has been printed and discussed in isolation from the rest of the novel.

Even when critics have offered to consider *Go Down, Moses* as a whole their fascination with "The Bear" has often led them to ignore or underestimate the extent to which a proper understanding of that chapter depends upon its being read in the context not only of the other hunting episodes but of the novel as a whole. A recent critic who seizes on several important aspects of the book—notably, its enactment of successive variations on the concepts of freedom and bondage—nevertheless allows his interpretation of the discussion in the fourth section of "The Bear" to lead him into an obvious misreading of the conclusion of "The Old People," where, he says, Cass refuses to believe Ike's account of the encounter with the buck:

He dismisses the incident as merely a buck-fever hallucination on Isaac's part. But the reader, given no previous or subsequent hints which cast doubt on the actuality of that salute, is inclined to feel

that Cass is thus represented as becoming more and more blinded
by and enslaved to practical matters, even while Isaac is becoming
liberated from the merely practical, by Sam Fathers.[6]

Such an interpretation seems not to take into account the chapter's
final paragraphs:

> "But I saw it!" the boy cried. "I saw him!"
> "Steady," McCaslin said. For an instant his hand touched the
> boy's flank beneath the covers. "Steady. I know you did. So did I.
> Sam took me in there once after I killed my first deer." (p. 187)

The point about the argument between Cass and Ike is precisely that
they are so alike in so many ways, virtually two sides of the same
Southern coin. The closeness of Ike's personal relationship to Cass—
"rather his brother than cousin and rather his father than either"
(p. 4)—is insisted upon at the very beginning of the book, and reiterated on many subsequent occasions. Cass, Sam Fathers, and the
wilderness itself are the main sources of Ike's education, and Cass, as
the conclusion of "The Old People" makes clear, has himself, in his
earlier day, learned from Sam Fathers and from the woods. It was Cass
who interpreted for Ike the reasons why he had refrained from killing
Old Ben, concluding with the words which are of central significance
for an understanding of the whole novel:

> 'Courage and honor and pride, and pity and love of justice and of
> liberty. They all touch the heart, and what the heart holds to
> becomes truth, as far as we know truth. Do you see now?' (p. 297)

The extent to which Ike accepts Cass's views appears during the
conversation in the commissary, when he repeats, almost word for
word, several of Cass's earlier statements about the nature of truth,
and indeed their discussion is for the most part not so much an argument as a joint exploration of possible approaches to certain crucial
issues which face them both as Southerners, as landowners, and as
heirs of old Carothers McCaslin.

It is of the utmost importance, here as throughout Faulkner's
work, not to regard any single character as a mouthpiece for the
author's own views: Faulkner never expresses himself directly in this
way but only in terms of a book's total pattern. Thus Cass is
not present simply as a foil to Ike; his position is no less firmly based
than Ike's and in certain ways it is he who gets the better of the discussion. Ike's emphasis throughout is on "pity and love of justice
and of liberty," his attempt is to expiate through repudiation of his
inheritance the sins of his grandfather, old Carothers McCaslin, and
of the whole history of the South. Cass, while not denying the exist-

ence or importance of the qualities on which Ike insists, nevertheless lays greater stress on "Courage and honor and pride," qualities which also "touch the heart" and hence constitute some part of "truth." There is dignity in Ike's position, but it clearly represents a withdrawal from the realities and the difficulties of life not unlike that displayed by Horace Benbow and Quentin Compson. It is a position grounded in pathetic compromise—the monthly pension which Ike accepts from Cass as a "loan"—and involving, in Ike's relationship with his wife, an insistence on principle which ultimately emerges as sterile and life-denying, somewhat in the manner of Charlotte Rittenmeyer's inflexible demand for an abortion in *The Wild Palms*.

A certain toughness and hard-headedness is essential to Cass's whole nature, and he is not always an attractive character, but his determination to run the plantation, to eschew what he regards as the luxury of repudiation, is rooted in reality and in life in a way that Ike's solution is not. When Ike declares himself to be "free," Cass retorts that the Southern white man will never be free of the Negro, nor the Negro of the Southern white man, and goes on to assert that he himself could never take any other position: "Even you can see that I could do no else. I am what I am; I will be always what I was born and have always been. And more than me." (pp. 299-300) The conversation ends with the two positions unreconciled but neatly in balance: Ike has idealism on his side, but by his act of repudiation, of withdrawal, he disqualifies himself from making any effective contribution to the developing historical situation, so that even Roth Edmonds, whom Ike so bitterly condemns in "Delta Autumn," has previously won at least some measure of our sympathy by his unimaginative but not insincere or inhumane attempts to cope with the difficult practical situations presented to him as the present owner of the McCaslin plantation in "The Fire and the Hearth"—situations such as Ike himself has never been called upon to confront.

There is a revealing interchange in an interview which Faulkner gave in 1955. Having learned from the interviewer that Isaac McCaslin was her favourite among his characters, Faulkner asked her why she admired him:

> INT: Because he underwent the baptism in the forest, because he rejected his inheritance.
> WF: And do you think it's a good thing for a man to reject an inheritance?
> INT: Yes, in McCaslin's case, he wanted to reject a tainted inheritance. You don't think it's a good thing for him to have done so?
> WF: Well, I think a man ought to do more than just repudiate. He should have been more affirmative instead of shunning people.[7]

Ike's life is a failure, primarily because he allows himself to rest in negation, in repudiation, and rejects all opportunities for affirmation. And so the fourth section of "The Bear" draws to a close with the comic story of Hubert Beauchamp's "legacy"—an ironic counterpoint to Ike's rejection of his McCaslin inheritance—and with the details of Ike's compromise over the loan and of the agony and waste of his relationship with his wife.

Yet this is not in the least to deny Ike's essential goodness, nor the quality of his idealism. "Sam Fathers set me free," (p. 300) Ike declares at the end of his long debate with Cass, and the invocation of Sam's name at this crucial point reminds us that the context of this section, which is almost entirely concerned with slavery and miscegenation and McCaslin family history, is an account of the hunting of an old bear and of the gradual disappearance of the wilderness in which he lived. Ike's experience as a hunter has played a vital part in his education, in the process of his becoming the man capable of renouncing his inheritance. In the other sections of "The Bear," Ike's skill as a woodsman and hunter is repeatedly insisted upon, and it is also made plain that he has learned thoroughly all that Sam Fathers has had to teach him about the proper rituals of the hunt, about loving and respecting the creatures who are pursued and killed. Faulkner's most direct attempt to link Ike's experience in the wilderness with his repudiation of the plantation occurs in "Delta Autumn," as Ike, an old man, lies in his tent and recalls his past life, beginning with the moment (recorded in "The Old People") when he shot his first buck:

Old Sam Fathers was alive then, born in slavery, son of a Negro slave and a Chickasaw chief, who had taught him how to shoot, not only when to shoot but when not to; such a November dawn as tomorrow would be and the old man led him straight to the great cypress and he had known the buck would pass exactly there because there was something running in Sam Fathers' veins which ran in the veins of the buck too, and they stood there against the tremendous trunk, the old man of seventy and the boy of twelve, and there was nothing save the dawn until suddenly the buck was there, smoke-colored out of nothing, magnificent with speed: and Sam Fathers said, 'Now. Shoot quick and shoot slow:' and the gun levelled rapidly without haste and crashed and he walked to the buck lying still intact and still in the shape of that magnificent speed and bled it with Sam's knife and Sam dipped his hands into the hot blood and marked his face forever while he stood trying not to tremble, humbly and with pride too though the boy of twelve had been unable to phrase it then: *I slew you; my bearing must not shame your quitting life. My conduct forever onward must become your death*; marking him for that and for more than that: that day and himself and McCaslin juxtaposed not against the wilderness but against the tamed land, the old wrong and shame itself, in repudiation and denial at least of the land and the wrong and shame even if he couldn't cure the wrong and eradicate the shame, who at fourteen when he learned of it had believed he could do both when he became competent and when at twenty-one he became competent he knew that he could do neither but at least he could repudiate the wrong and shame, at least in principle, and at least the land itself in fact, for his son at least: and did, thought he had: then (married then) in a rented cubicle in a back-street stock-traders' boarding-house, the first and last time he ever saw her naked body, himself and his wife juxtaposed in their turn against that same land, that same wrong and shame from whose regret and grief he would at least save and free his son, and saving and freeing his son, lost him. (pp. 350-351)

If Ike has achieved any kind of freedom, it is only that of loss itself; at best, it is the quasi-freedom of withdrawal and escape, such as Cass had accused him of seeking and such as Sam Fathers himself would surely not have approved. In *Go Down, Moses* the linking of the wilderness material with the themes of white-Negro relationships and of the ownership of the land is sometimes thought to be rather forced; but the tenuousness of the connection between the hunting episodes and the rest of the novel may be in some measure a direct and deliberate reflection of Faulkner's conception of Ike and of Ike's idealism. There seem to be some grounds for arguing that Ike's attempt to carry over into the practical workaday world the lessons Sam Fathers taught him in the wilderness was bound to fail, that the values he had learned from Sam Fathers, though fine in themselves, were already outmoded, and became steadily more obsolescent with the passing of the years. Certainly Ike's declaration that Sam Fathers had set him free has a hollow ring in the context of other examinations of the meaning of "freedom"[8] which Faulkner offers in the fourth section of "The Bear": the other character who declares herself to be free is Fonsiba, hopelessly enslaved though she is by appalling poverty and by the delusions of her husband, and we come to see, though Ike does not, that the husband himself, reading with his lensless spectacles and relying on his pension cheque while his farm stagnates, is not so many steps removed from Ike himself.

Although it is obviously an over-simplification, there is a sense in which it is true of Ike that what he *says* is right, but what he *does* is wrong. Nowhere is this distinction more valid than in "Delta Autumn," the one chapter of the novel in which the various themes merge and fuse not solely in terms of argument but also, and with profoundly moving effect, in terms of action, situation, and naturally invoked symbol. Roth's killing of the doe at the end of the chapter offers a wholly satisfying image of the white-Negro theme in the terms of the wilderness and hunting themes, and suggests at the same time that Ike has failed to pass on to younger men even the practical training he received from Sam Fathers. But the point at which all the threads of the novel seem to cross, at which the whole pattern of the book emerges with final and absolute clarity, is that of Ike's encounter with Roth's mistress. At the moment when we see the completion of the terrible circle initiated by old Carothers McCaslin—"the gnarled, bloodless, bone-light bone-dry old man's fingers touching for a second the smooth young flesh where the strong old blood ran after its long lost journey back to home" (p. 362)—we realise that not even Ike himself has succeeded in breaking out of that circle. For all his fine statements about love earlier in the chapter, Ike fails to recognise it in the young Negress. For all his admiration for the Negro, his hatred of his grandfather's sin, his repudiation of his inheritance, Ike at this moment of confrontation can only muster the traditional reactions: in effect he ratifies the solution offered by Roth Edmonds, the man he has affected to despise, by passing on the money to the girl; he can suggest no course of action other than her going North with the child and marrying "a black man . . . who would ask nothing of you and expect less and get even still less than that, if it's revenge you want." (p. 363) Ike's use of the word "revenge" indicates his own failure to recognise the strength and quality of the girl's love and points to the dignity of the Negro refusal to take revenge. It also shows a kind of muddled thinking on his part, since it should presumably be on a white man that she would seek revenge, and this confusion in its turn perhaps reveals the degree to which Ike is still trapped within traditional patterns of thought: he apparently sees revenge as a gesture against the world in general, and, in effect, he recommends the girl to hurt someone who is racially her inferior (Ike says, "a black man," and we already know that the girl is almost white) as a means of making good the hurt she has received from someone racially, and socially, her superior.

In the light of Ike's advice to the girl to go North, his presentation to the child of General Compson's hunting horn, a symbol of the wilderness and its values, becomes an almost meaningless gesture, while in the book's final chapter, "Go Down, Moses," the point is underlined that going North, with its consequent deracination, is unlikely to provide a satisfactory solution to any Negro's problems. From "Go Down, Moses" it appears that Ike's advice to the girl represents a further ratification of action previously taken by Roth, since Roth had first been responsible for sending Lucas and Molly's grandson away: "Roth Edmonds sold my Benjamin," Molly cries. (p. 380) The last chapter thus has its thematic function in relation to the whole work; it also has a structural importance, as a kind of epilogue, functionally linked with the somewhat detached prologue provided by "Was" and with the similarly detached yet immensely powerful central episode of "Pantaloon in Black." Gavin Stevens in "Go Down, Moses" occupies a role as uncomprehending outsider to the Negro way of life, thought, and feeling which is somewhat similar to that occupied by the deputy in "Pantaloon in Black". Stevens, unlike the deputy, is sympathetic, within his limits as a white man, and he is certainly well-meaning: indeed, he appears in a better light than Ike McCaslin, for all of Ike's advantages, at least to the extent that he takes positive action to help one particular Negro. At the same time, he completely fails to understand, or seriously to affect, either the situation or old Molly herself: "I wants hit all in de paper. All of hit," (p. 383) she insists, and nowhere in the whole of Faulkner's work is there a more persuasive dramatisation of the gulf dividing the white man's mind from the Negro's than the scene in which Stevens, confronted by Molly's grief, flees from the house in a kind of terror. In all this Stevens compares unfavourably with Cass, the man who had been fully committed to the practical situation, and the last words of the book seem to suggest that Stevens would have been better advised to confine himself to the job which he is paid, and presumably competent, to perform: " 'Come on,' he said. 'Let's get back to town. I haven't seen my desk in two days.' " (p. 383)

Considered in abstract terms, the two major themes of white-Negro relationships and of the destruction of the wilderness are inextricably linked: the wilderness disappears to make way for a system based on physical or economic slavery, and Ike's education in the wilderness fosters a sense of values which prompts him to a repudiation of that system and of the concept of land-ownership upon which it is based. Faulkner's expression of this dialectic is far richer than such an abstraction would suggest; in part this is because Ike's actions and assumptions are questioned and explored, not simply endorsed, because the technical scope of the book permits of great variety in the selection and presentation of characters and episodes, and because the novel possesses, despite its disrupted chronology, a firm underlying framework of historical continuity. One of the chief functions of "Was" is to supply historical perspective in terms of a superbly imagined vignette of a certain stratum of Mississippi society in the year 1859, while in subsequent chapters, and above all through the evocative device of the commissary books in the fourth section of "The Bear," Faulkner builds up—obliquely, by implication and slow accretion of detail, rather than by direct statement—a rich contextual presentation of a land and a society undergoing a process of slow but inevitable change. Faulkner spoke of his attitude towards this process in answer to a questioner at the University of Virginia:

> What the writer's asking is compassion, understanding, that change must alter, must happen, and change is going to alter what was. That no matter how fine anything seems, it can't endure, because once it stops, abandons motion, it is dead. It's to have compassion

for the anguish that the wilderness itself may have felt by being ruthlessly destroyed by axes, by men who simply wanted to make that earth grow something they could sell for a profit, which brought into it a condition based on an evil like human bondage. It's not to choose sides at all—just to compassionate the good splendid things which change must destroy, the splendid fine things which are part of man's past too, part of man's heritage too, but they were obsolete and had to go. But that's no need to not feel compassion for them simply because they were obsolete.[9]

This combination of regret for a vanishing past with a clear recognition of the necessity for change is a fundamental source of that internal tension and conflict which characterises the whole of Go Down, Moses, and which is reflected most obviously in the structure of the novel and in its constant interplay of comic and tragic elements.

The strength and vitality which Go Down, Moses derives from this interplay, and from the broad range of scene, action and character which the structure of the book permits, emerge with particular clarity in terms of a comparison with Big Woods (1955), a skilfully compiled anthology of hunting material from Go Down, Moses and elsewhere. "The Bear" reappears (without the fourth section), as do "The Old People" and a revised fragment of "Delta Autumn"; also included are "A Bear Hunt" and parts of "Red Leaves," "A Justice," and "Mississippi," the article which first appeared in Holiday magazine; but the only story to be collected for the first time is "Race at Morning," first published in the Saturday Evening Post earlier in 1955. Faulkner achieves in Big Woods an effective unity of scene, subject, and theme, but the book's singleness of mood, the consistency with which it sustains the elegaic note, tends to limit our sense of its engagement and breadth of relevance. The handsome format of the book and the Edward Shenton drawings with which it is decorated serve to emphasise that Faulkner did not intend it to be anything other than a celebration of the wilderness and a lament for its disappearance. At the same time, we can see how the isolation of the wilderness material in Big Woods, its separation from the tragic implications of the white-Negro theme, produces a dilution of both intensity and significance at crucial moments of the action (when Roth Edmonds shoots the doe in the final episode, for example), and we thus gain a fuller appreciation of the way in which the linking and merging of the racial and wilderness themes in Go Down, Moses help to make it one of the most dynamic of Faulkner's novels.

Go Down, Moses, indeed, is dramatic and swift-moving even in sections concerned with argument and the evolution of philosophical positions. In the fourth section of "The Bear" Faulkner achieves this effect through his characteristic device of dialogue, working out in terms of a conflict between two people the various facets of what is in fact one man's problem. This is a technique which Faulkner had used in the Quentin section of *The Sound and the Fury*, externalising Quentin's dilemmas in terms of remembered or imaginary dialogues, and, with remarkable success, in the Quentin-Shreve interchange of *Absalom, Absalom!*: it is a marvellously flexible device, allowing him to dramatise even the processes of ratiocination, to manipulate time sequences, withold information until the moment when its revelation will have the greatest impact, and, in sum, to extort narrative excitement from the most recalcitrant material. The sheer pace of *Go Down, Moses* is also enhanced by the sharp contrasts between succeeding chapters, and this too can be seen not as an innovation but as a culmination of techniques developed over several years and in a number of different novels. Juxtaposition, often of an abrupt and sharply ironical kind, had always been a favourite device of Faulkner's, from *Soldiers' Pay* onwards. In some of his major novels—*The Sound and the Fury*, *As I Lay Dying*, *Light in August*, and, most obviously, *The Wild Palms*—it becomes one of the basic organising principles. For Faulkner, as we have seen, the problem of organisation is primarily one of the disposition of large blocks of material, and it would be unwise to assume that the apparently episodic structure of *Go Down, Moses* is the result or reflection of any lack, on Faulkner's part, either of interest or of effort: it is more fruitful to see that structure as a logical step in his persistent effort to hold in suspension a single moment of experience, action, or decision and to explore the full complexity of that moment by considering, in particular, its total context of past, present and future, and its emergence as the often paradoxical product of many contrasted forces and pressures.

INTRUDER IN THE DUST

Intruder in the Dust, published in September 1948, was the first book of Faulkner's to appear since *Go Down, Moses*, more than six years previously. But the contract for *Intruder* had been signed as early as May 1940,[1] while Faulkner was working on *Go Down, Moses*, and there is a strong sense of continuity between the two books: both are largely concerned with the problem of white-Negro relationships; both have Lucas Beauchamp as a major character; and the final chapter of *Go Down, Moses* seems directly to anticipate the principal emphases and even something of the action of the later novel, with the figure of Gavin Stevens serving as an active and thematic link between the two. Stevens plays a larger role in *Intruder in the Dust*, however, and the prevalence of his voice in the final sections has done more than anything else to prompt discussion of the novel—on its first appearance, and often since—as a work of propaganda, a deliberate contribution to the contemporary debate on civil rights.

It seems unlikely, for reasons we shall consider, that this was Faulkner's primary intention. At the same time, such early reviews as those of Edmund Wilson and Elizabeth Hardwick[2] cannot be judged entirely irrelevant. To a degree never approached in Faulkner's earlier work, and only to be exceeded in *Requiem for a Nun* and *A Fable*, there are grounds for considering *Intruder in the Dust* as a kind of moral fable, as deliberate polemic—a dramatised parable designed to point the lessons verbalised by Gavin Stevens. It is true that Stevens is a created character with whose views Faulkner cannot be directly identified; it is also true that in the early stages of the novel Stevens suffers from those characteristic limitations of his time, class, and environment which Charles Mallison manages, through youth and innocence, to transcend. But Stevens takes to himself the truths his nephew discovers, absorbs them into his thinking, and speaks in the later sections of the novel with the authority of this new wisdom. In these pages there is a repeated insistence on the precise agreement and extraordinarily sensitive understanding between the man and the boy—"once more his uncle spoke at complete one with him and again without surprise he saw his thinking not be interrupted but merely swap one saddle for another" (p. 153)—and it is Stevens who helps Charles to his final affirmative vision of the South. The whole pattern of the novel appears to be manipulated in such a way as to confirm and ratify the validity of Stevens's concluding statements, and Charles's actions themselves become the practical text for his uncle's sermons on the South, its essential community, its need and ability to solve its own problems in its own way and its own time.

The programme seems specific, political, and frankly contemporary. But it is necessary to add that Stevens's overall "message" bears a close resemblance to the one which Faulkner delivered in his own person at Stockholm in 1950: "Some things [Stevens tells Charles] you must always be unable to bear. Some things you must never stop refusing to bear. Injustice and outrage and dishonor and shame. No matter how young you are or how old you have got. Not for kudos and not for cash: your picture in the paper nor money in the bank either. Just refuse to bear them." (p. 206) In the context of the whole book, this can only be taken at a positive valuation, and although the moral commitment had been fully apparent in Go Down, Moses—indeed, in almost all his work—Faulkner seems to speak out in Intruder in the Dust with a new explicitness. Since the novel was written and published during the period when Faulkner was working on A Fable, on what he hoped would become the crowning achievement of his career, this explicitness was perhaps deliberately sought after and consciously achieved.

Certainly there is ample evidence that Faulkner worked carefully towards the final form of Intruder in the Dust, and portions survive of what appear to be several different versions of the novel. A page from one of the rejected typescript versions is reproduced in the Faulkner number of the Princeton University Library Chronicle[3] and shows very extensive holograph revisions; it is by no means an untypical example, and other typescript pages carry in fact an even greater number of alterations. The typescript setting copy of the novel contains a number of minor holograph corrections, substitutions, and additions; it also reveals considerable revision carried out in the course of the actual typing, with passages cancelled in ink or pencil and immediately rewritten without interruption to the overall continuity of the text. The preparation of a fresh typescript was always for Faulkner a process of revision; in the following extract from the setting copy of Intruder in the Dust, square brackets have been used to indicate Faulkner's excisions, and the passage provides an example of the characteristic method of immediate reworking which Faulkner employed in preparing not only this typescript but those of many other novels as well:

So (moving: he had not stopped since the first second's fraction while he closed the office door) he flung himself bodily with one heave into [a calm, sagacious, an even deadly rationality of pro and con. The reason he was going out there tonight was that not even Sheriff Hampton and his uncle (vide Will Legate and the shot-gun stationed in the hall of the jail like a lighted stage scene where anyone approaching would have to see him long before they even reached the gate) were absolutely convinced that the Gowries and their kin and friends would not try to take Lucas out of the jail tonight and so if they were all in town tonight trying to lynch Lucas there wouldn't be anybody hanging around to catch him digging up the grave] a kind of deadly reasonableness [and] of enraged calculation, a calm sagacious and desperate rationality not of pros and cons because there were no pros : the reason he was going out there was that somebody had to and nobody else would and the reason somebody had to was that not even Sheriff Hampton (vide Will Legate and the shotgun stationed in the lower hall of the jail like on a lighted stage where anybody approaching would have to see him or them before they even reached the gate) were completely convinced that the Gowries and their kin and friends would not try to take Lucas out of the jail tonight and so if they were all in town tonight trying to lynch Lucas there wouldn't be anybody hanging around out there to catch him digging up the grave and if that was [true then] a concrete fact then its obverse would be concrete too : . . .[4]

Intruder in the Dust lacks the energy and intensity of Faulkner's best work, and despite meticulous revision of this kind, where Faulkner has retyped a long passage in order to change just one or two words, some of the writing remains unusually inert. What concerns us immediately obtrusive the eventual "message" of the book. Certainly the desire for clarity and explicitness which it seems to suggest. It is even tempting to see Faulkner's use of detective-story conventions in Intruder in the Dust as a means of making more acceptable and less immediately obtrusive the eventual "message" of the book. Certainly the crime-fiction element, apparent in the rather flashy title, is sustained as an essential part of the narrative framework, and Gavin Stevens doubles, or merges, his didactic role with his other role— already familiar from the stories later collected in Knight's Gambit— of an "amateur Sherlock Holmes,"[5] on whom we are ultimately dependent for an explanation of the crime and a solution of the problem of guilt.

At first sight it is also tempting to attribute to a desire for direct affirmative statement those elements in the book which appear either sentimental or simply implausible : the melodramatic churchyard scene, for instance, in which the boy, his Negro companion, and a seventy-year-old spinster succeed in digging up the grave; the whole fortunate outcome of the story, with Lucas proved innocent and set free; the reassuring way in which even old man Gowrie turns out to be an admirable character. Our sense both of sentimentality and of improbability begins to diminish, however, if we see Intruder in the Dust in terms not of narrowly averted tragedy but rather of prevailing comedy interspersed with darker moments. Viewed from this angle, what before seemed incongruous begins to take on a new and more ambiguous significance. The description of the three conspirators of virtue digging up the grave at night recalls, and perhaps deliberately so, the graveyard scene in *Tom Sawyer*, reminding us that, like Twain, Faulkner has little hesitation in juxtaposing effects of comedy and horror. The exhumation episode in *Intruder in the Dust* is grim, macabre, and frightening, and we naturally admire the courage of the three people, all so obviously unsuited to the task, who undertake to prove Lucas's innocence in defiance of risk and personal suffering. We do not doubt the authenticity of the terror, and we share Charles Mallison's sense of outrage at the monstrous burden which he and his companions have to bear. Yet the very incongruity of the scene gives it a humorous aspect, and this Faulkner also exploits. A more unlikely trio of exhumers it would be difficult to imagine, and there is something ludicrous about the whole business of swapping bodies in and out of the same hole. Moreover, once old Gowrie has revealed himself as a man dedicated to his own stern notions of integrity and honour, previous events begin to appear in a slightly different light and we may even wonder whether Charles, Aleck Sander, and Miss Habersham, far from being the most inappropriate investigators of the crime, were not in fact the only people who could with impunity have ventured into Beat Four at all: even a Gowrie, certainly old Gowrie himself, would hesitate before harming two children and an old woman.

The presence of these ambiguities in *Intruder in the Dust* must call into question any criticism of the book as sentimental and any description of it as unqualified moral fable. Undoubtedly Faulkner took the opportunities offered by the development of his narrative in order to offer direct and indirect comment on a situation which was, in a broad sense, contemporary and of which *Go Down, Moses* had already shown him to be very deeply aware; we may even detect in *Intruder in the Dust* some sense of the rhetorical and speculative elaboration of material that is, at base, both simple and melodramatic. But, as so often in his work, Faulkner's choice of narrator affords the most reliable indication of the book's central preoccupation. As Andrew Lytle observes, "By focusing [the thematic impetus] in the moral destiny of a boy, the story becomes dramatic instead of didactic: that is, a novel and not propaganda."[6] The use of Charles Mallison as narrator forces us to view the events of the novel in terms of his own experience of them, an experience which we are apparently intended to see as a progressive initiation into manhood and for which the predicament of Lucas Beauchamp provides not so much the cause as the context—the occasion and the particular circumstances.

Lucas occupies, of course, the point in the novel at which all the lines of the narrative cross; if he seems also to dominate the book, that is largely because he looms with such superhuman largeness in Charles

Mallison's childish vision. Whatever Lucas's representative importance, his particular and intensely personal significance for Charles himself is brilliantly established by the early scenes at the creek and in Lucas's house. As Charles, then aged twelve, clambered out of the creek into which he had fallen,

> he saw two feet in gum boots which were neither Edmonds' boy's nor Aleck Sander's and then the legs, the overalls rising out of them and he climbed on and stood up and saw a Negro man with an axe on his shoulder, in a heavy sheeplined coat and a broad pale felt hat such as his grandfather had used to wear, looking at him and that was when he saw Lucas Beauchamp for the first time that he remembered or rather for the first time because you didn't forget Lucas Beauchamp; gasping, shaking and only now feeling the shock of the cold water, he looked up at the face which was just watching him without pity commiseration or anything else, not even surprise. (p. 6)

The technique here perhaps suggests an influence from the cinema, but it achieves an effect comparable to that of Pip's first encounter with Magwitch at the beginning of *Great Expectations*. On Lucas's occasional appearances later in the book Faulkner provides only an external view of the man and his personality, never a comprehensive portrait. Deliberately so: the majority of the inhabitants of Yoknapatawpha County regard Lucas not as an individual but as a type, automatically categorising him as a "nigger murderer" and expecting him to receive the treatment prescribed by local custom for all such; those who have been forced to recognise him as an individual are grateful for the opportunity of thinking of him in the same convenient terms, glad to be able to put him "in his place" at last and thus "solve" the problem he has always presented. In another sense, too, the externality of Lucas's characterisation is not only deliberate but crucial. Lucas is fundamentally unknowable, and no more than anyone else does Charles succeed in penetrating the barrier of that "face pigmented like a Negro's but with a nose high in the bridge and even hooked a little and what looked out through it or from behind it not black nor white either, not arrogant at all and not even scornful: just intolerant inflexible and composed." (p. 13)

Charles, it is true, has an acute awareness of Lucas's individuality. But he is aware primarily of Lucas's sheer impenetrability, and certainly it is no commitment to individualism or to the idea of human dignity which first impels him to act on Lucas's behalf. His principal motivation, it appears, is his irritated recollection of an indebtedness to Lucas which his white pride insists that he discharge, but which Lucas's even more stubborn, and more resourceful, pride has consistently frustrated him from discharging. The progress of Charles's initiation is charted very largely in terms of his rejection of his original motive, which derived in large measure from the racial difference between Lucas and himself, in favour of a positive and even passionate awareness of the need to preserve human dignity and avert the shame of mob-violence. Comparisons between Charles Mallison and Huck Finn would here seem to be in order, but the analogy has obvious limitations. Lucas Beauchamp is no Nigger Jim. Where Jim is engaging, affectionate, and ultimately dependent upon Huck and other white men, Lucas is none of these things. Lucas, indeed, cannot even be cast as a victim, since he utterly refuses to recognise himself in that role, and since he is, in a real sense, the conscious instigator of the book's principal narrative events. This utter atypicality of Lucas, his invincible independence and impenetrability, is what finally undermines any conception of *Intruder in the Dust* as a straightforward moral fable. Quite apart from the novel's many other sources of ambiguity, it seems inconceivable that Faulkner could intend to present as typical of white-Negro relationships as a whole a situation focused exclusively upon Lucas Beauchamp and lacking the kind of diversification of character and episode essential to the broader range and larger scale of a novel like *Go Down, Moses*. Nowhere in *Intruder in the Dust* does this seem more obvious than in the splendidly ironic conclusion, where Lucas's insistence on being given a receipt, on keeping affairs between himself and his white "benefactors" on a strictly business footing, makes it clear that he does not intend his recent experience to affect his behaviour in the slightest degree and that he will not even release Charles from that indebtedness, that sense of being always at a disadvantage, which prompted the boy to his original intervention on Lucas's behalf.

REQUIEM FOR A NUN

Requiem for a Nun was published on September 27, 1951, more than seventeen years after a novel of Faulkner's with that title had first been announced for publication. In March 1934 that first abortive *Requiem* was reported as have been postponed,[1] no part of any manuscript or other version of it seems to have survived, and the narrative and thematic material which Faulkner then had in mind may have borne no relation to the material incorporated in the volume of 1951. Indeed, *Requiem for a Nun* could conceivably have been intended as the title for quite another work—for the novel which Faulkner once spoke of developing out of *Miss Zilphia Gant*,[2] for instance, or for the subsequently abandoned original version of *Absalom, Absalom!*. It is tempting, however, to see in this early mention of the title a confirmation of that intimate relationship between *Sanctuary* and *Requiem* which the later book makes everywhere apparent.[3] In the process of reworking *Sanctuary* into its final form, Faulkner had organised the book more firmly around the figure of Temple Drake and set against Temple's apparent withdrawal into immunity the institutionalised injustice of Goodwin's conviction and the lawless savagery of his lynching. He must have glimpsed at this stage, if not earlier, the importance of those themes of guilt and injustice implicit in the very plot of *Sanctuary*, but he was presumably unable or unwilling to embark on an extended exploration of them within the context of *Sanctuary* itself. The themes must have continued to haunt his imagination, but it was not until many years later that he returned to them, bringing them finally into focus in *Requiem for a Nun*.

Central to the whole structure and meaning of *Requiem for a Nun* as published is the figure of Gavin Stevens, who becomes in this book virtually the grand inquisitor of Faulkner's particular brand of humanism, at once leading and forcing Temple along the road towards what he believes to be her salvation; alternatively we can think of him, in Olga Vickery's phrase, as "a Socratic midwife presiding over the moral dialectic which focuses on Temple Drake."[4] This central action of the novel is presented in the form of a three-act play. The drama moves forward in time, apart from the flashback presented in the second scene of the second act, but the movement of the dialogue is regressive: as directed by Stevens, the discussion proceeds in ineluctable retrospect towards the exposure of Temple's deepest degradation, towards that final self-revelation and confessional which, by a trick of the theatre, Temple makes not to the impersonal figure of the State Governor but to Gowan Stevens, her own husband. The "plant" finally confirms that the concerns of the novel are with individual rather than with social responsibility: Nancy's fate is already sealed; Temple's, however, is still very much in the balance, and it is her salvation, not Nancy's, that provides the object of Gavin Stevens's elaborate exercise. Stevens's manipulation of the situation and of the course of the dialogue, and the relentlessness of the dialectical process and its emotional cost to Temple herself, are skilfully and sometimes quite movingly evoked. The adaptation to moral investigation of the detective-story techniques which Faulkner had earlier used in *Intruder in the Dust* and *Knight's Gambit* also lends these dramatic sections of the book a certain narrative strength. They are not, however, especially dramatic.

Faulkner's problem is that the whole drama centres not simply upon but within Temple Drake herself: the only really important things that happen are those which we understand to have taken place inside her. The device of dramatising internal conflict in terms of a dialogue which Faulkner followed in the commissary conversation between Ike and Cass in *Go Down, Moses* is here extended to take in a third participant: at the same time its effect is diluted, in that Stevens and the Governor cannot sensitively verbalise any aspect of Temple's dilemma and are therefore in no position to take over any significant portion of her moral or conversational burden. In the central scenes involving Temple, Stevens, and the Governor, there is no substantial conflict among the characters on stage: Stevens goads Temple, the Governor listens to her; they are both anxious to let her take the central role, and in order to sustain the illusion of a dialogue in progress, Faulkner has sometimes to create artificial opportunities for Stevens to speak—"Wait. Let me play too," (p. 126) he says at one point, and at another: "No, I'm going to talk a while now." (p. 160)[5] Faulkner also attempts to relieve his difficulties by allowing Temple to indulge in excessive self-dramatisation and to contrast herself, the present Mrs. Gowan Stevens, with the Temple Drake of eight years earlier. By an interesting though rather clumsy extension of this technique, Faulkner permits Temple to contrast herself with Maria, the heroine of Hemingway's *For Whom the Bell Tolls*:

> You know: somebody—Hemingway, wasn't it?—wrote a book about how it had never actually happened to a gir—woman, if she just refused to accept it, no matter who remembered, bragged. (p. 154)

A little later Stevens takes up this allusion and makes it more explicit, but it is obvious that Faulkner in no way ratifies the idea and that, on the contrary, he insists on its absurd irrelevance to Temple's situation: Temple, unlike Maria, had embraced corruption, and she had never been able to free herself from the influence of that corruption, or even genuinely to desire to free herself. For Temple, supremely, Stevens's dictum is true: "The past is never dead. It's not even past." (p. 92)

Temple's enforced confrontation of her own guilt commands our interest and, to a limited degree, our sympathy. But other aspects of these dramatic sections of the book are less convincing, and especially those involving Nancy. At the University of Virginia Faulkner made it clear what kind of significance he intended Nancy to possess. Confirming that Nancy, not Temple, was the nun of the title, Faulkner observed that despite the "tragic life of a prostitute which she had had to follow simply because she was ... just doomed and damned by circumstances to that life," Nancy "was capable within her poor dim lights and reasons of an act which whether it was right or wrong was of complete almost religious abnegation of the world for the sake of an innocent child."[6] But it is almost impossible to accept on any terms the murder of Temple's child: Nancy's self-sacrifice is overshadowed by an act whose symbolic portentousness is destroyed by the outrage it commits not simply upon our moral sensibilities but on our credulity. Faulkner insists on Nancy's ignorance and on the simplicity of her faith, but the murder seems the act of a fanatic, worthy rather of a Doc Hines than of the Dilsey whom Nancy in many ways suggests.

The action of these dramatic sections of the novel, as of the actual stage-version published in 1959, is highly formal and almost ritualistic, proceeding as if in a series of merging tableaux. The writing, too, seems ponderous and heavily stylised, sadly lacking in dramatic life, but it has been much admired by certain critics, and notably by Albert Camus in his preface to Maurice Coindreau's French translation of the book:

Or, le style de Faulkner, avec son souffle saccadé, ses phrases interrompues, reprises et prolongées en répétitions, ses incidences, ses parenthèses et ses cascades de subordonnées, nous fournit un équivalent moderne, et nullement artificiel, de la tirade tragique. C'est un style qui halète, du halètement même de la souffrance. Une spirale, interminablement dévidée, de mots et de phrases conduit celui qui parle aux abîmes des souffrances ensevelies dans le passé, Temple Stevens aux délicieux enfers du bordel de Memphis qu'elle voulait oublier, et Nancy Mannigoe à la douleur aveugle, étonnée, ignorante, qui la rendra meutrière et sainte en même temps.[7]

Camus offers an eloquent justification of the style—and, in that final sentence. a well-stated positive view of Nancy's role—and it is perhaps possible to suggest that Faulkner's technique has more in common with the classical tradition of French tragedy than with the most characteristic forms of English tragic drama. Certainly the great success which the stage-version of *Requiem* enjoyed in France was not repeated either in London or on Broadway.[8]

To most American and English critics the narrative interchapters of *Requiem for a Nun*, recording the story of Jefferson and of Jackson, capital of Mississippi, from their earliest settlement to the middle of the twentieth century, have seemed more generally successful than the book's dramatically-presented core. The prologue to Act One, "The Courthouse (A Name for the City)," is a slightly over-extended but always vigorous piece of story telling, part of which actually made its first appearance in *Harper's* in short-story form.[9] The story, entitled "A Name for the City," began at a point corresponding to the opening of the novel and concluded neatly at the point (on page 29 of the book) where Peabody says, "Only her name's Jefferson now. We cant ever forget that any more now." Though not one of Faulkner's best short stories, it was a thoroughly competent piece of work and entirely capable of independent existence. There are many differences of detail between story and novel versions, but the one substantial discrepancy appears in the introductory paragraphs of each: in the story we discover that the narrator, though unidentified, must in fact be Charles Mallison, and that the source of his information is his Uncle Gavin—Gavin Stevens—whose well-instructed historical imagination has preserved this story of the past. The fundamental anti-modernism of Uncle Gavin's attitudes is made quite explicit in the opening paragraph of the story when he contrasts the ever-increasing speeds at which man travels around the world with the image of "blind Homer, unable to quit the Athenian stone he sat on without a child to lead him, yet plumbed and charted the ultimate frontiers of passion and defeat and glory and ambition and courage and hope and fear,"[10] and it is perhaps worth noting, as one source of that thematic unity which Faulkner sought in the book as a whole, that although the interchapters of the novel are narrated in terms of the conventions of third-person objectivity, the attitudes they embody are close to those expressed by Gavin Stevens in the dramatic sections as well as those specifically identified as emanating from Stevens in the *Harper's* short story. Gavin Stevens, it would appear, is effectively the controlling intelligence throughout the whole of *Requiem for a Nun*, but his role here is quite different from the one he plays in such later books as *The Town* and *The Mansion*. In those novels, as we shall see, he is himself a participant in the central action, a protagonist in the fullest sense, and as such he is very critically viewed; in *Requiem*, however, as in *Knight's Gambit* and *Intruder in the Dust*, he is an agent, an instrument, rather than a participant—not himself the central figure but one of the means by which attention is focused on that figure—and although Faulkner's presentation of Stevens is never free of ambiguity it would seem possible in these instances to accept him at a positive valuation.

The second of the interchapters, "The Golden Dome (Beginning Was the Word)," is much shorter than the first and somewhat different both in content and in manner. Instead of dealing with Jefferson alone, it concerns itself, succinctly and almost racily, with the history of Mississippi as a whole and with the growth of Jackson, its capital city. Its first pages are reminiscent of the broad historical sweep so brilliantly achieved in the opening of *The Hamlet*; towards the end, there is a progressive narrowing of scope, a deliberate proliferation of petty detail and insignificant data, until the final, laconic, guidebook-style description of present-day Jackson in which all sense of individuality disappears and Jackson is made to sound indistinguishable from any town of comparable size anywhere in the United States. The last of the interchapters, the prologue to Act Three, "The Jail (Nor Even Yet Quite Relinquish—)," is slightly longer than the prologue to Act One, and it returns, rather repetitiously at times, to the story of Jefferson itself. Its central episode, the story of Cecilia Farmer, recalls an earlier moment in the history of the jail in which Nancy Mannigoe now awaits execution, and we see how a frail girl, simply by scratching her name on the jail window one day in 1861, ensured the perpetuation of her memory down the years, thus continuously repeating in her "clear undistanced voice" the simple affirmation: *"Listen, stranger; this was myself: this was I."* (p. 262)

Cecilia Farmer's act may remind us of Faulkner's definition of the artist as one who "knows he has a short span of life, that the day will come when he must pass through the wall of oblivion, and he wants to leave a scratch on that wall—Kilroy was here—that somebody a hundred, a thousand years later will see."[11] More immediately however, it seems to anticipate the even simpler affirmation of Nancy Mannigoe—"Believe" (p. 282)—in that final scene of *Requiem for a Nun* which follows immediately afterwards. There are many other interconnections between the dramatic and narrative sections of the novel, and Faulkner once explained that the narrative sections were designed to give the book "the contrapuntal effect which comes in orchestration, that the hard give-and-take of the dialogue was played against something that was a little mystical, made it sharper, more effective, in my opinion. It was not experimentation, it was simply because to me that seemed the most effective way to tell that story."[12] The effect achieved in the book is one of a constant reverberation between the dramatic and the narrative, between the private and public worlds. Both serve to emphasise the continuity of cause and effect in human history, as well as the impossibility of calculating— let alone of controlling—the ultimate ramifications of even the most insignificant actions. Both also emphasise the decline of individuality, and the most effective symbol of this decline, the guidebook description of Jackson, at once looks forward to the ensuing action in the office of the State Governor and harks back to the more extended narrative of the prologue to Act One, which told how the attempt to shake off responsibility for the loss of a useless padlock had led directly to the growth of the modern town of Jefferson. Faulkner uses this sequence of events to demonstrate the progressive erosion of the individualistic idea: man yields up first his responsibilities and ultimately his rights to impersonal institutions; flexibility and humanity disappear and human lives are increasingly dominated by abstract and often arbitrary principles and laws. The implications for the central action of the novel are clear; in a world where personal responsibility has disappeared, man is never forced to enquire too deeply into his own conscience: guilt is social, and can be socially discharged; crimes which society does not specifically recognise may go equally unrecognised by their perpetrators. Society permits and indeed encourages Temple to play the role of the bereaved mother; it is Gavin Stevens's self-imposed task to bring her to a recognition of her own ultimate guilt for the death of her child.

A FABLE

A *Fable* opens powerfully. Scene and setting are created swiftly and firmly; an atmosphere of heavy foreboding is immediately evoked; by the end of the opening chapter the major elements of the basic situation are already present, and some of the main figures have been glimpsed, as in a tableau, in their relative positions of power and rank. Above all, there has been the silent momentary exchange between the old General, supreme commander of the war machine of France and of its Allies, and the imprisoned Corporal, symbol and agent of opposition to everything that the old General represents. Only later do we learn that the Corporal is the General's illegitimate son, and although Faulkner once remarked that the heart of A *Fable* was the tragedy of the father who has to decide whether his son shall live or die,[1] it is not until the end of the book that they actually meet. The final, and only, interview between the old General and his son is of central importance for the philosophical and allegorical content of the novel; it is also the moment of the greatest dramatic and emotional tension. But the unsatisfactoriness of much of the book makes it hard to resist the feeling that Faulkner too long delays this confrontation, that he might have fulfilled sooner the dramatic promise of the opening chapter and especially of that first meeting of eyes.

In the interview between the old General and the Corporal, Faulkner, as so often before, employs dialogue not only as an expression of a particular human situation but as a means of dramatising ideas, and his method here is most immediately reminiscent of the discussion between Ike McCaslin and his cousin, Cass Edmonds, which occupies most of the fourth section of "The Bear" in *Go Down, Moses*. The similarity, indeed, is not simply one of technique. The attitudes, ideas, and relative positions of Cass and Ike correspond in interesting ways to those of the General and the Corporal. Cass and the General are men of authority, rank, and social responsibility, who see it as their role and their duty to confront directly the immediate, practical problems of the present time and place, the here-and-now; they are natural defenders of the *status quo*. The General and the Corporal are father and son, and it is stressed throughout *Go Down, Moses* that Ike's relationship to Cass is virtually a filial one. Both Ike and the Corporal are men with a deep allegiance to the land, who respond passively rather than actively to human problems, who walk the path of abnegation and martyrdom; Ike's search is more self-conscious and intellectual than that of the Corporal, and much less successful, but it is noteworthy that the latter plays a very subdued and silent role in A *Fable*, making few positive gestures of leadership, affecting others more by what he is than by what he says or does. The similarity between the two conversations, in Go *Down, Moses* and in A *Fable*, is suggestive in several ways. It serves to emphasise, for example, the degree to which the interview between the General and the Corporal, for all Faulkner's subsequent insistence on the father-son relationship, is primarily an exposition of two opposed attitudes towards the problems of existence, of human conduct, and of war and peace: it is even possible to see the interview, like that in Go *Down, Moses*, as a dramatic externalisation of a conflict that might be conceived of as existing within the mind of a single person. Despite the emotional charge given to the scene by our knowledge of the relationship of the two men, both the General and the Corporal seem so firmly fixed in their ideological positions that the exchange has something of a ritualistic quality, reminiscent of *Everyman* and other medieval morality plays in which personified virtues and vices are presented as struggling for an individual soul.

Whatever Faulkner's original intentions with regard to the structure of Go *Down, Moses*, it seems possible that he subsequently took the published book as a model for certain structural aspects of A *Fable*; he began writing A *Fable* shortly after finishing Go *Down, Moses*, and we can assume, with some assurance, that "The Bear" was the last part of Go *Down, Moses* to be completed. Both Go *Down, Moses* and A *Fable* might be considered as examples of "expressive form": both are made up of unnumbered chapters of widely varying lengths, and in each book chronology is manipulated and action suspended to meet the needs, not so much of character or plot development, but of thematic exposition. The outstanding structural peculiarity of A *Fable*, the intrusion of the long story of the lame racehorse, is in some measure prefigured by the relationship between the hunting episodes in Go *Down, Moses* and the crucial discussion between Ike and Cass in the commissary. The injured horse, like the crippled bear, old Ben, is apparently a symbol of natural freedom, and his story—which the groom's devotion marks as a kind of love-story—is portentously heralded by the invocation of mythological and literary references such as are associated, in *The Hamlet*, with the idyllic story of Ike Snope's love for the cow:

> the old Negro telling it, grave and tranquil, serenely and peacefully inconsequential, like listening to a dream, until presently the runner five years afterward was seeing what the Federal deputy marshal had five years ago while in the middle of it: not a theft, but a passion, an immolation, an apotheosis—no gang of oppor-

tunists fleeing with a crippled horse whose value, even whole, had ceased weeks back to equal the sum spent on its pursuit, but the immortal pageant-piece of the tender legend which was the crowning glory of man's own legend beginning when his first paired children lost well the world and from which paired proto-types they still challenged paradise, still paired and still immortal against the chronicle's grimed and bloodstained pages: Adam and Lilith and Paris and Helen and Pyramus and Thisbe and all the other recordless Romeos and their Juliets, the world's oldest and most shining tale limning in his brief turn the warp-legged foul-mouthed English horse-groom as ever Paris or Lochinvar or any else of earth's splendid rapers: the doomed glorious frenzy of a love-story, pursued not by an unclosed office file nor even the raging frustration of the millionaire owner, but by its own inherent doom, since, being immortal, the story, the legend, was not to be owned by any one of the pairs who added to its shining and tragic increment, but only to be used, passed through, by each in their doomed and homeless turn. (pp. 153-154)

The phrase "pageant-piece" directly recalls the reference in *Go Down, Moses* to the "yearly pageant-rite" (p. 194) of the hunt for old Ben, and suggests that the horse too is a symbol not merely of freedom but of what might be called natural decorum, the proud, unostentatious fulfilment of a destined role.

Considered in this light, the thematic relationship between the racehorse story and the rest of the novel seems much less arbitrary. Ike McCaslin in *Go Down, Moses* tries to find a means of expressing in human and social terms the lessons he has learned from the wilder-ness and from old Ben; in *A Fable*, though the situation is not precisely comparable, it might be said that the problem of the Cockney groom, after the death of the horse, is to reawaken in himself the impulses to self-sacrifice which the horse had so powerfully stimulated and to liberate those impulses in the human sphere, making them effective in the world of men. Such a liberation seems finally to be achieved when the Runner embroils the groom, in his military role as the Sentry, in the advance across no-man's-land made by the unarmed British troops towards the equally unarmed Germans. Certainly the Sentry is forced, in the moment before the arrival of the obliterating barrage, to a recognition of his essential kinship with his fellow men:

'No!' he cried, 'no! Not to us!' not even realising that he had said 'we' and not 'I' for the first time in his life probably, certainly for the first time in four years, ... (p. 321)

There are many similarities in theme and technique between *Go Down, Moses* and *A Fable*, but the later book is much the more consciously integrated of the two. It is true that the incorporation of the large block of *Notes on a Horsethief* material presents very considerable difficulties in linear terms, but Faulkner devotes great care to the establishment and maintenance of overall patterns of recurrent themes and symbols and to the interconnection of incidents and phrases which may be widely separated within the actual context of the book. The carefully-articulated time sequence suggests, as does the scale, subject, and formality of the book, a conceivable debt to *The Sound and the Fury*, or possibly to *Light in August*, the latter offering additional resemblances to *A Fable* in its concurrent development of several quite distinct plot elements. In *Light in August* the long flashback of Christmas's life is poised upon the moment when he goes into the house to kill Miss Burden; in *A Fable* the retrospective account of the stolen racehorse and its adventures belongs in the book's "time present" to the period on the Tuesday night when the Runner has been kicked unconscious by the Sentry, the groom of the racehorse story. It is interesting that Hodding Carter should recall that *Notes on a Horsethief* was originally submitted to the Levee Press as "A Dangling Participle from Work in Progress" and punctuated in such a way as to constitute only one or two sentences;[2] if punctuation of this kind had been retained when this material was incorporated into *A Fable* it would have served to emphasise the element of time-suspension involved.

Faulkner's manipulation of time in *A Fable* is deliberate and, up to a point, successful. Obviously, the sequence of the action is based in large measure upon an extended parallel with the events of the Christian Holy Week, but in the first part of the book, up to page 211, Faulkner radically disrupts this basic chronology, moving blocks of material backwards and forwards in time, apparently in an attempt to achieve, through devices of suspense and juxtaposition, an intensification of emotional effect at critical moments and an enrichment of the book's total meaning. On page 212, however, almost exactly halfway through the 437-page book, Faulkner returns to the scene of the first chapter and to just a few hours later in time, and it is perhaps not too much to say that not merely the story of the racehorse but the whole of the first half of the book can now be seen to have been organised, at once radial and concentric, about that opening scene. There is ample evidence here of Faulkner's structural skill, of his nice management and neat interlocking of a large body of highly diversified material. But we may wonder, as with James Gould Cozzen's *By Love Possessed*, another long novel organised in much the same meticulous way, whether so much structural self-consciousness is not the enemy of fictional life. *A Fable*, alone among Faulkner's mature books, is sadly lacking in narrative excitement, in that inflammation of our desire to follow events to a conclusion which normally constitutes one of Faulkner's simplest and greatest strengths.

This lack in A Fable has been attributed to the way in which events are seen more and more obviously to be following a symbolic pattern with whose sequence and outcome we are fully familiar; yet the presence of such a pattern is not clearly felt until the second half of the book, and it is this latter portion which actually offers the greater narrative vitality. From the moment on page 214 when the young girl of the opening scene meets the foreign women, one of whom is quickly identified as Marthe, the Holy Week parallels, only lightly touched upon heretofore, become both frequent and insistent; from this point too, the action moves more swiftly and more nearly chronologically, though with interruptions such as the retrospective account of the old General's past and with frequent shifts from one plot line to another. There is a noticeable acceleration of narrative pace as the Corporal's death approaches, and this is largely due to the way in which the sub-plots at this point either come to an end or merge with the central action : the Runner's attempt to bring about an actual meeting of unarmed troops from both sides reaches its disastrous conclusion; Levine, the young pilot officer, commits suicide; the Quartermaster-General's allegiance to the old General is finally shattered. Of the Holy Week parallels themselves it might be said that a certain interest is provoked by successive revelations of the precise manner in which the pattern is to be repeated, but that the parallels too often draw attention to themselves by their ingenuity—the barbed-wire "crown of thorns," for instance—rather than by any suggestive or moving aptness.

The sluggishness of much of the book, however, is impossible to deny, and it seems to be largely the product of the technique, of the way in which the interest aroused by the opening scene is allowed to founder in the succeeding mass of expository material whose significance and relevance is only clarified at a later stage. The first section of The Sound and the Fury makes heavy demands upon the reader, but it does provide, in however fragmentary a fashion, a framework for the ensuing action, and the novel as a whole seizes the imagination not simply by virtue of its language and content but also because it offers the reader the exciting experiences of participation and exploration—participation in the mental processes of its characters, exploration of the meaning of the human situation thus displayed. There is relatively little analysis of consciousness in A Fable: its mode is not exploratory but expository; its statements are general and abstract, humane but often lifeless.

This concern with general abstract truths rather than with particular human situations reveals itself very clearly in the detail of the style. In writing A Fable Faulkner submitted himself to an extremely rigorous aesthetic discipline, and evidence of this is provided not only by the mass of deleted pages from early and rejected versions of the

book which are now in the Alderman Library but also by the texture
of the published work itself. Faulkner's writing is here denuded of
much of that verbal and metaphorical richness, poetic in quality,
vigorous in movement, which marks alike the dialogue and the
continuous prose of his novels of the 'thirties and early 'forties. Images
no longer shift, extend themselves, merge one with another, but tend
to be deliberately controlled and patterned; often they are built up
painstakingly into elaborately paragraphic effects. In the opening
scene of the novel, for example, the first emergence of the people from
their sleeping places and their gradual gathering into a crowd in front
of the Hôtel de Ville is described in terms of water imagery—stream,
river, wave, flood—and the basic figure is sustained and developed
over several pages, so that on page 6 we read :

> he forced the horse on, feinting and dodging the animal through
> the human river which made no effort to avoid him, which accepted
> the horse as water accepts a thrusting prow. Then he was gone.
> Accelerating now, the crowd poured into the boulevard. It flung
> the cavalry aside and poured on, blotting the intersecting streets
> as it passed them as a river in flood blots up its tributary creeks,
> until at last that boulevard too was one dense seething voiceless
> lake.

The presence of such passages in the first chapter produces an effect
somewhat similar to the opening of a late Dickens novel, and they
establish in their symbolic portentousness something of the tone,
manner, and scale of the whole book. They also establish something of
its overall pattern, for although this water imagery is never again so
elaborately developed, it reappears each time the crowd is mentioned
or described. This recurrence, which can be seen to a lesser degree
in many other strands of imagery, notably those of excretion and
rigidity, is like the re-entry of a theme in music and serves to emphasise
the highly formal character of the book, since the reiterated imagery
is being used, not to enhance the concreteness of the description, but
rather to make the actuality more abstract, to drain it of particularisa-
tion and reduce it to a motif in a larger pattern.

Further evidence of the formality of A Fable appears in the profusion of elaborate similes—it is tempting to think of them as "heroic"
—and in the evident set-pieces which occur throughout the book :
Levine's vision of what the end of the war will be like, for example,
and the more extended analysis of the military hierarchy, with its
complex pattern of different ranks, channels, and functions, and of
the whole vast range of people and groups with a vested interest in
war. Alike in the overall pattern of the book and in the detail of every
page the deliberation and self-consciousness of Faulkner's effort is
everywhere apparent, until one doubts whether A Fable can usefully

or fairly be discussed as a novel at all, whether it should not be judged as what it proclaims itself to be—fable, allegory, morality, *exemplum.*

Faulkner's comments on A *Fable*, as on so many of his books, are not always consistent one with another, but what appears to be the most considered of his observations clearly demonstrates that he saw the book very largely in allegorical terms. Answering a question from Jean Stein about his use of Christian allegory in A *Fable*, Faulkner commented that "the Christian allegory was the right allegory to use in that particular story, like an oblong square corner is the right corner with which to build an oblong rectangular house." He continued:

> No one is without Christianity, if we agree on what we mean by the word. It is every individual's individual code of behavior by means of which he makes himself a better human being than his nature wants to be, if he followed his nature only. Whatever its symbol—cross or crescent or whatever—that symbol is man's reminder of his duty inside the human race. Its various allegories are the charts against which he measures himself and learns to know what he is. It cannot teach man to be good as the textbook teaches him mathematics. It shows him how to discover himself, evolve for himself a moral code and standard within his capacities and aspirations, by giving him a matchless example of suffering and sacrifice and the promise of hope. Writers have always drawn, and always will draw, upon the allegories of moral consciousness, for the reason that the allegories are matchless—the three men in Moby Dick, who represent the trinity of conscience: knowing nothing, knowing but not caring, knowing and caring. The same trinity is represented in A Fable by the young Jewish pilot officer, who said, "This is terrible. I refuse to accept it, even if I must refuse life to do so"; the old French Quartermaster General, who said, "This is terrible, but we can weep and bear it"; and the English battalion runner, who said, "This is terrible, I'm going to do something about it."[3]

This leads us admirably to the book's central meaning and plainly indicates its didactic purpose, its dedication to an explicit message. The mention of Moby Dick also suggests the kind of literary pattern Faulkner may have had in mind, although Billy Budd would in fact seem to offer a closer overall analogy: the relationship between Captain Vere and Billy Budd, as well as the whole context, occasion, and outcome of that relationship, offers remarkable parallels with that between the General and the Corporal, and we encounter in both books a deliberate and sustained invocation of Christian imagery. Faulkner's intention, clearly, was to make large, general statements, and to present them both as abstractions and as conclusions proceeding irresistibly from the dramatically presented human situation; he sought to deal in symbol and allegory, but to root them in the dramatic context, as Melville had done so effectively in *Moby Dick* and *Billy Budd*. The relative failure of Faulkner's attempt seems partly explicable in terms of a comment he made at the University of Virginia:

> That was *tour de force*. The notion occurred to me one day in 1942 shortly after Pearl Harbor and the beginning of the last great war. Suppose—who might that unknown soldier be? Suppose that had been Christ again, under that fine big cenotaph with the eternal flame burning on it? That He would naturally have got crucified again, and I had to—then it became *tour de force*, because I had to invent enough stuff to carry this notion.[4]

A *Fable* remained too obviously a *tour de force*, becoming a novel in form but not in spirit—since Faulkner seems to have denied himself any deeply imaginative exploration of the human situations so deliberately invented to provide the vehicle for his vision and his message. The message was paramount, and it was of such a kind, and of such urgency to Faulkner himself, that the attempt to convey it in terms of fiction was perhaps ill-conceived. It has often been noted that there appear in A *Fable* several words and phrases which also appear in the Nobel Prize Speech, and in large measure the book and the speech are products of the same passionate endeavour. But it is the very brevity and directness of the speech which gives it such memorable force. We may yet come to place a higher valuation on A *Fable*, and some European critics have already spoken in its defence,[5] but from our present perspective it is difficult not to see Faulkner's words at Stockholm as the cumulative, authoritative statement, and the ten-year labour of A *Fable* as a kind of extended gloss upon it.

THE TOWN

The Town is perhaps the most domestic of Faulkner's novels, the work which approximates most nearly to the characteristic forms of American social fiction. It displays neither the bland tenor, nor the obsessive notation, of books by J. P. Marquand or John O'Hara, but it is, outstandingly, the novel of Faulkner's which deals most closely and consistently with "ordinary" human beings leading reasonably "normal" lives within a precisely delineated social situation. Eula commits suicide, it is true, but emphasis is placed not on the act itself but on its moral and symbolic implications, and on its practical significance for the lives of other people; like every other action in the book, it is not an isolated incident but the culmination of long processes of cause and effect, the outcome of a continual interplay of personal and social factors. Throughout the novel there is a powerful sense of Jefferson, the town itself, as a living social entity, an operative community. As in *Sartoris*, Faulkner creates an active social world, with an intricate interlocking of social and personal relationships, and it is a mark of *The Town's* especial richness that we know so intimately the life of one particular family: we know what the Mallisons do and think, what and when they eat, what their day-to-day life is like; we see the tensions that exist between them as members of a single family inhabiting the same house; we are aware of them individually, seeing Maggie as the family's energetic and cohesive centre, seeing even her husband, though so lightly touched in, not merely as a background figure, simply part of the social scenery, but as a significant element in Gavin Stevens's total situation and as very credibly the father of young Charles. In a wider view, of course, the Mallison family merges into the larger pattern of Jefferson itself, and nothing happens in the novel which has not been conditioned by the social environment which Jefferson provides, and which does not reverberate in turn upon the sounding-board of Jefferson public opinion.

Faulkner, indeed, incorporates this human sounding-board as an integral part of the novel's structure. Charles Mallison explains on the opening page: "So when I say 'we' and 'we thought' what I mean is Jefferson and what Jefferson thought." (p. 3) It may seem a little arbitrary for Faulkner to confront us with a narrator who has to explain that he had not been born when many of the events of the novel occurred, that he is often a second- or third-hand source of information, but Faulkner's intention is precisely to employ Mallison as a simple, uncomplicated reflector and recorder of external events and of the public reaction to them. Inevitably, Mallison establishes himself as a character, an individual voice, especially when he himself is old enough to participate in the events he describes, and as a nephew of Gavin Stevens, living in the same house, he often has what might be considered an insider's view. Nevertheless, we can perceive clearly the distinctions between the respective narrative points of view of Charles Mallison, Gavin Stevens, and V. K. Ratliff as Faulkner reviewed them in answer to a question asked him at the University of Virginia; he had wanted, he said, to look at the object from three vantage-points, in terms of three different mentalities:

> That was—one was the mirror which obliterated all except truth, because the mirror didn't know the other factors existed. Another was to look at it from the point of view of someone who had made of himself a more or less artificial man through his desire to practice what he had been told was a good virtue, apart from his belief in virtues, what he had been told, trained by his respect for education in the old classical sense. The other was from the point of view of a man who practiced virtue from simple instinct, from—well, more than that, because—for a practical reason, because it was better. There was less confusion if all people didn't tell lies to one another, and didn't pretend. That seemed to me to give a more complete picture of the specific incidents as they occurred if they could be [viewed] three times.[1]

The narration is given to Charles Mallison, the "mirror," for rather more than half the book, and it is he who provides most of the basic narrative of events. Mallison also recounts the episodes of the brass stolen from the power-station, of the mule loose in Mrs. Hait's yard, and of the arrival and rapid departure of Byron Snopes's Indian children. These episodes are based upon material previously published in short story form as, respectively, "Centaur in Brass," "Mule in the Yard," and "The Waifs,"[2] and while they differ widely from each other in method and in tone, each is masterly after its own manner: the first has its narrative intricacy and its splendidly ironic reversals; the second, one of Faulkner's greatest comic *tours de force*, has its furious crescendoes of farcical activity; the third, striking a note less familiar in Faulkner's comic writing, offers a kind of savage grotesquerie— Byron Snopes's Indian children, according to Charles Mallison, "didn't look like people. They looked like snakes. Or maybe that's too strong too. Anyway, they didn't look like children." (p. 360) When Faulkner incorporates this short-story material into *The Town*, he distributes the relatively self-contained comic episodes in such a way that they operate within the book's aesthetic pattern as discrete, static elements set off against the flow of the narrative which contains them, while in social and thematic terms they serve as reminders of what Snopesism means in practice and are ironically counterpointed against the irrelevance and ineffectuality of Gavin Stevens's anti-Snopes crusade. Because they are so discrete and self-contained, and because we may be aware of their previous independent existence as short stories, these episodes perhaps retain something of the character of set-pieces; yet they have structural and contextual functions beyond those of the simple comic interlude, and each of them is linked with the main action of the novel, marking another step in the career of Flem Snopes.

Charles Mallison's role as major supplier of factual information frees for other purposes the narratives of Stevens and Ratliff, and it is in terms of a kind of dialogue between these two narratives, reinforced by the passages of actual dialogue between Stevens and Ratliff which occur throughout the book, that Faulkner dramatises some of the crucial conflicts of The Town. After Mallison (54 per cent), Stevens has the next largest share in the narration; his sections amount to approximately 38 per cent of the whole, leaving Ratliff with a mere 8 per cent. If Ratliff is felt as a much more significant presence in the novel than these proportions would suggest, that is partly because he figures in conversations reported by both Mallison and Stevens, but mainly because his very brevity, itself an expression of his intelligence and practical good sense, provides so effective, so deflationary, a contrast to the windy speculations of Gavin Stevens. It would be an over-simplification to speak of the distinction between the points of view of Mallison, Stevens, and Ratliff as one between, respectively, fact, theory, and truth, but there are important respects in which such a categorisation could be justified, and certainly this placing of Stevens, the identification of him as the odd man out in the trio, seems crucial to any understanding of his role in the novel as a whole.

Gavin Stevens, after all, is the central character of The Town: he has often been regarded simply as an analytical tool in Faulkner's hands, yet it would appear that he is himself the main subject for analysis. Despite the complexities of his personal relationships with his uncle, Charles Mallison's major function as a narrator is to set the scene for Stevens's thoughts and actions, while Ratliff's function is to scrutinise these thoughts and actions and pronounce upon their adequacy, or otherwise, to the demands of the changing situation. That Stevens should occupy so central a position is made possible, and in some degree necessary, by the prior existence of The Hamlet. The Town is a very different book from The Hamlet, and in writing it Faulkner seems to have referred back only rarely to the earlier book; he certainly seems to have made no particular effort to ensure narrative consistency and continuity. But The Town nonetheless builds upon The Hamlet; the events of The Hamlet lie behind all the situations of the later novel, and there can be no doubt of Faulkner's intention that they should be read in sequence, as the first and second volumes of a trilogy. Hence he found it neither necessary nor desirable to devote particular attention in *The Town* to the characterisation of Ratliff or of Flem Snopes : *The Hamlet*, insofar as it is a continuous narrative, offers a progressive revelation of both Ratliff and Flem as well as a record of that conflict between them which culminates in Ratliff's defeat. Following his defeat Ratliff has lost none of his courage, nor abated any of his fundamental opposition to Snopesism; his role in *The Town*, however, is more subdued and at the same time more subtle— he is the first to realise, for example, that Flem Snopes himself can be relied upon to rid Jefferson of the cruder varieties of Snopesism, and it is he who takes the practical step of giving financial support at a crucial moment to the anti-Snopes forces represented by Wallstreet Panic Snopes and his wife.

In *The Town* the avowed, and enthusiastic, opponent of Flem Snopes is Gavin Stevens, but any conflict between the two, at least in the sense of an active engagement, is more apparent than real. Ratliff in *The Hamlet* represented for Flem a serious threat which had to be contained and defeated; Gavin Stevens in *The Town* engages in a fantasy combat, aiming blows which Flem does not even need to avoid. The progress which Flem makes in Jefferson is the result not so much of his success in competition with others as of his internal, personal achievements of increased social awareness and renewed tactical flexibility; the outward evidence of his progress through *The Town* is provided not, as in *The Hamlet*, by economic victories over his rivals or his neighbours, but rather by a series of extremely memorable visual images : the water-tank, for example, which turns out to be, in Charles Mallison's words, not Flem's monument but his footprint; Flem's headgear, the cap giving way to the "hot-looking black politician-preacher's hat" (p. 141); Flem himself at his station in the bank, as immobile and apparently as permanent as Mrs. Jenny Du Pre's rubber plant; Eula's monument with the inscription which Flem himself has chosen. Flem displays, indeed, an adaptability, a capacity to learn, to change with changing circumstances, which Stevens himself would have done well to emulate. Stevens, of course, unlike Flem Snopes, is a man of principle, but it is the very rigidity of his principles which disables him as an effective opponent of Snopesism. Indeed, although the overt, the public theme of the novel may be the battle between Stevens and Flem Snopes, the real business of the book reveals itself as the internal conflict within Stevens himself between, on the one hand, the principles inculcated into him by his background and his education, and, on the other, the often contradictory demands of actual living. Trapped and immobilised by these opposing pressures, Stevens is reduced to ineffectuality, and it is one of the most pointed ironies of the novel that whenever Stevens achieves some form of positive action he does precisely what will assist Flem Snopes: his failure as an opponent of Snopesism is more radical even than Ratliff's had been in The Hamlet, and a good deal more culpable.

"Because he missed it. He missed it completely," (p. 153) says Ratliff at one point: indeed, at this particular point that is all he says. A subsequent section spoken by Ratliff contains no more than a similar assertion of Steven's persistence in error, while another begins: "No no, no no, no no. He was wrong. He's a lawyer, and to a lawyer, if it aint complicated it dont matter whether it works or not because if it aint complicated up enough it aint right and so even if it works, you don't believe it." (p. 296) Ratliff is speaking in this instance of Stevens's speculations about the means which Flem has apparently found for bringing pressure on Will Varner with a view to establishing himself as president of the bank, and the violence of Ratliff's rejection is necessitated, for the reader as for Ratliff himself, by the initial persuasiveness of Stevens's highly circumstantial yet wholly unsubstantiated projections. Stevens, like Miss Rosa Coldfield in Absalom, Absalom!, is an irrepressible fabulist, and, again like Miss Rosa, his brilliant but unreliable interpretations set an indelible stamp upon the book in which he appears. Only the closest reading of The Town reveals the full dangers of a literal dependence upon Stevens's excited, melodramatic, and, as often as not, entirely erroneous versions of events. Stevens's tendency is to see himself, Flem, Eula, and Linda as if they were all figures in a pattern, characters of myth, fable, or morality play: at one point he sees himself, bitterly, in the role of "family friend to Flem Snopes who had no more friends than Blackbeard or Pistol, to Eula Varner who no more had friends than man or woman either would have called them that Messalina and Helen had." (p. 205) Eula, for him, is "that damned incredible woman, that Frenchman's Bend Helen, Semiramis—no: not Helen nor Semiramis: Lilith: the one before Eve herself who earth's Creator had perforce in desperate and amazed alarm in person to efface, remove, obliterate, that Adam might create a progeny to populate it." (p. 44) So persistent is this mythologising tendency in Stevens's imagination that it comes as a shock to him, and to the reader, to discover that Eula is of normal size, to be confronted with the crude physical facts of Eula's affair with De Spain, to realise that Flem and Eula, having lived together for eighteen years, must necessarily talk to each other from time to time and come to agreements about practical, everyday affairs. And Eula, whatever Stevens's imagination told him, did have friends, among them Ratliff himself: when Eula casually refers to Ratliff as Vladimir, Stevens, who knows him only as V. K., has to exclaim "Vladimir? Did you say Vladimir? V. K. Is his name Vladimir?" (p. 322)

Together with Stevens's habit of abstraction, of speculation entirely beside the facts, or excessively beyond them, goes his sheer blindness to what is going on around him, and the novel offers a constant ironic interplay between what we gather from Mallison, from Ratliff, or from inference, to be the facts of the situation, and what Stevens imagines has happened, is happening, or will happen. It comes as a complete surprise to Stevens that Ratliff has gone into partnership with Wall Snopes; he has to learn from Eula, of all people, what Ratliff's initials stand for. Not only does Eula lead a day-to-day social and domestic life of which Stevens has not the slightest conception, she actually knows a good deal more of what is happening in Jefferson, and to Stevens's friends, than Stevens does himself. Indeed, Eula becomes in *The Town* a representative figure not only, as in *The Hamlet*, of superabundant vitality, but also of practical intelligence: in a quite down-to-earth way she embodies not only life but capacity for living. And some of her remarks during her three crucial interviews with Stevens operate no less effectively than Ratliff's warnings as a corrective to Stevens's abstracting imagination:

"You dont know very much about women, do you?" she said. "Women aren't interested in poets' dreams. They are interested in facts. It doesn't even matter whether the facts are true or not, as long as they match the other facts without leaving a rough seam." (p. 226)

Again Eula says: "I dont like scenes. You dont have to have scenes. Nobody needs to have a scene to get what you want." (p. 321) And on yet another occasion:

"You spend too much time expecting," she said. "Dont expect. You just are, and you need, and you must, and so you do. That's all. Dont waste time expecting." (p. 94)

Stevens does not know much about women, as Ratliff also tells him, in a remark that seems almost to echo Eula's; he becomes involved, upon his own initiative, in a series of foolish and unnecessary scenes, having committed himself, as often as not, to the defence of the manifestly indefensible; and he spends a large proportion of his time in expectation, in vain speculation, rather than in actual living. Consequently, although his whole position has been grounded in a desire to aid, support, and defend Eula Varner, Stevens ultimately fails her, as all the other men in her life have done. Stevens is the last person to see Eula before her suicide, and because he refuses to give her the assurances about Linda for which she asks, we shall see that he can be said, from one point of view, to bear a portion of the responsibility for her death. He goes to great lengths to help Eula's daughter, Linda, but at the end of the book he seems only to have succeeded in deracinating her. He sees himself as Eula's ally against Flem Snopes, but in practice he repeatedly finds himself assisting Flem in the furtherance of his aims, even to the point of undertaking the erection of that monument to Eula which is to stand as a symbol of Flem's unimpeachable respectability. By a final irony, it is Stevens who finds himself driven to swear to Linda that Flem is in truth her father, even though in so doing he jeopardises that very faith in his veracity which has made Linda appeal to him.

Faulkner himself admirably defined this aspect of Stevens's character and situation in answering another question at the University of Virginia. In *The Town*, said Faulkner, Stevens had "got out of his depth":

> He had got into the real world. While he was—could be—a county attorney, an amateur Sherlock Holmes [as in *Knight's Gambit*], then he was at home, but he got out of that. He got into a real world in which people anguished and suffered, not simply did things which they shouldn't do. And he wasn't as prepared to cope with people who were following their own bent, not for a profit but simply because they had to. That is, he knew a good deal less about people than he knew about the law and about ways of evidence and drawing the right conclusions from what he saw with his legal mind. When he had to deal with people, he was an amateur, he was —at times he had a good deal less judgment than his nephew did. Which is not against education. Probably the passion he had for getting degrees, for trying this and trying that and going all the way to Europe to get more degrees, to study more, was in his own nature, it was the same character that made him shy away from marriage, he was probably afraid to be married. He might get too involved with the human race if he married one of them.[3]

There can be no question of Stevens's inadequacy for life, nor of the validity of the judgments passed upon him by Eula Varner—explicitly in her interviews with him, implicitly by the very fact of what she is and how she behaves—or by Ratliff: speaking of Stevens's ignorance of women and of the world, Ratliff observes, "You never listened to nobody because by that time you were already talking again." (p. 229) But *The Town* is not a simple exposition of Stevens's folly. Indeed, Stevens is not wholly foolish, and in certain respects he is both attractive and admirable. His quixotry is often wrong-headed, ludicrously in excess of the facts or wilfully in opposition to them, but it always springs from principle, a will towards virtue, and a fundamental goodness of heart. Good intentions are never enough by themselves in the Faulknerian scale of values, but Warren Beck, in his fine study of the Snopes trilogy, defines this aspect of Stevens's personality in very positive terms:

Gavin Stevens' chivalry, then, is fundamental, in that he is protagonist of the ethic which is most explicit in putting women and children first but which applies in defense of all common human rights and of any decency, civility, and gentility conservative of such rights. Gavin's quixotism is not an aberration but simply an extravagance, a generous expenditure in the direction of the humane, setting the perhaps possible above the probable, and if it is cavalier, it is gallantly so, sensing honor vitally as something beyond position and assumption, to be lived up to in progressive conduct.[4]

Stevens's chivalry, as Beck calls it, certainly leaves us in no doubt of his essential goodness as a man, and in another of his comments about *The Town* at the University of Virginia Faulkner said that although the picture of Stevens fighting De Spain—"the knight that goes out to defend somebody who don't want to be defended and don't need it"— was both "sad and funny," it also showed "a very fine quality in human nature. I hope it will always endure."[5] Much of the complexity of *The Town* derives from the uncomfortable co-existence of this fundamental goodness of Stevens's with his ineffectuality and sheer wrongness in practical matters. He may mean well, but he does badly.

In fairness to Stevens, it must be said that in some of the situations where he is called upon to make a decision, no wholly satisfactory solution is possible: the most that can be hoped for is the choice of the lesser evil. At such moments our personal involvement in the novel is at once close, poignant, and salutary. Should Stevens have made love to Eula when she offered herself to him? Should he have married Linda at Eula's request, or at least have said that he would do so? Was he right in allowing Linda to go on thinking that Flem was her father? Was he wise to take the initiative in sending Linda away from Jefferson, and in the end to Greenwich Village? Judged by all the pragmatic and life-enhancing values embodied in the figure of Eula Varner, the decision which Stevens makes in each of these issues would appear to be the wrong one: Stevens was a fool and a coward not to take what Eula was willing to give; if he had promised to marry Linda he would presumably have prevented Eula's suicide; it was both dishonest and repulsive that he should tell Linda that Flem was her father; Linda was even less likely to find in Greenwich Village than in Jefferson the stability and love she needed, and which Stevens himself said he wanted for her. And yet, even without exploring to the full the ambiguities involved, it is clearly possible to take up quite contrary positions on all these issues. Stevens, it might be said, was right to refuse Eula's offer precisely because it meant so little to her; he was right not to promise Eula that he would marry Linda for the simple reason that marriage to Stevens would manifestly not have been the right solution for Linda herself; he could do no other than assure Linda that Flem was her father in view of what he had promised Eula in that final interview, and in view, indeed, of the reasons for which Eula had chosen suicide; he was right to encourage Linda to go away from Jefferson because she would have had no chance there of fulfilling herself, of realising her potentialities as a human being. These arguments may all have about them a touch of the cautious, the prudential, even the priggish, but they are not arguments lightly to be put aside.

A case for Stevens, then, can certainly be made out, and, in any event, he would command our sympathy as a suffering human being in the intolerable choices with which he is faced. Stevens's limitations appear, however, precisely in the degree to which he is so often unaware that there is a choice to be made. He does not begin to appreciate the complexities of the situations with which he concerns himself; he never realises what may be at stake for some of the characters involved (for example, that Eula, during that last interview, could be contemplating suicide); gifted fabulist though he is, ingenious though his intellectual processes undoubtedly are, Stevens lacks that capacity for sympathetic imaginative identification which alone could enable him to approach the truth. His reactions are automatic, trained, inflexible. As Faulkner said of him in a passage already quoted, he "had made of himself a more or less artificial man," basing his conduct not upon any sensitive apprehension of the needs of actual living, but upon what he had been educated to believe was right and virtuous in all circumstances. In one sense, Stevens is an example of that moral rigidity which Faulkner had rejected in so many of his books, most notably in *Light in August* and in the sad figure of Ike McCaslin in *Go Down, Moses*. Even more immediately, Stevens recalls the trained incapacity for life which Faulkner had dramatised in the figure of Horace Benbow,[6] although it is not until *The Mansion* that we see Stevens in the final withdrawal and cushioned domestication of his marriage with Melisandre Backus.

But in seeing Stevens as finally a somewhat pathetic figure we must not fall into the error of thinking him contemptible. If we find his quixotry irrelevant and even comic, as Faulkner clearly intended us to do, we must remember that Don Quixote himself was one of Faulkner's favourite characters,[7] and that Faulkner had no intention of questioning the nobility or humanity of the principles to which Stevens so resolutely held. Above all, it is important not to overlook Stevens's final speech, as he weighs and then accepts Ratliff's suggestion that Eula killed herself because she was bored:

"Bored," Uncle Gavin said. Then he said it again, not loud: "Bored." And that was when he began to cry, sitting there straight in the chair behind the desk with his hands folded together on the desk, not even hiding his face. "Yes," he said. "She was bored. She loved, had a capacity to love, for love, to give and accept love. Only she tried twice and failed twice to find somebody not just strong enough to deserve, earn it, match it, but even brave enough to accept it. Yes," he said, sitting there crying, not even trying to hide his face from us, "of course she was bored." (pp. 358-359)

The passage beautifully epitomises Stevens's peculiar combination of strength and weakness; it epitomises, too, the ambivalence of Faulkner's attitude towards him. Stevens is still wrong, terribly wrong, about Eula and about the reasons for her death; he is still incapable of realising the role which he himself has played. Yet he does show himself to be capable of experiencing deeply humane emotions—pity, the sense of tragic waste—and to be capable, too, of displaying those emotions frankly and without shame. Although remaining incapable of a full involvement in the life around him, Stevens nevertheless gains dignity from the totality of his commitment to some of the most permanent and positive of man's ideals.

THE MANSION

The Mansion, the final volume of the Snopes trilogy, was published in November 1959. Read in the sequence of the trilogy, immediately following *The Hamlet* and *The Town*, it may seem a less vital book than either of its predecessors. *The Town* had been a lesser work than *The Hamlet*, and very different in tone and technique, but its superbly controlled ambiguities and sheer profusion of incident and notation had made it unmistakably a major work; in *The Mansion*, however, the narrative of Gavin Stevens's relationship with Linda Snopes becomes tedious and even, in the New York and Pascagoula episodes, imaginatively unpersuasive, and, despite the liveliness of the account of old Meadowfill and the hog, there is some flagging of the comic invention—even at the time of Ratliff's disposal of Senator Clarence Snopes. Yet *The Mansion* in no sense shames the rest of the trilogy: it is a thoroughly competent piece of work with individual qualities which distinguish it from both *The Hamlet* and *The Town* and mark it out as being in important respects another kind of book altogether. Where *The Hamlet* and *The Town* concern themselves with worlds strictly limited both in social and in geographical terms, *The Mansion* ranges much further afield, presenting a wide range of characters and social types in many different settings, and achieving an almost picaresque variety and progression, most notably in the account of Mink's journey from Parchman to Jefferson. Mink's diverse encounters with good men and bad—with the storekeeper, the mad Goodyhay, the crooked pawnbroker, the two Memphis policemen, the Negro farmer—all serve to emphasise his Rip Van Winkle aspect, his remoteness from a world he last saw thirty-eight years previously, but they also mark the stages of his progress towards Jefferson and Flem.

The characterisation of Mink and the evocation of his slow but inevitable movement across the land are so powerful and disturbing that Mink's story, though suspended for the whole of the long central section, casts a peculiar excitement over the whole book. But if Mink is *The Mansion's* greatest triumph he is not its central figure. The core of the book is supplied by Stevens's continuing, though singularly unprogressive, relationship with Linda, and Faulkner both sustains and deepens the deliberate ambiguity of his presentation of Stevens, ultimately bringing to bear upon him pressures more testing even than those of *The Town*. Stevens reaps in *The Mansion* the consequences of the mistakes he made in *The Town*. Linda apparently loved Barton

Kohl and believed in him, and to that extent the New York experiment justified itself. Yet her suffering, deafness, and eventual decline as a human being are also seen as following—not inevitably, perhaps, but in practice—upon her deracination, which was in turn the outcome of Stevens's refusal to marry her and his insistence that she should go away from Jefferson. As in *The Town*, the arguments are nicely balanced. Nobody pretends that a marriage between Stevens and Linda would be an ideal solution, and it becomes less feasible as the years go by. At the same time, it offers itself as an eminently practical way of resolving a number of difficulties, and we can scarcely overlook Ratliff's frequent, and clear-sighted, warnings that the ultimate course of events will prove more disastrous than the marriage could ever have been.

When, on page 232 of *The Mansion*, Ratliff agrees to Charles Mallison's statement that Linda is not going to marry Stevens, he adds: "It will be worse than that." He repeats the remark, again in conversation with Charles, at the end of the "Linda" section of the novel, and in each case it is not of Linda that they are principally thinking, but of Stevens himself: it is for Stevens that things are going to be "worse"; it is Stevens who must bear the final burden of pity, disillusionment, and guilt. The main function of Ratliff and Charles as narrators, in *The Mansion* as in *The Town*, is to throw light on Stevens and his dilemma, and the somewhat offensive undergraduate tone which Charles adopts is closely related to his ambivalent feelings about Stevens and Linda: he apparently finds Linda physically attractive, but his main concern is with Stevens, whom he loves, in exasperated fashion, and tries to protect. Ratliff, whose voice in this novel as in its predecessors is that of intelligence and sanity, says to Charles on one occasion:

> "Look-a-here, what you want to waste all this good weather being jealous of your uncle for? Somebody's bound to marry him sooner or later. Someday you're going to outgrow him and you'll be too busy yourself jest to hang around and protect him. So it might jest as well be Linda." (p. 219)

Ratliff, significantly, can speak of Charles outgrowing Stevens, and he is prepared to see Stevens marry Linda. Equally significant is Ratliff's attitude towards Linda herself. As he tells Charles on one occasion, although the mementoes in his room are immediately connected with Linda, it is the memory of Eula Varner which he wishes to enshrine. Stevens, in *The Mansion*, seems largely to have forgotten about Eula, the urgency of his quixotry having seized upon Linda with at least equal enthusiasm, but Ratliff maintains a clear distinction between mother and daughter, and we come gradually to realise the degree to which Linda cannot match her mother in emotional

and moral stature any more than in physical appearance. Eula would
never have allowed herself to encourage Stevens in his fey notions
of a love which did not need physical expression; she would have seen
clearly that this was yet another of Stevens's excuses for escaping
involvement, just one more of his chivalric self-justifications for
avoiding sexual confrontation. That Stevens does find Linda attractive
is evident from their last embrace:

> he holding her, his hand moving down her back while the
> dividing incleft outswell of her buttocks rose under the harsh khaki,
> as had happened before now and then, the hand unchallenged—it
> had never been challenged, it would never be, the fidelity unthreat-
> ened and secure even if there had been nothing at all between the
> hand and the inswelling incleft woman flesh, he simply touching
> her, learning and knowing not with despair or grief but just sorrow
> a little, simply supporting her buttocks as you cup the innocent
> hipless bottom of a child. (pp. 423-424)

On this particular occasion Stevens is in fact holding Linda with
"terror," having just fully comprehended her responsibility for Flem's
death; he realises that her eyes are "not secret, not tender, perhaps not
even gentle." Faulkner clearly intends us to see how far Stevens's illu-
sions about Linda have been related to his adolescent sexual attitudes
and behaviour—his pride in sustaining a "fidelity" upon which Linda
herself places only a minimal value, his capacity for comparing Linda's
body to that of a child when, by ironic reversal, it is Linda who is
now the experienced partner in their relationship and Stevens himself
the innocent, the child.

Stevens shrinks from the facts and even the terminology of physical
love—he is shocked at hearing Linda use "the explicit word" (p. 238)
—and where Flem is impotent through physical disability Stevens
seems no less effectively to emasculate himself through his inhibitions
and intellectualisations: in this respect, at least, he resembles the
Prufrock figures of Faulkner's earlier fiction. Stevens's eventual
marriage to Melisandre Backus is a sadly middle-aged affair, and we
see that he has left everything too late: indeed, one of the most ironic
aspects of Stevens's career is that for him to have taken Linda, slept
with her, even married her at any late state of their relationship would
have been out of the question, simply because it would have nullified
the long years of refraining, made meaningless the previous refusal
not only of Linda but of Eula before her.

The pressures upon Stevens reach their climax at the very end of
the book, when the major themes and narrative threads of the whole
trilogy are brought triumphantly together in the description of Flem's
death and of the events leading up to it, and in this closing section
Faulkner seems to indicate his desire for unambiguous statement by

rejecting all his available first-person narrators and choosing instead, as in *The Hamlet*, the conventions of third-person narration. The whole episode recalls, in its complexity and in the illumination it sheds upon characters and events, the scene in the "Delta Autumn" chapter of *Go Down, Moses* in which Ike McCaslin meets Roth Edmonds's Negro mistress. Flem Snopes dies full of years, of wealth, and even of honour: he is president of the bank, deacon of the Baptist church, owner of the old De Spain mansion; he is given "a big funeral," (p. 419) attended not only by the town but by the county too, thus posthumously receiving a tribute to his achievement in comparison with which the water-tank, Eula's monument, and the mansion itself had been no more than footprints. Flem is killed by Mink, the dedicated instrument of vengeance, but it is Linda who has set that instrument in motion two years in advance of its due time, and Gavin Stevens, District Attorney, champion of justice and humanity, has allowed himself to be made an accessory to the murder. There is an apparent poetic justice in Flem's death at the hand of another Snopes, as if Snopesism were finally self-defeated. Yet the act for which Mink holds Flem guilty took place thirty-eight years in the past, making the revenge almost as anachronistic as Mink himself, while, by a final irony, Flem seems actually to welcome the death which Mink brings him: he does nothing to prevent Mink's early release, takes no steps to protect himself, and makes no effort to prevent Mink from taking a second shot when the first misfires. Mink and Linda, it would appear, may actually have done Flem a favour by killing him, and Gavin Stevens may once again have trapped himself into playing Flem's game.

Linda's share of the guilt for Flem's murder is in a real sense greater than Mink's, in that she acts deliberately, whereas Mink operates almost instinctively from a deep-rooted sense of what he *must* do if he is to remain a man. The deterioration of Linda as a human being is further indicated by her purchase of the white Jaguar. The foreignness of the car, its speed, colour and sheer ostentation, the mere fact that it is a vehicle in which, given her deafness, she can only be a danger to herself and to others—all this makes it clear that the car and the manner of its purchase in advance of Flem's death are intended by Linda as a flagrant symbol of her determination to cast off not only Flem but Jefferson and Gavin Stevens as well. For Stevens himself the conclusion of the novel, and of the trilogy, is bitterly ironic. He had collaborated in securing Mink's release, refusing to acknowledge even to himself what Linda's motives might be, and only the sight of her new car forces upon him the recognition of her guilt, and hence of his own. Stevens is now bereft of the two women round whom so much of his life has revolved; he is bereft, too, through self-betrayal, of that very body of principle upon which all his conduct had been based, and he has still failed to attain knowledge either of himself or of the world. His retreat into marriage with Melisandre Backus, living in a luxury made possible by the ill-gotten gains of Melisandre's first husband, a highly successful bootlegger, seems a pathetic conclusion for a man of Stevens's pretensions. Yet Stevens's goodness, his high ethical commitment, are still felt as positive, valuable elements: his tragedy lies in his inability to make these elements effective in action.

As Stevens and Ratliff drive out after the murder to try and find Mink Snopes, Ratliff forces him to confront what Linda has done, at the same time providing an interpretation of her action—as revenge for Eula's suffering—which will make it seem more comprehensible to Stevens, or at least more readily susceptible of rationalisation. Stevens weeps, and of these tears Warren Beck observes:

> His is no mere conventional regret or shock that the cherished Linda has been accessory before the fact of a murder and has similarly involved him. It seems rather a lament for all that Linda has been through, and he with her, the loss and grief and ghastly wrongs endured with that fortitude which is also a numbing, perhaps a hardening, and above all a distortion. What Linda is driven to mirrors what it has been like for her to have been so driven. Thus the grotesque becomes the pathetic; irony in its very detachment is the more comprehending; the absurd is lifted to the level of the tragic by humane regret.[1]

There is perhaps more defeat, and more despair, in Stevens's tears than this analysis allows. Nevertheless, Beck's point is well taken, and the interpretation he offers is undoubtedly one way of viewing the passage, one aspect of the intricate ambiguities of the book's conclusion. We do pity Linda for what she has had to suffer; we recognise what she does as in some measure the result of what the world has done to her; and we see the pathos implicit in the contrast between what, as Eula's daughter, she might have been, and what she has in fact become. Stevens, too, despite his defeats, has an important positive role to play: his failures as a man do not invalidate the ideals he seeks to uphold; his chivalry, like Don Quixote's, is not destroyed by its irrelevance to some of the situations in which it is invoked. Though the different sections of the novel carry the names of Mink, Linda, and Flem, Stevens himself is the real focus of its major concerns. It is largely through his humanity, his sensitivity both to the promise of life and to its pity, that we apprehend the book's deeper levels of suffering and anguish. And it is largely in terms of his own demanding scale of values, his high estimation of man's possibilities, that the characters of the novel, himself among them, are ultimately judged.

At the very end of *The Mansion*, however, the positive values are embodied primarily in the strange figure of Mink Snopes. After a lifetime of labour, suffering, and unceasing struggle against known and unknown powers, all of them infinitely stronger and better equipped than himself, Mink returns at the close towards that earth which he fears, but with which he has always been associated, approaching a final mingling with the myriads of the dead:

> himself among them, equal to any, good as any, brave as any, being inextricable from, anonymous with all of them: the beautiful, the splendid, the proud and the brave, right on up to the very top itself among the shining phantoms and dreams which are the milestones of the long human recording—Helen and the bishops, the kings and the unhomed angels, the scornful and graceless seraphim. (pp. 435-436)

In this fine concluding passage, the culmination of the whole trilogy, with its deliberate echoes of Ike Snopes's idyll with the cow, Faulkner makes perhaps his most moving plea for minimal humanity—more moving, for example, than the grandiloquent plea of A Fable since it gains authority from the abundant life of the trilogy as a whole and from the strength of Mink's characterisation. Faulkner never denies Mink's animality, his instinctive propensity for savage violence, all those qualities in him which lead Ratliff to define him as the only absolutely "mean" Snopes. Yet Mink more and more compels our reluctant admiration, and in displaying so great a capacity for dignity and endurance even in a man otherwise utterly vicious and degraded Faulkner makes a magnificent gesture of admiration and faith towards mankind as a whole. If Mink's combination of radically opposed characteristics sometimes recalls Joe Christmas, he is not associated with any of the Christian imagery which Faulkner invoked in Light in August. Mink is not a Christ-figure, simply a man.

One aspect of The Mansion we have not so far considered is its recapitulation, sometimes in rather leisurely fashion, of events chronicled in the two earlier books. The position of The Mansion in the trilogy and in his own career—when he began the book he had already written seventeen novels—must naturally have inclined Faulkner to review the broad ground already covered, to knit up loose ends, to fit together previously discrete elements so that they might be seen as parts of an overall pattern. Even at the time of the preparation and publication of The Portable Faulkner, he had shown an interest in the possibility of drawing together all the threads of the Yoknapatawpha material, and in the last years of his life he spoke frequently of writing a Domesday Book of Yoknapatawpha County, a kind of genealogy of the different families, possibly somewhat along the lines of the Compson genealogy he wrote for The Portable Faulkner.[2] In The Mansion there are signs that Faulkner may have begun reviewing his whole œuvre with such an end in view. We encounter once again in The Mansion —usually by hearsay or in narrative summary—such characters as

Pat Stamper, Miss Joanna Burden, Skeets McGowan, Colonel John Sartoris, Bayard Sartoris and his son Benbow. A man called Spoade is mentioned, grandson of the Spoade whom Quentin Compson had known at Harvard in *The Sound and the Fury*; we learn what happens to Benjy, how he eventually burns down the Compson house and himself with it; we discover that the store of which Jason Compson eventually becomes the proprietor originally belonged to Ike Mc-Caslin; we see Jason himself defeated in an economic contest with Flem Snopes. In this last instance, Faulkner skilfully uses another character who prided himself on his business acumen as a means of giving a fresh emphasis to Flem's own shrewdness, but for the most part these reminiscences, recapitulations and reworkings of earlier material seem to have little functional justification in terms of the novel as a whole, whatever interest they may have in relation to Faulkner's developing conception of Yoknapatawpha County. But if this constant retrospection often seems merely to dilute or delay the narrative progress and the exploration of the moral dilemmas, there is nevertheless something satisfactory about the very tidiness of the process, the piecing together of the jig-saw. Some of the pieces had to be altered in certain ways before they could be fitted into place, and Faulkner himself recognised this in the note with which he prefaced the novel, explaining that the "contradictions and discrepancies" between *The Mansion* and its predecessors were "due to the fact that the author has learned, he believes, more about the human heart and its dilemma than he knew thirty-four years ago; and is sure that, having lived with them that long time, he knows the characters in this chronicle better than he did then."

James B. Meriwether recalls that some of the inconsistencies between *The Hamlet* and *The Town* were removed by Faulkner when his attention was drawn to them at the time when the later novel was in galley proof. When Faulkner submitted the typescript of *The Mansion*, however, the discrepancies between the new book and its two predecessors were pointed out to him before type was set up, and he made a considerable effort to eliminate them: "Not only did he make a lot of small changes, but in at least one chapter he did some rather substantial rewriting to bring it into closer accordance with *The Town* and *The Hamlet*."[3] Certain changes demanded by consistency Faulkner refused to make, using the argument he later embodied in his preface to the published book and which he had used several years before in writing to Malcolm Cowley about the inconsistencies between the Compson genealogy and *The Sound and the Fury*: he said that he had simply changed his mind about some incidents and characters, and that it was now *The Hamlet* which needed to be rewritten in order to bring it into line with *The Town* and *The Mansion*.[4] What is important here is not that Faulkner failed to remove all discrepancies but that he should have concerned himself at all with matters of this kind. Faulkner's interest in questions of continuity and consistency may suggest that his mind was turning towards a rationalising review of his previous work. It certainly indicates the high value which he set upon the Snopes trilogy as a whole, the work with which he had lived the longest and in which he had concerned himself, more consistently than elsewhere, not so much with the extreme, the violent, or the perverted—to use the terms so favoured by those of his readers who have read little of his work and relished only *Sanctuary*—but rather with the ordinary, the humble, and even the abject representatives of mankind. "Art is simpler than people think [Faulkner wrote to Cowley in 1945] because there is so little to write about. All the moving things are eternal in man's history and have been written before, and if a man writes hard enough, sincerely enough, humbly enough, and with the unalterable determination never never never to be quite satisfied with it he will repeat them, because art like poverty takes care of its own, shares its bread."[5]

THE REIVERS

IN *The Reivers*, as in *The Mansion*, Faulkner returns again and again to incidents, settings, and characters first created in earlier novels and stories, often elaborating, reworking, and even revaluing his previous treatment of such material. The mood of the book is genial, nostalgic: not for nothing is it sub-titled "A Reminiscence." We re-encounter Boon Hogganbeck and his wild shooting, Mr. Buffaloe and his motor-car, Miss Reba, Minnie and the Memphis brothel; we hear mention of Flem Snopes, Thomas Sutpen, and Major De Spain; we meet in the flesh the Mr. Binford who in *Sanctuary* had been no more than a maudlin memory; Miss Corrie turns out to have been christened Everbe Corinthia, the name Faulkner gave years before to the English lock-keeper's daughter in "Leg." The Priest family, to which Lucius, the narrator, belongs, has not previously appeared in Faulkner's work, but the Priests are closely connected to the McCaslins, and if some of the relationships within the family seem rather familiar that may be partly because *The Reivers*, dedicated to Faulkner's grandsons, draws heavily on those autobiographical sources previously exploited in *Sartoris* and *The Unvanquished* and in the *Holiday* magazine piece on "Mississippi." Uncle Ned and Aunt Callie are apparently based on Falkner family servants of the same names; Lucius is one of four brothers, as was Faulkner; Lucius's father, Maury, owns a livery stable, as for many years did Faulkner's father, Murry. These and other parallels are obvious enough, and do a good deal to explain the warm, intimate note of the whole book.

We have already seen, however, that Faulkner's nostalgia in *The Reivers* is for his own early work as well as for his own early life. Especially interesting in this respect is the return to the characters and setting of the brothel scenes in *Sanctuary*, but at a time somewhat earlier than the events of that novel—a time when Mr. Binford was alive, Miss Reba still young, and the world, though sinning lustily, somehow more innocent than it later became. It is almost as though Faulkner, remembering the notoriety of *Sanctuary*, had deliberately replaced the corruption of that novel with images, perhaps not of sweetness and light but at least of common sense and charity. Indeed, Miss Reba's practical wisdom and sheer strength of character establish her, in *The Reivers*, as a figure scarcely less portentous or less admirable than Grandmother Millard in *The Unvanquished*. Such inversions and revaluations seem to have been deliberately intended by Faulkner:

they must have contributed to the mood of obvious enjoyment in which the book was written, and they constitute an important source of pleasure for the reader already familiar with Faulkner's earlier work.

Similar in intention and effect are those episodes in which Faulkner seems to run dangerously close to sentimentality while actually maintaining a tight and wholly unsentimental control. Thus when Everbe Corinthia reforms, gives up her trade, marries Boon and gives him a son, there may seem some justice in Leslie Fiedler's remark that Faulkner, who had earlier divided women "into the viable (to him) categories of mothers and whores," had succeeded in *The Reivers* in "proving to his own satisfaction that the whores are mothers too."[1] But Faulkner is fully aware of the comic aspects of the situation, and frankly exploits them in his descriptions of the utterly different but equally disruptive impacts made by Otis and Lucius upon Miss Reba's brothel and in the richly comic final scene, in which the reformed whore proudly displays what is all too plainly her husband's son to the young Lucius Priest who had been the instrument of her reformation :

> "Well?" she said. "What do you think?"
> I didn't think anything. It was just another baby, already as ugly as Boon even if it would have to wait twenty years to be as big. I said so. "What are you going to call it?"
> "Not it," she said. "Him. Cant you guess?"
> "What?" I said.
> "His name is Lucius Priest Hogganbeck," she said. (p. 305)

Superficially, as Faulkner is well aware, the moment out-Hollywoods Hollywood, but when played off against the cool realism of Lucius's own reactions the apparent sentimentality dissolves into sheer comedy.

The contest between Boon and Ludus in the opening chapter is another of the book's many and varied comic episodes—*The Reivers* becomes, indeed, almost an anthology of the most characteristic types of Faulknerian humour. Boon's ineffectiveness with a pistol is matched by the inadequacy of his powers of verbal self-expression, and the chapter contains splendid examples of what might be called the rhetoric of inarticulation, as Boon struggles to explain to Ludus the outrageousness of his remarks :

> "He insulted me," Boon said. "He told Son Thomas I was a narrow-asted son of a bitch."
> Now Mr Hampton looked at Ludus. "All right," he said.
> "I never said he was norrer-asted," Ludus said. "I said he was norrer-headed."

"What?" Boon said.

"That's worse," Judge Stevens said.

"Of course it's worse," Boon said, cried. "Cant you see? And I aint even got any choice. Me, a white man, have got to stand here and let a damn mule-wrestling nigger either criticise my private tail, or state before five public witnesses that I aint got any sense. Cant you see? Because you cant take nothing back, not nothing. You cant even correct it because there aint nothing to correct neither one of them to." (pp. 15-16)

Shortly before this exchange takes place, Ludus has been removed from his job at the livery stable: officially, he has been dismissed; in fact, by an unspoken convention, he knows, as does everyone else, that he has merely been suspended for a week. Towards the end of the chapter he shatters both convention and the patience of Lucius's father by speaking the unspoken—what, in the context of the whole episode, has become virtually the unspeakable :

"I could come back now, without waiting to Monday," Ludus said. "Iffen you needs me."

"No," Father said. (p. 17)

Later in the novel comes the precisely* described physical action of the horse-racing, the whole affair subtly managed by Ned with a skill and resourcefulness worthy of comparison with Pat Stamper's trading in "Fool About a Horse," or Uncle Buddy's poker-playing in "Was." There is, too, the initial motor-trip to Memphis, splendidly sustained as narrative, and richly diversified with incidents whose farcical elements, though always present, are allowed to emerge gradually and without over-emphasis. The "mudfarmer" who keeps Hell Creek bottom ploughed up in order to keep himself in business is a fine comic invention, but no less remarkable, here as throughout the book, is the verbal humour, the comedy achieved directly through the dialogue. When Boon and the mudfarmer haggle over the fee for pulling the car out of the mud, Boon's protest at the increase in the rate for pulling the same car out of the same mud-hole is answered with splendid illogic couched in the most logical of terms: "That was last year. There's more business now. So much more that I cant afford not to go up." (p. 90) And at the very end, when the mudfarmer is insisting on two dollars for each passenger, Boon protests that Lucius is only a child :

"Walking back to Jefferson might be lighter for him," the man said, "but it wont be no shorter."

"All right," Boon said, "but look at the other one! When he gets that mud washed off, he aint even white!"

The man looked at distance awhile. Then he looked at Boon. "Son," he said, "both these mules is color-blind." (p. 91)

These frankly comic allusions to the fact that Ned is a Negro are indicative of one important strand in the book's varied but unstrenuous treatment of white-Negro relationships. We are never allowed to forget that the action is not contemporary, and the whole strategy of the narrative point of view serves to stress the character of the novel as an affectionate evocation of a world that cannot return. Seen from this angle, it becomes irrelevant to speak of the portrait of Uncle Parsham as sentimentalised, or to complain of the obsolescence of the standards by which white behaviour towards Negroes appears to be judged: the ways in which Miss Reba acts towards Minny, for example, and Colonel Linscomb towards Ned, are intended to confirm our impression of them as admirable characters. In any case, we are touched by Miss Reba's solicitude for Minny, and it certainly seems appropriate that Otis and Butch, on the other hand, should be marked out by the contemptuousness with which they treat Ned and others of his race. Again, however, it is characteristic of *The Reivers* that Otis and Butch should alone incur condemnation, and even the caricatured figure of Otis becomes in the long run primarily a comic instrument. Butch's threat is ultimately deflected by Miss Corrie—in what may have been a conscious or unconscious reminiscence of Maupassant's "Boule de Suif"—but Faulkner's painfully convincing presentation of him remains the one serious disturbance of the book's overall geniality.

Other sources of disturbance, however, underlie the light surface, even though they only occasionally disrupt it. Chief among these are the frequent reminders of what this rush of events and experiences must mean for Lucius himself: Faulkner repeatedly holds in check the purely farcical elements of the action in order to insist on the implications for Lucius himself, to show how intolerable is the burden of knowledge and responsibility "which a boy of only eleven should not really be called to shoulder." (p. 224) The quotation exemplifies the virtues of Faulkner's choice of narrator. Strictly speaking, Lucius is an old man remembering, and reflecting upon, what it was like to have been the boy to whom these things happened; at the same time, his reporting of the boy's experience, and of the boy's reactions to it, seems so precise and sensitive that Faulkner manages to achieve both nostalgic retrospect and narrative immediacy, and achieve them simultaneously. The book evokes in affectionate terms the grandfather's memories of what the world was like in the days of his youth; it also offers an always eventful and sometimes moving narrative of the boy's precocious initiation into the facts of life; and it does both in terms of a narrative point of view capable of encompassing the nearness to experience of total recall as well as the ability to comment on experience which comes only with maturity. Faulkner never under-estimates the capacity of children for swift comprehension, for logical thought and purposive action, and he never over-estimates their capacity for articulation. Lucius Priest, as the boy, speaks only rarely, but he sees all, and even as a child he understands a good deal; reminis-cing as an old man, he can give coherence, shape, and meaning to the whole experience.

Lucius's initiation suggests in certain respects an ironic reversal of Ike McCaslin's in *Go Down, Moses*, in that Ike's introduction was to positive values, Lucius's to what the world calls sin. Closer analogies to Lucius's situation can be found in other of Faulkner's first-person narrators: Charles Mallison, for example, in *The Town*; Bayard Sartoris in *The Unvanquished*; and, perhaps more relevant than either of these, Quentin Compson in stories like "That Evening Sun" and "A Justice." As a story both of a boy's initiation and of young innocence triumphant, *The Reivers* also recalls *Intruder in the Dust*, while Faulkner can hardly have been unaware of the analogies between *The Reivers* and *Huckleberry Finn*. The boy-narrator and his older but less intelligent companion, the adventurous journey of escape, the eventual assumption of effective authority by a supremely gifted manipulator (perhaps ironically, it is a Negro, Ned, who fulfils the Tom Sawyer role), the establishment of close ties of loyalty between the boy and his companion—all these features *The Reivers* has in common with *Huckleberry Finn*. Most notable of all, perhaps, is the correspondence between Huck's famous decision to go to Hell for Jim's sake and Lucius's deliberate choice of what he calls Non-virtue as he allows Boon to drive past the turning to McCaslin and continue on towards Memphis: "So I said nothing; the fork, the last frail impotent hand reached down to save me, flew up and passed and fled, was gone, irrevocable; I said *All right then. Here I come.*" (p. 68) As with Huck, the world to which Lucius is so abruptly introduced is a wicked one, a world of whores, thieves, trickery, and lies where kindness, affection, courage, pity, and honour may nevertheless be encountered—indeed, in the same people who are responsible for the whoring, thieving, tricking, and lying. Lucius, entering into this world all unprepared, has rapidly to discover for himself a set of values by which to judge both the world and its inhabitants, and, as with *Huckleberry Finn*, the moral drama of the novel lies primarily in the hero's progressive creation of such a scale of values in response to the varied experiences which come his way.

In remembering the enthusiasm which greeted the publication of *The Reivers* only a few weeks before Faulkner's death, we may be tempted to ironic speculation as to whether the praise and over-praise which *The Reivers* received was in some degree a reflection of the relief which certain reviewers may have felt at encountering a Faulkner novel which they could read, understand, and enjoy in easy and effortless fashion. Sir Charles Snow, interviewed by the New York Times on the occasion of Faulkner's death, said that Faulkner "was enormously admired all over the world. Possibly he was admired more than read."[2] The observation was a shrewd one, for it is undoubtedly true both that Faulkner's reputation was largely the creation of literary opinion outside America, and especially in continental Europe, and that many of those who subscribed to the general estimate of Faulkner's greatness did so without particular enthusiasm and often with little intimate knowledge of his work. For such people The Reivers may well prove the most approachable of Faulkner's books; if so, they will gain from it a pleasant but very misleading impression. The Reivers is not one of Faulkner's most notable achievements, and it is scarcely to be compared with The Sound and the Fury, As I Lay Dying, Light in August, Absalom, Absalom!, The Hamlet, Go Down, Moses, or even Sanctuary, to which it so often harks back. Yet it remains an extremely funny book, and an engagingly happy one; and it seems, in retrospect, an entirely appropriate final volume in that long row of novels and short-story collections which demonstrates, merely at a glance, the security of Faulkner's claim to major stature.

SHORT STORIES

FAULKNER'S short stories warrant a treatment at once more extended and more detailed than the scope of the present study permits; at the same time, any account of Faulkner's achievement as a whole must make some acknowledgment of his mastery of the short-story form and of the importance in his career of the successive volumes in which the majority of his stories were collected. In considering *These 13* (1931), *Doctor Martino and Other Stories* (1934), *Knight's Gambit* (1949), and *Collected Stories* (1950), it is essential to think of them not simply as aggregations of individual stories but as volumes which may conceivably possess a discernible internal organisation of their own. Extremely relevant in this context is a letter which Faulkner wrote in the early autumn of 1948 to Malcolm Cowley, with whom he had recently stayed for a short period. Describing the slow flight South in an aircraft which seemed to stop at every possible airfield, Faulkner commented:

> It wasn't too dull because I spent the time thinking about the collection of stories, the which the more I think about, the better I like. The only book foreword I ever remembered was one I read when I was about sixteen, I suppose, in one of Sienckewicz (maybe that's not even spelled right), which, I dont even remember: Pan Michael or what, nor the actual words either: something like 'This book written in ... [sic] travail (he may have said agony and sacrifice) for the uplifting of men's hearts.' Which I believe is the one worthwhile purpose of any book and so even to a collection of short stories, form, integration, is as important as to a novel—an entity of its own, single, set for one pitch, contrapuntal in integration, toward one end, one finale.[1]

The passage offers an admirable statement both of Faulkner's seriousness of purpose in all his work and of his essential conception of fictional form. The idea of Faulkner extending this conception to the arrangement of the short-story collections may appear surprising at first, but he seems to have said something similar, if less precise, to Marshall Smith in 1931:

> When I saw him Faulkner was working on a new book, a collection of short stories. He believes that a book of short stories should

be linked together by characters or chronology. This collection was to be called *These Thirteen*, the stories dealing with the war, the imaginary town of Jefferson, and a few in other settings.[2]

These 13, published by Cape and Smith on September 21, 1931, has three main divisions, clearly marked in the first edition, which correspond to the broad categories mentioned in Smith's last sentence:

I
Victory
Ad Astra
All the Dead Pilots
Crevasse

II
Red Leaves
A Rose for Emily
A Justice
Hair
That Evening Sun
Dry September

III
Mistral
Divorce in Naples
Carcassonne[3]

Clearly the three indicated divisions have been made primarily in terms of geography and subject-matter: the four war stories, the six Yoknapatawpha County stories, and the final trio of stories about Americans abroad which fall into neither of these categories. When the list is inspected more closely, and with Faulkner's letter to Cowley in mind, other patterns begin to emerge. In titling the book Faulkner may have had in mind Balzac's *Les Treize*, but he was no doubt also aware of the traditional connotations of the number thirteen. There are few humorous stories in the volume, the sections are organised in such a way that the comic elements receive relatively little emphasis, while the concluding sentences of the final stories in each of the sections seem to represent variations on a single sombre theme:

Above his voice the wounded man's gibberish rises, meaningless and unemphatic and sustained. (p. 123)
The dark world seemed to lie stricken beneath the cold moon and the lidless stars. (p. 280)
Steed and rider thunder on, thunder punily diminishing: a dying

star upon the immensity of darkness and of silence within which, steadfast, fading, deepbreasted and grave of flank, muses the dark and tragic figure of the Earth, his mother. (p. 358)

It also seems significant that Faulkner should have ended the book with "Carcassonne." He once spoke of his fondness for the story,[4] and it perhaps represents an attempt to capture in words the anguish and ecstasy of the creative experience, or at least of the creative ambition: the buckskin pony seems to suggest an American-bred Pegasus, while Carcassonne itself apparently stands for the world of the imagination. Taken together with the culminating stories of the two previous sections, "Carcassonne" should perhaps be regarded as expressing a commitment to an ultimately tragic vision of life, and this commitment may possibly be linked with the book's dedication, "To Estelle and Alabama." Alabama was the name of Faulkner's great-aunt, Mrs. McLean, but it was also the name which Faulkner and his wife had given to that first daughter whose birth and swift death had occurred earlier in 1931, the year of publication of These 13.

The arrangement of the stories within each of the sections also seems to have been planned with some care. "Victory," although one of the weakest stories in the volume, is perhaps placed before the other war stories because of its time-span, which embraces the whole war and its immediate aftermath, and because it dramatises, in peculiarly violent terms, those sad and bitter ironies to which the subadar gives explicit expression in the succeeding story, "Ad Astra": " 'Those who have been four years rotting out yonder—' he waved his short thick arm—'are not more dead than we.' " (p. 69) The same note is sounded in the third story, "All the Dead Pilots," while the fourth, "Crevasse," refers back to "Victory," of which it was at one time a part,[5] and presents a concentrated image of horror and disgust which provides the occasion and justification for the concluding sentence we have already quoted.

In the second and longest section Faulkner seems deliberately to have rejected the opportunities for making the obvious connecting links between one story and another. "Red Leaves" and "A Justice," the two stories about Indians, are not placed together, nor is "A Justice" juxtaposed with "That Evening Sun," although Quentin Compson is the narrator in both. Miss Emily Grierson and Miss Minnie Cooper are similar characters, yet the stories in which they appear, "A Rose for Emily" and "Dry September," are placed some distance apart, while Faulkner also ignores the possibility of placing side by side "Hair" and "Dry September," the two stories in which Hawkshaw the barber appears as a central character. The clue to Faulkner's method is perhaps to be found in a phrase from his letter to Malcolm Cowley: "contrapuntal in integration." To have used the obvious connections between stories as a series of simple links would in fact have tended to fragment the collection into a number of smaller units. The experience of reading the central section according to Faulkner's scheme is one of continual recognition and awareness of reverberation: the recurrence of characters, setting, situations, and themes provokes the recollection and hence the continuing coexistence of the earlier story or stories and produces a total effect of progressive enrichment.

The last three stories form a more enigmatic group. All three, however, are concerned with the enlargement or extension of experience, and "Mistral" and "Divorce in Naples" are concerned, in a sense, with education. Carl and, to a limited extent, George in "Divorce in Naples" resemble the two young Americans in "Mistral" in that they are forced out of the innocence of inexperience into knowledge which must change them and which they must absorb before they resume the former pattern of their lives. When the dancing starts again, when the walking tour is continued, things are not the same as they were: Carl's loss of virginity, implicitly acknowledged in his decision to buy a present for his whore, finds its counterpart in "Mistral" in the young men's new awareness of "the secret nostalgic sense of frustration and of objectless and unappeasable desire." (p. 329) In "Carcassonne," as in the two previous stories, the protagonist is uprooted, out of his home environment, and the theme of the story, though pursued with much greater depth and complexity, resembles the themes of "Mistral" and "Divorce in Naples" in so far as it centres upon the idea of experience, of transcending the familiar. In other respects, as we saw earlier, its concern with the world of the imagination gives it a special position in the book, as if it were a final statement, both culminating and retrospective, of overall artistic intention.

Of the first and third groups in *These 13*, only one story, "Ad Astra," had previously been published; of the central group, only "A Justice" had not appeared in print before. And it is the stories of this group, and especially "Red Leaves," "A Rose for Emily," "That Evening Sun," and "Dry September," which represent the peak of Faulkner's achievement in the short story form—work which he was occasionally to equal, as in "Wash" and "Barn Burning," but never to surpass. That this achievement was, like all of Faulkner's work, the result of revision, of discipline, of an increasingly sophisticated technical mastery, becomes apparent from a study of manuscript and typescript material relating to some of these stories.

Norman Holmes Pearson has admirably demonstrated how, in revising "That Evening Sun," Faulkner eventually saw the need to omit certain passages of explicit comment on Nancy's situation: "like Hemingway," Professor Pearson observes, "Faulkner came to understand that what is created by presentation need not be repeated by statement."[6] A similar process of salutary revision can be studied in "Dry September" and "A Rose for Emily." The manuscript of "Dry

September" bears the title "Drouth," as does a surviving carbon type-script of the story; the leader of the lynching party, called McLendon in *These 13*, has the name Plunkett in these pre-publication versions and in the version published in *Scribner's* in January 1931.[7] There are more substantial changes, however. In the manuscript the order of the first two sections is reversed, so that the story opens with the description of Miss Minnie Cooper and then moves into the scene in the barber's shop: a great improvement is effected in later versions by opening dramatically with the tension among the men in the barber's shop and then juxtaposing the description of Minnie against an already created mood of violence. Even more important was the deletion from versions subsequent to the manuscript of two para-graphs which originally stood at the beginning of the third section, and which evoked in somewhat rhetorical terms the social context of the action. The opening sentences of the second of these paragraphs are characteristic: "Life in such places is terrible for women. Life in all places is terrible for women."[8] The advantages gained through omitting the paragraphs are obvious, since their abstract statements were presented powerfully and concretely elsewhere in the story in terms of the lives of the people involved in the action.

An even more striking example of this process of rejecting otiose abstract formulations is to be seen in the pre-publication versions of "A Rose for Emily," the first of Faulkner's full-length stories to be published and perhaps still the best-known. Half-way down the final page of the manuscript appears a conversation between Miss Emily and her Negro servant shortly before her death.[9] No trace of this conversation survives in published versions of the story, but the con-versation does appear, and in expanded form, in an extant carbon typescript. In this version the conversation begins at a point corres-ponding to the end of the present fourth section:

> ... her gray head propped on a pillow yellow and moldy with age and lack of sunlight, her voice cold and strong to the last.
> "But not till I'm gone," she said. ...

At the end of the conversation, the text leads directly into that of the published versions:

> ... she appeared to muse intently, as though she were listening to dissolution setting up within her. "Hah," she said.
> Then she died, and the negro met the first of the ladies at the front door ...[10]

The conversation itself occupies rather more than two pages of type-script. Miss Emily, expecting to die soon, talks of the shock the townspeople will have when they open the upstairs room, and the

Negro servant indicates that he knows what the room contains. Miss Emily also says that the Negro will be glad to have the money for the house, which she has bequeathed to him according to the agreement they had made thirty-five years before, since he will then be able to go to Chicago as he had always wanted to do: the terms of the agreement were apparently that if he died first she would bury him in a coffin bearing his name on a gold plate, and that if she died first he would inherit the house in her will. But the Negro replies that he wants neither house nor money because he is going to the poorhouse, where he can sit and watch the trains go by.

Not only would the retention of this material have diluted the final episodes and too long delayed the climactic revelation, but the direct presentation of Miss Emily, the preferred insight into personality and motive, would have greatly diminished the fruitful ambiguities of the narrative and the situation and tended to undermine the emphasis on the central theme of withdrawal into unreality and illusion. It should also be noticed that the conclusion of the typescript version of the story is more explicitly ghoulish even than the conclusion of the published versions. In the typescript the penultimate paragraph begins:

> The man himself lay in the bed; for a long while we just stood there, looking down at that profound and fleshless grin cemented into what had once been a pillow by a substance like hardened sealing-wax. One side of the covers was thrown back, as though he were preparing to rise; we lifted the covers completely away, liberating still another sluggish cloud of infinitesimal dust, invisible and tainted. The body had apparently once lain in the attitude of an embrace, but now . . .[11]

Here again the published version is undoubtedly preferable, and in these revisions of "A Rose for Emily" we can find the clearest possible evidence of Faulkner's growing sophistication as an artist, and specifically of his realisation of the advantages, especially in the short-story form, of allowing the narrative to make its own points, to establish its own ambiguities and implications, without elaborate underscoring.

In 1931 *Idyll in the Desert* was published in a slim volume from Random House, and in 1932 the Book Club of Texas brought out *Miss Zilphia Gant* in somewhat similar form: neither can be considered as anything other than a short story, and although both are competently done, with a touch in *Miss Zilphia Gant* of that grotesquerie which has marked so much of recent Southern fiction, neither is of any particular distinction. Throughout the early 1930's Faulkner continued to publish short stories in the magazines—eight in 1931, seven in 1932, three in 1933, nine in 1934—so that he had no difficulty in getting together another volume of stories for the spring of

1934: where seven stories had appeared for the first time in *These 13*, *Doctor Martino and Other Stories* contains only two stories, "Black Music" and "The Leg," which had not been previously published. *Doctor Martino* was much inferior to *These 13*. Apart from "Wash," which was closely related to *Absalom, Absalom!*, and "The Hound," which was not subsequently reprinted because of the use which Faulkner made of the same material in the Mink Snopes sections of *The Hamlet*, none of the stories showed Faulkner at his best. Nor does he appear to have given very serious thought to the internal organisation of the volume: it seems impossible, at least, to discern any clear pattern either of a contrapuntal or of a straightforward sequential nature, and we can more profitably discuss the stories as they reappear in the carefully articulated context of *Collected Stories*.

Faulkner's next collection of short stories after *Doctor Martino* did not appear until 1949, and although *Knight's Gambit* cannot be considered as possessing more than minor importance it has perhaps been too readily dismissed as simply a miscellaneous collection of not especially distinguished detective stories. The volume does have a certain thematic unity, and we can perceive in it some of the stages by which Faulkner worked towards the more overt social, moral and even political engagement characteristic of much of his later work, and towards his final conception of Gavin Stevens, the figure in or through whom that engagement was so frequently dramatised.

One of the barriers impeding fuller appreciation of *Knight's Gambit* is its opening story, "Smoke." Faulkner first published the story in *Harper's* in April 1932, but it had apparently been written—and several times rewritten—early in 1930.[12] It was republished in *Dr. Martino*, and it is the only one of the six stories in *Knight's Gambit* which had previously been collected. Yet it is surely the weakest of the six, and it seems extraordinary that Faulkner should have been so attached to so undistinguished a work: the only substantial reason for its inclusion in *Knight's Gambit* would seem to have been his need to use every one of the Gavin Stevens stories in order to fill out what proved, even so, to be only a short book. "Smoke" is a detective story in the tradition of Poe and Conan Doyle, with clues and, indeed, vital information withheld from the reader in such a way as to allow the final dénouement to rest entirely in the hands of the all-wise detective—Dupin, Sherlock Holmes, Gavin Stevens. This type of detective story has generally gone out of fashion in the present century, but what is more serious in the context of *Knight's Gambit* is that "Smoke" is by no means typical of the stories which follow it. Standing at the beginning of the volume, it inevitably does much to establish the tone and character of the whole; the difficulty is that it strikes a false note and creates expectations—or limitations of expectation—which are inappropriate to a proper understanding of the subsequent stories. All of them have the underlying structure of a detective story; but whereas "Smoke" must be judged almost entirely upon its merits as a representative of that particular genre, the later stories often have other, and more valuable, qualities— qualities which might easily be overlooked by the reader whose approach has been limited and channelled by the initial encounter with "Smoke."

"Monk" and "Tomorrow," for example, although not good stories, are sometimes moving ones, and none of the qualities which give them interest derive from their "detective" aspects. What we notice in these stories, however, is an apparently wilful refusal to develop those elements which seem to possess the richest human potentialities. In "Tomorrow" Faulkner creates in almost minimal terms at least one character, Jackson Fentry, whom he could readily have built up into a much more impressive figure, and the case of "Monk" is even more remarkable. This story, first published in 1937, anticipates, especially in its setting, certain aspects of both *The Hamlet* and *Intruder in the Dust*, but it also seems to draw in its characterisation of Monk himself, the near-idiot, upon the presentation of Benjy in *The Sound and the Fury*: like Benjy, Monk has "no comprehension of bereavement, irreparable finality." (p. 44) There is no attempt to make Monk an attractive figure; at the same time, Faulkner devotes to him, as to all his idiots, half-wits and mental incompetents, a special compassion, enabling Monk to emerge as a repulsive yet also a pathetic figure, with even a kind of earth-given strength which we are forced to recognise as admirable. At the end of the story, therefore, it seems appropriate, and in some measure a reminder and celebration of Monk's peculiar strength, that Gavin Stevens, quitting the tainted air of the prison and the even more tainted atmosphere of the Pardon Board, should evoke his sense of regained freedom and cleanliness in terms of the land with which Monk is continually associated.

It would seem clear that Faulkner has in Monk the outlines of a major character—such a character, say, as Mink Snopes, whom Monk resembles in so many ways. Yet this is not, in the end, Monk's story, but Gavin Stevens's. In his treatment of the strangely pathetic events leading to Monk's execution Faulkner is concerned to emphasise not so much the event themselves and their effect on Monk but rather the manner and circumstances in which Gavin Stevens finds them out. Stevens's detective work provides an opportunity for an attack upon the cynical manipulation of human lives for sordid political ends, but its relation to Monk and his fate seems extremely tangential.

It is interesting to speculate on Faulkner's reasons for refusing to develop in these stories the full potentialities of his material. "Tomorrow," of course, was not published until 1940, and Faulkner may have felt that by that time, and especially in *The Hamlet*, published in April of the same year, he had treated sufficiently of characters of Jackson Fentry's general type and background and of that quality of endurance which Fentry primarily embodies: "The lowly and invincible of the earth—to endure and endure and then endure, tomorrow and tomorrow and tomorrow." (p. 104) It might be said, indeed, that in his presentation of Fentry, as in those words of Gavin Stevens's, Faulkner was drawing on work which was already behind him, which had been absorbed into his creative equipment as part of his repertoire, his always available stock-in-trade. To some extent, in fact, he was merely "coasting" in these stories, not working at full pressure, relying on devices, phrases, characters he had already employed in previous novels and stories. Apart from "Smoke," the stories in *Knight's Gambit* apparently belong to the middle years of Faulkner's career: "Monk," the second in chronological order, appeared in 1937; the next, "Hand upon the Waters," followed in 1939, "Tomorrow" in 1940, and "An Error of Chemistry" in 1946. By the time he wrote these stories Faulkner already had much of his major work behind him; the detective story form seems to have been one which excited his ingenuity without calling out the full extent of his powers; and it seems likely that when writing "Monk" and the three succeeding stories he sketched in certain parts somewhat lightly and casually for the simple reason that they did not especially engage his attention.

Faulkner, however, may have been drawn to the detective story precisely because of the opportunity it offered for the minimal presentation of such characters as did not interest him. The essence of the Sherlock Holmes type of detective story, as we have seen, is its concentration of interest upon a single figure, that of the detective himself, and although Faulkner may have found a variety of satisfactions in using the form—not least that delight in the orderly resolution of disorder, the final clicking of things into place, which had played a part in the structuring of even such novels as *The Sound and the Fury* and *Absalom, Absalom!*—there seems little doubt that the stories in *Knight's Gambit* must be seen primarily as a series of more or less deliberate exercises on the way to his final conception and characterisation of Gavin Stevens. Considered in this light, the limited presentation of Jackson Fentry and Monk Oglethorp can be seen as functional rather than merely casual; instead of lamenting the human inadequacies of the stories, we ought perhaps to be praising their leashed power. This was perhaps the quality which impressed the editors of *Ellery Queen's Mystery Magazine* when they awarded second prize in their First Annual Detective Short-Story Contest to "An Error in Chemistry." As a detective story, "An Error in Chemistry" seems neat enough, but crudely melodramatic and not especially plausible; the particular interest it does possess was indirectly and somewhat paradoxically indicated by the editors when they spoke of it as a "strange story of almost pure detection ... stylised, morbid, mystical, and sharply and brilliantly narrated."[18] The editors' use of the epithets "strange" and "mystical" was no doubt a response to their sense that something quite other than "pure detection" was in fact involved—a somewhat puzzled tribute to the story's conclusion, in which Gavin Stevens speculates on the reasons why the former circus illusionist, Signor Canova, should have risked and even courted discovery after committing his triple murder:

> "What else could the possession of such a gift as his have engendered, and the successful practising of it have increased, but a supreme contempt for mankind? You told me yourself that he had never been afraid in his life."
> "Yes," the sheriff said. "The Book itself says somewhere, *Know thyself*. Ain't there another book somewhere that says, *Man, fear thyself, thine arrogance and vanity and pride*? You ought to know; you claim to be a book man. Didn't you tell me that's what that luck-charm on your watch chain means? What book is that in?"
> "It's in all of them," Uncle Gavin said. "The good ones, I mean. It's said in a lot of different ways, but it's there." (p. 131)

At the point where this passage occurs, the demands of the story as one of "almost pure detection" have already been met. But Faulkner also has two self-imposed demands to meet: that of his irrepressible fascination with the character of the murderer—a character so far scarcely touched upon for the simple reason that his identity has been concealed—and that of his concern to make the story subserve a final moral purpose.

The element of direct moral intention involved here is directly related to the developing presentation of Gavin Stevens. The book's title is taken from its final story, the only one not to have been previously published, and refers explicitly to a move in chess; but by the time we discover this we have already become gradually aware that Gavin Stevens is himself a knight of many gambits, an embodiment of justice, a fearless, skilful and yet compassionate campaigner for the right. Seen in this light, the statements at the end of "An Error in Chemistry" appear to take on an importance that is central to the pattern and meaning of the whole book; Signor Canova's ultimate crime consists in his "supreme contempt for mankind" and the moral of his fate emerges as: "Man, fear thyself, thine arrogance and vanity and pride." The values Gavin Stevens upholds are, in contrast, the humanistic ones which Faulkner invokes in his Nobel Prize speech and so often elsewhere and to which Stevens himself briefly alludes earlier in this same story when he speaks of his own interest not so much in truth as "in justice and human beings." (p. 111)

What is remarkable in *Knight's Gambit* is the demonstration of Stevens acting upon these values in a context which affords them little obvious sustenance. In these stories, apart from

"Knight's Gambit" itself, life is lived at a low level, not only in economic terms but intellectually, morally, and sometimes emotionally, and it is almost as though Faulkner were trying out Gavin Stevens, testing him under a variety of difficult conditions, facing him with the problems and agonies involved in helping, simply because they are human beings, people who do not seek help, who seem almost beyond help, and who will not give thanks for help rendered. *Knight's Gambit* might appropriately have been entitled "The Education of Gavin Stevens," and Stevens's special distinction is his sheer persistence, the simple fact that after all his experiences with these pitiful and vicious people, after all his often unsuccessful and usually unappreciated attempts to come to their assistance, he nevertheless goes on, splendidly quixotic and undefeated. Here, again, we can see another advantage for Faulkner of the detective-story form: Gavin Stevens, in his role of detective, is, uniquely, the man who knows, and it is essential to Faulkner's larger conception of him that he should act as he does, be the man he is, not in ignorance of the true situation or of the real characters of the people with whom he deals, but in the context of a full possession of the facts.

In "Smoke" Stevens is little more than an inferior and mildly moralistic Sherlock Holmes, but in "Monk" he is already something of a crusader for justice, and in "An Error of Chemistry," as we have seen, he is a staunch upholder of humanistic values. He retains, of course, many of his Sherlock Holmes characteristics, but as the book proceeds he also carries an increasing burden of representative significance. The stories in *Knight's Gambit* are ranged in the order of their original publication, with the previously unpublished "Knight's Gambit" bringing up the rear, but this chronological sequence corresponds in large measure to the perceptible development of Gavin Stevens. This may, of course, be entirely coincidental, but it seems reasonable to speculate on the degree to which the stories in *Knight's Gambit* can be considered as a series of increasingly deliberate exercises revolving upon Gavin Stevens in both his investigatory and his crusading roles. *Knight's Gambit* was published after *Intruder in the Dust*, but the stories in the later volume, including the original version of "Knight's Gambit" itself, were all written before the novel;[14] *Intruder in the Dust*, indeed, should perhaps be regarded as the end-product of the development reflected in the successive stories of *Knight's Gambit*.

The title story of the book seems to stand somewhat apart from its predecessors. Obviously it cannot be ignored, if only because it occupies little less than half of the whole volume, but it is loosely constructed, over-extended, and sadly lacking in vitality. Considered in the context of the book as a whole, the chief importance of "Knight's Gambit" lies in its presentation of Gavin Stevens, who appears here as a more elaborately developed character and as a somewhat different one. In the earlier stories, the emphasis has been on his role as investigator and interpreter of events which do not involve him directly, and the stories have remained within the detective story convention at least insofar as they offer little, if any, analysis of the effect of these events and experiences upon Stevens himself. In "Knight's Gambit" the whole apparatus of the story—the limited setting of Stevens's room in which much of the action takes place, the way in which the various characters come there to see Stevens, the overt presence of a narrator, Chick Mallison—forces us continually to note the effect which the events have on Stevens himself; the conclusion of the story, too, constitutes a dénouement of Stevens's personal story as well as of his investigatory activities, which here, for the first time, actually achieve the detection and prevention of a crime before it has taken place. At the same time, Stevens is provided with a pattern of family relationships, and his garrulity and romanticism, scarcely hinted at in earlier stories, are played upon to an even greater degree than in *Intruder in the Dust*. What we have in "Knight's Gambit," in fact, is an early sketch for the Gavin Stevens of *The Town* and *The Mansion*—a man deeply involved in his own personal affairs and emotions as well as concerned for more abstract questions of justice and humanity.

Knight's Gambit was apparently conceived as a by-product of the process which led to the preparation and publication of *Collected Stories*,[15] a volume which occupies an extremely important place among Faulkner's major works. It is of course true that all the forty-two stories had been previously published, but seventeen of them had not been previously collected, and among these were the superb "Barn Burning," perhaps the most deeply and movingly realised of all Faulkner's stories, and the comic masterpiece "Mule in the Yard." Above all, the mere act of bringing together the stories into one volume made it possible for the first time to survey the full range of Faulkner's achievement in the short-story form, and his organisation of the stories into six separately titled sections made it necessary to read each of them in a new context.

In his 1948 letter to Cowley Faulkner outlined the plan of *Collected Stories*, a plan which embodied his belief that a collection of stories should have "form, integration" no less than a novel, "an entity of its own, single, set for one pitch, contrapuntal in integration, toward one end, one finale." The stories in the first section, "The Country," all deal with the countryside of northern Mississippi and its inhabitants—Indians, hill-farmers like the McCallums, and poor whites like the Griers and Ab Snopes's family. "Barn Burning" comes first, an induction to the section and to the book as it had once been intended as an induction to *The Hamlet*, establishing patterns of conflict which echo throughout the volume—white vs. Negro, poor vs. rich, family vs. outsiders—and exploring themes which also recur: the opposition between the emotional ties of home and family and the urgent need for escape and self-determination, the complexities of the father-son relationship, the tension between social values and those which are primarily moral or aesthetic. "Shingles for the Lord" follows "Barn Burning" not simply because of the contrast between deliberate and accidental arson, or between the two versions of the father-son relationship, but also because both stories exemplify the same qualities in the poor whites. "Shingles for the Lord" speaks more explicitly of these qualities, and the need for such explicitness underlines its relative weakness as a story, but the terms "indestructibility, endurability" (p. 42) here applied to Whitfield could equally be used of Ab Snopes in "Barn Burning" as well as of other men in "Shingles for the Lord" itself. These same qualities are depicted in somewhat obtrusively heroic terms in the third story, "The Tall Men," and further emphasis is obtained through Faulkner's exploitation of the alien and strongly contrasted figure of the Government investigator : we see the McCallums more plainly because we see them largely through the investigator's appalled vision.

The fourth story, "A Bear Hunt," is not really the tale of hunting which its title might seem to suggest, but rather the story of a practical joke, a tall tale, involving Indians living in the recesses of the woods and two main characters, Ratliff and Provine, who apparently come from much the same background as the characters of other stories in this section. It offers, too, a contrast in mood both with its predecessor and with the fifth story, "Two Soldiers," in which the small boy (the second soldier of the title) becomes the chief embodiment of those qualities of simple determination, endurance, and courage which Faulkner finds so admirable in these people. The mother's instructions to Pete as he goes off to the war echo those of Buddy McCallum to his sons, and the qualities they both emphasise are the necessity for a proper dignity and pride in one's name and for a right pattern of behaviour in relation to the superior authority of the State. The Grier family, central characters in "Shingles for the Lord" and "Two Soldiers," appear again in "Shall Not Perish," the sentimental story which ends the section. What is notable about this story is the degree to which it seems to echo many of the motifs of "Barn Burning" : both stories, for example, contain references to the Civil War, close delineations of social differences, and descriptions of poor whites entering the De Spain mansion. But the entrance made by the Griers is very different from that made by Ab Snopes. Time has gone by and much has changed; the United States is engaged in World War II, and the Civil War has receded further into the past. What the story shows, and what Mrs. Grier makes explicit, is that Southerners have now grown beyond the old limited loyalties : she and De Spain are separated by a social gulf as wide as that which separated Ab Snopes and the De Spain of "Barn Burning," but where Ab could only assert his own worth in opposition to De Spain, Mrs. Grier can bridge the gulf by her assertion of human values: the removal of the Confederate flag becomes symbolic, and the galloping men on the cinema screen which the boy's grandfather identifies with Confederate cavalry the boy himself can identify with the strength of the single nation which is the contemporary United States. "The Country" thus shows overall progression of theme and of chronology as well as internal variety of mood and treatment. None of the stories had been previously collected, and the section as a whole displays a degree of unity, of mutual reverberation between stories, not exceeded by any of the later sections.

The second section, "The Village," is built up about a core of four stories taken from the second section of *These 13*—"A Rose for Emily," "Hair," "Dry September," and "That Evening Sun"—and the juxtaposition of "Hair" with "A Rose for Emily" at the beginning of the section seems to suggest that Faulkner was making the kind of opportunistic connections between one story and the next (here, between the last word of "A Rose for Emily" and the title of "Hair") which he had rejected in *These 13*. But instead of "Hair" being immediately followed by "Dry September," the other story in which Hawkshaw appears, a previously uncollected story, "Centaur in Brass," is allowed to intervene. Apparently Faulkner was anxious to establish more firmly the sense of Jefferson itself as a place, a social entity, before going on, in subsequent stories, to explore in detail a series of incidents revelatory of different aspects of life in the town. The first person narrator in "Centaur in Brass," as in "A Rose for Emily," seems to represent the generalised voice of Jefferson, as Charles Mallison was later to do in *The Town*, the novel into which "Centaur in Brass" itself was subsequently incorporated. Just as "Centaur in Brass" opens with the words "In our town," (p. 149) so the first sentence of "A Rose for Emily" contains a reference to "our whole town," (p. 119) while later in the story there occurs a frequent use of "we" and an allusion to ladies calling on bereaved families, "as is our custom." (p. 123) The first-person narrator of "Hair" is rather carefully individualised through colloquialism and personal reference, but the story does treat of certain aspects of Jefferson life over a number of years: it evokes the image of the barber shop as a centre of gossip, for example, and contains allusions to "all the men in town" (p. 134) and to "the young fellows, the loafers that pitch dollars all day long in the clubhouse yard, waiting for the young girls to come giggling down to the post office and the soda fountain in the late afternoon." (p. 141)

In "Dry September," the fourth story, the presence of Jefferson is immediately established in terms of the barber shop setting, but the story's main concern is with the actions of isolated individuals—especially Hawkshaw, McLendon, and Minnie Cooper—as they are played out against the background of the town and of the oppressive September heat. Most of the subsequent stories concentrate on isolated individuals in much the same way, and the theme of isolation—most poignantly, perhaps, in two such different stories as "Death-Drag" and "That Evening Sun"—becomes the more apparent and the more appalling in the context of the continuing cohesive life of the small town. The precise reasons which underlie the organisation of the later stories in the section are sometimes difficult to discern, but Faulkner seems once more to have worked on "contrapuntal" principles, seeking a continual variation of mood—with constant shifts between tragic, tragi-comic and comic—and of narrative point of view, as well as that spacing out of interconnected themes and characters which we saw in *These 13*: he again keeps Miss Emily Grierson and Miss Minnie Cooper apart and avoids juxtaposing Hawkshaw's two appearances, the two Snopes stories, or the two stories, "Dry September" and "That Evening Sun," in which Negroes appear in the role of victim.

The four stories about Indians which comprise the third section, "The Wilderness," have a unity of setting and of tone which seems sufficiently self-evident, and much the same can be said of the following section, "The Wasteland," with its stories about World War I. The section is very similar to the opening section of *These 13*, although a fifth story, "Turnabout," has been added and the two stories about airmen, "Ad Astra" and "All the Dead Pilots," are here placed in the framing positions formerly occupied by "Victory" and "Crevasse."

The fifth section, "The Middle Ground," is the longest in the book; of its eleven stories, six had appeared in *Doctor Martino* while the remainder had previously been uncollected. Like *Doctor Martino* itself, the section seems somewhat miscellaneous. Nearly all the stories, however, concern themselves with themes of deracination and disillusion, with the loss of familiar bearings—either with tragic implications, as in "Wash," or in more comic terms, as in the quixotic absurdity of the situations into which Lieutenant Backhouse's romantic gallantry leads him in "My Grandmother Millard and General Bedford Forrest and The Battle of Harrykin Creek." In entitling the section "The Middle Ground," Faulkner may have had nothing more in mind than this experience of upheaval and uprooting—geographical, social, intellectual, or emotional—undergone by the central characters in all the stories: by the lost and defeated couple of "The Brooch," for instance, by the "lost woman" of "Fox Hunt," the homeless pair in "Pennsylvania Station" and the homeless poet in "Artist at Home." But "The Middle Ground" may correspond to "the middle of the journey," and it seems worth noting that all the stories contain a death. In most of them it is an actual physical death—in "Wash," for example, in "Doctor Martino," "Pennsylvania Station," "Artist at Home," "The Brooch," "There Was a Queen," "Mountain Victory"— but in the others some kind of symbolic death is enacted: the killing of the fox in "Fox Hunt," the "death" which Monaghan of "Honor" had suffered, with all the other pilots, during World War I, the official "death" which Lieutenant Backhouse undergoes in "My Grandmother Millard" before he can be reborn under the less offensive name of Backus, the death in life to which the grandmother in "Golden Land" resigns herself in the final sentence of the story.

The first three stories of the final section, "Beyond," seem to move onwards from the deaths of the previous section to a preoccupation with the world of the supernatural—the ghosts of "Beyond," the faun of "Black Music," the ghost and dual existence of "The Leg." These three stories had previously been collected in *Doctor Martino*; the three final stories of the section and of the volume, "Mistral," "Divorce in Naples," and "Carcassonne," we have already discussed in the context of *These 13*, in which they appeared in the same order and in the same concluding position. As we saw earlier, "Mistral," "Divorce in Naples," and "Carcassonne" all deal with moments of initiation, recognition, and transcendence; the three stories now placed alongside them can also be considered in these terms, although they employ, as the others do not, the methods of fantasy. In "Beyond," which can perhaps be linked with "Carcassonne" as representing something of a personal statement for Faulkner himself, the old Judge, faced with the need for decision and choice, rejects the consolations of religion in favour of a stern humanistic commitment similar to that which runs through all of Faulkner's work. "Black Music," which seems to have some connection with "Carcassonne," at least in terms of the setting and the central character, is the story of a man who has "been something outside the lot and plan for mortal human man to be." (p. 805) "The Leg" seems more nearly a straightforward ghost story than either of its predecessors, but we are perhaps intended to see the narrator as being finally confronted—in a manner somewhat reminiscent of James's story "The Jolly Corner"—with the image of what might in some sense be his other self, the exponent of his own deep and unacknowledged desires. The stories have other points of similarity, and one possible justification for the section's title could be found in the fact that all of them, with the debatable exception of "Beyond," are set outside the United States. But it is clear that Faulkner had more than mere geography in mind. An earlier title of the story "Beyond" was "Beyond the Gate,"[16] apparently a straightforward allusion to death. In shortening the title to "Beyond" before the story was published in 1933, Faulkner may well have sought to eliminate the element of cliché in the original; he may also have preferred the single word because of its wider range of suggestion and possible meaning. In the manuscript of *As I Lay Dying*, at the point where Darl speaks of emptying himself for sleep, there appears in the margin, in Faulkner's hand, the one word "Beyond."[17] The Judge in "Beyond" also talks of emptying himself for sleep, and confronts his own problems of personal identity in terms and language very similar to Darl's. In applying the title to the whole of the final section of *Collected Stories* Faulkner perhaps intended to emphasise the degree to which they were all concerned with awareness of personal identity, and with the attempts made by the protagonists to define their own identity in terms of the strange, the unfamiliar, the supernatural, or death itself. Of "Carcassonne," the final story, Faulkner once said that he was "still writing about a young man in conflict with his environment."[18] The solution his protagonist finds is to transcend environment, to move beyond it into the world of the imagination. Essentially, as we saw in discussing *These 13*, it is the solution of the creative artist, of Faulkner himself, and speaking at Charlottesville of the resurgence of writing in the South following World War I, Faulkner observed: "I myself am inclined to think it was because of the bareness of the Southerner's life, that he had to resort to his own imagination, to create his own Carcassonne."[19]

THE ACHIEVEMENT

THE ACHIEVEMENT

"DO you love the South?" someone asked Faulkner when he was in Japan in 1955, and his reply virtually paraphrased the famous concluding paragraph of *Absalom, Absalom!*: "Well, I love it and hate it. Some of the things there I don't like at all, but I was born there, and that's my home, and I will still defend it even if I hate it."[1] It is only in the context of entirely unsentimental statements such as this that it seems useful to talk of Faulkner's "rootedness" in the South and in Mississippi. The term was first used by Phil Stone in the Preface to *The Marble Faun*, and while we must remain fully aware of Stone's contribution to Faulkner's career, our present perspective allows us to discern in the Preface the limitations of his understanding of Faulkner both as a man and as a writer. "These are primarily the poems of youth and a simple heart," wrote Stone in the opening sentence. He continued:

> They are the poems of a mind that reacts directly to sunlight and trees and skies and blue hills, reacts without evasion or self-consciousness. They are drenched in sunlight and color as is the land in which they were written, the land which gave birth and sustenance to their author. He has roots in this soil as surely and inevitably as has a tree.

*   *   *

> The author of these poems is a man steeped in the soil of his native land, a Southerner by every instinct, and, more than that, a Mississippian. George Moore said that all universal art became great by first being provincial, and the sunlight and mocking-birds and blue hills of North Mississippi are a part of this young man's very being.[2]

After such an introduction, the poems themselves may come as something of a surprise. Some of the images of *The Marble Faun*, some of the details of natural description, undoubtedly derived from Faulkner's direct experience of the Mississippi countryside, but the volume as a whole is essentially artificial, deliberately literary both in inspiration and in intention:

279

> As the tumbling sunlight falls
> Spouting down the craggy walls
> To hiss upon the frozen rocks
> That dot the hills in crouching flocks,
> So I plunge in some deep vale
> Where first violets, shy and pale,
> Appear, and spring with tear-stained cheeks
> Peeps at me from the neighbouring brakes,
> Gathering her torn draperies up
> For flight if I cast my eyes up. (p. 14)

This is scarcely the landscape of northern Mississippi; it more closely resembles the Arcadian landscapes of traditional pastoral, or, more specifically, the adaptations of these which appear in the verse of Keats and Swinburne. As George P. Garrett has shown, Faulkner's dependence upon the conventionally "poetic" is the main source of the poem's failure; Garrett also insists, however, upon the ambitiousness and sophistication of Faulkner's structural conception in *The Marble Faun*: "It could scarcely have been attempted by an unlettered, accidental poet."[3] Stone's remarks about Faulkner's lack of self-consciousness in treating of natural beauty are justified by certain passages in the poem, but they clearly suggest that he had not fully appreciated the kind, and degree, of artifice, of technical experimentation, in which Faulkner was already engaged.

The poem of Faulkner's which seems closest in feeling to Stone's Preface is not *The Marble Faun* itself but the much shorter "My Epitaph," which was apparently written at about the same time as the Preface,[4] although it was first published in 1932 and appeared in its final form the following year, as the concluding poem of *A Green Bough*. It seems further evidence of Stone's failure to appreciate Faulkner's real qualities as a writer that in December 1931, as we saw earlier, he could look forward to the publication of *A Green Bough* as a fuller expression of Faulkner's rootedness in local soil than any of the novels had proved to be; Stone added, in the same letter to Louis Cochran: "My present discouragement about him is as to whether or not this part of him will ever be articulate in prose."[5] "My Epitaph," like *The Marble Faun*, may now appear to have represented, more than anything else, a literary pose, a position adopted for artistic purposes and in response to literary influences: certainly we may find it difficult to believe that Faulkner ever experienced any deep sense of personal commitment to the romantic, not to say sentimental, notions of intimate communion with the native soil which the poem celebrates. Faulkner's rootedness in the South and in Mississippi is of course crucial to his work, and Katherine Anne Porter, consciously or otherwise, used an image from "My Epitaph" in answering a television interviewer's question about Faulkner and the South:

"Oh, yes, he is rooted as a tree; almost as natural, almost as organic. He is a natural force. And of course, he has—he does get the strength of the man that stands on his native earth and knows who he is and where he is and what he's doing."[6]

But the last point which Miss Porter makes is the essential one: the South becomes for Faulkner a solid basis, a firm place to start from, a point of departure. It is not itself the end in view.

The importance of understanding Faulkner's native environment was one of the points Phil Stone insisted upon in the second of a series of articles on "William Faulkner, the Man and his Work," which he contributed to the *Oxford Magazine* in 1934:

It is a country of not a great deal of riches and of almost no poverty. Situated in the northern part of Mississippi, not far from the Tennessee line, it is a country broken to some extent, with many little creek bottoms and some small river bottoms, both of which have a soil of fair fertility, a country of hills with no mountains, a country with many lovely trees and countless birds, with a climate variable but mostly temperate as to both cold and heat and with few days of the year that cannot be spent comfortably out of doors. It is a country of abundant rainfall and of a general plenty without that luxuriousness of the Delta counties which lie to the west of it.

The red-clay subsoil, Stone continued, had "great possibilities," but the topsoil contained "a great deal of sand" and the cutting down of the timber and subsequent bad farming had led to much erosion and hence to a decline in the "general prosperity" of the countryside: "Still I have yet to meet the man who knows of his own knowledge of any person in North Mississippi who has ever starved to death."[7] Towards the end of the third article, Stone spoke in lyrical vein of the beauty of the countryside, "where one can find the unspoiled golden peace of legendary days," and attributed to Faulkner as well as to himself the feeling "that Oxford and the country around it have done enough for a man when they permit him to live here." Stone went on to explain the grounds for this attitude:

Here, out of the contemporary mad rush, we have time and quiet to think and savor the taste of things without having to gulp them down. Here we can see the stars. Here on frosty nights of fall we have only to listen to hear, faint and afar, the bay of the hunting hound, as in "Sartoris"—"mournful and valiant and a little sad." Here, as I sit writing this, it is quiet enough to hear the cool rustle of the leaves of the ancient oaks and the mellow liquid call of the whippoorwill from the front yard.[8]

We may freely allow of these passages that they evoke one important aspect of Faulkner's environment, the rich if unspectacular beauty of the hill-country of northern Mississippi. We may also recognise that Stone was writing out of a deep affection for the land which was his as well as Faulkner's. We may acknowledge, too, that something of the feeling which pervades Stone's paragraphs does appear in *Sartoris*, the novel which he mentions by name, and the only one of Faulkner's novels about which he seems to have been consulted during the actual process of composition. And there is the evidence of such works as *The Hamlet*, *Go Down, Moses* and *Big Woods* to show that Faulkner never lost his sense of the land's fecundity and beauty, that he never ceased to see the actions of men in the long and diminishing perspective of the land's permanence and ultimate inviolability. But even in *Sartoris* Faulkner draws upon other elements of his environment, and in his work as a whole the scenic beauty and rural calm of Mississippi provide only one aspect of the total impression. The one-sidedness of Stone's evocation can be indicated by juxtaposing with it a passage from *Old Times in the Faulkner Country*. John Cullen also describes with enthusiasm the land that he and Faulkner had both known, although it is of the Mississippi Delta country that he mainly writes—and in tones of regret for something that has passed away and will not return : "There never was and never again will be on this earth such a paradise for hunting dogs and men as the miles and miles of great virgin forests and jungles of the Big Bottoms."[9] But elsewhere in the book he recalls in considerable detail the lynching of Nelse Patton, in September 1908, the incident on which, he believes, Faulkner based the death of Joe Christmas in *Light in August*. Patton had murdered a white woman with a razor—her head, says Cullen, "had been severed from her body, all but the neck bone"[10]—and he was captured after being shot by John Cullen himself, then a boy of fourteen. That night a mob incited by former United States Senator W. V. Sullivan broke into the jail :

> When the mob finally got through and broke the lock off the murderer's cell, Nelse had armed himself with a heavy iron coal-shovel handle. From a corner near the door, he fought like a tiger, seriously wounding three men. He was then shot to death and thrown out of the jail. Someone (I don't know who) cut his ears off, scalped him, cut his testicles out, tied a rope around his neck, tied him to a car, and dragged his body around the streets. Then they hanged him to a walnut-tree limb just outside the south entrance to the courthouse. They had torn his clothes off dragging him around, and my father bought a new pair of overalls and put them on him before the next morning.[11]

And in the morning, according to the contemporary report in *The*

Lafayette County Press which Cullen goes on to quote, "the passerby saw the lifeless body of a negro suspended from a tree—it told the tale, that the murder of a white woman had been avenged—the public had done their duty."[12] If this ripe journalistic sententiousness seems even more horrifying than Cullen's eye-witness account, both pall beside the remarks of Senator Sullivan, quoted by Cullen from the Jackson *Daily Clarion-Ledger*:

> "Cut a white woman's throat? and a negro? Of course I wanted him lynched.
> "I saw his body dangling from a tree this morning and I am glad of it."[13]

Faulkner himself was only eleven at the time of the lynching, but he was already living in Oxford and, as Cullen suggests, it seems extremely likely that he heard many stories about the incident both at the time and in following years, and that it became an important source for Christmas's death in *Light in August* and for similar episodes elsewhere in his work—we may note, for example, that the death of Patton took place in September, and that Faulkner may conceivably have had this in mind in writing "Dry September."

The lynching of Nelse Patton suggests only too plainly that there may be another side to Stone's idyllic portrait of Oxford and its countryside; the use which Faulkner apparently made of the incident provokes the larger question of the relationship between the real world of Lafayette County, Mississippi, and the fictional world of Yoknapatawpha County which provides the scene and setting for so much of Faulkner's work. As we saw earlier, there can be no doubt of the frequency with which Faulkner drew upon members of his own family in creating characters for his novels and stories, especially in the early stages of his career and most notably in *Sartoris*. *Mosquitoes* also shows in very obvious form Faulkner's readiness to make direct use of people he knew, while in *The Reivers*, a late but essentially retrospective book, he seems occasionally to be transposing actual people into fictional characters with only minimal gestures towards disguise. In *Pylon* Faulkner exploited, within a few months of their occurrence, events of which he had himself been a witness, and the topography of New Orleans is clearly discernible under the thin disguise of the modified street names of the fictional New Valois. Not surprisingly, there have been many attempts to identify the real-life sources of characters, incidents, and places which appear in novels and stories with a Yoknapatawpha County setting. Nor is it at all surprising that some of these attempts have met with a good deal of success. Because Faulkner conceived of Jefferson as not simply a Southern but specifically a northern Mississippi small town, it had to have a rough geographical site, and he seems to have thought of it, at least at the time when he was writing his early novels, as situated in the position occupied by the actual town of Ripley, Mississippi, where his family had lived before their removal to Oxford. But Jefferson then proceeded to grow, change, proliferate new landmarks and inhabitants, alter in size, population, and outline—all in response to the constantly developing demands of Faulkner's subsequent work—and he inevitably tended to take what he needed from Oxford, the town he knew best.[14]

The whole point about Jefferson, however, is precisely that it is fictional, imaginary, and therefore indefinable in any terms or contexts other than those provided by the novels and stories themselves, and investigation of Faulkner's sources can offer little assistance in answering the more important critical question as to how far he thought of the imaginary world of Yoknapatawpha County as a single unified whole. There has been much talk of a "Yoknapatawpha Saga," and it is true that towards the end of his career Faulkner spoke of the overall "design" which ought to appear in the "whole output or sum of an artist's work";[15] he also showed some interest in the possibility of a comprehensive, rationalising review of his whole œuvre, designed to tidy up all the loose ends and fit everything into place. But the difficulties he encountered in attempting to revise *The Mansion* with the two other books of the Snopes trilogy in mind suggest only too clearly how self-frustrating such an undertaking might have proved, while the contrast between this tendency towards retrospection and his earlier refusal to return to work already behind him may give us some grounds for thinking that Faulkner's motions towards a "Golden Book" of Yoknapatawpha County were symptoms of a flagging creative vitality. There is evidence that Faulkner, at quite an early stage of his career, had seen that he might one day have to pay some attention to questions of consistency; in an unfinished autograph note which Meriwether dates from "1931 or not long after," Faulkner observed: "as you say, I am availing myself of my prerogative of using these people when and where I see fit. So far, I have not bothered much about chronology, which, if I am ever collected, I shall have to do."[16] In fact, Faulkner continued throughout his career to use his characters when and where he saw fit: the same names occur in different books, but even when the characters who bear them are recognisably the same, minor discrepancies continually appear. Considering the Yoknapatawpha material as a whole, it is impossible to pretend that Faulkner achieves or even attempts consistency and continuity. The Snopes trilogy is the one instance in Faulkner's work in which individual novels are overtly presented as a linked sequence, and we have seen that even here Faulkner finally allowed many of the inconsistencies to stand, despite the fact that at the time of completing *The Mansion* the retrospective mood was strongly upon him. Elsewhere, many of the errors and misplaced emphases of Faulkner criticism have sprung from a too casual conflation of the appearances made by a single character (single at least in name) in various books, or from such unjustifiable short-circuiting as reading the Compson Appendix as though it were an integral part of *The Sound and the Fury*.[17] Faulkner's novels and stories set in Yoknapatawpha County do demonstrate an overall unity; it is not, however, a unity which can be adequately defined in chronological, geographical, or sociological terms, nor in the literary terms of expanded chronicle or linked sequencer; it is rather a unity of inspiration, of a single irradiating tragi-comic vision—a vision, indeed, which informs all of Faulkner's work, but which perhaps takes on a special intensity when focused on materials drawn from Faulkner's own corner of the world, his "own little postage stamp of native soil."[18]

Answering a question about Yoknapatawpha at the University of Virginia in 1957, Faulkner said: "No, it was not my intention to write a pageant of a county. I simply was using the quickest tool to hand. I was using what I knew best, which was the locale where I was born and had lived most of my life."[19] Here, as elsewhere, Faulkner speaks of his creation of Yoknapatawpha County in the same terms, the same metaphors from carpentry, as he habitually used when speaking of his use of violence, of Christian imagery, of historical events: he refers to it simply as a means to a larger end, a by-product of other, more central preoccupations. Obviously this must not be overstated. That Faulkner was a Southerner is clearly of the first importance, not least because it gave him that "sense of an organic community" of which Cleanth Brooks speaks in *The Hidden God*,[20] and in March 1936 Thomas Wolfe could write to Stark Young: "And I agree utterly with your estimate in your letter—that what he [Faulkner] writes is not like the South, but that yet the South is *in* his books, and in the spirit that creates them."[21] But Wolfe concedes what has since become more generally recognised, the irrelevance of seeking in Faulkner's fiction for precise sociological and political correspondences with the actual world of Lafayette County or, more broadly, of the South, and whatever assessment we make of the significance of Yoknapatawpha County it seems at least clear that Faulkner did not think of himself as creating that "legend of the South" of which Malcolm Cowley spoke in the Introduction to *The Portable Faulkner*.[22]

The importance, critical and historical, of *The Portable Faulkner* is beyond question, and when Faulkner had seen Cowley's introduction he wrote back to congratulate him: "It's all right, sound and correct and penetrating." Later in the same letter, however, he added a note of qualification: "I don't see too much Southern legend in it."[23] Faulkner's reservation seems extremely significant, suggesting further that he may not have altogether recognised himself in Cowley's definition of "an epic or bardic poet in prose, a creator of myths that he weaves together into a legend of the South."[24] We have suggested that Faulkner was never seriously concerned to chronicle, let alone to hymn, to celebrate, the land as an end in itself; but Cowley's terminology raises questions of technique as well as of theme. In calling Faulkner a bardic poet he seemed to be stressing elements of looseness, of infinitely extensible (and infinitely heroic) vistas of the Southern past. Yet the whole structural tendency of Faulkner's work is not outwards but inwards, not centrifugal but centripetal. At the Nagano Seminar he remarked that he might have invented Yoknapatawpha County for "the same reason that is responsible for the long clumsy sentences and paragraphs. I was still trying to reduce my one individual experience of the world into one compact thing which could be picked up and held in the hands at one time."[25] Faulkner had made the same point much more fully in one of his early letters to Cowley himself:

> As regards any specific book, I'm trying primarily to tell a story, in the most effective way I can think of, the most moving, the most exhaustive. But I think even that is incidental to what I am trying to do, taking my output (the course of it) as a whole. I am telling the same story over and over, which is myself and the world. Tom Wolfe was trying to say everything, get everything, the world plus 'I' or filtered through 'I' or the effort of 'I' to embrace the world in which he was born and walked a little while and then lay down again, into one volume. I am trying to go a step further. This I think accounts for what people call the obscurity, the involved formless 'style', endless sentences. I'm trying to say it all in one sentence, between one Cap and one period. I'm still trying, to put it all, if possible, on one pinhead. I dont know how to do it. All I know is to keep on trying in a new way. I'm inclined to think that my material, the South, is not very important to me. I just happen to know it, and dont have time in one life to learn another one and write at the same time. Though the one I know is probably as good as another, life is a phenomenon but not a novelty, the same frantic steeplechase toward nothing everywhere and man stinks the same stink nomatter where in time.[26]

In the light of this remarkable passage we can perhaps see more clearly the intention and function informing some of the most characteristic devices of Faulkner's fiction: the long sentences, for example, to which Faulkner himself refers and which enable him to hold a single moment in suspension while its full complexity is explored; the tableau-like epiphanies, and the other images of arrested time and arrested motion; the circular and centripetal structural techniques of novels like *The Sound and the Fury* and *As I Lay Dying*; the familiar concentrative device, most brilliantly used in *Go Down, Moses*, of allowing the revealing confrontation of character in extended dialogue to become also a dramatisation of moral themes. We have had frequent occasion to notice Faulkner's tendency to work in blocks of material, so that the structural process became primarily a question of achieving the optimum disposition of relatively discrete units: we can now understand that he always sought for effects of ironic juxtaposition and illuminating interreflection, for that constant reverberation to and fro within the novel which makes for thematic as well as emotional intensification. Faulkner reminds us again in the passage that his use of a Mississippi setting, his creation of Yoknapatawpha County, was essentially subservient to his larger concerns, an available device for enhancing that sense of epitomisation for which he strove, microcosmic not of the South but of all mankind in all ages—so that even in the Snopes trilogy Faulkner was engaged not in writing a fictionalised chronicle of Mississippi social history but in making his most sustained attempt to explore, dramatise and affirm what in the Nobel Prize address he called "the old verities and truths of the heart, the old universal truths lacking which any story is emphemeral and doomed—love and honor and pity and pride and compassion and sacrifice." His whole effort is directed towards the crystallisation of these "verities," towards making the abstractions actual and concrete in the intensely particularised world of his fiction. His endeavour may be compared to that of Blake, who sought to "Hold Infinity in the palm of your hand/And Eternity in an hour." It was, perhaps, the endeavour of a poet. But not of a bardic poet.

Thus Faulkner's major concerns, like those of all great artists, were ultimately moral, and there is little value in abstract discussions of his ideas which fail to take this into account. It is sometimes said, for example, that Faulkner was obsessed with time, but this would seem to be true only insofar as he was inevitably aware of time as the medium in which men live and events happen. His emphasis is not on time itself but on the never-ending ramifications of all actions which occur in time. "For was, and is, and will be, are but is," says Princess Ida in Tennyson's *The Princess*,[27] and Faulkner used the same simple terminology to express his own conception of time's fluidity. For him, however, the all-important point consisted in the idea that there could be no such thing as "was": since time constituted a continuum the chain of cause and effect could never be broken, and every human action must continue to reverberate, however faintly, into infinity. Hence the all-importance of conduct, of personal responsibility for all one's actions—the kind of moral issue which Faulkner treated most explicitly in *Requiem for a Nun* but which runs in fact through all his work.

It is necessary to emphasise that Faulkner in his best work is not concerned with ideas in any abstract sense. His preoccupations are not intellectual but moral; what he offers is not philosophy but wisdom. At the same time, his public statements are in no sense divorced from his literary achievement. The Nobel Prize Speech has sometimes been regarded as very much a *post hoc* statement, a deliberate effort on Faulkner's part to match with his own grandilo-quence the grandeur of the occasion. It should properly be seen as a distillation, necessarily couched in abstract terms, of the kind of state-ments and moral judgments which had been implicit in his work from the very first. As Faulkner wrote to Warren Beck in 1941: "I have been writing all the time about honor, truth, pity, consideration, the capacity to endure well grief and misfortune and injustice and then endure again ..."[28] Like the people of Oxford, so many of Faulkner's critics have failed to understand, in the words of "Mac" Reed, that Faulkner was "their closest friend who was trying to show them in his own peculiar way that they must appreciate the good life better."[29]

The crucial failure of much Faulkner criticism, however, and the one which underlies so many misreadings and misjudgments of his work, has been the continuing underestimation of Faulkner as an artist. The case against Faulkner was made out by Wyndham Lewis in his book, *Men Without Art*, published in 1934. In a chapter sub-titled "The Moralist with the Corn-Cob," Lewis attacked Faulkner for his presentation of "demented" characters[30] and fiercely criticised his style, accusing him of injecting poetic effects to liven up listless passages of his prose, and arguing of his repeated use of such words as "myriad" and "sourceless" that such repetition was not deliberate but merely revealed "the character of this slipshod and redundant artistic machine."[31] The various critics who have echoed Lewis's observations down the succeeding years have done so with little of his brilliance, much less of his justification, and nearly all of his mis-statements. Meanwhile the small but distinguished body of serious Faulkner criticism has increasingly revealed the intricate structural and imagistic patterns which operate within the novels, and shown that the elaboration of the style, with its repetitions and rhetorical flourishes, possesses an organic relationship with the material of the novels and with their moral and emotional themes. The overall tendency of such criticism has been to establish Faulkner as a deliberate, conscientious, and highly sophisticated literary artist, who, though not always successful, was always fully aware of what he was doing and always absolutely in control of material, characterisation, structure, and style.

That these conclusions can continue to be ignored by critics who still adhere to Lewis's line of attack can perhaps be attributed to Faulkner's much-criticised and widely-misunderstood "provinciality," his isolation in a part of the United States which the rest of the nation has agreed to call backward. Nothing could be less illumi-nating than to think of Faulkner as a kind of American primitive, a sort of literary and less engaging Grandma Moses, a wild untutored genius of the backwoods. It is not helpful even to see him as self-educated, lacking in literary culture, cut off from literary tradition, suffering as an artist because of his isolation from a sophisticated milieu such as he might have found in New York, London, or Paris. The early part of this book may perhaps have suggested that Faulkner had seen more of the world at an earlier age than has usually been assumed, and certainly that it did not take him long to see all that he needed to see of urban cultural centres and particularly of the literary and publishing world of New York. Louis Cochran recalls Faulkner saying, on his return home from his 1931 trip to New York, that he "had never been so tired of literary people in his life."[32] Faulkner was well aware of that diffusion of creative energy in talk which constitutes the seductive but fatal danger inherent in the life of literary circles, and his self-isolation in Oxford represented not a negative act of withdrawal but a positive commitment to literature, to the act of writing. That long shelf of Faulkner's books would surely have been a good deal shorter if he had not stayed at home and written with intense concentration for long periods of time: it is staggering to think, for example, that in a period of about eight years, from 1928 to 1936, Faulkner wrote four major novels (*The Sound and the Fury*, *As I Lay Dying*, *Light in August*, and *Absalom, Absalom!*), three other novels (*Sartoris*, *Sanctuary*, and *Pylon*), and a large number of short stories; he may also have made considerable progress towards an early version of *The Hamlet* at this time.

But if Faulkner isolated himself, and with good reason, from the contemporary literary world, he did not isolate himself from historical literary tradition. Indeed, it would seem fair to say that in certain important respects Faulkner was more actively aware of American and European literary traditions than any other important American novelist of this century, Hemingway not excluded. In one of the interviews at the University of Virginia, Faulkner said: "I read *Don Quixote* every year. I read the Old Testament. I read some of Dickens every year, and I've got a portable Shakespeare, one-volume Shakespeare, that I carry along with me. Conrad, *Moby-Dick*, Chekhov, *Madame Bovary*, some of Balzac almost every year, Tolstoy ... Gogol. Most of the Frenchmen of the nineteenth century I read in every year."[33] In assessing Faulkner's answers to questions of this nature it is always necessary to make due allowance for his sense of humour, and it seems highly questionable whether he had in fact read these books as recently or as frequently as he pretended. Faulkner often described his reading in similar terms, however, and there seems no reason to doubt that he had read at some time—probably during his youth or early manhood—the books and authors he mentions: Richard P. Adams, indeed, has traced echoes from many of them in Faulkner's work,[34] and the influence of the Old Testament and Shakespeare is almost everywhere apparent. There can be no doubt whatever of the breadth and sheer quantity of Faulkner's reading during the years of his apprenticeship, and the importance of Phil Stone's help and guidance at this stage of his career can hardly be over-estimated. In the course of the critical essays and reviews which Faulkner contributed to the *Double Dealer* and *The Mississippian* in the early 1920's we find mentioned, usually with reference to specific texts, several of the classic authors of English, French and American literature, and a large number of contemporary writers, notably Edward Arlington Robinson, Conrad Aiken (whom he especially admired), Amy Lowell (whom he especially disliked), Sinclair Lewis, John Masefield, Robert Frost, George Bernard Shaw, Eugene O'Neill, Ezra Pound, and D. H. Lawrence. Even when allowance has been made for a young writer's natural inclination to parade his reading, the impression remains—and it is reinforced by the kind of experimentation which he attempted in the prose sketches written in New Orleans —that Faulkner had read a good deal of recent writing, both American and European, and that he had made a shrewd assessment of the contemporary literary climate.[35]

The first two novels, *Soldiers' Pay* and *Mosquitoes*, show signs of influence from T. S. Eliot, Sherwood Anderson, James Branch Cabell, James Joyce, and possibly from Aldous Huxley, Scott Fitzgerald and Thomas Beer. In *Sartoris* Faulkner first began to find a voice distinctively his own, and in *The Sound and the Fury*, despite the continuing presence of Joyce, he achieved it, with astounding abruptness and completeness. Following the all-important initial breakthrough represented by the brilliant technical success of *The Sound and the Fury*, Faulkner seems to have gone beyond the range of direct literary influences. He no longer needed to fall back on the patterns created by his contemporaries or immediate predecessors, or even to seek encouragement in their example. He moved on, with superb assurance and technical sophistication, to the multiple viewpoints of *As I Lay Dying*, the rhetorical splendour and intricate, deliberately unresolved narrative patterns of *Absalom, Absalom!*, the violent juxtapositions of *The Wild Palms*, the rich, varied, and precisely calculated stylistic and thematic patterning of *The Hamlet*, the complex interrelationships and interactions of *Go Down, Moses*, the play-within-a-novel of *Requiem for a Nun*, the austere parable of *A Fable*.

Of *The Sound and the Fury* itself it has to be said not only that it is a book of outstanding individuality which no one but Faulkner could have written, but also that Faulkner himself could not have written it if he had not been a Southerner, indeed a Mississippian, born at a particular moment in time. Yet one does not need to underrate either Faulkner's originality or his Southerness in order to see that the novel is far from what it has too often been taken to be— a series of daring and almost random experiments made in isolation from the main streams of the novel in America and in Europe. On the contrary, *The Sound and the Fury* is a deliberately conceived and superlatively executed work of great technical sophistication: it is set in the American South, but it stands in the direct tradition of the modern psychological and experimental novel. Once we accept Faulkner's awareness of other writers and their innovations—perhaps Dostoevsky, probably Flaubert and James, certainly Conrad, and most importantly Joyce (whether or not Faulkner had read the whole of *Ulysses* at the time of beginning work on his own novel)—then the experiments he makes in *The Sound and the Fury* take on a double significance, for they can be seen not as a series of blind leaps in the dark, the speculative adventures of an isolated genius, but as the result of definite choice. Well informed of experiments which previous novelists had made, Faulkner did not simply evolve home-made solutions for his own problems but chose particular solutions rather than others of which he was also aware. His explorations broke new ground because they were not groping forays but planned expeditions which took the achievements of others as their starting-point.

It is important that the influences which almost certainly lie behind *The Sound and the Fury* were primarily European, even allowing for the possibility of certain minor influences from Sherwood Anderson and John Dos Passos. In discussing *Absalom, Absalom!* we discerned a possible influence from Charlotte Brontë, in discussing *Light in August* it seemed necessary to refer to Dickens and Hardy; elsewhere Conrad and Balzac are indisputable formative presences. There are obvious dangers, in fact, in attempting to place Faulkner in any exclusively American tradition. His literary environment includes Melville, Hawthorne, and James, but it also includes—to name only the most significant for Faulkner himself—Dostoevsky, Balzac, Flaubert, Verlaine, Cervantes, Shakespeare, Keats, Shelley, Swinburne, Wilde, Joyce, Synge, Eliot, Conrad, and the King James Bible. Much has been written about Faulkner as a humorous writer in the tradition of the American Southwest, and certainly the tall tale figures largely in his work from the first sketches written in New Orleans to his last book, *The Reivers*, which might be considered as one long tall tale. Yet we saw in discussing *The Hamlet* that when Faulkner employs the tall tale he does so with precisely calculated literary objectives in view: he uses it with a full knowledge of its antecedents and with a sophisticated awareness of its contribution to the elaborate interplay of traditional and experimental features which constitutes the complex multiple presentation of his novels. He is not committed to the tall tale in any uncritical way, as an essential element in a literary tradition to which he owes and recognises allegiance, and it remains only one of many devices which he can deploy and manipulate at will. Further warning against taking a purely Southern or even purely American view of Faulkner is provided by his remark, in 1922, that Mark Twain was "a hack writer who would not have been considered fourth rate in Europe, who tricked out a few of the old proven 'sure fire' literary skeletons with sufficient local color to intrigue the superficial and the lazy."[36] As time went on Faulkner came to rank Twain more highly, at least for *Huckleberry Finn*,[37] but the early comment at least emphasises how European was Faulkner's outlook at this period. It suggests, too, that if Faulkner did later resume some of the characteristic features of Twain's work, and of the work of other American figures, he did so consciously and discriminatingly, as a viable method of treating the material offered by that corner of native earth with which he had elected to deal.

Faulkner's achievement can be adequately estimated only by our seeing him as a great novelist in the context not merely of the South, or even of the United States, but of the whole western tradition. His deep identification with his own region is one of his greatest strengths, especially as it emerges in the marvellous sense of place, whether it be the heart of the wilderness or the interior of Miss Reba's brothel, and in the rich evocation of the world of Yoknapatawpha County; and certainly the intensity of his tragic power in novels such as *The Sound and the Fury*, *Light in August*, and *Absalom, Absalom!* derives both from this profoundly localised sense of social reality and from a poignant awareness of the proud and shameful history of the courageous, careless, gallant and oppressive South. At the same time, to concentrate too exclusively on this aspect of his work is to be in danger of mistaking means for ends and of seeing Faulkner as a lesser figure than he really is. The solidity of Faulkner's provinciality provides the unshakable foundation for his immensely ambitious exploration of the fundamental human themes with which he is always primarily concerned, and the examples of Hardy and Emily Brontë may suggest that Faulkner is not alone among novelists in pursuing the universal in terms of the intensely local. But it is Dickens whom Faulkner most resembles, in the passionate humanity of his tragi-comic vision, in the range and vitality of his characterisation and the profusion of his social notation, in the structural complexity of his novels and their broad symbolic patterns. It is also Dickens whom Faulkner most resembles in the sheer quantity and sustained quality of his achievement, and it is alongside Dickens, the greatest of the English novelists, that Faulkner must ultimately be ranked.

NOTES

NOTES

THE CAREER

1. Faulkner to Cowley, 16. The Faulkner-Cowley correspondence is deposited in the Yale University Library. Faulkner's letters are, with one exception, undated but have been numbered and catalogued in the sequence in which Malcolm Cowley placed them. Future references will give simply this number. John Faulkner, *My Brother Bill: An Affectionate Reminiscence* (New York, 1963), pp. 210-211, gives a broadly similar account of the variations in the spelling of the family name. One of the stations on Colonel Falkner's railroad was called Falkner, as Faulkner says, but it does not appear to have been the family's "place of . . . origin."

2. Annie Brierre, "Faulkner Parle," *Nouvelles Littéraires*, October 6, 1955, p. 6.

3. The quotation is from p. 4 of Thomas L. McHaney's unpublished M.A. thesis, "The Image of the Railroad in the Novels of William Faulkner, 1926-1942" (University of North Carolina, 1962), upon which I have drawn for my account of Colonel Falkner's railroad.

4. *My Brother Bill*, p.10.

5. *My Brother Bill*, pp. 11-13.

6. *My Brother Bill*, pp. 15, 126-127, 142. See also Phil Stone, "William Faulkner and His Neighbors," *Saturday Review*, XXV (September 19, 1942), 12.

7. See, for example, pp. 7-11, 30-34, 53-59.

8. Faulkner to Cowley, 16. See also Stone, "William Faulkner and His Neighbors."

9. Phil Stone, "William Faulkner, the Man and His Work," *Oxford Magazine*, 1, 2 (1934). Quoted in James B. Meriwether, "Early Notices of Faulkner by Phil Stone and Louis Cochran," forthcoming article in *Mississippi Quarterly*. Professor Meriwether kindly made available to me a copy of this article in advance of its publication.

10. *My Brother Bill*, p. 130. According to John Faulkner, Faulkner did not enter the bank until 1916, when he was nineteen and had already left school for two years.

11. *Forum*, LXXXIII (April 1930), lvi.

12. Stone graduated from Yale in 1914 and received his law degree from there in 1918 (*Bulletin of Yale University: Alumni Directory Number*, New Haven, 1956).

13. Stone, "William Faulkner, the Man and His Work," *Oxford*

Magazine, I, 3 (1934). Quoted Meriwether, "Early Notices of Faulkner."

14. Robert Coughlan, *The Private World of William Faulkner* (New York, 1954), p. 48.

15. *My Brother Bill*, p. 130.

16. Richard P. Adams, "The Apprenticeship of William Faulkner," *Tulane Studies in English*, XII (1962), 114.

17. See Joseph L. Blotner, ed., *A Catalogue of the Library of William Faulkner*, to be published by the University Press of Virginia. Professor Blotner has generously allowed me to make use of the typescript of this catalogue, which I shall in future refer to simply as *Catalogue*. Appendix A, based on information supplied by Professor James B. Meriwether, lists books ordered by Stone from the Brick Row Bookshop. For Faulkner's Hergesheimer review see Carvel Collins, ed., *William Faulkner: Early Prose and Poetry* (Boston, 1962), pp. 101-103. For the allusion to Élie Faure, see below, p. 20.

18. Quoted Meriwether, "Early Notices of Faulkner." My discussion of the Faulkner-Stone relationship owes a great deal to suggestions made by Professor Meriwether in conversation or in letters.

19. Ibid., quoted Meriwether, "Early Notices."

20. Stone, "William Faulkner and His Neighbors."

21. Stone to Louis Cochran, December 28, 1931, quoted in Meriwether, "Early Notices." Cochran's article, "William Faulkner, Literary Tyro of Mississippi" (Memphis *Commercial Appeal*, November 6, 1932, Section IV, p. 4), is also reprinted in full in Meriwether's article.

22. For all the works mentioned in this paragraph see Collins, ed., *William Faulkner: Early Prose and Poetry*.

23. *Early Prose and Poetry*, p. 45.

24. Collins, *Early Prose and Poetry*, p. 4, records that Faulkner worked from April 1 to June 15, 1918, at "an armament company in Connecticut"; Stone, in his letter to Cochran of December 28, 1931, mentions the Winchester Arms Company by name (see Meriwether, "Early Notices").

25. *My Brother Bill*, p. 134.

26. *Early Prose and Poetry*, p. 4; Mr. G. Price-Stephens informs me that Faulkner entered the recruits' depot on July 10.

27. Foreword, *The Faulkner Reader* (New York, 1954), p. x.

28. *My Brother Bill*, p. 134. Coughlan says Faulkner was rejected because he was too short (*Private World*, p. 50).

29. See *Early Prose and Poetry*, especially p. 78. The notebook itself is in the Alderman Library.

30. *My Brother Bill*, p. 135. Mr. Price-Stephens, however, has drawn my attention to the information in Alan Sullivan, *Aviation in Canada, 1917-1918* (Toronto, 1919), which seems to suggest that

Faulkner could not have completed the full pilot's course in the time available; see, for example, pp. 76-77, 169, 173.

31. *Early Prose and Poetry*, pp. 5-6; Mr. Price-Stephens tells me that Faulkner was officially demobilised on January 4, 1919. With Faulkner's notebook in the Alderman Library is a letter, dated November 12, 1920, from the Air Ministry in London notifying Faulkner that his honorary commission had been gazetted the previous March. See *The London Gazette*, March 9, 1920, p. 2911; also Mr. Price-Stephens's article, "Faulkner and the Royal Air Force," forthcoming in *Mississippi Quarterly*.

32. *Private World*, p. 51. I am grateful to Mr. Coughlan for his kindness in identifying, here and elsewhere, the sources of his information.

33. *My Brother Bill*, pp. 138-139. John Faulkner says that the crashed aircraft was a Sopwith Camel, which he earlier (p. 135) describes as "the orneriest airplane ever built." From Alan Sullivan, *Aviation in Canada, 1917-1918*, however, it seems almost certain that Faulkner would have flown only basic training aircraft, probably the Canadian version of the Curtis JN-4 or "Jenny"; see, for example, p. 47.

34. Faulkner to Cowley, 20.

35. Henry Nash Smith, "Writing Right Smart Fun, Says Faulkner," *Dallas Morning News*, February 14, 1932, Sect. IV, p. 2.

36. *Early Prose and Poetry*, pp. 6, 19.

37. A. Wigfall Green, "William Faulkner at Home," in Frederick J. Hoffman and Olga W. Vickery, edd., *William Faulkner: Two Decades of Criticism* (East Lansing, 1951), p. 40.

38. Faulkner to Cowley, 16.

39. The dates "April, May, June, 1919" appear on the final page of *The Marble Faun* (Boston, 1924). Professor Meriwether, however, has suggested to me that the carbon typescript of the book which he describes in *The Literary Career of William Faulkner: A Bibliographical Study* (Princeton, 1961), p. 10, was prepared later than 1919, and that since this typescript was considerably revised and expanded before publication it seems doubtful that *The Marble Faun* existed in anything like its final form as early as 1919.

40. The texts are accessible in *Early Prose and Poetry*, pp. 57-59, 61.

41. *Early Prose and Poetry*, pp. 13-16.

42. *Ole Miss*, 1920-1921, XXV, 135. This page is reproduced in *Early Prose and Poetry*, p. 80, since the decorative border was apparently drawn by Faulkner, but the list of names has been blocked out.

43. *Literary Career*, pp. 8-9. See also *Early Prose and Poetry*, pp. 17-18.

44. *Literary Career*, Fig. 1.

45. *Catalogue*, where the book is listed as Wilde, *Salomé: A Tragedy in One Act*. Translated from the French of Oscar Wilde, pictured by Aubrey Beardsley (Boston, 1912). The volume was auto-

graphed by Faulkner, a sign, Professor Blotner has suggested, that he attached some particular importance to it. See Blotner, "William Faulkner's Name Was in the Books He Loved Best," *New York Times Book Review*, December 8, 1963, pp. 4-5, 45.

46. Stone to Cochran, December 28, 1931. Quoted Meriwether, "Early Notices."

47. *My Brother Bill*, p. 142.

48. Cf. *Literary Career*, p. 14.

49. Marshall J. Smith, "Faulkner of Mississippi," *The Bookman*, LXXIV (December 1931), 416.

50. Stark Young, "New Year's Craw," *New Republic*, XCIII (January 5, 1938), 283.

51. Young, loc. cit.

52. Smith, loc. cit.; Young, loc. cit.

53. Information in a letter to the author from Professor Walter B. Rideout of the University of Wisconsin, December 14, 1963.

54. *Early Prose and Poetry*, pp. 20-21.

55. Stone to Cochran, December 28, 1931. Quoted Meriwether, "Early Notices."

56. Alderman Library.

57. *Early Prose and Poetry*, pp. 24, 26.

58. Faulkner to Cowley, 16. See also *Private World*, p. 53; *My Brother Bill*, pp. 147-148, 152-153.

59. *Private World*, p. 53.

60. *Literary Career*, p. 35. Meriwether also records on the same page a much later typescript of the story which Faulkner inscribed for Phil Stone's son, his own godson, at Christmas, 1948.

61. "The Wishing-Tree," typescript in Alderman Library, p. 42. Cf. Carvel Collins, ed., *New Orleans Sketches: William Faulkner* (New Brunswick, N.J., 1958), p. 29; also *Early Prose and Poetry*, p. 18. In *New Orleans Sketches*, p. 29, Collins says that "Mayday" was written later than 1925; if so, then "The Wishing-Tree" may also date from about 1926 rather than from 1923 or 1924.

62. *Literary Career*, pp. 86-87. These stories are all in the Alderman Library.

63. "Love," typescript, Alderman Library, p. 1.

64. *Literary Career*, p. 87.

65. "Moonlight," carbon typescript, Alderman Library, p. 5.

66. Texts accessible in *Early Prose and Poetry*.

67. Cf. *Early Prose and Poetry*, pp. 22, 30-31; *Literary Career*, pp. 88 (for "Spring"), 91 (for "Cleopatra"). See also James B. Meriwether, comp., *William Faulkner: An Exhibition of Manuscripts* (Austin, Texas, 1959), p. 11. As Meriwether observes, there is ample evidence in manuscript material now at the University of Texas to show that Faulkner had written most of the poems in *A Green Bough* before the publication of *The Marble Faun*.

68. Texts available in *Early Prose and Poetry*.

69. See note 39 above. The Faulkner collection at the University of Texas includes a copy of this bound typescript and many miscellaneous typescript sheets of octosyllabic couplets.

70. Quotations in this paragraph taken from the Catalogue for Sale No. 622, Swann Galleries, New York, April 25, 1963, pp. 1-2.

71. Editorial, I (March 1921), 83. Quoted Frederick J. Hoffman et al., *The Little Magazine: A History and a Bibliography* (Princeton, N.J., 1947), p. 192.

72. Cf. Sherwood Anderson, *Memoirs* (New York, 1942), p. 351: "We used to gather in the office of the magazine once a month, make a night of it, bring drinks in and go over manuscripts. When there wasn't enough to make up a number of the magazine we sat and wrote pieces to enable it to go to press."

73. La Farge's novel *Laughing Boy* was in Faulkner's library at the time of his death (*Catalogue*).

74. Anderson, *Dark Laughter* (New York, 1925), p. 76.

75. Howard Mumford Jones and Walter B. Rideout, edd., *Letters of Sherwood Anderson* (Boston, 1953), p. 87.

76. Information supplied in letter from Professor Rideout, December 14, 1963.

77. Basso, "William Faulkner: Man and Writer," *Saturday Review* XLV (July 28, 1962), 11.

78. James K. Feibleman, interview, February 4, 1963.

79. James K. Feibleman, *Philosophers Lead Sheltered Lives* (London, 1952), p. 24.

80. Jean Stein, "William Faulkner" [interview], in Malcolm Cowley, ed., *Writers at Work: The Paris Review Interviews* (New York, 1958), p. 137. Cf. Carvel Collins, "The Pairing of *The Sound and the Fury* and *As I Lay Dying*," in Faulkner number of *Princeton University Library Chronicle*, XVIII (Spring 1957), p. 123: "Some of the artistic and literary people whom William Faulkner knew at New Orleans in the mid-twenties have pointed out to me the extent to which they discussed Freud, Joyce, and Frazer."

81. Smith, "Writing Right Smart Fun."

82. *Catalogue*. Cf. Blotner, "Faulkner's Name . . .".

83. Cf. Richard Ellman, *James Joyce* (New York, 1959), p. 307n. Stone ordered a copy of *A Portrait* from the Brick Row Bookshop in January 1926 (*Catalogue*).

84. Adams, "The Apprenticeship of William Faulkner," pp. 114, 139.

85. Ellman, op. cit., pp. 543, 593n.; *Letters of Sherwood Anderson*, p. 148.

86. Marshall Smith, "Faulkner in Seclusion, Writing Movie Script," *Memphis Press-Scimitar*, December 1, 1931, p. 11. Mrs. Faulkner was quoted as saying: "When we were married in 1928

[sic], he began what he termed my education. He gave me James Joyce's 'Ulysses' to read. I didn't understand it. He told me to read it again. I did and understood what Mr. Joyce was writing about."

87. *Letters of Sherwood Anderson*, p. 148. Possibly Faulkner bought his copy in Paris in 1925 : see p. 22.

88. La Farge, *Raw Material* (Boston, 1945), p. 127.

89. Interview, February 3,1963.

90. Basso, "William Faulkner : Man and Writer," p. 12; cf. *Private World*, p. 64.

91. Faulkner, "Sherwood Anderson," in *Princeton University Library Chronicle* (Faulkner number), p. 93; Faulkner's article first appeared in the *Dallas Morning News*, April 26, 1925, Part III, p. 7. See also *New Orleans Sketches*, p. 18.

92. "Once Aboard the Lugger," *Contempo*, I (February 1, 1932), pp. 1, 4; "Mississippi," *Holiday*, XV (April 1954), 33-47. But see p. 23.

93. *Early Prose and Poetry*, pp. 114-118; quotations, p. 117.

94. *New Orleans Sketches*, pp. 27-29.

95. The "New Orleans" sketches which Faulkner contributed to the January-February 1925 issue of the *Double Dealer* may well have been influenced by Wilde's *Poems in Prose* (it is also interesting to compare Faulkner's sonnet "Hermaphroditus," first published in *Mosquitoes*, p. 252, with the lines about Salmacis in the twenty-first stanza of Wilde's poem "The Burden of Itys"). It may have been through George Moore, whom he had certainly read by this time (see *Princeton University Library Chronicle*, Faulkner number, p. 93, and p. 21 below) and whose *Lewis Seymour and Some Women* he seems to have received as a Christmas present in 1918 (*Catalogue*), that Faulkner was introduced to Mallarmé's prose poems (cf. Moore, *Confessions of a Young Man* [London, 1917], pp. 178-181) and to Gautier's *Mademoiselle de Maupin*, which he quotes both in *Mosquitoes* (p. 340) and in "Wealthy Jew," the first of the "New Orleans" pieces. Compare the opening sentence of "Wealthy Jew"—" 'I love three things : gold; marble and purple; splendor, solidity, color.' " (*New Orleans Sketches*, p. 37)—with page 211 of *Mademoiselle de Maupin* (Paris, 1878): "Trois choses me plaisent : l'or, le marbre et la pourpre, éclat, solidité, couleur." Faulkner owned a copy of a 1918 edition of *Mademoiselle de Maupin* (*Catalogue*), and his familiarity with a book to which the Symbolists attached such importance may itself be significant of his aesthetic attitudes at this period.

96. Faulkner, "Sherwood Anderson : An Appreciation," *Atlantic*, CXCI (June 1953), 28; cf. Anderson, *Memoirs*, p. 474.

97. *Letters of Sherwood Anderson*, p. 136.

98. Information in letter from Professor Rideout, December 14, 1963. Cf. *New Orleans Sketches*, p. 18.

99. Swann Galleries Catalogue, p. 2.

100. Rideout, letter, December 14, 1963.

101. Rideout, letter, December 14, 1963.

102. *Early Prose and Poetry*, p. 32; *New York Times*, July 7, 1962, p. 6. For the drawings see *Early Prose and Poetry*, pp. [104]-[106].

103. Swann Galleries Catalogue, p. 2.

104. Rideout, letter, December 14, 1963.

105. *Letters of Sherwood Anderson*, pp. 139-140; "Elmer," manuscript page in Alderman Library headed "Elmer and Myrtle," also typescript in Massey Collection, pp. 8ff. Anderson said in his letter that he intended to use the incident of the boy's experience of a fire in *Tar: A Mid-West Childhood*, but he seems not to have done so.

106. For the two letters see *Literary Career*, Figures 27-29, and *Letters of Sherwood Anderson*, pp. 162-164. For discussion of the Al Jackson material see H. Edward Richardson, "Faulkner, Anderson, and Their Tall Tale," *American Literature*, XXXIV (May 1962), 287-291, and more especially the reply by Walter B. Rideout and James B. Meriwether, "On the Collaboration of Faulkner and Anderson," *American Literature*, XXXV (March 1963), 85-87.

107. Frederick L. Gwynn and Joseph L. Blotner, edd., *Faulkner in the University: Class Conferences at the University of Virginia 1957-1958* (Charlottesville, Virginia, 1959), p. 232.

108. *Private World*, p. 60.

109. When in late 1931 Louis Cochran sent Phil Stone the draft of his article on Faulkner, Stone challenged a good deal of what Cochran had said but not the statement that Faulkner had taken to New Orleans with him a half-completed novel. See Meriwether, "Early Notices," and note 21 above.

110. Rideout, letter, December 14, 1963. Cf. *Faulkner in the University*, pp. 21-22, and Anderson, *Memoirs*, p. 356.

111. *Letters*, p. 146.

112. Reprinted in *Princeton University Library Chronicle* (Faulkner number), pp. 89-94.

113. *Atlantic* (June 1953), p. 28.

114. Drawing reproduced in *Literary Career*, p. 11. The book was published in New Orleans by the Pelican Bookshop Press, 1926.

115. *Atlantic* (June 1953), p. 28.

116. *Letters*, p. 155.

117. Rideout, letter, December 14, 1963.

118. *Letters*, pp. 145-6.

119. *New Orleans Sketches*, p. 31.

120. *Literary Career*, p. 81.

121. Typescript, Alderman Library, p. 3. This typescript material comprises passages from several different versions, all of them fragmentary, and there is some duplication of page numbers.

122. Typescript, Alderman Library, pp. 21, 22. Faulkner wrote,

apparently while he was in Paris, a humorous "Ode to the Louver":
see *William Faulkner: An Exhibition of Manuscripts* (Texas), p. 6.

123. Typescript, Alderman Library, p. 1; reproduced as Fig. 7 of
the *Literary Career*.

124. *New Orleans Sketches*, pp. 31, 33; a number of these manuscripts are now in the Faulkner Collection of the University of
Texas.

125. *New Orleans Sketches*, p. 31.

126. *New Orleans Sketches*, pp. 31-32.

127. Typescript, Alderman Library, p. 104.

128. *New Orleans Sketches*, p. 32.

129. Faulkner mentioned Guynemer in his Foreword to *The
Faulkner Reader* (see p. 6, above), and he may conceivably have
known, in French or in translation, Henry Bordeaux, *Le chevalier de
l'air: vie héroïque de Guynemer* (Paris, 1918); Bordeaux's invocation
of the names and terminology of medieval chivalry in describing aerial
combat sometimes resembles certain passages in *Sartoris*.

130. "The Apprenticeship of William Faulkner," p. 128.

131. Information in a letter to the author from Mr. Odiorne,
December 10, 1963.

132. Typescript, Alderman Library, pp. 88-93. One of the characters
in the episode is an excessively mean English peer, Lord Wysbroke,
who borrows a servant's bicycle in order to get to the railway station.
On pp. 90-91 Lord Wysbroke is in London. According to John
Faulkner (*My Brother Bill*, p. 155), Faulkner visited London on his
way home from Paris.

133. "Elmer," typescript, Alderman Library, unnumbered page.

134. "Portrait of Elmer Hodge," p. 22.

135. "Elmer," typescript, Alderman Library, p. 23.

136. "Portrait of Elmer Hodge," p. 57.

137. *Literary Career*, p. 81.

138. "Elmer," typescript, Alderman Library, p. 44. Cf. Quentin's
obsession with the factory smokestack and with Herbert Head's cigar.

139. "Elmer," typescript, Alderman Library, pp. 18, 8. Faulkner
returned many times to the theme of virginity, and it is interesting
in this respect to read Elmer's youthful image of his ideal woman: "a
Dianalike girl with an impregnable integrity, a slimness virginal and
impervious to time or circumstance. Darkhaired and small and proud,
casting him bones fiercely as though he were a dog, coppers as if he
were a beggar, looking the other way ..." (Typescript, Alderman
Library, p. 47; final periods in the original).

140. *Faulkner in the University*, p. 58.

141. *My Brother Bill*, p. 155.

142. Swann Galleries Catalogue, p. 2.

143. *New Orleans Sketches*, p. 33. John Faulkner (*My Brother Bill*,
p. 155) says that his brother came home "steerage, with a beard. He

smelled like steerage too. When he came in Mother said, 'For heaven's sake, Billie, take a bath.' "

144. Manuscript, Alderman Library, p. [2]. Cf. *The Sound and the Fury*, pp. 330, 364.

145. *Literary Career*, p. 81.

146. *New Orleans Sketches*, pp. 33-34; further information supplied by Mr. William B. Wisdom, interview, February 3, 1963, and by Mrs. Robert Crager, interview, February 4, 1963.

147. *New Orleans Sketches*, p. 33.

148. See James B. Meriwether, "Sartoris and Snopes: An Early Notice," *Library Chronicle of the University of Texas*, VII (Summer 1962), 36-39.

149. Quoted Meriwether, ibid., p. 37.

150. In the Arents Collection of the New York Public Library.

151. Cantwell, "The Faulkners: Recollections of a Gifted Family," *New World Writing: Second Mentor Selection* (New York, 1952), p. 306.

152. Robert N. Linscott, "Faulkner Without Fanfare," *Esquire*, LX, 1 (July 1963), 38.

153. Faulkner to Cowley, 15.

154. *My Brother Bill*, pp. 70, 16.

155. Stone to Mrs. Bess Stoner Landon, undated, quoted in O. B. Emerson, "William Faulkner's Literary Reputation in America," (unpublished Ph.D. dissertation, Vanderbilt University, 1962), p. 649. The dissertation is a valuable source of information about Faulkner's American reception.

156. See Conrad Aiken, *A Reviewer's ABC* ([New York], 1958), pp. 197-200.

157. James B. Meriwether, "Notes on the Textual History of *The Sound and the Fury*," *Papers of the Bibliographical Society of America*, LVI (1962), 288 and note. See also pp. 81-85, below.

158. Typescript in Alderman Library, p. [5]: first two sentences quoted *Literary Career*, p. 16. Meriwether ("Textual History," p. 289n) suggests that the piece may have been "a version of the introduction Faulkner wrote for an unpublished, limited edition of *The Sound and the Fury*." See also ibid., pp. 305,308, and Faulkner to Cowley, 20.

159. Coindreau, preface to *Le bruit et la fureur*, translated by Maurice E. Coindreau (Paris, 1949), p. 14: "Ecrit alors que l'auteur se débattait dans des difficultés d'ordre intime, ..."

160. Draft introduction [?], pp. 4, 3; first passage quoted in *Literary Career*, p. 16.

161. Meriwether, "Textual History of *The Sound and the Fury*," p. 289.

162. Meriwether, ibid., p. 292.

163. A copy of Art Young's *On My Way* was signed and dated by Faulkner: "Oxford, Miss./12 Dec. 1928" (*Catalogue*).

164. The contract was dated February 18, 1929 (Meriwether, "Textual History," p. 292n).

165. Lenore Marshall, "The Power of Words," *Saturday Review*, XLV (July 28, 1962), 16.

166. Meriwether, "Textual History," p. 292. Harrison Smith (interview, March 28, 1963) confirmed this account, but admitted that his memory of such matters had become extremely faint.

167. *Literary Career*, p. 66; see p. 114, below.

168. *My Brother Bill*, p. 159.

169. Judge Falkner's candidacy was announced in the *Oxford Eagle*, December 27, 1928, p. 1; his defeat was reported in the same paper on February 21, 1929, p. 1. According to the *Oxford Eagle*, January 24, 1929, p. 1, not even heavy rains kept Judge Falkner from driving around in his Chrysler to campaign. Information supplied by Mr. Thomas L. McHaney.

170. *Faulkner in the University*, p. 233.

171. *My Brother Bill*, pp. 158-159.

172. *Oxford Eagle*, June 27, 1929, p. 5.

173. See below, pp. 93-94.

174. *My Brother Bill*, pp. 160-161; the page is in the Mississippi Room at the University of Mississippi.

175. He told Marshall Smith ("Faulkner of Mississippi," pp. 415-416) that the hum of the dynamo fascinated him: "Some day I'm going to buy a dynamo and put it in my workroom."

176. See below, pp. 108-109.

177. *Literary Career*, p. 168.

178. *Literary Career*, pp. 168-169.

179. Unbound carbon typescript, Alderman Library, p. 7.

180. Meriwether, "Textual History of *The Sound and the Fury*," p. 288n; see also *Literary Career*, p. 167.

181. Information supplied in a letter to the author from Professor Meriwether, January 17, 1964.

182. *My Brother Bill*, pp. 162-163; *Private World*, p. 22.

183. Marshall Smith, "Faulkner in Mississippi," p. 412; Henry Nash Smith, "Writing Right Smart Fun." Cf. Anthony Buttitta, "William Faulkner, That Writin' Man of Oxford," *Saturday Review*, XVIII (May 21, 1938), 7.

184. *Catalogue*. Cf. Blotner, "Faulkner's Name . . ."

185. Below, pp. 114-117.

186. Frederick J. Hoffman, Introduction to Frederick J. Hoffman and Olga W. Vickery, edd., *William Faulkner: Three Decades of Criticism* (New York and Burlingame, 1963), pp. 1-18.

187. *Letters*, p. 252.

188. Allen Tate, interview, September 3, 1963.

189. Stone to Cochran, December 28, 1931. Cochran himself spoke of Faulkner as one who, "beyond mild semi-annual libations, enjoyed

with some boyhood crony who never read a book in his life, looks but rarely upon the cup that cheers" (Meriwether, "Early Notices").

190. "Faulkner of Mississippi," pp. 411-412.

191. So Spratling's drawing would suggest: see p. 26, above. The point of the obviously humorous reference, however, may have been Faulkner's preference for Mississippi "moonshine"; Sherwood Anderson (*Memoirs*, p. 473) recalls Faulkner asking if he could leave some of his things in Anderson's house while he was looking for somewhere to stay in New Orleans: "His 'things' consisted of some six or eight half gallon jars of moon liquor he had brought with him from the country and that were stowed in the pockets of the big coat." The bulging of the coat had made Anderson think, at first sight, that Faulkner must be deformed.

192. *Private World*, p. 105.

193. "Faulkner Without Fanfare," p. 36.

194. *My Brother Bill*, p. 149.

195. John B. Cullen, in collaboration with Floyd C. Watkins, *Old Times in the Faulkner Country* (Chapel Hill, N.C., 1961), p. 17.

196. Malcolm Cowley, interview, March 26, 1963.

197. *My Brother Bill*, pp. 149-150.

198. Carl Van Vechten, interview, April 6, 1963.

199. Information from Professor Meriwether; apparently Faulkner reached New York by sea.

200. *Memphis Press-Scimitar*, December 1, 1931, p. 11; see p. 14, above.

201. Carvel Collins, "Nathanael West's *Day of the Locust* and *Sanctuary*," *Faulkner Studies*, II (Summer 1953), 23.

202. *Catalogue*. Coughlan (*Private World*, p. 110) has a story of Faulkner attending a party at Connelly's, whom he had perhaps met through Roark Bradford (see p. 13, above).

203. Ben Wasson, interview, February 2, 1963.

204. *Literary Career*, p. 175.

205. Buttitta, "William Faulkner, That Writin' Man of Oxford," p. 7.

206. *Literary Career*, p. 67.

207. Draft introduction [?], pp. 2-3.

208. Ibid., p. 4.

209. *Contempo*, I (February 1, 1932), p. 2. Most of the poems were subsequently incorporated into A *Green Bough*; the story, "Once Aboard the Lugger," has never been collected.

210. Oliver Wells, ed., *An Anthology of the Younger Poets* (Philadelphia, 1932), pp. 122-126. *Salmagundi* was published in Milwaukee, 1932.

211. *Nouvelle revue française*, XXXVI (June 1, 1931), 926. French criticism of Faulkner was, from the beginning, distinguished and perceptive: see Thelma M. Smith and Ward L. Miner, *Trans-*

atlantic Migration: The Contemporary American Novel in France (Durham, N.C., 1955), pp. 122-145, and, more especially, the excellent account in S. D. Woodworth, William Faulkner en France (1931-1952) (Paris, 1959).

212. According to Coughlan (Private World, p. 106), an approach, spearheaded by Tallulah Bankhead, was made to Faulkner at the Charlottesville Conference; Mrs. Faulkner, in the Press-Scimitar interview of November 30, 1931, said that her husband was working on a script for Tallulah Bankhead.

213. George R. Sidney, "Faulkner in Hollywood: A Study of his Career as a Scenarist" (unpublished Ph.D. dissertation, University of New Mexico, 1959), p. 36. For information about Faulkner's work in Hollywood I have relied upon this important dissertation and upon Meriwether's Literary Career, pp. 155-163.

214. "Faulkner in Hollywood," pp. 37-38 (for comment on The Story of Temple Drake, see pp. 230-231, 234); Literary Career, pp. 156-158, 161.

215. Writers at Work, p. 126. Cf. Private World, pp. 111-114.

216. New York Times, December 25, 1932, Sect. IX, p. 5.

217. "Faulkner in Hollywood," p. 203; Literary Career, p. 160.

218. An Exhibition of Manuscripts (Texas), p. 10.

219. The Double Dealer, VII (April 1925). This was the issue in which Faulkner's essay "On Criticism" appeared, and the mention of "A Greening Bough" appears in the editorial note on him as a contributor (no page number).

220. Contempo, III (June 25, 1933), 1; the text was italicised.

221. For the influence of Swinburne on Faulkner, see Faulkner, "Verse Old and Nascent: A Pilgrimage," Double Dealer, VII (April 1925), 129-131; text available in Early Prose and Poetry, pp. 114-118. See also Adams, "Apprenticeship of William Faulkner," p. 120.

222. New York Times, June 26, 1933, p. 12.

223. My Brother Bill, pp. 8, 222. Cf. Maurice Coindreau, Preface to Le bruit et la fureur, p. 14n: "Les profondes secousses morales sont un facteur puissant dans l'inspiration de William Faulkner. C'est après avoir perdu un de ses enfants qu'il écrivit Light in August ..." See also p. 26, above.

224. "Writing Right Smart Fun."

225. My Brother Bill, pp. 167-170. Cf. Olivia Browne, "The Flying Faulkners," Memphis Commercial Appeal, November 8, 1959, Sect. IV. See pp. 138-141 below.

226. New York Times, November 11, 1935, p. 3.

227. My Brother Bill, pp. 217-219. See Private World, p. 99, for Faulkner's story of how, after the crash, he "put [Dean's] body together in a bathtub." Cf. "Faulkner in Hollywood," pp. 53-54.

228. "Faulkner in Hollywood," pp. 41-45; Literary Career, p. 157.

229. Lavon Rascoe, "An Interview with William Faulkner,"

Western Review, XV (Summer 1951), 302 (quoted "Faulkner in Hollywood," p. 86). There is some question as to Faulkner's part in writing *Slave Ship* : see "Faulkner in Hollywood," pp. 84-86.

230. B. R. Crisler, "Film Gossip of the Week," *New York Times*, August 2, 1936, Sect. X, p. 3.

231. See below, pp. 150-151. Coindreau, Preface to *Le bruit et la fureur*, p. 14n, states that *Absalom, Absalom!* was written in the weeks following Dean's death.

232. Some of the limited edition certificate of issue statements mentioned on p. 68 of *Literary Career* are dated from Los Angeles on October 19, 1936.

233. For the letter, see *Princeton University Library Chronicle* (Faulkner number), Plate II; for Coindreau's account of his visit, see ibid., pp. 108-109. Cf. John Faulkner on "Earnest Trueheart" (*My Brother Bill*, p. 172).

234. Faulkner dated a book at Rowanoak on September 1, 1937 (*Catalogue*).

235. The novel could conceivably have been *The Hamlet*, however.

236. Cantwell, "The Faulkners," p. 305.

237. Information in letter from Professor Meriwether, January 17, 1964.

238. *My Brother Bill*, pp. 186-190, etc.

239. *Old Times in the Faulkner Country*, p. 49.

240. Ibid., p. 13.

241. *My Brother Bill*, pp. 156-157.

242. *Old Times*, p. 13.

243. Ibid., pp. 13-14; cf. *Private World*, pp. 96-99.

244. *New York Times*, January 19, 1939, p. 15.

245. See Aiken, *A Reviewer's ABC*, pp. 200-207.

246. For the composition of *The Hamlet* see below, pp. 180-185.

247. Brennan, "Journey South," *University of Kansas City Review*, XXII (Autumn 1955), 15.

248. There is an official letter (dated May 23, 1941) relating to this matter among the papers in the Alderman Library.

249. See p. 234, below.

250. In a letter to the author, dated December 17, 1963, Professor Meriwether states that Faulkner's correspondence with his agent, Harold Ober, in the years 1941 and 1942 reveals him to have been in urgent need of money.

251. Faulkner to Cowley, 4; George Wickes, ed., *Lawrence Durrell and Henry Miller: A Private Correspondence* (London, 1963), p. 174. See also Sidney, "Faulkner in Hollywood," pp. 45-46.

252. Faulkner to Cowley, 24.

253. "Faulkner in Hollywood," pp. 45-46; *Literary Career*, pp. 157, 159, 160. For Humphrey Bogart, see *Writers at Work*, pp. 125-126.

254. Faulkner to Cowley, 4.

255. "Faulkner in Hollywood," pp. 46-47; for "Revolt in the Earth" see *Literary Career*, pp. 92-93, 160.

256. Faulkner to Cowley, 2.

257. "Faulkner in Hollywood," p. 46.

258. Faulkner to Cowley, 19 and 24.

259. *Literary Career*, pp. 93, 159.

260. "Faulkner in Hollywood," pp. 48, 94-95; *Literary Career*, p. 157. Faulkner got screen credit for his work on the screen play.

261. Faulkner apparently spent some time in Paris and Rome before arriving in Egypt: see, for example, A. M. Dominicis, "An Interview with Faulkner," *Faulkner Studies*, III (Summer-Autumn 1954), 33-37.

262. Linscott, "Faulkner Without Fanfare," p. 36.

263. Cynthia Grenier, "The Art of Fiction: An Interview with William Faulkner—September, 1955," *Accent*, XVI (Summer 1956), 173.

264. *New York Times*, February 16, 1947, Section VII, p. 8.

265. Faulkner to Cowley, 11.

266. *Writers at Work*, p. 125.

267. Robert A. Jelliffe, ed., *Faulkner at Nagano* (Tokyo, 1962), p. 114.

268. *Writers at Work*, p. 126.

269. *Private World*, p. 109. For additional comment on Faulkner's attitudes towards Hollywood, see Sidney, "Faulkner in Hollywood," pp. 214-230, 239.

270. Information supplied in letter from Professor Meriwether, December 17, 1963.

271. Faulkner to Cowley, 4 and 24.

272. For Aiken see note 245 above; the most important of several articles on Faulkner which Beck published in 1941 and 1942 was "William Faulkner's Style," *American Prefaces*, 6 (Spring 1941), 195-211 (reprinted in Hoffman and Vickery, edd., *Three Decades*, pp. 142-156). For French criticism of Faulkner during the late 1930's see Woodworth, *William Faulkner en France*, pp. 47-56.

273. Cowley to Faulkner, July 22, 1944; Cowley's letters to Faulkner are also in the Yale University Library.

274. Faulkner to Cowley, 2; Faulkner himself dated this first letter to Cowley: "Hollywood, Sunday, 7 May".

275. Faulkner to Cowley, 13.

276. Faulkner to Cowley, 7.

277. Faulkner to Cowley, 11.

278. Faulkner to Cowley, 18.

279. Faulkner to Cowley, 23. For the relationship of the appendix to the novel see Meriwether, "Textual History of *The Sound and the Fury*," pp. 310-313.

280. See below, pp. 285-286.

281. Faulkner to Cowley, 24.

282. Reprinted in *Three Decades*, pp. 109-124.

283. Cowley to Faulkner, August 9, 1945.

284. Information about *A Fable* and *Intruder* from Professor Meriwether.

285. Information in a letter from Mr. Albert Erskine of Random House, November 6, 1963.

286. *New York Times*, November 7, 1948, Sect. VII, p. 8.

287. *Private World*, pp. 116-119.

288. See below, pp. 259, 270-275.

289. *New York Times*, November 24, 1948, p. 44.

290. *American Academy of Arts and Letters: Proceedings*. Second Series. Number One (New York, 1951), p. 18.

291. Quoted by Hodding Carter, "Faulkner and His Folk," *Princeton University Library Quarterly* (Faulkner number), p. 99.

292. *Old Times in the Faulkner Country*, p. 18.

293. *New York Times*, November 11, 1950, p. 14.

294. *New York Times*, November 28, 1950, p. 10; *Private World*, pp. 134-135.

295. *New York Times*, December 8, 1950, p. 27. For the ceremonies in Stockholm see ibid., December 11, 1950, p. 10.

296. *New York Times*, January 29, 1961, Sect. VII, p. 8.

297. *New York Times*, March 7, 1951, p. 30, and October 27, 1951, p. 8; a manuscript of the brief acceptance speech, in French, which Faulkner made on the latter occasion is reproduced in the Faulkner number of the *Princeton University Library Chronicle*, Plate I.

298. Marian Nancy Dew, "A Study of William Faulkner's *Requiem for a Nun*" (unpublished M.A. thesis, University of North Carolina, 1962), pp. 18-19.

299. Dew, op. cit., p. 20; the letter from Ayers is in the Alderman Library.

300. See Smith and Miner, *Transatlantic Migration*, pp. 144-145, for a report of Faulkner's extraordinarily enthusiastic reception at the final session of the Œuvres du XXe Siécle festival, May 30, 1952 (the report is quoted in *Three Decades*, p. 28).

301. *New York Times*, October 19, 1952, Sect II, p. 1 (quoted Dew, op. cit., p. 20).

302. Bouvard, "Conversation with William Faulkner," *Modern Fiction Studies*, V, 4 (Winter 1959-1960), 361-364.

303. See *New Yorker*, February 28, 1953, pp. 18, 19, 20.

304. *Literary Career*, p. 162.

305. *New York Times*, April 12, 1953, Sect. II, p. 11. Cf. Sidney, "Faulkner in Hollywood," p. 48n.

306. *Literary Career*, pp. 162-163.

307. *New York Times*, August 10, 1954, p. 17, and August 22, 1954, p. 84. For remarks made by Faulkner in Brazil, see *Time*, August 23, 1954, p. 76.

308. *Faulkner at Nagano*, p. 130.

309. Hodding Carter, "Faulkner and His Folk," p. 102.

310. *New York Times Book Review*, February 6, 1955, p. 2.

311. Ibid., p. 24. The final sentence is added in holograph at the end of the 3-page carbon typescript of the speech now among the Faulkner papers in Princeton University Library.

312. *Harper's*, CCXI (July 1955), 37.

313. "Faulkner and His Folk," p. 102.

314. Speech printed in Memphis *Commercial Appeal*, November 11, 1955, p. 8; expanded version in *Three Views of the Segregation Decisions* (Atlanta, 1956), pp. 9-12.

315. Russell Howe, "New Civil War if Negro Claims are Pressed," London *Sunday Times*, March 4, 1956, p. 7. The remark as quoted makes little sense when read in context.

316. "If I Were a Negro," *Ebony*, XI (September 1956), 71.

317. "On Fear: The South in Labor," *Harper's*, CCXII (June 1956), 30.

318. *My Brother Bill*, p. 268.

319. *New York Times*, April 16, 1956, p. 8; Faulkner's refusal was announced two days later (April 18, p. 29).

320. See, for example, the interview at Princeton reported in *New York Times*, March 8, 1958, p. 19: "It's always been my belief that the white folks and the colored folks simply don't like one another. ... It seems to me that simple. In making the integration decision, the Supreme Court ignored this."

321. Jelliffe, ed., *Faulkner at Nagano*, p. v; Miss Hide Ishiguro, interview, December 1, 1963. See Gay Wilson Allen, "With Faulkner in Japan," *American Scholar*, XXXI (Autumn 1962), 566-571, especially p. 569: "The talk was natural, unaffected, colloquial, at times ungrammatical. ... he showed no evasion, no condescension, and occasional flashes of wit without flippancy."

322. *New York Times*, August 29, 1955, p. 17.

323. *New York Times*, September 18, 1955, p. 74.

324. See Annie Brierre, "Faulkner Parle," pp. 1, 6; also Cynthia Grenier, "The Art of Fiction," pp. 167-177, and Madeleine Chapsal, "A Lion in the Garden," *Reporter*, XIII (November 3, 1955), p. 40.

325. *New York Times*, October 13, 1955, p. 27.

326. *New York Times*, October 7, 1956, p. 20.

327. *Literary Career*, p. 51; *New York Times*, March 29, 1957, p. 19.

328. *Literary Career*, p. 36n; Dew, "Study of Requiem," p. 37.

329. *New York Times*, May 23, 1957, p. 39. Faulkner apparently found the proceedings somewhat tedious, and in presenting the medal he shortened his prepared speech to a statement of notable brevity: " 'No man deserves it more,' said Mr. Faulkner, 'and few have waited longer for it.' "

330. *New York Times*, June 9, 1959, p. 35.

331. Elliott Chaze, "A Short Visit with Faulkner," *Life*, LI (July 14, 1961), p. 11.

2. See, for example, the one reproduced as Fig. 1 of *Literary Career*.

332. *My Brother Bill*, pp. 214-219; *Old Times*, pp. 50-51; William Van O'Connor, *The Tangled Fire of William Faulkner* (Minneapolis, 1954), p. 168.

333. Sources for paragraph: *New York Times*, March 4, 1958, p. 31; November 13, 1958, p. 20; October 3, 1959, p. 3; April 21, 1962, p. 21; April 30, 1962, p. 19; May 19, 1962, p. 12. Several books inscribed for Faulkner by South American writers during the Venezuelan trip are listed in *Catalogue*. For the West Point visit, see Joseph L. Fant and Robert Ashley, edd., *Faulkner at West Point* (New York, 1964).

334. *My Brother Bill*, p. 1; *Oxford Eagle*, July 12, 1962, Sect. I, p. 7.

335. *Oxford Eagle*, July 12, 1962, Sect. II, p. 1; see the comment by Julian Mitchell, "Chronicler," *Spectator*, September 21, 1962, p. 409.

336. *New York Times*, July 9, 1962, p. 5.

337. *New York Times*, July 7, 1962. p. 7.

338. *Proceedings*, Second Series, 1 (1951), p. 19.

SOLDIERS' PAY

1. Carvel Collins (*Early Prose and Poetry*, p. 11) mentions a copy of "The Lilacs" dated January 1, 1920; the poem was later published as *A Green Bough*, I.

3. See p. 11, above.

4. Quotations from *Jurgen* (London, 1921): pp. 112, 12, 145, 16. Blotner (*Catalogue*) lists a 1923 edition of *Jurgen*, together with three other books by Cabell.

5. Collins (*New Orleans Sketches*, p. 30) reports that Faulkner once intended to entitle the novel *Mayday* (cf. Fitzgerald's story, "May Day," also about returned servicemen, first published in 1922 in *Tales of the Jazz Age*). We have already seen that Faulkner probably knew something of Frazer's work (above, p. 14 and note) and that he had read *Jurgen*, in which much humorous play is made with nature myths, but an equally likely source would seem to be *The Waste Land*: for the influence of Eliot on Faulkner see Adams, "The Apprenticeship of William Faulkner," pp. 116-117, Frederick L. Gwynn, "Faulkner's Prufrock—and Other Observations," *Journal of English and Germanic Philology*, LII (January 1953), 63-70, and Ruth Gasser Fourier, "The 'Prufrock' Theme in the Novels of William Faulkner" (unpub. M.A. thesis, University of South Carolina, 1948), passim.

6. George P. Garrett, Jr., "An Examination of the Poetry of William Faulkner," in *Princeton University Library Chronicle* (Faulkner number), p. 125.

7. Possible sources of influence in this respect would seem to include Cabell, Fitzgerald (see above, p. 4), and Wilde (see above, p. 16 and note); Faulkner's description of the rain's "silver lances" recalls Wilde's use of the same image in the fourth stanza of "The Burden of Itys." In *Faulkner at the University*, p. 20, Faulkner speaks of Conrad and Thomas Beer as early influences: for Conrad see Adams, "Apprenticeship," pp. 129-135; the work of Beer's which Faulkner may have had especially in mind is *Sandoval: A Romance of Bad Manners* (New York, 1924), e.g., pp. 130, 218-219.

MOSQUITOES

1. *New Orleans Sketches*, pp. 22-23.
2. See above, p. 15.
3. *New Orleans Sketches*, p. 23. Other information from interviews with Mrs. McClure and Professor Feibleman. For Sam Gilmore, see *Literary Career*, p. 24.
4. Olga W. Vickery, *The Novels of William Faulkner: A Critical Interpretation* (Baton Rouge, La., 1959), pp. 8-10. See also Hyatt H. Waggoner, *William Faulkner: From Jefferson to the World* (Louisville, Ky., 1959), pp. 8-19, for another valuable discussion of the novel.
5. Bound typescript in Alderman Library, p. 248.
6. Ibid., pp. 204-207.
7. Ibid., p. 235.
8. Adams, "Apprenticeship," p. 132, observes that David may be impotent or, since he is attracted by Patricia's "flat boy's body," homosexual.
9. *Princeton University Library Chronicle* (Faulkner number), p. 91.
10. See above, p. 17.
11. *Faulkner in the University*, p. 257.
12. Cf. Fourier, "The 'Prufrock' Theme," pp. 20-22, 29.
13. See above, p. 300.
14. See above, p. 4.

SARTORIS

1. *Writers at Work*, p. 141; cf. Cantwell, "The Faulkners," p. 306.
2. *Collected Stories*, p. 428. Cf. *Collected Stories*, pp. 511-512, opening of "All the Dead Pilots."
3. Manuscript, p. 01, reproduced as Fig. 9 of *Literary Career*.
4. Meriwether, "Textual History of *The Sound and the Fury*," p. 289; interview with Mr. Wasson, February 2, 1963.
5. Bound carbon typescript, Alderman Library, pp. 222-223.
6. Reproduced as Fig. 8 of *Literary Career*.

7. Typescript, Alderman Library, p. 294.

8. This material is also present in the manuscript, Alderman Library, pp. 52-d and 52-e.

9. Typescript, Alderman Library, p. 374.

10. Ibid., p. 443.

11. *Literary Career*, p. 65.

12. Random House propose to publish *Flags in the Dust* in its uncut form, and Mr. Albert Erskine tells me that Faulkner knew and approved of this plan. Sidney, "Faulkner in Hollywood," pp. 212-213, notes that Faulkner's screenplay for "War Birds" (see above, p. 35) explores the relationship between young Bayard and his brother John and supplies some of Bayard's actions with elements of motivation which are less obvious in *Sartoris*.

13. *Faulkner in the University*, p. 285.

THE SOUND AND THE FURY

1. The deposit of the Massey Collection in the Alderman Library has happily reunited the original first page of the manuscript of *The Sound and the Fury* with the remainder; page 5 is still missing (see *Literary Career*, p. 65).

2. Quentin's experience seems strongly reminiscent, in certain respects, of the "weird seizures" suffered by the Prince in Tennyson's *The Princess*: see, for example, III. 167-173; see also the Prince's injury, VI. 1-3, and especially VII. 30-35, in which the word "twilight" twice occurs.

3. See *A Green Bough*, X, entitled "Twilight" on its first publication in *Contempo*, I (February 1, 1932), 1.

4. Anderson, *Winesburg, Ohio* (New York, n.d.), pp. 4-5.

5. Faulkner's *Dallas Morning News* article on Anderson, in *Princeton University Library Chronicle* (Faulkner number), p. 90. See William L. Phillips, "Sherwood Anderson's Two Prize Pupils," *University of Chicago Magazine*, XLVII (January 1955), 12.

6. Faulkner to Cowley, 4.

7. *Faulkner at Nagano*, pp. 103-105.

8. Coindreau, Preface to *Le bruit et la fureur*, p. 7; cf. *My Brother Bill*, pp. 69, 125.

9. *Literary Career*, p. 175.

10. Coindreau, op. cit., pp. 9-12.

11. Manuscript, Alderman Library, p. 26.

12. See George R. Stewart and Joseph M. Backus, " 'Each in Its Ordered Place': Structure and Narrative in 'Benjy's Section' of *The Sound and the Fury*," *American Literature*, XXIX (January 1958), 440-456; their conclusion, after discovering that "a change in type does not always indicate a break between units and that a new unit can

be introduced without a change in type," is that Faulkner's device becomes "worthless" (p. 446).

13. Meriwether, "Textual History," pp. 294-299.

14. Faulkner to Wasson, undated, in Massey Collection.

15. Manuscript, Alderman Library, p. 34 (reproduced as Fig. 10 of *Literary Career*).

16. *Faulkner in the University*, p. 6.

17. *Faulkner at Nagano*, p. 72.

18. Faulkner to Cowley, 7.

19. Ibid.

20. Cf. Scott, *Quentin Durward* (London, n.d.), p. 63. When Quentin first introduces himself he is asked whether Durward is "a gentleman's name":

"By fifteen descents in our family," said the young man; "and that makes me reluctant to follow any other trade than arms."

"A true Scot! Plenty of blood, plenty of pride, and right great scarcity of ducats, I warrant thee."

21. *Portable Faulkner*, pp. 745-746.

22. E.g., *Writers at Work*, p. 130.

23. Linscott, "Faulkner Without Fanfare," p. 38.

AS I LAY DYING

1. See especially Carvel Collins, "The Pairing of *The Sound and the Fury* and *As I Lay Dying*."

2. I am indebted for this last point to Professor Meriwether, who also drew my attention to the important early essay by Valery Larbaud, "Un Roman de William Faulkner," in *Ce vice impuni, la lecture . . . domaine anglais* (Paris, [1936]), pp. 218-222.

3. E.g., *Faulkner in the University*, p. 87.

4. *Literary Career*, pp. 65-66. The manuscript and carbon typescript are in the Alderman Library; the typescript setting copy is at the University of Texas.

5. Garrett, "Some Revisions in *As I Lay Dying*," *Modern Language Notes*, LXXIII (June 1958), 414-417.

6. Manuscript, Alderman Library, p. 94.

7. Simon Claxton, "William Faulkner: an Interview," *The Cate Review*, June 1962, p. 6.

8. Grenier, "The Art of Fiction," p. 172.

9. *Writers at Work*, p. 129.

10. Grenier, loc. cit.

11. *Writers at Work*, p. 129; cf. *Faulkner in the University*, p. 87.

12. Larbaud, *Ce vice impuni*, p. 219. The final allusion is presumably to Lief Ericsson, Scandinavian discoverer of America.

13. Interview, September 3, 1963.

14. *New Orleans Sketches*, p. 26; cf. "The Pairing," p. 115.

15. Manuscript, pp. 75, 45.

16. *Writers at Work*, p. 129.

17. "American Drama: Eugene O'Neill," *The Mississippian*, February 3, 1922, p. 5 (*Early Prose and Poetry*, p. 88); Faulkner here misquotes the speech of Christy Mahon, from the last act of *The Playboy*, in which occurs the phrase "mitred bishops," echoed in *The Hamlet*, *The Mansion*, and elsewhere.

18. In John M. Synge, *Plays, Poems, and Prose* (London, 1946), p. 107.

SANCTUARY

1. Letter to Bessie Zaban Jones, February 7, 1934, in Blair Rouse, ed., *Letters of Ellen Glasgow* (New York, 1958), p. 150; see also pp. 188-190.

2. *Faulkner at Nagano*, pp. 64-65; see also James B. Meriwether, "Some Notes on the Text of Faulkner's *Sanctuary*," *Papers of the Bibliographical Society of America*, LV (1961), 192-206.

3. See *Literary Career*, p. 66, and Linton R. Massey, "Notes on the Unrevised Galleys of Faulkner's *Sanctuary*," *Studies in Bibliography*, VIII (1956), 195-208.

4. *An Exhibition of Manuscripts* (Texas), pp. 13-14; see also reproduction of galley sheet, p. 7, and cf. *Sanctuary*, pp. 4-5.

5. Manuscript, Alderman Library, p. 39, which bears deleted headings for Chapter I and, apparently at a later stage, for Chapter II.

6. Manuscript, p. 131; reproduced as *Literary Career*, Fig. 12.

7. Massey, op. cit., pp. 205-208. In the first table, part of the conclusion of Chapter VI of the unrevised galleys is accidentally listed as having been incorporated into Chapter VI of the published book; in fact, as the second table correctly shows, Chapter VI of the book is based entirely on Chapter VIII of the galleys, and those portions of Chapter VI which Faulkner retained, intact or in revised form, are all to be found within Chapter XVII of the book.

8. The following chapters of the book are composed of material taken almost directly from the galleys: IV, V, VI, VII, XI, XII, XIII, XVIII, XXI, XXII, XXIII, XXIV, XXV, XXVIII.

9. *The Story of Temple Drake*, released by Paramount Productions, Inc., in 1933 (see *Literary Career*, p. 161).

10. Massey, op. cit., p. 201.

11. Collins, "A Note on *Sanctuary*," *Harvard Advocate*, CXXXV (November 1951), p. 16; Collins explains that "in the real, perverted

rape the implement was so fantastically unnatural that compared
to it the implement used by the fictional gangster in the most notorious
episode of the novel seems well along the way towards normalcy ..."
See also, Robert Cantwell, "Faulkner's 'Popeye'," Nation, CLXXXVI
(February 15, 1948), 140-141, 148. A bootlegger called Popeye appears
in Faulkner's unpublished story, "The Big Shot" (see below, p. 159):
"a slight man with a dead face and dead black hair and eyes and a
delicate hooked little nose and no chin, crouching snarling behind the
neat blue automatic. He was a little, dead-looking bird in a tight black
suit like a vaudeville actor of twenty years ago, with a savage falsetto
voice like a choir-boy, and he was considered quite a personage in his
own social and professional circles." (Typescript, Alderman Library,
pp. 1-2).

12. *Faulkner at Nagano*, p. 63.

13. Quoted in Woodworth, *William Faulkner en France*, p. 39.

14. Cleanth Brooks, "Faulkner's *Sanctuary*: The Discovery of Evil,"
Sewanee Review, LXXI (Winter 1963), 1-24, is able to demonstrate the
flaws in Peter Lisca's argument ("Some New Light on Faulkner's
Sanctuary," *Faulkner Studies*, II [Spring 1953], 5-9) that the Drake
family was alone responsible for Temple's perjury at the trial. But
Brooks takes the view that Temple's family were completely uninvolved; he argues that Eustace Graham makes no attempt to preserve
Temple's reputation and that in the following passage Temple is
forced to reveal that she has been staying at Miss Reba's whorehouse:

"Where have you been living since May twelfth of this year?"
Her head moved faintly, as though she would see beyond him. He
moved into her line of vision, holding her eyes. She stared at him
again, giving her parrotlike answers.
"Did your father know you were there?"
"No." (p. 343)

It seems unlikely, however, that Faulkner would have dealt so ob-
scurely with so crucial an issue, that the revelation Brooks assumes
to have been made would not have caused a commotion in the court,
or that Graham could have gone on to make emotional pleas about
"this ruined, defenseless child." (p. 346) Temple has already said that
her "home" is in Memphis; presumably she now gives the District
Attorney, as the first of her prepared, "parrotlike" answers, a Memphis
address, probably fictitious and certainly one which Faulkner, for
reasons of convenience, would choose not to supply; presumably, too,
Graham has to "hold her eyes" precisely because she is having to lie.
Moreover, Graham goes on to speak of the place simply as a haven to
which Temple has escaped ("You were in hiding, then, because something had happened to you and you dared not—" [p. 343]), language
which is scarcely applicable to Miss Reba's but which perhaps con-

tains an ironical glance at the novel's title. The Memphis lawyer is apparently acting for Popeye, as Brooks remarks, but this would not necessarily exclude other sources of corruption. The details seems obscure, but it is at least clear that ranged against Horace are several forces all of whom are anxious to see Goodwin convicted and Popeye's rôle played down: Popeye himself; Eustace Graham, who is primarily concerned with the political advantages to himself of securing a conviction; and Judge Drake, who is anxious to minimise his daughter's, and his family's, public shame. At the very least, Judge Drake's subsequent actions in withdrawing Temple from the courtroom and, indeed, from the country, would seem to constitute an implicit endorsement of her perjury.

15. Robert E. Lee and Lucius Quintus Cincinnatus Lamar. Lamar, at one time a lawyer in Oxford, Mississippi, became Secretary of the Interior under President Cleveland and an Associate Justice of the United States Supreme Court. Ward L. Miner, *The World of William Faulkner* (New York, 1959), pp. 94-95, notes that Faulkner gave Lamar's initials and Christian names to more than one of his characters: L. Q. Peabody, for example, and Lucius Quintus Carothers McCaslin.

16. Collins, "The Pairing of *The Sound and the Fury* and *As I Lay Dying*," p. 123.

17. *Measure for Measure*, II. ii. 162-177. Other sources for the title have of course been suggested: Cleanth Brooks, for example (op. cit., p. 20), refers to a passage from Conrad's *Chance*. Another attractive possibility would seem to be the following passage from Wilde's *Salomé*, which Faulkner certainly knew (see pp. 8-9, above):

> HERODIAS: You are looking again at my daughter. You must not look at her. I have already said so.
> HEROD: You say nothing else.
> HERODIAS: I say it again.
> HEROD: And that restoration of the Temple about which they have talked so much, will anything be done? They say the veil of the Sanctuary has disappeared, do they not?
> HERODIAS: It was thyself did steal it. Thou speakest at random. I will not stay here. Let us go within.
> HEROD: Dance for me, Salomé.

(G. F. Maine, ed., *The Works of Oscar Wilde* [London and Glasgow, 1948], pp. 551-552).

18. E.g., the lawyer who takes advantage of Ruby Lamar, the "Jew lawyer from Memphis," (p. 338) and probably Judge Drake himself.

19. Albert Camus [letter], *Harvard Advocate*, CXXXV (November 1951), p. 21.

LIGHT IN AUGUST

1. *Faulkner in the University*, p. 77.

2. See Darrel Abel, "Frozen Movement in *Light in August*," *Boston University Studies in English*, III (Spring 1957), 32-44, and Norman Holmes Pearson, "Lena Grove," *Shenandoah*, III (Spring 1952), 3-7.

3. Cowley to Faulkner, September 17, 1945.

4. *Faulkner in the University*, p. 45.

5. It seems worth noting the close resemblance between the final sentence in this quotation and the fourth section of "Dry September" (*Collected Stories*, p. 180).

6. *Portable Faulkner*, p. 652 (cf. Faulkner to Cowley, 9).

7. See Alfred Kazin, "The Stillness of *Light in August*," in *Three Decades*, especially pp. 252-253.

8. *Faulkner in the University*, p. 72.

9. Quotations in this paragraph: manuscript, Alderman Library, pages unnumbered. See *Literary Career*, p. 87.

10. Typescript, Alderman Library, p. 26; see below, pp. 159-161.

11. For a reproduction of the first of these manuscript pages see *An Exhibition of Manuscripts* (Texas), pp. 8-9.

12. Mr. Albert Erskine has pointed out to me, however, that the name is not uncommon in Mississippi.

13. *Faulkner in the University*, p. 75; see also p. 45.

14. Draft introduction to *The Sound and the Fury* [?], pp. 2-3 : see p. 33, above.

15. The manuscript in the Alderman Library seems originally to have been entitled "Dark House" (*Literary Career*, p. 67), possibly an allusion to section VII of Tennyson's *In Memoriam*; cf. M. Coindreau's comment that the book was written in the aftermath of the death of Faulkner's first child (Preface to *Le bruit et la fureur*, p. 14n, quoted above, p. 306).

16. *Faulkner in the University*, p. 199.

17. See Robert M. Slabey, "Myth and Ritual in *Light in August*," *Texas Studies in Literature and Language*, II (Autumn 1960), 328-349, for an extremely interesting discussion of mythic elements in the novel.

18. Kazin, op. cit., p. 249, speaks of this incident as "virtually an annunciation."

19. J. G. Frazer, *The Golden Bough: A Study in Magic and Religion* (London, 1911), Part I, Vol. 1, pp. 12-14. The present action of *Light in August* apparently takes place in 1932 (see William H. F. Lamont, "The Chronology of *Light in August*," *Modern Fiction Studies*, III [Winter 1957-1958], 360-361), and it is perhaps worth noting that in that year August 13, the date of Diana's festival, fell on a Saturday;

Joe Christmas waits for midnight on the Friday night before going into the house to kill Miss Burden in the early moments of the Saturday.

20. *The Golden Bough*, Part I, Vol. 1, pp. 8-11.

21. Cf. ibid., p. 14: "The Christian Church appears to have sanctified this great festival of the virgin goddess by adroitly converting it into the festival of the Assumption of the Blessed Virgin on the fifteenth of August." This first chapter of *The Golden Bough* offers many extremely suggestive points of comparison with *Light in August*.

PYLON

1. *My Brother Bill*, pp. 273-274.

2. *New York Times*, February 10, 1934, p. 18; also February 4, 1934, Sect. VIII, p. 8. Cf. *Pylon*, pp. 17-18, and photograph in New Orleans *Item*, February 4, 1934, p. 4.

3. See photograph New Orleans *Times-Picayune*, February 10, 1934, p. 1; also *New Orleans City Guide*, written and compiled by the Federal Writers' Project of the Works Progress Administration for the City of New Orleans (Boston, 1938), p. 297.

4. W. Adolphe Roberts, *Lake Pontchartrain* (Indianapolis, 1946), pp. 338-339; cf. Harold Sinclair, *The Port of New Orleans* (Garden City, New York, 1942), p. 325.

5. *Times-Picayune*, February 9, 1934, p. 11, and February 10, 1934, p. 3.

6. *Times-Picayune*, February 11, 1934, p. 14, and February 12, 1934, p. 1; February 15, p. 4.

7. *Times-Picayune*, February 17, 1934, p. 3.

8. Cf. *Pylon*, pp. 38-40, 164.

9. Cf. *Pylon*, pp. 229-231. Faulkner seems to have had De Troyat especially in mind, however: in one of his stunts De Troyat "thrilled the crowd by driving his plane at nearly 100 miles an hour down one of the runways, with first one wheel and then the other touching the ground" (*Times-Picayune*, February 15, 1934, p. 4). Cf. *Item*, February 10, 1934, p. 2, for an account of similar "crazy flying" stunts performed by a flier named Dick Granere.

10. *New York Times*, February 15, 1934, p. 11; cf. *Times-Picayune*, February 15, 1934, p. 1, and especially Merlin Kennedy, "Eye-Witness Describes Fatal Plunge of Captain Nelson," *Item*, February 15, 1934, p. 6. Nelson feared that he would be killed and left a note behind him directing that his ashes should be scattered over the lake (see below, p. 320). His aircraft, apparently an ordinary light plane with fireworks attached to the fuselage, was perhaps the one to which John Faulkner refers (*My Brother Bill*, p. 274); in the *Item* report (p. 6), however, it

is described as a "red biplane" which was "completely equipped for night flying."

11. *Times-Picayune*, February 16, 1934, pp. 1, 3.

12. *New York Times*, February 17, 1934, p. 6; *Times-Picayune*, February 17, 1934, pp. 1, 3.

13. *Times-Picayune*, February 16, 1934, p. 3.

14. *Times-Picayune*, February 18, 1934, pp. 1, 4.

15. There is no suggestion of self-sacrifice, however, in the very full account of the accident in the New Orleans *Item-Tribune*, (Sunday) February 18, 1934, pp. 1, 16; the account, signed by Faulkner's friend Hermann B. Deutsch, a reporter on the *Item*, is written in dramatic manner: Jack Storey, "the wise-cracking announcer," was describing the race; then, "In the midst of a sentence, he stopped. The crowd began to make that peculiar moaning sound which every packed mass of humanity gives forth at times of horror." (p. 1) Also on the first page is a remarkable photograph of Ben Grew's falling body stretched between his opened emergency parachute and the parachute which had become entangled in the aircraft. Deutsch's assumption is that Kenily simply jumped, was knocked unconscious by his twisting machine, and so failed to open his parachute. Note, however, that in the unsigned *Item* report (February 17, p. 2) of Neuman's forced landing the pilot is said to have "kicked the fragile plane deliberately into a puddle of standing water when he saw there was a danger of his crashing towards the stands otherwise."

16. *Times-Picayune*, February 19, 1934, p. 4. See also the remarkable account of Nelson's funeral, "Wishes of Nelson Fulfilled As Ashes Are Flung To Winds," by Hermann B. Deutsch, in the *Item*, February 19, 1934, pp. 1, 2:

> A gay cavalier of the skies, whose whole life had been a carefree challenge to death, made his last gay gesture this morning through the hands of a friend and the power of man over the air [the last fourteen words, with the single alteration of "air" to "elements," are repeated at the very end of the report].
>
> The ashes of Captain Merle Nelson, veteran of the war-time army air service and noted stunt flier, were scattered from the scudding clouds in a blast of wind that was the product of man and nature combined.
>
> Within less than an instant they had vanished from sight, driving off in a gale as invisible particles almost as swiftly as the man of whose pulsing tissues they had once formed a living part had roared cloudward in the fine tingle of zestful living. (p. 1)

There are obvious stylistic similarities between this and the first of the accounts of Schumann's death which the Reporter composes at the end of *Pylon* (cf. the style of the unsigned description of preparations for Nelson's funeral in the *Item*, February 17, pp. 1, 2). Also relevant to *Pylon* are the ideas expressed in an unsigned article on Shushan Airport in the *Item-Tribune*, (Sunday) February 4, 1934, p. 15; two pilots, Lee Miles and Art Chester, rivals in the 100-mile race, are here described as helping each other out in times of trouble: "They aid each other. They help whenever the other needs it. As does each and every one of the men who live by the air." It seems possible that it may have been Hermann B. Deutsch's evident enthusiasm for flying which gave Faulkner the idea of using a newspaper reporter as the main centre of consciousness in his novel.

17. *Times-Picayune*, February 19, 1934, p. 2.

18. *Faulkner in the University*, p. 36.

19. Typescript setting copy, Alderman Library, pp. 228, 262, 70.

20. Galleys, University of Texas; see especially sheets 53-54. Elsewhere in the galleys it is interesting to note Faulkner's rejection of the weak substitutions suggested by his editors for some of the strong Anglo-Saxon words he had used, preferring instead to print the appropriate number of dots—four on pages 200 and 258 of the book, for example, and five (for a plural noun) on page 58.

21. There are also similarities in their backgrounds: Lena had lived with her brother (twenty years her senior) and his wife, Laverne with her sister (twenty years her senior) and her husband, and both were driven out by the men in the house, Lena's brother acting self-righteously, Laverne's brother-in-law hypocritically.

22. See John R. Marvin, "Pylon: The Definition of Sacrifice," *Faulkner Studies*, I (Summer 1952), 20-23.

23. Torchiana, "Faulkner's *Pylon* and the Structure of Modernity," *Modern Fiction Studies*, III (Winter 1957-1958), 307.

24. O'Connor, *The Tangled Fire of William Faulkner*, pp. 92-93: the term "half-metallic" in the passage by Torchiana is quoted from O'Connor, p. 93.

25. Dos Passos, *Airways, Inc.* (New York, 1928), e.g., pp. 86-94. It is perhaps worth noting that the newspapers reporting the events at Shushan Airport often carried on other pages long accounts of the proceedings of a Senate investigating committee which was inquiring into allegations of corruption in the granting of air mail contracts. See, for instance, *Item-Tribune*, February 18, 1934, p. 8 (report of Kenily-Grew crash is on pp. 1, 16).

26. *Times-Picayune*, February 14, p. 1; fuller description of parade on p. 3.

27. T. S. Eliot, *Collected Poems, 1909-1935* (London, 1936), p. 63.

28. Ibid., p. 15. Cf. Fourier, "The 'Prufrock' Theme," p. 22.

29. "Folklore of the Air," *American Mercury*, XXXVI (November 1935), 372.

30. *Collected Stories*, p. 198.

ABSALOM, ABSALOM!

1. *An Exhibition of Manuscripts* (Texas), p. 13.
2. *Faulkner in the University*, p. 76.
3. Reproduced in *The Book Collector*, IV (Winter 1955), facing p. 279.
4. Typescript setting copy, Alderman Library, p. 102.
5. For Faulkner's retention of a passage, compare p. 9 of rejected version (reproduced in Fig. 14 of *Literary Career*) with p. 13 of the published book; comparison of the same two pages shows that in response to an editorial complaint that it was confusing to have a "musing" ghost Faulkner actually intensified the stylistic and syntactical extravagance of the passage. For still another version of the first chapter, see "Absalom, Absalom!" *American Mercury*, XXXVIII (August 1936), 466-474; the chapter was published as one of a number of excerpts from work in progress by American writers.
6. Marginal note to typescript setting copy, p. 13 (reproduced in *Literary Career*, Fig. 14).
7. *Faulkner in the University*, pp. 273-274. Cf. quotation from *Winesburg, Ohio*, pp. 87-88, above.
8. Cf. comparison of *Absalom, Absalom!* with *The Atheist's Tragedy* in Anthony C. Hilfer, "William Faulkner and Jacobean Drama: A Comparison" (unpublished M.A. thesis, Columbia University, 1960), pp. 36-56.
9. Cf. Ilse Dusoir Lind, "The Design and Meaning of *Absalom, Absalom!*," in *Three Decades*, p. 283; this reading of the novel is extremely interesting throughout.
10. *Faulkner in the University*, p. 75.
11. Cf. Faulkner's comment on the role of the short convict in *The Wilds Palms* in *Faulkner in the University*, p. 179.
12. Faulkner to Cowley, 4: "[Quentin] grieved and regretted the passing of an order the dispossessor of which he was not tough enough to withstand. But more he grieved the fact (because he hated and feared the portentous symptom) that a man like Sutpen, who to Quentin was trash, originless, could not only have dreamed so high but have had the force and strength to have failed so grandly."
13. Cf. Lind, *op. cit.*, p. 281; Vickery, *The Novels of William Faulkner*, pp. 89-90. Evelyn Roddey Taylor, "A Comparative Study of Hawthorne and Faulkner" (unpub. M.A. thesis, Drake University, 1960), points to resemblances between *Absalom, Absalom!* and *The House of the Seven Gables* and between both of these works and the *Agamemnon* of Aeschylus (see especially, pp. 43-52, 108). See also Lennart Björk, "Ancient Myths and the Moral Framework of Faulkner's *Absalom, Absalom!*," *American Literature*, XXXV (May 1963), 197-199.

14. *Literary Career*, p. 170.
15. *Faulkner in the University*, p. 73.
16. "The Big Shot," typescript, Alderman Library, pp. 6-7.
17. Ibid., pp. 10, 9, 13.
18. *Faulkner in the University*, pp. 48-49.
19. *Faulkner in the University*, p. 73.
20. *Faulkner in the University*, p. 56.
21. See especially Richard Chase, *The American Novel and Its Tradition* (London, 1958), pp. 205-236.
22. Taylor, loc. cit.
23. *Faulkner in the University*, p. 243.
24. See, for example, *Faulkner in the University*, p. 50, and cf. Adams, "The Apprenticeship of William Faulkner," passim.
25. Charlotte Brontë, *Jane Eyre* (London, 1954), p. 414.
26. *Jane Eyre*, p. 303.
27. *Faulkner in the University*, p. 202.
28. See the arguments cogently advanced by John Hagan, "Fact and Fancy in *Absalom, Absalom!*," *College English*, XXIV (December 1962), 215-218. Mr. Hagan's view that it was from Henry Sutpen himself that Quentin learned why he had shot Bon (not because of the octaroon mistress, nor because of the incestuous nature of his proposed marriage to Judith, but because of his Negro blood) receives further support from a passage which he does not quote: on p. 181 of the novel Quentin thinks that Shreve sounds *"just like father ... Just exactly like father if father had known as much about it the night before I went out there as he did the day after I came back ..."* The Chronology which Faulkner supplied for the novel provides additional evidence to show that Bon's Negro blood is one of the solid facts of the novel and not mere speculation on the part of Quentin and Shreve; against the year 1831, we read: "Sutpen learns his wife has negro blood, repudiates her and child." It is conceivable of course that the Chronology is unreliable as evidence, and it does contain two apparent errors. One of these, the dating of the visit of Rosa and Quentin to Sutpen's Hundred as 1910 instead of 1909, is apparently a simple, and understandable, slip. The other involves a more substantial discrepancy: on p. 210 of the book we learn that Charles Etienne Saint-Valery Bon and Judith die of yellow fever; in the Chronology their death is ascribed to smallpox. That this was due neither to carelessness nor to a desire for ambiguity is suggested in "The Focus of William Faulkner's *Absalom, Absalom!*" (unpub. M.A. thesis, University of Virginia, 1959), p. 29, by Arlyn Bruccoli, who notes that in this instance Faulkner apparently used the Chronology to correct an error in the book. In *Absalom, Absalom!* (p. 210) Judith is said to have contracted the disease from Etienne and to have been buried apart as if it was feared that others might "contract the disease from her"; but yellow fever, Bruccoli observes, is not a contagious

disease, although smallpox is, and it is perhaps worth adding that the manuscript version of the Chronology, now in the Alderman Library, simply records the deaths of Etienne and Judith without specifying the disease. Thus, while we may perhaps regret that Faulkner felt it necessary to supply a Chronology, there seems no reason to doubt its reliability as evidence.

29. It is conceivable that in placing at this point the conclusion of Mr. Compson's letter, the first part of which appears just over 200 pages earlier (pp. 173-174), Faulkner intended to point towards the moment six months later when Quentin committed the suicide of which we have already learned from *The Sound and the Fury*. Mr. Compson, reporting the death of Miss Coldfield, observes:

> *Surely it can harm no one to believe that perhaps she has escaped not at all the privilege of being outraged and amazed and of not forgiving but on the contrary has herself gained that place or bourne where the objects of outrage and of the commiseration also are no longer ghosts but are actual people to be actual recipients of the hatred and the pity.* (p. 377)

Mr. Compson is being his usual whimsical self, but for the ghost-tormented mind of Quentin his remarks might well have assumed a deeper significance, as offering, in fact, that solution and resolution which had so far proved elusive.

THE UNVANQUISHED

1. "An Odor of Verbena," manuscript, Alderman Library, p. 6.
2. "An Odor of Verbena," typescript, Alderman Library, p. 13.
3. *Saturday Evening Post*, CCVII (September 29, 1934), 81.
4. *Faulkner in the University*, p. 252.
5. Brooks, *The Hidden God: Studies in Hemingway, Faulkner, Yeats, Eliot, and Warren* (New Haven and London, 1963), pp. 30-34; Waggoner, *William Faulkner: From Jefferson to the World*, pp. 170-183; Collins, Foreword to *The Unvanquished* (New York, 1959), pp. vii-xii; Meriwether, "The Place of *The Unvanquished* in William Faulkner's Yoknapatawpha Series," (unpublished doctoral dissertation, Princeton University, 1958), passim.
6. Meriwether, "Faulkner and the South," in Richard K. Meeker, ed., *The Dilemma of the Southern Writer* (Farmville, Va., 1961), pp. 143-163.
7. Faulkner, "Beyond the Talking," *New Republic*, LXVII (May 20, 1931), 23.
8. *Faulkner in the University*, p. 252.
9. *Faulkner in the University*, p. 2.

THE WILD PALMS

1. Typescript setting copy, Alderman Library, unnumbered title page (see *Literary Career*, pp. 28, 69).

2. Joseph J. Moldenhauer, "Unity of Theme and Structure in *The Wild Palms*," in *Three Decades*, p. 312.

3. It should perhaps be noted that two of these models represent characters which were among Faulkner's favourites—Don Quixote and Falstaff (cf. *Writers at Work*, p. 137).

4. *Faulkner at Nagano*, p. 80.

5. *Writers at Work*, p. 133.

6. *Faulkner at Nagano*, p. 80.

7. Typescript setting copy, Alderman Library : see especially pp. 31 and 67, 66 and 89-A.

8. *Faulkner in the University*, p. 178.

9. *Faulkner in the University*, p. 180.

10. Faulkner owned a copy of Lyle Saxon's *Father Mississippi* (New York, 1927) at the time of his death (*Catalogue*), and it seems likely that he had earlier drawn upon it for some details of the "Old Man" material; see especially Saxon's description of one of the Indian mounds used as places of refuge during the 1927 floods, p. 66, and cf. *The Wild Palms*, pp. 229-232.

11. See M. Coindreau's brilliantly suggestive "Préface aux *Palmiers sauvages*," *Temps Modernes*, VII (January 1952), 1187-1196.

12. Cowley to Faulkner, November 2, 1945.

13. Faulkner to Cowley, 13.

THE HAMLET

1. *Faulkner in the University*, pp. 14-15.

2. Faulkner to Cowley, 7.

3. Meriwether, "Sartoris and Snopes : an Early Notice," p. 37; see above, p. 24.

4. Ibid., p. 38.

5. This point corresponds to the top of p. 19 of the Arents Collection manuscript and to p. 348 of the published book. The second page of the manuscript is reproduced as Fig. 18 of *Literary Career*.

6. *Literary Career*, p. 173.

7. *Literary Career*, p. 174 (see under "Peasants").

8. *Literary Career*, p. 171.

9. *Faulkner in the University*, p. 90.

10. In the Alderman Library are two pages, numbered 18 and 19,

of a typescript entitled "Abraham's Children" (see *Literary Career*, Fig. 19, for a reproduction of p. 18); a third page, numbered 29, has been grouped with these but should perhaps be better described as belonging to a version of "Father Abraham." Both this page and p. 19 of "Abraham's Children" are almost identical with p. 29 of the "Father Abraham" typescript also in the Alderman Library, and it seems possible to suggest that "Abraham's Children" may represent an abbreviated version of "Father Abraham" produced by a single drastic deletion of the long opening descriptions of Flem, Eula, and Frenchman's Bend. These descriptions occupy approximately 11½ pages of "Father Abraham" typescript; allowing for the introductory material necessary to establish the situation for short-story purposes (as in the *Scribner's* version of "Spotted Horses"), this would account for the pagination of "Abraham's Children" running about ten pages behind. It is necessary to emphasise, however, that these speculations are extremely tentative (more of this early Snopes material may yet come to light) and that in any case the fact that "Abraham's Children" is narrated in the third-person makes it unlikely to have been an immediate source for the published "Spotted Horses."

11. *Scribner's*, LXXXIX (June 1931), 587, 586.

12. Ibid., p. 585.

13. Evidence for this conclusion can be obtained from comparison of the various versions of the material available in the Alderman Library: see *Literary Career*, pp. 69-70, and Figs. 20 and 21.

14. Starke, "An American Comedy: An Introduction to a Bibliography of William Faulkner," *The Colophon*, XIX (1934), [15].

15. Ibid., p. [16].

16. This material is all in the Alderman Library: see *Literary Career*, pp. 70-73.

17. Typescript setting copy, Alderman Library, p. 179.

18. Professor Meriwether has suggested to me that Faulkner may have seen "Wash" as related, with the Mink Snopes material, to an exposition of the desperate plight of such men and of their capacity for a kind of dignity; the Wash Jones episode might then have balanced the Mink episode at the end of *The Mansion* and emphasised even more strongly that Flem was not necessarily typical of his class. Cf. Robert Penn Warren, "William Faulkner," in *Three Decades*, p. 120.

19. The first page of the manuscript is reproduced as Fig. 15 of *Literary Career*; for the typescript, also in the Alderman Library, see *Literary Career*, p. 70.

20. The evocation of the De Spain mansion and of its significance for the boy would also have looked forward to Flem's purchase and occupation of the building in the later books of the trilogy.

21. Cf. two of the most recent books on Faulkner: Peter Swiggart, *The Art of Faulkner's Novels* (Austin, Texas, 1962), p. 195, repeats the familiar view that *The Hamlet* is "based upon a number of short

stories published originally in the early thirties," and Lawrance Thompson, *William Faulkner: An Introduction and Interpretation* (New York, 1963), p. 135, speaks of Faulkner "choosing to perform a scissors-and-paste job, patching together pieces or wholes of six short stories [Thompson includes "Afternoon of a Cow," which has only incidental similarities with the Ike Snopes episodes and nothing textually in common with them] which had previously existed as unrelated units"—a job, Thompson adds, which seems to have been done with "a cavalier laziness." The inadequacy of such views has been evident for some time from Faulkner's own remarks recorded in *Faulkner at the University* and from the information collected by James B. Meriwether in *Literary Career*.

22. See Burton Rascoe's analysis of the climax of the "Fool About a Horse" episode recounted by Ratliff and his comment that "Mr. Faulkner never even suspects that New York reviewers can be so ignorant of physiology that they accept such a tale literally and don't know you can't pump up a horse with a bicycle pump" (Rascoe, "Faulkner's New York Critics," *American Mercury*, L [June 1940], 246).

23. *Three Decades*, p. 123.

24. This passage in the novel (part of a section omitted from the English edition) has been revised, and greatly improved, from the version which appears on p. 146 of the manuscript :

"But I still dont see why I got to pay $15.00—"
"Because you got 4 children and you make 5, and 5 times 3 is 15.["]
"I aint got but 3 yet," Eck said.
"But you got the meat and hide." I.O. said. "Cant you even try to keep from forgetting that?"

25. The rejected typescript version of p. 1 which bears the pencilled note "Rec'd 3/20/39" (see p. 185, above) also bears the title "THE PEASANTS/BOOK ONE/Chapter I".

26. Grenier, "The Art of Fiction," p. 174.

27. *Faulkner in the University*, p. 34.

28. Warren Beck, "Faulkner: a Preface and a Letter," *Yale Review*, LII (October 1962), 159.

GO DOWN, MOSES

1. For the genealogy, see *Literary Career*, p. 31; Faulkner, however, says that the genealogy "developed itself" (*Faulkner in the University*, p. 97).

2. *Faulkner in the University*, pp. 4, 273.

3. Mr. Albert Erskine of Random House (letter, November 6, 1963) recalls Faulkner telling him that the book was a novel and that the words "and Other Stories" should never have appeared.

4. Mr. Erskine, loc. cit., states that the letter must have been from Robert Haas, who had brought Faulkner to Random House when the firm of Smith and Haas was taken over and had retained some editorial responsibility for his work; according to Mr. Erskine, Faulkner replied to the letter towards the end of January, confirming the suggestions but saying that he saw no necessity for adding numbers to the chapter titles.

5. *Portable Faulkner*, p. 226.

6. Lawrance Thompson, *William Faulkner: An Introduction and Interpretation*, p. 87.

7. Grenier, "The Art of Fiction," p. 175. Cf. *Faulkner in the University*, p. 246.

8. Cf. Thompson, op. cit., 81.

9. *Faulkner in the University*, p. 277.

INTRUDER IN THE DUST

1. Information supplied by Professor James B. Meriwether.

2. Edmund Wilson, "William Faulkner's Reply to the Civil-Rights Program," in *Classics and Commercials* (New York, 1950), pp. 460-470; Elizabeth Hardwick, "Faulkner and the South Today," in *Two Decades*, pp. 244-250.

3. *Princeton University Library Chronicle* (Faulkner number), Plate VII.

4. Typescript, pp. 92-93 (Alderman Library). The plural "were" following the bracket is retained in the final text (p. 83), although Faulkner's (perhaps accidental) omission of "and his uncle" in the process of revision left "Sheriff Hampton" as the verb's single subject; it is possible that Faulkner allowed the phrase "not even Sheriff Hampton" to imply plurality.

5. See below, p. 241.

6. For the comic aspects of *Intruder*, see Eudora Welty, "In Yoknapatawpha," *Hudson Review*, I (Winter 1949), 596-598.

7. Lytle, "Regeneration for the Man." in *Two Decades*, p. 254.

REQUIEM FOR A NUN

1. Dew, "A Study of William Faulkner's *Requiem for a Nun*," p. 2.
2. *Literary Career*, p. 22.

3. In a letter Faulkner wrote to Harrison Smith in the early 1930's he said that *Requiem for a Nun* was about "a nigger woman" (information from Mr. Albert Erskine).

4. Vickery, *Novels of William Faulkner*, p. 123.

5. Shreve uses the same phrases in *Absalom, Absalom!*, but in that novel the element of joint participation in the task of narrative reconstruction is inseparable from the total pattern.

6. *Faulkner in the University*, p. 196.

7. Albert Camus, Preface to *Requiem pour une nonne*, translated by M. E. Coindreau (Paris, 1957), p. xii.

8. Dew, op. cit., pp. 37-38.

9. "A Name for the City," *Harper's*, CCI (October 1950), [200]-202, 204, 206, 208, 210, 212-214.

10. Ibid., p. 200.

11. *Faulkner in the University*, p. 61.

12. Ibid., p. 122.

A FABLE

1. *Faulkner at Nagano*, p. 159.

2. *Literary Career*, p. 38.

3. *Writers at Work*, pp. 132-133; cf. the similar comments Faulkner makes in discussing Ike McCaslin's relinquishment of his inheritance, *Faulkner in the University*, pp. 245-246.

4. *Faulkner in the University*, p. 27.

5. E.g. Heinrich Straumann, "An American Interpretation of Existence: Faulkner's A Fable," in *Three Decades*, pp. 349-372.

THE TOWN

1. *Faulkner in the University*, pp. 139-140.

2. "Centaur in Brass," *American Mercury*, XXV (February 1932), 200-210; "Mule in the Yard," *Scribner's*, XCVI (August 1934), 65-70; "The Waifs," *Saturday Evening Post*, CCXXIX (May 4, 1957), 27, 116, 118, 120. "The Waifs" was in fact an extract from the novel, printed from the galley proofs: see *Literary Career*, p. 44.

3. *Faulkner in the University*, pp. 140-141.

4. Beck, *Man in Motion* (Madison, 1961), p. 136.

5. *Faulkner in the University*, p. 141.

6. Cf. p. 118, above.

7. *Writers at Work*, p. 137.

THE MANSION

1. Beck, *Man in Motion*, p. 173.

2. *Writers at Work*, p. 141; also letter to author from Mr. Albert Erskine, November 6, 1963.

3. James B. Meriwether in *Approaches to the Study of Twentieth-Century Literature* (East Lansing, 1961), p. 43. Mr. Albert Erskine informs me that Faulkner made further alterations to *The Mansion* after the book had been published.

4. Meriwether, ibid., p. 44.

5. Faulkner to Cowley, 4.

THE REIVERS

1. Leslie A. Fiedler, "The Last of William Faulkner," *The Guardian*, September 28, 1962, p. 6.

2. *New York Times*, July 7, 1962, p. 7.

SHORT STORIES

1. Faulkner to Cowley, uncatalogued letter. For *Pan Michael*, see Faulkner's Foreword to *The Faulkner Reader*; Joseph L. Blotner, "William Faulkner's Name," p. 45, has pointed out that the phrases come in fact from the final page of *Pan Michael* and that a copy of an 1898 edition, inscribed with the name of his grandfather, was among Faulkner's books at the time of his death.

2. Smith, "Faulkner of Mississippi," p. 416. It seems possible that Faulkner had in mind the precedent of Anderson's *Winesburg, Ohio* or of Hemingway's *In Our Time* (or of both).

3. Volume Two of the *Collected Short Stories of William Faulkner* (London, 1958) is entitled *These Thirteen*: the stories it contains are the same as in *These 13*, but they are printed in the order in which they occur in the one-volume *Collected Stories* (New York, 1950; London, 1951).

4. *Faulkner in the University*, p. 22; for the title cf. Ford Madox Ford, *A Man Could Stand Up—*, in *Parade's End* (New York, 1961), p. 506, also *Absalom, Absalom!*, p. 160.

5. *Literary Career*, p. 86.

6. Pearson, "Faulkner's Three 'Evening Suns'." *Yale University Library Gazette*, XXIX (October 1954), 66.

7. Manuscript and carbon typescript in Alderman Library (*Literary Career*, p. 83).

8. Manuscript, unnumbered page.

9. Manuscript, Alderman Library, p. 5; the manuscript is incomplete. On p. 1 Faulkner has changed Miss Emily's surname from Wyatt to Grierson.

10. Carbon typescript, Alderman Library, pp. 13, 15.

11. Ibid., pp. [16-17].

12. *Literary Career*, p. 175.

13. *Literary Career*, p. 34.

14. The records of Faulkner's agent, Harold Ober, reveal that a first (22-page) version of "Knight's Gambit" was received in January 1942 and that a revised version still failed to sell in 1946 (information in a letter from Professor Meriwether, December 17, 1963); cf. Faulkner to Cowley, 10.

15. Letter from Mr. Albert Erskine, November 6, 1963.

16. *Literary Career*, p. 81.

17. Manuscript, Alderman Library, p. 31.

18. *Faulkner in the University*, p. 22.

19. *Faulkner in the University*, p. 136.

THE ACHIEVEMENT

1. *Faulkner at Nagano*, p. 26.

2. Preface to *The Marble Faun*, pp. 6, 7.

3. Garrett, "An Examination of the Poetry of William Faulkner," p. 125.

4. Cf. *Early Prose and Poetry*, pp. 30-31.

5. Stone to Cochran, December 28, 1931, in Meriwether, "Early Notices"; see above, p. 5.

6. Transcript of interview, WCBS-TV, October 14, 1956, p. 18 (copy in Princeton University Library).

7. Quoted Meriwether, "Early Notices."

8. Ibid.

9. *Old Times in the Faulkner Country*, p. 25.

10. Ibid., p. 90; Cullen, p. 93, points the comparison with *Sanctuary*, p. 135.

11. *Old Times*, pp. 91-92.

12. Ibid., p. 96.

13. Ibid., p. 97.

14. Cf. G. T. Buckley, "Is Oxford the Original of Jefferson in William Faulkner's Novels?" *Publications of the Modern Language Association of America*, LXXVI (September 1961), 447-454; Calvin S. Brown, "Faulkner's Geography and Topography," ibid., LXXVII (December 1962), 652-659. Both articles offer interesting material, but their theses seem unnecessarily narrow.

15. *Writers at Work*, p. 141.

16. *Literary Career*, p. 41.

17. A recent example is Martin Green, *Re-appraisals: Some Commonsense Readings in American Literature* (London, 1963), pp. 169-170, 172, 189-190.

18. *Writers at Work*, p. 141.

19. *Faulkner in the University*, p. 3; cf. *Faulkner at Nagano*, pp. 80-81.

20. Brooks, *The Hidden God*, p. 40.

21. Elizabeth Nowell, ed., *The Letters of Thomas Wolfe* (New York, 1956), p. 495.

22. *The Portable Faulkner*, p. 23.

23. Faulkner to Cowley, 15.

24. *The Portable Faulkner*, p. 23.

25. *Faulkner at Nagano*, p. 81.

26. Faulkner to Cowley, 4.

27. *The Princess*, III. 307.

28. Beck, "Faulkner: a Preface and a Letter," p. 159; see above, p. 200.

29. *New York Times*, July 7, 1962, p. 7; see above, p. 56.

30. Lewis, *Men Without Art* (London, 1934), p. 49.

31. Ibid., pp. 46-48.

32. Cochran, "William Faulkner, Literary Tyro of Mississippi," in Meriwether, "Early Notices." Cochran also attributes to Faulkner a description of New York as a place "where everybody talks about what they are going to write, and no one writes anything."

33. *Faulkner in the University*, p. 50.

34. Adams, "The Apprenticeship of William Faulkner," passim.

35. Cf. George P. Garrett, Jr., "Faulkner's Early Literary Criticism," *Texas Studies in Literature and Language*, I (Spring 1959), 3-10; the texts of the essays and reviews are available in *Early Prose and Poetry*.

36. Faulkner, "American Drama: Inhibitions 2," *The Mississippian*, March 24, 1922, p. 5, reprinted in *Early Prose and Poetry*, p. 94.

37. See, for example, *Faulkner in the University*, pp. 15, 281, but note that on p. 145 he speaks of "the clumsy method of Mark Twain and Dreiser."

INDEX

About the Author

MICHAEL MILLGATE was born in Southampton, England, in 1929. He studied at St. Catharine's College, Cambridge, at the University of Michigan, and at the University of Leeds, and for several years taught English and American literature at Leeds. He is now Professor of English at York University, Toronto. Previous publications include *William Faulkner* and *American Social Fiction: James to Cozzens*, as well as articles on various aspects of English and American literature.